Study Guide to Accom

The Legal, Ethical and International Environment of Business

Second Edition

Herbert M. Bohlman
Mary Jane Dundas

Prepared by:
Thomas D. Brierton
University of the Pacific

West Publishing Company
Minneapolis/St. Paul   New York   Los Angeles   San Francisco

WEST'S COMMITMENT TO THE ENVIRONMENT

In 1906, West Publishing Company began recycling materials left over from the production of books. This began a tradition of efficient and responsible use of resources. Today, up to 95% of our legal books and 70% of our college texts and school texts are printed on recycled, acid-free stock. West also recycles nearly 22 million pounds of scrap paper annually—the equivalent of 181,717 trees. Since the 1960s, West has devised ways to capture and recycle waste inks, solvents, oils, and vapors created in the printing process. We also recycle plastics of all kinds, wood, glass, corrugated cardboard, and batteries, and have eliminated the use of Styrofoam book packaging. We at West are proud of the longevity and the scope of our commitment to the environment.

Production, Prepress, Printing and Binding by West Publishing Company.

COPYRIGHT © 1993 by   WEST PUBLISHING CO.
610 Opperman Drive
P.O. Box 64526
St. Paul, MN 55164–0526

ISBN 0–314–01676–7

CONTENTS

Preface

The fundamental purpose of this Study Guide is to assist you in understanding the principles of law as presented in the Legal Environment of Business by Max Bohlman, Mary Jane Dundas, and Gaylord A. Jentz. I hope to guide you through the textbook by presenting each chapter in a readable and understandable manner. The materials in the Study Guide directly correspond to the materials in the textbook, providing you with a condensed version of the textbook which is easy to reference.

Legal concepts for most students can be difficult to comprehend. The language of the law tends to be very precise and somewhat complex. This Study Guide attempts to organize and define the concepts of law in a student's language. An overview of each chapter is presented to provide a perspective of how the concepts fit together. The overview will help you sort out the interrelationships between areas of law. The Study Guide highlights the major concepts from each chapter and provides you with a framework from which to study. The Study Guide also allows you to confirm your knowledge through a variety of test questions. The answers to all the questions are at the end of each chapter along with the page number of where the answer is found in the text.

The Study Guide includes the following items:

1. Part Summaries--A brief overview of the areas of law covered in each of four different parts.

2. <u>Major Concepts</u>--A brief summary of each chapter discussing the major concepts in the chapter, introducing the particular area of law.

3. <u>Chapter Outlines</u>--The chapter outlines describe the legal principles in the text and provide clarity to specific concepts.

4. <u>Fill-in-the-Blank Questions</u>--These questions place the concepts in a fact scenario. The questions deal with some of the more important concepts in the chapter.

5. <u>True-False Questions</u>--The true-false questions allow you to quickly test your knowledge on materials contained in the chapter. The true-false questions tend to test very specific facets of the law.

6. <u>Multiple-Choice Questions</u>--The multiple-choice questions are at varying degrees of difficulty. These questions will test your ability to memorize concepts as well as your ability to apply legal principles.

7. <u>Essay Questions</u>--The essay questions will help you think through a problem. The essay questions are open-ended to encourage students to talk through the issues with other students. Essay questions should be approached as problems to be solved by legal analysis.

<u>Acknowledgement</u>

I wish to thank Jeanette Biava for all her assistance in correcting and preparing this Study Guide.

Thomas D. Brierton

To my wife Julia M. Brierton
and our daughter, Abigail.

PART I
INTRODUCTION TO LAW

Part Summary

This segment attempts to acclimate students to the legal system of the United States. These chapters expose the student to the major aspects of the legislative, executive, and judicial branches of the government. Chapters 1, 3, and 5 discuss the foundations on which the legal system has been built. A study of the judicial system and the litigation process provides the student with a basic understanding of the common law and conflict resolution (further discussed in Chapter 4).

In addition, ethics and criminal law are carefully considered. Basic ethical theory is explained in Chapter 2. Chapter 7 discusses criminal law as it applies to business.

Administrative agencies are fully discussed in Chapter 6. Administrative agencies play an important part in the regulation of business activity.

Chapter 1
Sources of the Law

Over the centuries, lawyers, philosophers, and academicians have debated the meaning of the term "law". A wide variety of definitions have been asserted. A multitude of legal philosophies beginning about the time of Socrates have attempted to explain and define the concept of law.

American jurisprudence is deeply rooted in the natural law philosophy which emphasizes the higher law from a divine source. Other schools of thought have approached law through logic, realism, and economics.

The sources of American law are threefold. The dual sovereign system in the United States allows for the federal government and each state to have its own constitution, statutes, and common law. The primary source of law comes from the United States Constitution. Statutes are laws enacted by Congress or a state legislature and recorded in code books. The common law, also known as judge-made law, is created by federal and state courts. Judges, in settling disputes, may make laws which other courts will follow.

The law is not only classified according to its source but also according to how its content is applied and as to what relief the injured party is seeking. These classifications are helpful in clarifying the various aspects of the law in the United States.

This chapter will introduce the student to the legal environment of business. The chapter presents some essential concepts for understanding the American legal system. These concepts lay the foundation for the following twenty-three chapters in the book.

Chapter Outline

I.   Definition of Law--Law has been defined quite differently depending on the legal philosophy of the one doing the defining. Most legal philosophers agree that law is composed of rules which are designed to provide order to society and ensure justice through a moral code.

   A.   Schools of Legal Philosophy

      1.   The Natural Law School--Natural law proponents assert that a higher law exists and came from a divine origin. The Magna Carta, the Declaration of Independence, and the U.S. Constitution reflect natural law ideals.

      2.   The Historical and Sociological Schools--The historical school attempts to describe the law of the past and apply it to contemporary situations. The sociological school considers how people ought to conduct themselves in society.

      3.   The Analytical School--This school of thought attempts to formulate general principles through analyzing a legal code.

      4.   The Legal Realists--This legal philosophy emphasizes the pragmatic and empirical sides of the law. Legal realists attempt to influence the law through stressing the social end desired.

      5.   The Economic School--This legal philosophy gives economic theory priority in evaluating the law. The maximization of individual welfare plays an important part in a legal system, according to the economic school.

II. Sources of American Law

   A.   Constitutions--Each state and the federal government have a constitution which sets guidelines for the operation of government and protects individual rights and freedoms.

1. <u>U.S. Constitution</u>--The U.S. Constitution is the
    highest source of man-created law in the United
    States. The U.S. Constitution delegates power
    to three separate branches of government (i.e.,
    the Executive, Legislative, and Judicial
    branches). The U.S. Constitution, as drafted by
    the framers, limits the power of these three
    branches through various checks and balances.
    No one branch of the federal government may
    accumulate an excessive amount of power so as to
    thwart individual freedoms. The founding
    fathers sought to protect individual rights
    through the first ten amendments to the Consti-
    tution (i.e., Bill of Rights) and through
    limiting the power of government. In other
    words, a government by the people and for the
    people. (See Chapter 3 for additional informa-
    tion on the U.S. Constitution.)

2. <u>State Constitutions</u>--Every state in the nation
    has enacted a constitution to structure its gov-
    ernment. The U.S. Constitution reserves all
    powers not retained by the federal government to
    the states. In some cases, the states may regu-
    late areas concurrently with the federal govern-
    ment, although state constitutions and state
    laws that violate the U.S. Constitution are
    void.

B. <u>Statutes and Ordinances</u>--Congress and state legis-
    latures pass laws which are called statutes. Those
    enacted by Congress are published in the United
    States code. Statutes passed by state legislatures
    are published in state code books (e.g., Illinois
    Revised Statutes). Federal statutes are applicable
    in all 50 states, whereas state statutes may only be
    enforced in the state of enactment.

    <u>Example of a State Statute</u>--The uniform commercial
    code is a uniformly drafted code adopted in all
    states, the District of Columbia, and the Virgin
    Islands. The code creates a uniform body of law
    covering most commercial transactions. The code
    encourages the execution of business transactions by
    providing clarity and standardized rules.

    Ordinances are laws passed by cities and counties
    and may only be applied in the particular city or
    county where enacted.

C.   Common Law--Common law, also known as judge-made
     law, is created by judges. A judge may formulate
     common law by interpreting a statute or adopting a
     rule where no statute or ordinance exists. A legis-
     lature may affirm or change the common law through
     enacting new legislation.

     1. Stare Decisis--Stare decisis ("let the decision
         stand") requires the court to follow prior
         decisions (precedent) when deciding new cases.
         If a prior case was identical to a case now
         before the court, the judge will utilize the ex-
         perience and wisdom of the past decision to de-
         cide the case at hand.

         Stare decisis allows the court to be more effi-
         cient, uniform, and just. In addition, stare
         decisis makes the law more stable and predict-
         able.

         A judge may depart from following precedent when
         the rule is incorrect or not applicable.
         Changes in the rationale underpinning the rule
         usually cause the court to overrule precedent
         and adopt a new rule.

         State and federal appellate courts may create
         precedent, which all other inferior courts are
         required to follow. When the U.S. Supreme Court
         adopts a rule, all other courts in the United
         States must follow such rule, as all other
         courts in the United States are considered infe-
         rior. If the highest court in a state adopts a
         rule, all other state courts in that state must
         follow the same rule.

III. Classification of Law

A.   Substantive Law Versus Procedural Law--Substantive
     law defines and creates legal rights and obliga-
     tions. The law of contract which requires the
     parties to have contractual capacity to enter into a
     legally binding agreement is an example of a sub-
     stantive rule.

     Procedural law creates the means for enforcing
     rights and governs the process of administering jus-
     tice (e.g., the rules of evidence, number of jurors
     on a jury, statute of limitations, etc.).

B. <u>Public Law Versus Private Law</u>--Public law describes
and regulates the relationship between the people
and government, whereas private law deals with relationships between private individuals.

C. <u>Civil Law Versus Criminal Law</u>--Civil law defines the
legal rights and duties between individuals and
sometimes between individuals and government. Civil
law is generally compensatory in nature or seeks to
make a person whole when an injury has occurred.

Criminal law defines wrongs committed against society as a whole. Criminal law is defined in federal
and state criminal codes as well as local ordinances. The criminal law is punitive in nature or
seeks to punish a wrongdoer.

These classifications of law overlap one another,
and a law may fall into all three categories at one
time. For example, the Sherman Act prohibits "contracts, combinations, or conspiracies which restrain
trade;" this section of the Sherman Act is a substantive law which is also public and criminal.
Another section of the Sherman Act allows a competitor who has been injured to sue a violator of the
Act for treble damages (3 times the amount). This
is an example of a substantive law which is private
and civil.

IV. <u>Courts of Law Versus Courts of Equity</u>--The major distinction between a court of law and a court of equity is
the remedy available to the parties. The distinction is
mostly historical, and courts today have merged law and
equity into one court.

A. <u>Courts of Law</u>--In a court of law, the litigants may
only seek certain remedies for relief, usually money
damages.

B. <u>Courts of Equity</u>--In courts of equity, the litigants
may ask the court to order various forms of relief,
excluding money damages. The equity court will not
order an equitable remedy unless the remedy at law
is inadequate (i.e., money damages would be inappropriate).

The equity court may award specific performance to a
litigant who has entered into a contract for a
unique item and the seller has breached the contract. Or the equity court may issue an injunction

which prohibits someone from doing something or requires someone to do something.

Rescission is another equitable remedy which allows
a party to cancel a contract and be returned to the
status quo (i.e., have returned what was given).

C.   Distinctions--In courts of equity, the litigants do
not have a constitutional right to a jury as they
would in a court of law.

In courts of law, an individual must abide by the
statute of limitations or be barred from bringing a
lawsuit. A statute of limitation sets the time
period in which a party can bring a case. Courts of
equity, according to the doctrine of laches allow
individuals to bring their case in a reasonable time
or be barred from suing.

V.   Administrative Agency Regulations

A.   Administrative Agencies--An administrative agency is
created by Congress or a state legislature to exercise legislative, executive, and judicial power. An
agency may have the power to create rules and adjudicate cases. Generally, rules created by an administrative agency are enforceable as law.

VI. Locating Case Law

A.   Appellate Court Decisions--Most appellate courts
(courts of review) publish their opinions. Appellate courts review the decisions of the trial courts
if one of the parties to the original case requests
an appeal. The appellate court decisions are considered the common law and used by attorneys and
judges to decide new cases. The reported decisions
are published in volumes called Reports or Reporters
which are numbered consecutively.

Each reported appellate court case may be located by
its citation. The citation contains the volume
number, case name, and page the case begins on.
Both federal and state appellate court cases may be
found according to the proper citation.

Study Questions

Fill-in-the-Blank Questions

The Uniform Commercial Code Article 2 regulates the sales of goods. Article 2 of the code applies to the sales goods (i.e., defined as tangible personal property). Section 2-314 requires all goods sold by merchants to be of merchantable quality when sold. Merchants are sellers who deal in the goods of a kind or have a special skill or knowledge about the goods involved.

Arthur Smith purchases a new automobile from New World Auto for $22,000 and receives a written express warranty of 2 years or 24,000 miles. New World Auto is a merchant of automobiles.

Section 2-314 of the Uniform Commercial Code is an example of a _____ law.
               (substantive/procedural)

If a court interprets the term "sale of goods" to include new and used automobiles, this is an example of _____
_____ law.   (statutory/
   common)

Under the code, when a warranty is violated, the injured party may bring a lawsuit to recover money damages; this is an example of a _____ law action.
                 (civil/criminal)

If a judge orders the defendant to pay the plaintiff $5,000 in damages, this order came from a _____ court.
                          (law/equity)

True-False Questions

1. Roscoe Pound, a famous legal philosopher, believed society's moral ideas are taken from ethics which provide us with principles of law. _____

2. Jurisprudence is a philosophy of law. _____

3. The Natural Law School attempts to discover the principles of contemporary law through concentrating on the history of the legal system. _____

4. Legal Realists examine the structure and subject matter of a legal code to extract underlying principles through logic. _____

5. The U.S. Constitution does not delegate any legislative powers to the states. _____

6. The framers of the U.S. Constitution attempted to balance the national government's power in three separate branches. _____

7. Ordinances are laws created by state legislatures. _____

8. Common law is derived from usages and customs of society and from the judgments of courts. _____

9. The Uniform Commercial Code is a federal statute enacted by Congress in 1952. _____

10. Administrative law is an example of public law because it addresses the relationship between business and government. _____

Multiple-Choice Questions

1. The State of California enacts a law which prohibits non-resident automobile insurance companies from charging more than a set maximum rate for various categories of insureds. Several insurance companies not located in California challenge the statute as a violation of the U.S. Constitution. These insurance companies refused to follow the law. This law is an example of:

    a. common law.
    b. statute.
    c. ordinance.
    d. federal regulation.

2. Refer to question 1. If an appellate court decides the California law is constitutional and may be enforced against insurance companies, this is an example of:

    a. common law.
    b. statute.
    c. ordinance.
    d. federal regulation.

3. Refer to question 2. The insurance companies appeal the case all the way up to the U.S. Supreme Court after losing at the lower levels. The power of the U.S. Supreme Court to determine if the California law violates the U.S. Constitution is known as:

a.   stare decisis.
b.   precedent.
c.   equity.
d.   judicial review.

4.   Which of the following is an example of an order issued
     by a court of law?

     a.   The defendant must specifically perform a contract to
          sell a unique item.
     b.   The defendant must pay $25,000 as damages for breach
          of a contract.
     c.   The plaintiff is allowed to rescind the contract.
     d.   The defendant is ordered to stop causing a nuisance.

5.   The legal philosophy which evaluates law according to
     economic theory is:

     a.   the Analytical School.
     b.   the Legal Realists.
     c.   the Sociological School.
     d.   the Economic School.

6.   The U.S. Constitution accomplishes which of the follow-
     ing?

     a.   creates the powers of government
     b.   creates the structure of the federal government
     c.   limits the power of the federal government
     d.   all of the above

7.   The Natural Law School is based on which of the following
     principles?

     a.   customs of society
     b.   U.S. Constitution
     c.   basic ethical values
     d.   social science theories

8.   The concept of stare decisis does not provide which of
     the following to the American legal system?

     a.   stability
     b.   efficiency
     c.   inflexibility
     d.   predictability

9.   The highest court in the State of Arizona ruled that
     charitable organizations such as hospitals may be sued by
     injured parties. This decision overruled fifty years of

precedent which would not allow a charitable organization to be held liable for their own negligence.

Abigail Smith, while a patient in a Tempe hospital, was injured when she slipped and fell in the hallway due to water on the floor spilt by the janitor. Abigail sues the hospital; the hospital argues the suit should be dismissed. The court allows the case to go to trial. This is an example of:

a. check and balances.
b. stare decisis.
c. judicial review.
d. equity.

10. An example of a procedural law is:

a. the rule of contractual capacity.
b. negligence.
c. the crime of embezzlement.
d. the number of jurors on a jury.

11. Which of the following is an appropriate reason for departing from precedent?

a. changes in business practice
b. no longer applicable
c. technological change
d. all of the above

12. The separate but equal concept was overturned in which of the following cases?

a. Marbury v. Madison
b. Plessy v. Ferguson
c. Brown v. Board of Education
d. none of the above

13. Which of the following is a false statement concerning the concept of stare decisis?

a. Trial courts are constrained to follow the same rule in subsequent cases involving identical facts.
b. Relative certainty in the law.
c. Appellate courts must always follow precedent.
d. Established principles become well-known.

14. Which of the following statements is <u>false</u>?

a. Common law may not be changed by statute.
b. The plaintiff is the party bringing the lawsuit.

c. The defendant is the party responding to the plaintiff's claims.
d. The common law is relatively flexible.

15. Which of the following is not a proper way to classify
the law?

a. civil and criminal
b. substantive and procedural
c. public and private
d. all of the above are proper ways to classify the law

16. Bert Baxter lives next to a landfill where the city dumps
garbage collections every Tuesday and Thursday. Bert
notices that the paint on his house is peeling off due to
toxic fumes coming from the landfill. Bert is afraid to
use his backyard because of these fumes, and brings a
lawsuit against the landfill asking the court to enjoin
the landfill from disposing of toxic materials. If Bert
wins the case, the court will issue which of the following?

a. specific performance
b. rescission
c. laches
d. injunction

17. Refer to question 16. During the trial, Bert is not
entitled to which of the following?

a. a jury
b. equity
c. justice
d. all of the above

18. Refer to question 16. The landfill argues that Bert
Baxter has failed to bring his lawsuit promptly and asks
the court to dismiss the case. The landfill asserts that
toxic materials have always been disposed of at the site
since the landfill opened over ten years ago. If the
court dismisses Bert's lawsuit, this is an example of:

a. the statute of limitations.
b. specific performance.
c. the doctrine of laches.
d. the doctrine of clean hands.

19. The Federal Communications Commission (F.C.C.) creates a
rule which prohibits television advertisers from using

violence in commercials during prime time. The F.C.C.
was given the authority to make rules concerning television advertisers by Congress. This rule has the force of
law and is considered a:

a. regulation.
b. ordinance.
c. statute.
d. judge-made law.

20. The U.S. Constitution guarantees the citizens of the
United States many individual freedoms. In which of the
following might the U.S. Constitution have been violated?

a. A private company searches the desk of an employee.
b. A mother searches the room of her son.
c. A federal agent searches the office of a corporate
executive.
d. A security guard at a local mall searches an individual for shoplifting.

21. Which branch of the federal government has the responsibility of enforcing the law?

a. Congress
b. the executive
c. the courts
d. none of the above

22. Originally, courts of law could award which of the following remedies?

a. rescission
b. land
c. injunction
d. specific performance

23. Carl Caldwell has entered into a contract to buy 100
acres of prime land. Carl tricked the owner of the land
into selling it by making false representations about the
land and its value. The owner of the land later discovers that Carl was attempting to defraud him and refuses
to convey the property at the closing. Carl goes to
court asking for specific performance. The court refuses
because:

a. land is not a unique item.
b. specific performance does not apply.
c. money damages are available.
d. Carl does not have clean hands.

24. Which of the following are equitable maxims?

    a. Equality is equity.
    b. Whoever seeks equity must do equity.
    c. Equity will not suffer a right to exist without a remedy.
    d. All of the above.

25. Administrative agencies may have which of the following powers?

    a. legislative
    b. judicial review
    c. executive
    d. two of the above

Essay Question

1. The natural law philosophy is the basis for the Declaration of Independence and the U.S. Constitution. The Declaration of Independence was the official document which declared the colonies free from the governmental authority of the King of England. The Declaration of Independence severed the tie with England, enumerated the King's transgressions, and subsequently created a war. The American revolutionaries believed they were fully justified in denouncing the King and going to war. Why did the revolutionaries in the American Revolution believe they were justified in declaring war against England?

Answers to Study Questions

Fill-in-the-Blank Questions

Section 2-314 of the Uniform Commercial Code is an example of substantive law.

If a court interprets the term "sale of goods" to include new and used automobiles, this is an example of common law.

Under the code when a warranty is violated, the injured party may bring a lawsuit to recover money damages. This is an example of a civil law action.

If a judge orders the defendant to pay $5,000 to the plaintiff as damages, this order came from a law court.

True-False Questions

1. True (p. 16)

2. True (p. 16)

3. False. This is the Historical School of Thought. (p. 16)

4. False. This is the Analytical School. (p. 17)

5. False. All powers not delegated to the federal government are reserved for the states. (p. 18)

6. True (p. 18)

7. False. Ordinances are created by cities or counties. (p. 18)

8. True (p. 19)

9. False. The U.C.C. is a state statute, uniformly drafted. (p. 18)

10. True (p. 26)

Multiple-Choice Questions

1. b (p. 18)
2. a (p. 19)
3. d (p. 18)
4. b (p. 27)
5. d (p. 17)
6. d (p. 18)
7. c (p. 16)
8. c (p. 19)
9. b (p. 19)
10. d (p. 26)
11. d (p. 19)
12. c (p. 22)
13. c (p. 20)

14. a (p. 19)
15. d (p. 24)
16. d (p. 27)
17. a (p. 27)
18. c (p. 28)
19. a (p. 26)
20. c (p. 18)
21. b (p. 18)
22. b (p. 27)
23. d (p. 28)
24. d (p. 28)
25. d (p. 26)

Essay Question

1. The American Revolution was premised on the natural law ideal that "all men are created equal, that they are endowed by their Creator with certain unalienable rights." The revolutionaries believed that the Creator gave men

rights which could not be taken away by a governmental
body.   They believed the King had taken away their unalienable rights through various edicts.   Since the King
had transgressed upon their God-given rights, they were
justified in freeing themselves from such oppression.
The revolutionaries, believing in a higher authority over
the King, chose to follow a higher law.

The revolutionaries were not waging war to secure power
or wealth for themselves.   They believed in liberty and
equality for all and sought to make sure government
guaranteed it.   (p. 16)

Chapter 2
Ethics and Corporate
Social Responsibility

Major Concepts

Ethics and corporate social responsibility have received a
vast amount of attention during the last decade. Ethics
involves an individual's system of moral values and beliefs.
The moral value system adopted by an individual will direct
behavior when ethical issues are faced. Cultural background,
experiences, religion, and political beliefs all may influence
an individual's ethical behavior. In most instances, the law
is considered the minimum ethical level. Most legal activity
can also be labeled as ethical. Although in some cases,
equating legal with ethical and illegal with unethical produces absurd results.

Ethical issues require business to clarify goals and objectives among various interests. The corporation must consider
the shareholders, employees, customers, suppliers, and the
community when making decisions.

The law develops in response to societal values. As the
values of society change, the law will also change. A nation
may experience highs and lows in ethical behavior according to
the level of responsibility demanded by society. What was
legal and ethical twenty years ago may not be legal or ethical
today. Society is constantly reprioritizing what it values.

Chapter Outline

I.   <u>Ethical Conduct</u>--The concept of ethics has been debated
     for hundreds of years. Ethics may be defined as a set
     of rules of conduct in which we judge the behavior of
     others or our own. Ethics is the process of evaluating
     behavior to determine if it is wrong or right. An indi-
     vidual's ethics is based upon his or her value system.
     Most people value behavior which is fair, just, and
     socially desirable. Each person may have a different
     perspective on what is ethical. An individual's cul-
     tural background, experience, religious beliefs, and
     political beliefs formulate his or her value system and
     determine behavior. Despite wide differences in society
     concerning values, there must be a minimum behavioral
     level expected of all members of society. The law
     establishes the minimum duty required of all individuals
     and business. Conduct below the minimum is usually
     illegal.

     However, the law is not the absolute guide on ethics.
     Since the process of lawmaking is subject to corruption,
     the law may promote unethical conduct. In some cases,
     no law exists to govern the conduct of society in a par-
     ticular area. The law in most instances provides param-
     eters for society to operate within.

     A.   <u>Ethical Issues</u>--An ethical issue arises when a busi-
          nessperson is faced with making a decision in light
          of several competing interests among parties in-
          volved. Ethical dilemmas often involve employees
          who must decide whether or not to inform public of-
          ficials of unsafe or illegal activity of the employ-
          er. The dilemma stems from the conflict between the
          employee's legal duty of loyalty to the employer and
          the employee's moral responsibility to protect con-
          sumers or other employees from unsafe conditions.
          The employee must weigh the interests of all those
          involved to determine the proper response. In some
          states, the employer can terminate an employee-at-
          will (i.e., whistle-blower) without fear of legal
          recourse by the employee. Other states allow the
          employee to sue the employer for wrongful discharge.

     B.   <u>Changing Standards of Ethical Behavior</u>--The values
          of society are reflected in the law. The law
          responds to changes in society's values. If society
          places a high value on a drug-free workplace, the
          laws will reflect an intolerance to drug usage and
          drug dealing.

II. Theories of Ethical Conduct--Philosophers have debated a
     variety of ethical theories over the centuries. A
     knowledge of ethical theory is extremely useful to busi-
     ness managers in the decision-making process.

     A. Normative Ethics--The area of normative ethics con-
         siders the norm or the standard of correct behavior.
         Asking the practical questions of what should a
         person do in a particular situation is normative
         ethics. Deciding what is right and wrong. Norma-
         tive ethics is divided into deontological and teleo-
         logical theories.

         1. Deontology--The deontological theory is based
             upon the concept of duty or obligation of an
             individual. Moral values are known and abso-
             lute. A deontologist follows a moral code as a
             matter of duty to do the right action. This
             theory emphasizes the action itself as being
             right or wrong.

         2. Teleology--The teleological theory determines
             right and wrong by the consequences or end re-
             sult of a person's actions.

     B. Utilitarianism--The theory of utilitarianism empha-
         sizes pleasure or happiness as the desired end of
         all human action. A set of rules to maximize
         happiness all around is the basis of the theory.
         The basic premise of utilitarianism is "the greatest
         good for the greatest number."

III. The Corporation's Responsibility of Business Ethics--
     Management must consider the internal and external
     ethical dilemmas that may arise. The corporation must
     deal with ethical issues arising from the relationships
     with shareholders, employees, customers, suppliers, and
     the community or public at large.

     A. Shareholders and Ethics--The primary interest of
         shareholders is to maximize the profits of the cor-
         poration. Shareholders as owners of the corporation
         expect a return on their investment in the form of
         dividends. The objective of profit maximization is
         contrary to a decision by management to increase
         employee wages, lower prices, improve the quality
         and safety of a product for the consumer, or make
         large monetary contributions to the community. Any
         decrease in revenues and increase in costs will

lower profits and may conflict with short-term earnings per share expectations.

Some economists believe the sole responsibility of management is to maximize profits, although management must learn to balance the interests of all the parties involved.

The common law has provided management the freedom to make decisions without the pressure of shareholder demands, although management is responsible for exercising its business judgment in good faith.

Directors of a corporation have the power to declare a dividend or reinvest the earnings in the company for capital investment, increased wages, or improvement of the product. The court will not interfere in the management of the corporation, unless the directors or officers are guilty of fraud or misappropriation of corporate funds or abuse their discretion. The shareholders may force the corporation to declare a cash dividend when the directors have abused their discretion by not distributing cash when a large surplus exists.

B. Employees and Ethics--The employer has a responsibility to treat employees fairly. The employer must determine the appropriate wages and benefits to be paid to employees. The employer must provide a safe working environment for employees.

The Occupational Safety and Health Act requires the employer to provide working conditions free of recognized hazards. Providing safe working conditions may be costly to the employer. The higher the production costs the higher prices consumers will pay for the product. The employer will have to balance the employee's interest in safety against the consumer's interest in low-priced products.

Employers must treat employees fairly in hiring, training, compensation, and terminations. Under the Civil Rights Act of 1964, the employer is prohibited from discriminating against an individual because of race, color, national origin, sex, or religion. The Act covers employers with 15 or more employees. Subsequent acts of Congress prohibit age and handicap discrimination.

C. <u>Customers and Ethics</u>--Business must consider the well-being of the consumer when determining the quality of a product, the price, and how to advertise the product. It is in the best interests of the corporation to satisfy the consumer, as the consumer has the power to freely choose to buy or not to buy the products of the corporation.

Management is required to keep abreast of product research and inform the consumer if the product is defective or hazardous. Present theories of products liability favor the consumer. The law has placed the burden on business to produce products free of defects which could harm consumers.

What is the ethical responsibility of a corporation whose product is disapproved by the Food and Drug Administration for sale in the United States but legal to sell in other in countries? Should the corporation market the drug in other countries? Management must decide between short-term profits and the well-being of citizens of foreign nations.

D. <u>Suppliers and Ethics</u>--Business has an ethical responsibility to current suppliers when management is considering buying from a new supplier. In most cases, the decision to buy supplies from one source or another is based upon price. Ceasing to do business with a supplier may cause an adverse effect on the supplier and even bankruptcy.

E. <u>The Community and Ethics</u>--Most corporations donate to charitable organizations such as hospitals, universities, and the arts. At one time in the United States, it was illegal for a corporation to give to charity. The law has changed to vest the corporation with the power to engage in philanthropic activities.

The corporation must also consider the effect of polluting the air and water, doing business with South Africa, and the effect on a community if the corporation closes a plant.

III. <u>Legal Ethics</u>--Attorneys are required to follow a code of professional ethics. If an attorney breaches the code of ethics, he or she may be disciplined and disbarred.

Study Questions

Fill-in-the-Blank Questions

The United States Steel Corporation sold tubular products to the oil and gas industry. An employee of the U.S. Steel Corporation believed one of the company's products was defective and voiced his concern with management.

If the employee is terminated for attempting to make the product safer by notifying management, he may _____ _____ the employer.   (never sue/
  in some states sue)

The employee-at-will concept comes from _____ _____.   (the common law/
  a state statute)

The law must discourage frivolous lawsuits by employees which disrupt business but also encourage employees to _____ unethical, unsafe, or
    (expose/keep silent about)
illegal behavior.

An employee who informs a government official of his company's illegal activity is called a _____.
                    (whistle-blower/supplier)

True-False Questions

1. Ethical conduct is fair, just, and socially desirable. _____

2. Ethics and legality are one in the same. _____

3. Each person's definition of ethics depends on his or her unique cultural background, experience, religious and political beliefs. _____

4. A whistle-blower is one who informs public officials of an unsafe or illegal activity conducted covertly by a business. _____

5. All courts in the U.S. allow a whistle-blower to bring a cause of action against the employer. _____

6. The law is unchangeable despite changing societal values. _____

7. A corporate board of directors cannot be compelled to declare dividends. _____

8. OSHA is the federal administrative agency which requires employers to treat employees fairly in hiring. _____

9. Manufacturers may have a responsibility to notify consumers of the hazards of using a product. _____

10. Some economists believe the corporation's only responsibility is to maximize profits. _____

Multiple-Choice Questions

1. Which of the following individuals said, "There is one and only one social responsibility of business . . . to increase profits"?

   a. Daniel Patrick Moynihan
   b. Henry Ford
   c. Milton Friedman
   d. George Geary

2. Which of the following theories was founded by Jeremy Bentham?

   a. teleology
   b. normative ethics
   c. deontology
   d. utilitarianism

3. Which of the following is a proposition of utilitarianism?

   a. greatest happiness of greatest number
   b. legal duty
   c. of the obligation
   d. ends justify the means

4. The word "ethics" evolved from the Greek word "ethos." Ethics is defined as which of the following?

   a. habitual code of conduct
   b. custom
   c. a system of moral standards
   d. all of the above

5. The salary of a company's chief executive officer (CEO) may be several million dollars even though the company itself is not earning a profit. Which of the following regulates how much the CEO should be paid?

    a. Securities Exchange Commission
    b. Occupational Safety and Health Administration
    c. U.S. Attorney General
    d. none of the above

6. If shareholders believe corporate directors acted improperly by not declaring a dividend, they may:

    a. sue for personal damages.
    b. sue to compel the directors to declare a dividend.
    c. demand the board of directors resign.
    d. none of the above.

7. The board of directors of Ford Motor Company voted to market a new automobile called the Edsel. The board believed this new design would become a best-seller and increase Ford's market share. Based upon reasonable projections, sales of the new auto were to be highly profitable. The Edsel turned out to be a disaster for Ford, costing the company millions of dollars. The board of directors decided not to declare a dividend that year. A group of minority shareholders sued the board of directors. The court will not interfere unless:

    a. the directors committed fraud.
    b. there was misappropriation of funds.
    c. a surplus of net profits exists.
    d. all of the above.

8. Refer to question 7. If the shareholders are to win the case, they must prove which of the following?

      I. fraud
     II. abuse of discretion
    III. breach of good faith

    a. I only
    b. I or II
    c. I or II or III
    d. III only

9. The Occupational Safety and Health Administration has the authority to inspect and establish which of the following?

a. employee compensation
b. benefits for sick leave
c. hiring practices
d. safe working conditions

10. Employers have a legal duty to treat employees fairly in which of the following?

   I. hiring
  II. training
 III. compensating

a. I only
b. I and II
c. I, II, and III
d. I and III

11. Joan Murray desired to become an accomplished dancer. She auditioned at a local dance studio where the instructor told her she had great dance ability and potential. Joan signed up for $31,000 in dance lessons over a period of two years. Joan relied on the positive statements made by the instructor when purchasing additional dance lessons. Joan later discovered she has very little dance ability and wants to rescind the dance agreement. Which of the following theories of recovery will Joan assert?

a. negligence
b. fraud
c. abuse of discretion
d. business judgment rule

12. Refer to question 11. The instructor will attempt to assert which of the following defenses?

a. trade puffing
b. a mere opinion
c. a prediction
d. all of the above

13. In 1989, The Exxon Valdez spilled 11 million gallons of crude oil in Prince William Sound. Hundreds of lawsuits were filed as a result of the disaster. Which of the following is (are) causes of the damage?

a. cost reduction by Exxon
b. Congress' failure to have adequate procedures to deal with spills
c. Alaska's failure to have personnel and equipment to deal with spills
d. all of the above

14. Union Carbide operated a pesticide factory in Bhopal,
     India. Forty tons of toxic gasses were released from the
     plant, killing approximately 1,800 people. In 1989, the
     government of India settled with Union Carbide on behalf
     of the families for how much?

     a. $3.3 billion
     b. $500 million
     c. $470 million
     d. $5 million

15. Which of the following has drafted a code of ethics for
     attorneys?

     a.   American Bar Association
     b.   American Trial Attorneys Association
     c.   Office of Legislative Counsel
     d.   Department of Justice

Essay Question

 1. The Johns-Manville Corporation manufactured asbestos for
     several years before it was known that asbestos was haz-
     ardous to human health. The Johns-Manville Corporation
     filed for protection under the 1978 Bankruptcy Reform Act
     due to the large number of asbestos claims. The company
     estimates the claims as something over $2 billion when
     the net worth of the company is just over $1 billion.
     The reason for the company's large potential liability
     stems from products liability law. What was the ethical
     responsibility of the company before bankruptcy?

Answers to Study Questions

Fill-in-the-Blank Questions

If the employee is terminated for attempting to make the product safe by notifying management, he may <u>in some states sue</u>
the employer. (p. 39)

The employee-at-will concept comes from <u>the common law</u>.
(p. 39)

The law must discourage frivolous lawsuits by employees which
disrupt business but also encourage employees to <u>expose</u> unethical, unsafe, or illegal behavior. (p. 39)

An employee who informs a governmental official of his company's illegal activity is called a <u>whistle-blower</u>.   (p. 39)

True-False Questions

1. True (p. 34)

2. False. Ethics and legality have similar definitions but are not the same. (p. 35)

3. True (p. 34)

4. True (p. 39)

5. False. Not all courts in the U.S. allow wrongful discharge causes of action. (p. 39)

6. False. The law may change to reflect societal values. (p. 35)

7. False. A corporate board of directors can be forced to declare dividends. (p. 36)

8. False. OSHA has authority over worker safety not hiring practices. (p. 39)

9. True (p. 40)

10. True (p. 33)

Multiple-Choice Questions

1.	c (p. 33)		9.	d (p. 39)
2.	d (p. 35)		10.	c (p. 39)
3.	a (p. 35)		11.	b (p. 41)
4.	d (p. 34)		12.	d (p. 41)
5.	d (p. 38)		13.	d (p. 43)
6.	b (p. 37)		14.	c (p. 45)
7.	d (p. 37)		15.	a (p. 48)
8.	c (p. 37)			

Essay Question

1. Did the company know the dangers attached to the use of asbestos? If the company knew or had reason to know that the product could be hazardous, the law imposes a duty to warn consumers of the potential danger and remedy the

defect. Should the company have more extensively tested
the product to determine its safety? The courts have not
clearly answered the question of how much research must
be done before a company puts a product on the market.

Under strict tort liability, the company is liable for
damages if the product is defective, the defect made the
product unreasonably dangerous, and the defect proxi-
mately caused the injury. Strict liability does not
require the proof of fault by the manufacturer. Under
strict liability, Johns-Manville can be held responsible.
The products liability law seeks to provide an incentive
for manufacturers to improve product safety and to spread
the risk of injury. (p. 40)

Chapter 3
The Judicial System and Litigation

Major Concepts

The legal system in the United States is primarily a common law system. The courts play an important role in resolving disputes and interpreting the laws enacted by legislatures and the U.S. Constitution.

In order for a court to adjudicate a dispute, the court must have jurisdiction. Jurisdiction is the authority of a court to decide a controversy over a type of subject matter, a person, or property. Subject matter jurisdiction is the authority of a court to hear a particular type of case, such as a lawsuit involving the probate of a will or a traffic violation. In personam jurisdiction is the authority of a court to hear and decide a case over a specific person. The court must have in personam jurisdiction to order the defendant to pay damages. In rem jurisdiction is the court's authority to hear and decide a matter involving real or personal property.

The court system in the United States is comprised of federal and state courts. In both state and federal court systems, a plaintiff will have an opportunity to bring his or her case to trial at the court of original entry. A party may appeal to a higher level court where the appellate court will review the record of the trial. Appellate courts function as courts of review and do not hear new evidence or impanel juries.

The judicial process in a civil case involves a series of steps. The parties must receive adequate notice of the lawsuit and a copy of the complaint. The parties will have an opportunity to challenge the sufficiency of the complaint and the answer through pretrial motions. The parties are allowed to discover the evidence pertaining to the case. The trial will give each party an opportunity to prove their case.

Chapter Outline

I. Jurisdiction--A court must have jurisdiction in order to hear and decide a case. Jurisdiction is the authority of a court to decide a controversy over the subject matter of the case, the parties involved, and sometimes property. Judgments rendered by state courts where jurisdiction requirements have been met may be enforced in other states under the Full Faith and Credit Clause of the U.S. Constitution.

Jurisdiction is essential for a court to exercise its authority to order legal and equitable relief. Venue is the geographic location of the lawsuit. Venue may be changed if holding the trial in a certain locality is inconvenient to the parties or a defendant is not able to get a fair and impartial trial in a particular community.

A. In Personam Jurisdiction--The court must have in personam jurisdiction to decide a case and order a defendant to do or not do something. If the defendant is a resident of the state, the state court may assert in personam jurisdiction by personally serving the defendant with a summons and complaint. This method of giving a party actual notice of the legal action is called Service of Process. A corporation that has been incorporated in the state where the lawsuit is filed is subject to the in personam jurisdiction of that state's courts. State courts ordinarily can only obtain jurisdiction over persons or property located within the geographical boundaries of the state.

If the defendant is a nonresident of the state, the court may still exercise in personam jurisdiction over the defendant if the defendant has committed a tort in the state. State Long Arm Statutes allow state courts to obtain in personam jurisdiction over a nonresident when the nonresident defendant has committed a tort (civil wrong) within the state. The commission of a civil wrong (e.g., negligent operation of a motor vehicle) in the state is considered a minimum contact or a relationship with the

state.   The Due Process Clause of the U.S. Constitution requires there be minimum contacts between the
forum state (i.e., state where lawsuit is filed) and
the nonresident defendant for traditional notions of
fair play and substantial justice to not be of-
fended. Both the federal and state courts may uti-
lize a state's long arm statute to assert jurisdiction.

The state may also use the long arm statute where a
nonresident corporation does a substantial amount of
business in a forum state. Nonresidents must be
served with a summons and complaint either in person
or through the mails.

B.   In Rem Jurisdiction--A state court may take control
over real or personal property if the property is
located within the state. If the court has in rem
jurisdiction, the court has power over the property
at issue. If a defendant fails to pay after the
court has ordered the payment of damages to the
plaintiff, the plaintiff may seek to attack the
defendant's property and have it sold to pay off the
amount owed. The court must have in rem jurisdiction over the property of the defendant in order to
have the local law enforcement officers take possession of the defendant's property and subsequently
sell it at a public sale. A court located in one
state does not have in rem jurisdiction over real
property located in another state.

C.   Subject Matter Jurisdiction--State courts have general subject matter jurisdiction or, in other words,
very broad jurisdiction. Subject matter jurisdiction allows a court to have the authority to decide
certain types of cases. It is the subject matter of
the lawsuit which is important for determining subject matter jurisdiction. Some courts only have
subject matter jurisdiction up to a certain specified dollar amount (e.g., small claims court usually
up to $2,500) or according to a specific kind of
case, such as probate or bankruptcy. Each court
must have subject matter jurisdiction to hear and
decide a case. For example, a state trial court
would not have subject matter jurisdiction to discharge a debtor under federal bankruptcy law.

D.   Quasi In Rem Jurisdiction--Where a lawsuit does not
directly involve property, but the court renders a
judgment concerning the defendant's property.

II.   <u>Court Systems in the United States</u>--Each state and the
       federal government have independent court systems. In
       addition, the District of Columbia has its own federal
       court system. Rules of procedure are uniform among fed-
       eral courts but widely different among the states.
       Courts may generally be classified as either trial
       courts or appellate courts (i.e., courts of review). A
       plaintiff must initially enter at the trial court level
       before proceeding to an appellate court.

       The federal court system and most state court systems
       have three tiers. The bottom level consists of various
       trial courts which hear all the evidence presented by
       the plaintiff and defendant. The parties must be al-
       lowed an opportunity to prove their case. Once a
       decision is rendered by the trial court, either party
       has the right to appeal the case to the next level
       court. This intermediate appellate court will only
       review the trial court's decision. During the appeal,
       no new evidence is presented by the parties and in most
       cases a panel of judges will determine if the trial
       court applied the law correctly. The appellate court
       accepts the facts as provided by the trial court. If
       the appellate court finds some material error in appli-
       cation of the law by the trial court, the decision will
       be reversed and sometimes sent back (i.e., remanded) to
       the trial court for further deliberations. A party may
       appeal the decision of the appellate court to a higher
       level appellate court. As to decisions concerning state
       law where no federal issue is involved, the decision of
       a state's highest court is final.

   A.   <u>State Court Systems</u>--A state trial court may have
         either general or limited subject matter jurisdic-
         tion. If the court has general subject matter
         jurisdiction, then a vast array of cases may be
         heard by the court. Trial courts with limited
         subject matter jurisdiction may only hear specific
         types of cases. The trial court may have many
         names, such as district court, superior court,
         circuit court, and even supreme court. In many
         states, the supreme court is the highest level
         appellate court of that state.

         State appellate courts have jurisdiction to hear
         only appeals concerning issues of law. Appellate
         courts do not retry the case but decide if the trial
         court was in error.

B. <u>Federal Court System</u>--The federal court system is three-tiered consisting of trial courts called district courts, intermediate courts of appeals called courts of appeals, and the highest court called the Supreme Court.

    1. <u>District Courts</u>--Every state has at least one federal district court. There are ninety-five federal judicial districts. In some cases, a district covers the entire state, and in states with large populations, there may be several districts.

       Some district courts have very limited jurisdiction, such as the United States Tax Court and the United States Bankruptcy Court.

    2. <u>Courts of Appeals</u>--There are twelve appellate judicial circuits which hear cases from district courts located in the circuit. A thirteenth circuit has been created and is known as the Federal Circuit located in the District of Columbia. The courts of appeals do not have original jurisdiction but review lower court decisions in panels of three judges.

    3. <u>Supreme Court of the United States</u>--The highest court of the federal system is the U.S. Supreme Court with eight associate justices and one Chief Justice. The justices of the Supreme Court are appointed by the President with Senate confirmation and hold their office during good behavior. The Supreme Court usually operates as an appellate court reviewing the decisions of other federal courts.

        a. <u>Which Cases Reach the Supreme Court</u>--In most cases, an appeal to the Supreme Court is under a writ of certiorari requesting the high court to review the lower courts' decision where a federal issue is involved. No absolute right of appeal exists to the Supreme Court.

        b. <u>Writ of Certiorari</u>--The parties may petition the Supreme Court to issue a writ of certiorari which requires the lower court to send the record to the Supreme Court for review. The granting of the writ is in the discretion of the Supreme Court. Most cases under review involve substantial federal issues for resolve by the Supreme Court.

Approximately 5,000 petitions are submitted to the Supreme Court each year requesting an appeal, of these only 125 to 150 will be heard by the Court.

(1) <u>Issuance of Writ of Certiorari</u>--In five situations, the Supreme Court is likely to issue a writ of certiorari.

    (a) When a state supreme court has decided a substantial federal question.

    (b) When two federal courts of appeals disagree.

    (c) When a federal appeals court has decided an important federal question not yet decided by the Court or has decided a case in conflict with decisions of the Court or departed from usual judicial procedure.

    (d) When a federal court of appeals holds a state statute inviolation of federal law.

    (e) When a federal court holds an act of Congress unconstitutional and the federal government or its employee is a party.

c. <u>Judicial Review</u>--The power of judicial review is the Supreme Court's authority to review and declare unconstitutional the laws of Congress. It is the duty of the Court to say what the law is. The power of judicial review is not found in the U.S. Constitution. The Supreme Court in <u>Marbury v. Madison</u> decided it had such power.

4. <u>Jurisdiction in the Federal Court System</u>--Federal courts are courts of limited subject matter jurisdiction. Not every plaintiff has the right to file his or her case in federal district court. The two most common methods of subject

matter jurisdiction are federal question and diversity of citizenship.

a.   Federal Question Jurisdiction--A cause of action based on the U.S. Constitution, a treaty, or a federal law may be brought in a federal court because it raises a federal question. The plaintiff need not be suing for a minimum amount to bring the lawsuit.

b.   Diversity of Citizenship Jurisdiction--In a diversity of citizenship case, the plaintiff and defendant must be citizens of different states and the amount in controversy must exceed $50,000. Citizens of foreign countries qualify as citizens of different states for diversity purposes. No plaintiff and defendant can be citizens of the same state in a diversity of citizenship case.

In some cases, a state court and federal court may have jurisdiction over the parties and the subject matter at the same time; this is called concurrent jurisdiction. Where only one court has jurisdiction over a case, this is known as exclusive jurisdiction.

III. Judicial Procedures: Following a Case Through the Courts--The adversary system used in the United States promotes the fact finding function of the court. Judges act as independent overseers to this process allowing opposing parties to zealously present their side of the case. The procedures differ between state and federal courts as well as between civil and criminal cases. Most businesses at one time or another will be involved in a civil lawsuit either as a plaintiff or defendant.

A.   Trial Procedures in a Civil Case

1.   Pleadings--The pleadings are the initial legal documents which formulate the issues of a case. The basic documents known as the pleadings are the complaint, the answer, and the reply. The complaint is the formal document which generally alleges the plaintiff's case against the defendant. The complaint along with a summons is usually personally served on the defendant by local marshal or sheriff. The summons gives the defendant notice of the lawsuit and requires the

defendant to answer the complaint and appear in court on a specified date.

The answer is filed with the clerk of the court by the defendant. The answer outlines the defenses of the defendant and refutes the plaintiff's allegations. The defendant may wish to file a counterclaim alleging a cause of action against the plaintiff. If the plaintiff has failed to state a cause of action, the defendant may have the case dismissed. Where a counterclaim has been filed, the plaintiff must reply to the defendant's allegations.

2. Pretrial Motions--Either party may attempt to dispose of the case before it goes to trial through various motions. If no issue of fact needs to be resolved, the court may grant a summary judgment in favor of the plaintiff or defendant. Or if the plaintiff has failed to state a cause of action, the defendant may ask the court to dismiss the case.

3. Discovery--Before the trial, the parties attempt to gather all the evidence through examining records, documents, and witnesses. Either party may use depositions or written interrogatories to ask witnesses and parties to the case questions about the facts of the case. Depositions are taken under oath, a court official records the question asked of the witness and the answer provided. Interrogatories are a series of written questions served upon a witness or party that must be answered and returned to the opposing party.

4. Pretrial Hearing--Usually prior to the trial, a conference is held between the parties' attorneys and the judge. The pretrial hearing is intended to facilitate a settlement between the parties, avoiding the expense and time of a trial.

5. The Trial--If a settlement is not reached during the pretrial hearing, the case will proceed to trial. If a party requests a jury, the court will select a panel of citizens for jury duty. The attorneys and the judge will attempt to eliminate any potential jury member who may not be able to render an independent and fair decision.

The trial begins with opening statements by the opposing parties. The plaintiff's counsel makes the first opening statement, followed by the defendant's counsel. The plaintiff must prove his or her case by a preponderance of the evidence in a civil suit seeking money damages. In a criminal case, the plaintiff (i.e., government prosecutor) must prove the case beyond a reasonable doubt.

At the close of the plaintiff's case the defendant may ask the judge for a directed verdict. If the plaintiff fails to prove his or her case, the judge will grant the defendant's motion and the trial will be over.

Both parties may present closing arguments which summarize their side of the case. Each party will urge the judge and the jury to decide in their favor. In a jury case, the judge will instruct the jury as to the appropriate law to apply to the facts. The jury will decide the facts of the case, and the judge will decide the law to be applied. If no jury exists, the judge will decide both issues of fact and law.

A final decision made by the jury is called a verdict. The judge will sign an order incorporating the verdict which then becomes the judgment.

After the trial, a party may request the judge to overturn the jury's verdict (i.e., motion for a judgment notwithstanding the verdict) or have a new trial conducted or appeal the case to an appellate court.

IV. The Judiciary

A. State Judicial Selection Procedures--State judges may be elected or appointed to the bench depending on state statute. Usually, judicial appointments are based on a merit selection system which allows applicants to apply for openings. Judicial committees examine the applicant's qualifications, recommending a particular applicant for appointment.

B. Federal Judicial Selection Procedures--Openings in the federal court system are filled by Presidential appointments upon Senate confirmation. An appointment to the federal bench is usually for life.

Study Questions

Fill-in-the Blank Questions

The ABC Corporation entered into a contract with Business Systems Computer Corporations (BSCC) for the purchase of several business computers totalling $45,000. ABC takes delivery of the computers and pays half of the total amount owed. During the installation of the computers, ABC's president becomes dissatisfied with the system and refuses to pay BSCC the remaining amount owed.

BSCC brings a lawsuit against ABC by filing a _____ _____ with the clerk of the court.   (cross-claim/ complaint)

ABC believes they have been defrauded into buying a computer system which does not meet their needs. ABC wants to sue BSCC in the same lawsuit. ABC must file a _____ _____ with the clerk of the court.   (counterclaim/ reply)

In order for the court to decide the case, the court must have _____ jurisdiction. (In rem/subject-matter)

The _____ notifies the defendant that he (complaint/summons) or she must file an answer and appear in court on a specified date.

True-False Questions

1. In personam jurisdiction is the power the court has over real property. _____

2. The long arm statute is a federal statute allowing federal courts to obtain jurisdiction over nonresidents. _____

3. Venue is concerned with the geographic area where a lawsuit should be brought. _____

4. The federal court system is a three-tiered system. _____

5. State supreme courts are always the highest level court in the state. _____

6. Appellate courts are generally known as courts of review. _____

7. Trial courts have original jurisdiction in cases coming before the court for the first time. _____

8. The federal courts are generally courts with broad subject matter jurisdiction. _____

9. The appellant is the party bringing an appeal before an appellate court. _____

10. Under federal question jurisdiction, the plaintiff must be suing for more than $50,000. _____

Multiple-Choice Questions

1. The _____ of the Constitution requires the enforcement of judgments made in sister states.

    a. equal protection clause
    b. full faith and credit clause
    c. judicial review clause
    d. writ of certiorari

2. The long arm statute may be used by:

    a. state courts.
    b. federal courts.
    c. voir dire.
    d. two of the above.

3. The pleadings in a civil case do not include which of the following?

    a. writ of mandamus
    b. complaint
    c. answer
    d. reply

4. Which of the following is not a federal court?

    a. U.S. Bankruptcy Court
    b. U.S. Tax Court
    c. probate court
    d. District Court

5. In which of the following cases would a federal district court have subject matter jurisdiction?

a. Plaintiff sues alleging a violation of a federal statute by defendant.
b. Plaintiff sues for breach of contract by defendant.
c. Plaintiff sues to clear a defect of the title.
d. Plaintiff sues the defendant for negligently operating a motor vehicle. (Plaintiff and defendant are from the same state.)

6. When a case can be tried by only one court, it is said the court has _____ jurisdiction.

a. concurrent
b. exclusive
c. federal question
d. in rem

7. When the U.S. Supreme Court grants a writ of certiorari, the Court is:

a. retrying the case.
b. dismissing the case.
c. ordering the lower court to send the record for review.
d. remanding the case to the lower court.

8. Which of the following will be issued by a court to assist a party in collection of a claim?

a. a cross-claim
b. subpoena duces tecum
c. subpoena
d. writ of attachment

9. Jack Smith has brought a lawsuit against Acme Supply Co. for breaching a contract for the sale of $10,000 of office supplies. Jack has properly filed all the documents and appears in court on the day of the trial. Acme does not file an answer and fails to appear in court for the trial. The court will:

a. dismiss the case.
b. issue a default judgment.
c. issue a summary judgment.
d. issue a directed verdict.

10. If a party demands a jury trial, the jury will decide which of the following?

a. issues of fact
b. issues of jurisdiction

    c.   issues of law
    d.   all of the above

11.   In a lawsuit in which the defendant answers the plaintiff's complaint and files a counterclaim, the plaintiff must do which of the following?

    a.   the plaintiff need not do anything
    b.   file a reply
    c.   file a cross complaint
    d.   file a motion to dismiss

12.   Baxter, Inc. is suing John Smith, a former employee, for the conversion of company assets while on the job. Both the plaintiff and the defendant have filed the appropriate pleadings. Upon examination by the court of the complaint and the answer, it is discovered that no issues of fact need to be resolved. Either party may motion the court to:

    a.   issue a directed verdict.
    b.   order a new trial.
    c.   issue a summary judgment.
    d.   issue a writ of certiorari.

13.   Which of the following is not a procedural device to obtain information during the discovery stage?

    a.   oral depositions
    b.   written interrogatories
    c.   uniform interrogatories
    d.   voir dire

14.   The conference held prior to the trial, attended by opposing attorneys and the judge, to attempt a settlement is called:

    a.   pretrial hearing.
    b.   voir dire.
    c.   opening statements.
    d.   discovery.

15.   The burden of proof in a criminal case is:

    a.   by a preponderance of the evidence.
    b.   by clear and convincing evidence.
    c.   beyond a reasonable doubt.
    d.   beyond all doubt.

16. During the trial, the plaintiff called a witness to the stand to testify. After the direct examination of the witness by the plaintiff's attorney, the defendant's attorney may:

    a. redirect.
    b. rebut.
    c. cross-examine.
    d. recross-examine.

17. Ken Kaiser was injured when he fell down the stairs at a friend's house. The carpeting on the stairs had not been properly secured to the stairs causing Ken to slip and fall. Ken sues the homeowner for his injury and loses at the state trial court. Ken appeals the decision to the state's highest court of appeals. The court affirms the trial court's decision as to state law on homeowner liability. The court followed the rule of contributory negligence barring Ken from any recovery. Ken may now appeal the case to the:

    a. U.S. District Court.
    b. U.S. Court of Appeals.
    c. U.S. Supreme Court.
    d. Ken may not appeal.

18. Dick Jones is involved in an auto accident with Sally Smith on the expressway. Sally believes Dick was driving negligently when he cut in front of her without first signalling. Sally sues Dick in state court for the damage done to her brand new mini van. Sally will need to prove her case by:

    a. clear and convincing evidence.
    b. a preponderance of evidence.
    c. beyond all doubt.
    d. beyond a reasonable doubt.

19. Refer to question 18. Sally wins her case against Dick, and the court orders Dick to pay damages of $18,000. Dick wants to appeal the case to the next highest level appellate court. In order for the appellate court to reverse the lower court's decision, Dick will have to prove:

    a. an error was made by the judge in applying the law.
    b. the facts were incorrectly interpreted by the jury.
    c. Sally failed to prove her case beyond a reasonable doubt.
    d. none of the above.

20. Sue Clark purchased a new automobile from Autoworld, Inc. on credit. Sue agreed to pay $200 per month over four years. The dealer, Autoworld, failed to disclose the annual Percentage Rate in the contract Sue signed. This was a clear violation of the state Fair Credit Act, subjecting Autoworld to a fine of up to $10,000. Sue brings a private action for violation of the state statute. Does the federal district court have subject matter jurisdiction?

   a. Yes, because a statute was violated.
   b. Yes, because a federal question exists.
   c. Yes, because of diversity of citizenship.
   d. No, because there lacks a basis for federal jurisdiction.

21. Vincent was arrested by F.B.I. agents after he held up a federally insured savings and loan. Federal prosecutors will have to prove the case:

   a. by clear and convincing evidence.
   b. beyond a reasonable doubt.
   c. by a preponderance of the evidence.
   d. beyond all doubt.

22. Barney bought a brand new copy machine from Copy Inc. for use in his business. The copy machine never really worked right, and Copy Inc. refused to make the needed repairs. Barney, after months of frustration, filed a small claims case against Copy Inc. for breach of contract. The case came to trial without a jury, and Barney won a $2,000 judgment. Copy Inc. may pursue which of the following?

   a. appeal
   b. motion for judgment notwithstanding the verdict
   c. summary judgment
   d. motion to dismiss

23. Joseph, an Illinois resident, was involved in an auto accident with Molly, a California resident, in the state of Kansas. Joseph brought a lawsuit against Molly for the damage to his automobile and his personal injuries totalling $57,000. Does the federal court located in Illinois have subject matter jurisdiction to hear the case?

   a. Yes, because of diversity of citizenship.
   b. Yes, because of federal question.
   c. No, because the plaintiff is from Illinois.
   d. No, because the defendant is from California.

24.   Refer to question 23. If Molly is personally served with
      the summons and complaint while in California, will the
      federal district court in Illinois have in personam ju-
      risdiction?

      a.   Yes, because of diversity of citizenship.
      b.   No, because there is no federal question.
      c.   No, because the defendant does not have minimum con-
           tacts with Illinois.
      d.   Yes, because traditional notions of fairness are met.

25.   The New York State Welfare Commission has terminated the
      welfare benefits of Susan Smith. Susan believes her due
      process rights have been violated by the Welfare Commis-
      sion. Susan files her lawsuit in federal district court
      after appealing to the Commission. Does the federal
      district court have subject matter jurisdiction to hear
      the case?

      a.   Yes, because of diversity of citizenship.
      b.   Yes, because of a federal question.
      c.   No, because of minimum contacts.
      d.   No, because Susan was not entitled to welfare bene-
           fits.

Essay Question

1.   Hubert Howard is the regional sales representative for
     Comptrol Office Machines, Inc. Hubert is responsible for
     sales of Comptrol machines in three states. Comptrol's
     corporate headquarters is in Seattle, Washington.
     Hubert, one day while traveling in California to meet a
     client, was involved in an auto accident. Hubert
     inadvertently ran a red light and collided with Hugo
     Smith, a California resident. Hugo's car is totally
     destroyed, but he suffered only minor cuts and bruises.

     Hugo brings a lawsuit against Hubert and Comptrol for
     $100,000 in damages in a federal court located in
     California. Does the federal court have subject matter
     jurisdiction to hear the case?

Answers to Study Questions

Fill-in-the-Blank Questions

BSCC brings a lawsuit against ABC by filing a complaint with
the clerk of the court. (p. 63)

ABC wants to sue BSCC in the same lawsuit. ABC must file a
<u>counterclaim</u> with the clerk of the court. (p. 63)

In order for the court to decide the case, the court must have
<u>subject matter</u> jurisdiction. (p. 52)

The <u>summons</u> notifies the defendant that he or she must file an
answer and appear in court on a specified date. (p. 52)

<u>True-False Questions</u>

1. False. In rem jurisdiction is the power of the court
    over real property. (p. 52)

2. False. The long arm statute is a state statute. (p. 52)

3. True (p. 54)

4. True (p. 56)

5. False. A state supreme court may be a trial court in
    some states. (p. 55)

6. True (p. 56)

7. True (p. 55)

8. False. The federal courts have limited subject matter
    jurisdiction. (p. 59)

9. True (p. 56)

10. False. No jurisdictional amount is needed. (p. 59)

<u>Multiple-Choice Questions</u>

1. b (p. 52)	14. a (p. 68)	
2. d (p. 52)	15. c (p. 70)	
3. a (p. 63)	16. c (p. 70)	
4. c (p. 55)	17. d (p. 56)	
5. a (p. 59)	18. b (p. 70)	
6. b (p. 59)	19. a (p. 56)	
7. c (p. 59)	20. d (p. 59)	
8. d (p. 63)	21. b (p. 70)	
9. b (p. 64)	22. a (p. 56)	
10. a (p. 69)	23. a (p. 59)	
11. b (p. 63)	24. c (p. 53)	
12. c (p. 68)	25. b (p. 59)	
13. d (p. 68)		

Essay Question

1. Yes, the federal court has subject matter jurisdiction
    over Hubert and Comptrol as long as both defendants are
    not residents of California. Under Diversity of Citizen-
    ship jurisdiction, the case may be decided by the federal
    court if the requirements are met. The plaintiff and de-
    fendant must be citizens of different states, and the
    amount of controversy must exceed $50,000. This case
    meets the requirements because Hugo and Hubert are from
    different states and Hugo is suing for an amount greater
    than $50,000. (p. 59)

Chapter 4
Alternative Dispute Resolution Procedures

Major Concepts

Great concern has developed over the excessive burdens being placed on the parties to a lawsuit. The judicial system may take years to resolve a matter at great expense to the parties involved. In the interests of speed, economy, and justice, many parties are turning to alternative forms of settling disputes.

The costs of resolving a dispute through ADR methods are substantially less than litigating and usually much quicker. ADR affords the parties an opportunity to select the decision maker and the forum. The rules of procedure are relaxed and the setting is informal in most ADR cases.

The most popular alternative dispute resolution procedure is arbitration. The parties may agree to arbitrate a dispute before or after the conflict arises. The parties may contractually agree to arbitration or the court may order the parties to arbitrate.

Many other forms of ADR procedures may be utilized by parties to resolve their disputes. Most methods require the parties to voluntarily submit to an impartial third party to facilitate a settlement.

Chapter Outline

I. **Comparisons Between Alternative Dispute Resolution Procedures and the Judicial System**--Studies have compared ADR and the judicial system on six factors. The factors are money, time, privacy, formality, selection of the decision maker, and the forum.

A. **Financial Costs**--The costs of conducting a trial depends on the locality of the court. The costs range from $10,500 for a jury trial in California to $3,000 for a jury trial in Florida. Federal court costs average above $10,800. The costs of litigating is partially subsidized by court fees, but the majority of the expense is paid by the taxpayer.

The cost of private ADR averages as low as $275, and, if the arbitration is private, then the cost is paid by the parties.

Studies of the legal system have revealed that 43% of the plaintiffs were not awarded any money damages. The average award over a 20-year period was $84,000, but in only 19% of the cases did the plaintiff receive the average or higher. In one-fourth of the cases, the cost to hold a trial was more than the plaintiff recovered.

B. **Time Costs**--The time to litigate ranges from 5 years in Connecticut to 12 months in Arizona. In most litigations, the case never gets to trial because it is dropped or settled. The long delays are due to a backlog of cases, and sometimes because the parties have little incentive to resolve the dispute.

In private arbitration cases, it takes on the average 145 days to resolve a commercial case.

C. **Privacy Factor**--In civil court, legal documents filed with the court and the trial itself are open to the public. Most ADR methods are private and not open to public examination.

D. **Formality**--Judicial proceedings are usually formal, requiring strict adherence to procedural rules, whereas alternative dispute resolution procedures are informal and more relaxed.

E. **Selection of the Decision Maker**--In most judicial settings, the parties do not have the right to se-

lect the judge. In the ADR process, the participants usually select the decision maker.

F.   Choice of Forum--In a lawsuit, the parties have
     little control over where the case is litigated.   In
     an arbitration case, the parties may select the
     forum in advance.

II.   The Alternative Dispute Resolution Process

A.   Negotiation--Negotiation is where two or more par-
     ties discuss differences and move toward a settle-
     ment, acceptable to all the parties involved.
     Negotiation is the best resolution technique because
     the parties themselves have voluntarily reached a
     solution. Negotiation may occur at any time during
     the litigation process, even after a judgment has
     been rendered by the court.

B.   Conciliation--The process of bringing together the
     disputing parties for negotiation by a third party
     is called conciliation. The goal of conciliation is
     to reach a resolution between the parties.

C.   Mediation--The mediation process is entirely volun-
     tary by the parties. The goal of mediation is to
     create discussion between the disputing parties. An
     impartial third party attempts to facilitate the
     interchange between the parties. The mediator may
     suggest solutions to the problem but has no power to
     compel a solution or make a decision.

     In many commercial agreements, the parties have pro-
     vided for a combination of mediation and arbitra-
     tion. Mediation is first used to facilitate
     negotiation and arbitration if negotiation fails.

D.   Arbitration--The parties in arbitration submit their
     dispute to an impartial third person called an arbi-
     trator. The arbitrator is usually an expert in the
     area of the dispute. The decision of the arbitrator
     is binding on the parties. The American Arbitration
     Association (AAA) was founded for the purpose of
     fostering arbitration techniques and advancing the
     prompt and economical settlement of disputes.

     Under the Federal Arbitration Act, Congress has de-
     clared a policy favoring arbitration. The act gives
     the right to parties to agree to resolve disagree-
     ments by arbitration. Thirty states have passed the

Uniform Arbitration Act which validates the arbitration process as effective and efficient. The Act was drafted in 1955 by the National Conference of Commissioners on Uniform State Laws.

1. <u>Contractual Arbitration</u>--An agreement to arbitrate may be executed before or after the dispute arises. The parties include an arbitration clause in the initial contract which requires any future dispute to be submitted to arbitration, or the parties may enter into an agreement called a Submission to Arbitration when the dispute arises.

    The agreement to arbitrate must be entered voluntarily, and it must be in writing to be enforceable in court. Once the agreement is signed by both the parties, the parties cannot bring a legal action. The parties may resort to the courts after the arbitration process has been exhausted. If both parties refuse to arbitrate, the agreement is not binding.

2. <u>Judicial Arbitration</u>--The court may order the parties to arbitrate their dispute, or in some states the parties may voluntarily agree to arbitration after a lawsuit is commenced. Some states require arbitration if the alleged damages are less than a certain amount. A party who is dissatisfied with the arbitration award may appeal to the court.

    Many differences exist between contractual arbitration and judicial arbitration. The most important distinctions have to do with procedural rules. In judicial arbitration, the parties must follow the rules of evidence, have the right to full discovery, subpoena of witnesses, and the right to appeal the decision of the arbitrator. Under a contractual arbitration, the process is private. The parties do not have to comply with the rules of evidence, and costs the parties less.

3. <u>Arbitration Procedure</u>--Similar to litigation procedure, the arbitration must follow a series of steps to reach final resolution. There are five basic steps in the process of arbitrating a dispute.

a. Selection of the Arbitrator--The parties may
    have specified in the contract how the arbi-
    trator will be selected. If no agreement
    was made, the American Arbitration Associ-
    ation has designed a method for selecting an
    arbitrator. Each party is presented with a
    list of qualified arbitrators in which the
    parties cross out the names not wanted. The
    lists of the parties are then compared to
    determine a mutually acceptable arbitrator.

b. Preparation for the Hearing--The parties
    agree on the day and time of the hearing.
    All the evidence will be assembled by the
    parties in preparation for presentation
    before the arbitrator.

c. The Hearing--The proceeding is similar to a
    trial in that each side has the opportunity
    to present opening statements, direct evi-
    dence, and closing statements. Witnesses
    may be required to appear by court order.

d. The Award--The arbitrator will make the de-
    cision within 30 days after the hearing has
    ended. Once the award is made, it is final
    and cannot be changed unless the parties
    agree to reopen the case and restore the
    arbitrator's authority.

e. The Appeal--In a contractual arbitration,
    the parties have a limited right to appeal.
    If the arbitrator was involved in miscon-
    duct, fraud, corruption, undue means, or
    refused to hear all the evidence, the award
    may be appealed. Substantial prejudice or
    bias exhibited against either party is a
    basis for appeal.

    In judicial arbitration, either party may
    appeal the award for any reason and have a
    new trial ordered (i.e., a trial de novo).

    The arbitration process has been criticized
    as not providing clear-cut decisions and
    tending to compromise most disputes. In
    addition, the decisions of arbitrators are
    not based upon precedent, so a great amount
    of uncertainty exists in the case.

E.   Fact Finding--In some commercial settings, an inde-
     pendent third party will attempt to make a thorough
     investigation of the facts surrounding a dispute.
     Based upon the facts, the third party will make a
     recommendation to the disputing parties.

F.   Mini-Trial--The mini-trial is a voluntary procedure
     where the parties agree to allow an advisor to con-
     sider all the relevant documents, exhibits, wit-
     nesses, and written arguments to determine the
     issues. The advisor will then meet with the parties
     to issue rulings on discovery matters and attempt to
     resolve questions of procedure. Once the parties
     have learned all the facts, the dispute is usually
     settled.

G.   Private Judge--In some states, private parties may
     hire a judge to resolve a dispute. The judge is
     called a referee and has the full powers of a judge,
     except the authority to find a party in contempt of
     court. The parties may decide when the case will be
     heard.

     The case proceeds just like a trial, and all the
     rules of evidence apply. The parties pay the major-
     ity of the costs which can be substantial.

Study Questions

Fill-in-the-Blank Questions

Semco, Inc. is a manufacturer of consumer household products
in the southwest United States. Semco's management is concerned about increasing litigation costs and the length of
time it takes to resolve a matter through the judicial system.

The cost of using the courts to resolve a matter is
_____ than using ADR procedures.
   (greater/less)

The parties to a dispute _____ the right to
                              (have/do not have)
choose the decision maker and the forum in ADR.

In an ADR procedure, the parties are _____
                                          (required/not
_____ to follow the rules of evidence.
   required)

The decision of an arbitrator _____ binding on the
parties.   (is/is not)

True-False Questions

1. An arbitrator is considered a judge under federal law.
    _____

2. Congress in the Federal Arbitration Act declared a fed-
    eral policy in favor of arbitration. _____

3. Arbitration may only occur when it is ordered by the
    court. _____

4. An agreement to arbitrate need not be in writing to be
    enforceable. _____

5. The parties to an arbitration agreement must have entered
    into the agreement before the dispute arose. _____

6. A pre-trial hearing is the same procedure as a mini-
    trial. _____

7. Conciliation and mediation may be used interchangeably.
    _____

8. The fact finding ADR procedure is similar to the discov-
    ery process of the judicial system. _____

9. In all states, parties are prohibited from hiring private
    judges to resolve disputes. _____

10. In arbitration, the arbitrator makes an award which is
    binding on the parties. _____

Multiple-Choice Questions

1. Advocates of various alternative dispute resolution pro-
    cedures agree on which of the following goals?

    >   I. a speedy resolution
    > II. a just determination of the dispute
    > III. reasonable cost to the parties involved

    a. I only
    b. I and II
    c. I, II, and III
    d. I and III

2. Which of the following procedures is <u>not</u> considered an alternative dispute resolution?

    a. mini-trial
    b. arbitration
    c. mediation
    d. litigation

3. Courts have in some cases refused to support alternative dispute resolution procedures. If the parties agreed by contract to arbitrate all disputes that arose between them, the court might invalidate the agreement because:

    a. they are attempting to set up private tribunals.
    b. arbitration clauses are illegal.
    c. the arbitrator was not a lawyer.
    d. all of the above.

4. Which of the following is/are requirement(s) for an arbitration agreement to be enforceable in court?

      I. must be signed by the arbitrator
     II. the agreement must be written
    III. it must be entered voluntarily by the parties

    a. I only
    b. I and II
    c. I, II, and III
    d. II and III

5. A brokerage firm customarily entered into written arbitration agreements with clients. The agreement required arbitration of any controversy relating to the clients' accounts. Which of the following statutory claims can be resolved by arbitration?

    a. § 10(b) of the Securities Exchange Act of 1934
    b. Racketeer Influenced and Corrupt Organizations Act
    c. antitrust laws arising out of international commercial transactions
    d. all of the above

6. Which of the following states have <u>not</u> adopted the Uniform Arbitration Act?

    a. Arizona
    b. Illinois
    c. New York
    d. Utah

7. Which of the following is not a difference between con-
    tractual arbitration and judicial arbitration?

    a. right to the use of discovery techniques
    b. application of the rules of evidence
    c. award is binding
    d. the right to a jury

8. After an arbitrator hears all the evidence presented by
    the parties, the arbitrator makes a decision in:

    a. 30 days.
    b. 45 days.
    c. 60 days.
    d. 3 months.

9. The arbitrator's decision is based upon the facts pre-
    sented at the hearing. The decision is called:

    a. a judgment.
    b. an award.
    c. an order.
    d. a rule.

10. Acme Inc. entered into written employment contracts with
     its employees. A provision in the employment contract
     required all disputes to be submitted to arbitration con-
     cerning the employment of the employee. Bob Baker is
     discharged from Acme Inc. for no apparent reason. Bob
     believes he was wrongfully discharged and submits his
     claim to arbitration. The arbitrator decides the case in
     favor of Acme. Bob later discovers the arbitrator
     received a bribe to decide the case for Acme. Bob may
     appeal the case on which of the following grounds?

     a. refusal to hear all the evidence
     b. failed to follow precedent
     c. corruption
     d. two of the above

11. In a judicial arbitration, either party may appeal the
     decision of the arbitrator. The appeal is treated by the
     court as an entirely new case and a trial will be
     ordered. This is called:

     a. judicial review.
     b. trial de novo.
     c. summary judgment.
     d. mini-trial.

12. Broad Realty Co. sold a home to Arthur Young. The home
     was about ten years old and its basement flooded during
     heavy rains. The buyers did not know about the defective
     foundation which caused the basement to flood. The pur-
     chase contract contained an arbitration clause requiring
     arbitration of any claim between the parties. Arthur
     made a demand for arbitration, and the case was tried
     before an arbitrator. The arbitrator decided in favor of
     Arthur based upon a breach of implied warranty of habit-
     ability. Broad Realty argues that case precedent re-
     stricts the application of the implied warranty of
     habitability only to builders, and Broad was not the
     builder of this home. If Broad Realty appeals the
     decision, what is the likely outcome?

     a. A new trial will be held.
     b. The court will reverse the decision.
     c. The court will order a directed verdict.
     d. The court will affirm the arbitrator even if an error
         of law was made.

13. Refer to question 12. The arbitration clause in the pur-
     chase contract required disputes relating to defect of
     title to be arbitrated. The arbitrator decided in favor
     of Arthur based on breach of the implied warranty of
     habitability. Which of the following would be the best
     legal grounds for Broad Realty to use in appealing the
     decision?

     a. error in application of the law
     b. fraud
     c. prejudice
     d. arbitrator exceeded his/her authority

14. Which of the following alternative dispute resolution
     procedures is authorized under the Magnuson-Moss Product
     Warranty Act?

     a. mediation
     b. arbitration
     c. mini-trial
     d. fact finding

15. In some states, parties are allowed to hire a judge to
     privately resolve a dispute. The judge is called:

     a. a magistrate.
     b. a line judge.
     c. an arbitrator.
     d. a referee.

16. Which of the following is an advantage of the private judge alternative dispute resolution procedure?

    a. the parties can control when the case will be heard
    b. expense of the procedure
    c. availability in all states
    d. right to a jury

17. Which of the following is/are the major purpose(s) for utilizing an alternative method to resolve a dispute?

    a. to force the courts to decide a case quicker
    b. to avoid large judgments against defendants
    c. it is less expensive and more expeditious
    d. to decrease attorney fees

18. Which of the following is in favor of alternative dispute resolution procedures?

      I. the judiciary
     II. the business sector
    III. former Chief Justice Warren E. Burger

    a. I only
    b. I and II
    c. I and III
    d. I, II, and III

19. Which of the following is/are violation(s) of the American Arbitration Association Code of Ethics?

      I. The arbitrator is related to one of the parties in a case he has decided.

     II. The arbitrator received compensation for his services as an arbitrator.

    III. The arbitrator does not believe a witness's testimony after cross-examination.

    a. I only
    b. I and II
    c. I, II, and III
    d. I and III

20. Which of the following is designed to make legislation on arbitration more uniform throughout the country?

    a. Uniform Commercial Code
    b. Uniform Arbitration Act

    c.   American Arbitration Association
    d.   American Bar Association

21. Hank Smith files a lawsuit with the county clerk's office. Hank is suing Monica Simpson for breach of contract for the amount of $1,250.00. The court orders the case to be decided by an arbitrator. This is an example of:

    a.   compulsory arbitration.
    b.   mini-trial.
    c.   contractual arbitration.
    d.   private judge.

22. The courts have listed several reasons for refusing to enforce arbitration clauses. Which of the following is <u>not</u> one of those reasons?

    a.   less expensive to litigate
    b.   protection of a party's rights
    c.   unqualified arbitrators
    d.   the setting up of private tribunals

23. The cost of an average federal trial is:

    a. $3,000.
    b. $8,300.
    c. $10,500.
    d.   more than $10,800.

24. What percentage of lawsuits did the plaintiff win an award over $1,000,000?

    a.   1%
    b.   3%
    c.   5%
    d.   10%

25. The number of cases that are arbitrated each year is:

    a.   10,000.
    b.   20,000.
    c.   35,000.
    d.   over 50,000.

Essay Question

1. The J. R. Robinson Co. entered a contract to buy fifteen tons of sheet metal from Tifton Metal Products, Inc. The

contract clearly specified all the material terms of the sale and was signed by the presidents of both companies. Tifton, due to a shortage of raw materials, failed to deliver the order to J. R. Robinson Co. on time. Tifton subsequently delivered twelve tons of sheet metal. J. R. Robinson's president sent a letter to the president of Tifton; the letter stated that J. R. Robinson Co. would sue Tifton for breach of contract unless the remaining three tons of sheet metal were delivered immediately. Tifton's president called J. R. Robinson's president, and over the telephone the two companies agreed to arbitrate their dispute. Two weeks later J. R. Robinson Co. files a lawsuit against Tifton, Inc. for breach of contract. What is the result?

Answers to Study Questions

Fill-in-the-Blank Questions

The cost of using the courts to resolve a matter is <u>greater</u> than using ADR procedures. (p. 78)

The parties to a dispute <u>have</u> the right to choose the decision maker and the forum in ADR. (p. 80)

In an ADR procedure, the parties are <u>not required</u> to follow the rules of evidence. (p. 80)

The decision of an arbitrator <u>is</u> binding on the parties. (p. 90)

True-False Questions

1.   False. Arbitrators are not called judges. (p. 90)

2.   True (p. 83)

3.   False. Arbitration may be voluntary. (p. 85)

4.   False. Contractual arbitration agreements must be in writing. (p. 85)

5.   False. An arbitration agreement may be entered into after the dispute arises. (p. 88)

6.   False. A pre-trial hearing is a conference between the judge and attorneys to a case to attempt to reach a settlement. (p. 94)

7. False. Conciliation is different from mediation in several aspects. (p. 81)

8. True (p. 94)

9. False. In California, parties may hire a private judge. (p. 94)

10. True (p. 92)

Multiple-Choice Questions

1.	c (p. 78)	14.	a (p. 94)
2.	d (p. 81)	15.	d (p. 94)
3.	a (p. 78)	16.	a (p. 94)
4.	d (p. 88)	17.	c (p. 78)
5.	d (p. 83)	18.	d (p. 78)
6.	c (p. 85)	19.	a (p. 82)
7.	d (p. 90)	20.	b (p. 85)
8.	a (p. 91)	21.	a (p. 90)
9.	b (p. 91)	22.	a (p. 79)
10.	c (p. 92)	23.	d (p. 79)
11.	b (p. 92)	24.	a (p. 79)
12.	d (p. 92)	25.	d (p. 79)
13.	d (p. 92)		

Essay Question

1. The J. R. Robinson Co. will be allowed to proceed with the case in court. Even though the parties agreed to arbitrate their dispute, the agreement to arbitrate was oral and thus unenforceable by the court. Tifton may attempt to force J. R. Robinson to arbitrate under the agreement, but the court will refuse to recognize the arbitration contract. (p. 88)

Chapter 5
The Constitution and the Regulation of Business

Major Concepts

The founding fathers of the United States in 1787 forged a
document which would create a strong central government by
consent of the people. The U.S. Constitution created three
separate and distinct branches of government: the legislative, executive, and judicial. The first ten amendments to
the Constitution are known as the Bill of Rights. The Bill of
Rights were added in 1791 to protect individual freedoms
against governmental infringement and promote equality
(i.e., Doctrine of Selective Incorporation).

The founding fathers sought to protect individual rights
against the abuses of a strong federal government. The Bill
of Rights originally applied only to the federal government.
The U.S. Supreme Court has interpreted the Fourteenth Amendment as incorporating the Bill of Rights and thus guaranteeing
the protection of individual rights from infringement by the
states (i.e., Doctrine of Selective Incorporation).

The regulation of business by government comes under the
authority of the Constitution. Congress has the power to
enact laws which effect interstate commerce through the Commerce Clause, Article I section 8. State legislatures may
also regulate interstate commerce, subject to Congressional
authority to preempt a particular area of regulation.

Corporations and some partnerships have the legal right to
assert constitutional protections. Both of the above forms of
businesses are considered separate legal entities or persons

entitled to individual freedoms and equal treatment under law, although businesses do not have the Fifth Amendment protection against self-incrimination as natural persons do.

This chapter will review some of the major provisions of the U.S. Constitution as they relate to business.

Chapter Outline

I. <u>Articles of the Constitution</u>--The first three Articles of the Constitution delegate power to the legislative, executive, and judicial branches of the government, respectively. Each branch has only the authority as provided for in the Constitution. The other four Articles of the Constitution generally provide direction to the federal and state governments for the administration of law.

    A. <u>The Supremacy Clause</u>--Article VI of the Constitution establishes the Constitution, federal law, and U.S. treaties as the supreme law of the land. The Constitution and federal law have priority over all other state and local law. Congress may exclusively or concurrently regulate an area. If Congress intends to exclusively regulate an area and state and federal law conflict, federal law through the supremacy clause will preempt the state law. In some cases, the federal and state legislatures may constitutionally enact laws regulating the same area.

    B. <u>Separation of Powers</u>--The federal government is divided into three equal and separate branches. Article I created the legislature, Article II created the executive, and Article III created the judicial branch. The framers of the Constitution separated the three according to governmental function for the purpose of preventing one overly powerful central branch. A system of checks and balances has been created to limit the power of any one branch.

    C. <u>The Commerce Clause</u>--Article I section 8 lists the powers of Congress to legislate. The Commerce Clause gives Congress the authority to regulate interstate commerce and intrastate commerce, which has a substantial effect on interstate commerce.

    D. <u>State Regulation of Commerce</u>--The state may regulate interstate commerce through its police powers. The state has the authority to enact law which promotes the health, safety, morals, and general welfare of that state's citizens.

State regulation which substantially interferes with interstate commerce is invalid under the Commerce Clause. Congress, through the authority of the Commerce Clause, has the power to regulate the states in all aspects of their governmental functions.

E. The Taxing Power--Article I section 8 gives Congress the "power to lay and collect Taxes, Duties, Imposts and Exercises." The power to tax will be upheld as long as Congress was empowered to regulate the area being taxed. Congress may also impose a tax as a revenue-raising measure.

F. The Spending Powers--Congress has the authority "to pay the debts and provide for the common defense and general welfare of the United States." The spending power gives Congress wide discretion to disperse the funds collected through taxes. Taxpayers have been generally unsucessful in their attempts to challenge specific government spending (i.e., this is due to a lack of standing to bring the issue before a court of law).

G. Delegated Powers--The powers not specifically given to the federal government are reserved for the states under the Tenth Amendment. The powers of the federal government have been enumerated in Articles I, II, and III. The Tenth Amendment makes note of the powers explicitly given to the federal government and allows the government to do whatever is necessary and proper to carry out the powers granted.

II. The Bill of Rights in a Business Context

A. Business and the First Amendment--Freedom of speech as guaranteed by the First Amendment is not an absolute right. The government is allowed to place limitations on commercial and political speech.

1. Defamation--Individuals and businesses do not receive First Amendment protections if the statements are untrue. Defaming the integrity or character of another can subject the speaker to a lawsuit. Public figures and officials may

only hold an individual responsible for false
statements if actual malice is proven.

2. Commercial Speech--Both political and commercial
   expressions are protected by the First Amendment. Commercial speech is usually in the form
   of advertising and may be restricted to a
   greater extent than political speech.

   The states and the federal government may prevent the dissemination of commercial speech that
   is false, deceptive, misleading, or that proposes an illegal transaction. Otherwise, commercial speech cannot be restricted unless a
   substantial governmental interest is being
   directly advanced.

3. Freedom of Religion--The First Amendment guarantees the right to freely exercise religion and
   prohibits the government from establishing a
   state religion. The federal and state government must not significantly advance religion but
   may provide incidental benefits. Laws prohibiting certain business activities on Sunday and
   forbidding religious discrimination by employers
   have been upheld as not violating the
   Establishment Clause.

B. Search and Seizure--The Fourth Amendment prohibits
   unreasonable searches and seizures by the government. Subject to some exceptions, the government
   must obtain a warrant based upon probable cause
   before searching a person, house, or business. Even
   administrative agencies are required to secure a
   warrant from a magistrate before conducting a search
   of a business's premises. This provision of the
   Fourth Amendment protects an individual's right to
   privacy.

C. Self-Incrimination--The Fifth Amendment does not
   allow the government to coerce a person into testi-
   fying against himself or herself in a criminal case.
   It states no person "shall be compelled in any
   criminal case to be a witness against himself." The
   protection only relates to evidence that can be used
   against the accused, although an individual may be
   compelled to produce incriminating business records.
   Corporations and some partnerships are not protected
   by this provision of the Fifth Amendment. Business
   records in the custody of an attorney or accountant

must be surrendered when a search warrant is presented unless an exception exists.

D. Due Process--The Fifth and Fourteenth Amendments prohibit the government from depriving a person of life, liberty, or property without due process of law.

   1. Procedural Due Process--The government must administer justice fairly before taking a person's life, liberty, or property. The process must be fair in providing adequate notice to an individual and an opportunity for a hearing.

   2. Substantive Due Process--The Due Process Clause has been used to examine the constitutional validity of legislation affecting life, liberty, or property. This provision considers the substance of legislation and has allowed the U.S. Supreme Court to invalidate state statutes that are unreasonable.

E. Equal Protection--The Fourteenth Amendment requires the "equal protection of the laws" to all persons. The Equal Protection Clause requires the state government to treat similarly situated individuals in a similar manner.

Legislation which discriminates against a certain class of individuals or businesses must be rationally related to a legitimate state purpose which directly advances the state's interest to be upheld as constitutional. If a suspect classification is involved, such as a race, religion, or alienage, the statute must directly advance a compelling state interest to be upheld.

Study Questions

Fill-in-the-Blank Questions

The law firm of Able, Barker and Carlson placed an advertisement in The Wall Street Journal which covered half a page and read as follows:

   - Insider Trading Defense Attorney Money Back Guarantee If Convicted

                    - Painless Bankruptcy at the Lowest Rates in Town
                    - We Do Commercial Law Better

                      Call Now for a Free Consultation
                         Able, Barker and Carlson
                           Attorneys at Law

The New York State Bar prohibits attorneys from advertising as
part of the state ethical code of conduct. The New York State
Office of Registration has disciplined Able, Barker and
Carlson for violating the ethical code of conduct. Able,
Barker and Carlson believe their constitutional rights have
been violated.

The advertisement is a form of _____
speech.   (commercial/political)

The advertisement is protected by the _____
Amendment if it is true.   (First/Fifth)

The New York State Bar Association _____
                                    (has/does not have)
the right to prohibit all forms of attorney advertising.

The firm of Able, Barker and Carlson _____ required
                                          (is/is not)
to disclose all material information concerning the costs of
litigation in the advertisement.

True-False Questions

  1. The Supremacy Clause in the U.S. Constitution requires
      federal law to preempt all similar state laws. _____

  2. The federal legislative, executive, and judicial branches
      of government were created to function as one large and
      powerful central governmental unit. _____

  3. Congress is the only governmental body vested with the
      power to regulate interstate commerce. _____

  4. The states may regulate interstate commerce subject to
      some constitutional limitations. _____

  5. The police power is defined as the authority of the fed-
      eral government to collect taxes. _____

  6. The first ten amendments of the U.S. Constitution are
      known as the Bill of Rights. _____

7. The Bill of Rights have been incorporated into the Four-
    teenth Amendment by the U.S. Supreme Court through the
    doctrine of selective incorporation. _____

8. Corporations do not have the right to be protected by the
    Bill of Rights. _____

9. The Due Process Clause is found in the Fourth Amendment.
    _____

10. The government has the right to search the work premises
    of a private business with a warrant based upon probable
    cause which is specifically drawn. _____

Multiple-Choice Questions

1. The U.S. Supreme Court has the right to scrutinize the
    content of legislation through the doctrine known as:

    a. Full Faith and Credit.
    b. Selective Incorporation.
    c. Establishment Clause.
    d. Substantive Due Process.

2. When a state statute directly conflicts with the effects
    and purposes of a federal statute, the federal statute
    prevails. This is known as:

    a. Procedural Due Process.
    b. preemption.
    c. the police power.
    d. the reserved powers.

3. The State of Iowa enacts legislation which forbids the
    use of double tractor trailers on state highways. The
    Iowa legislature believes trucks pulling two semi trail-
    ers are hazardous. The Iowa legislature did not base the
    enactment of this law on fact. Trucks coming from out of
    state with double trailers must either go around Iowa or
    shed one of their trailers. The truck traffic on Iowa
    highways has been substantially decreased. The A.B.C.
    Freight Company seeks to challenge the law as a violation
    of the Constitution. A.B.C. Freight Company normally
    ships goods by double tractor trailer through the State
    of Iowa. If A.B.C. wants to challenge the Iowa statute
    in federal court, which constitutional provision will
    most likely be used?

    a.   Commerce Clause
    b.   Establishment Clause
    c.   Equal Protection
    d.   Double Jeopardy

4. Refer to question 3. If it can be shown that the Iowa legislature was attempting to give Iowa trucking companies a distinct advantage over nonresident trucking companies, this most likely violates the:

    a.   Supremacy Clause.
    b.   Privileges and Immunities Clause.
    c.   Due Process.
    d.   Free Exercise Clause.

5. Refer to question 3. The authority of the State of Iowa to promote the safe use of Iowa highways is called:

    a.   police power.
    b.   Substantive Due Process.
    c.   separation of power.
    d.   the spending power.

6. Refer to question 3. A.B.C. as a corporation cannot assert which of the following constitutional provisions?

    a.   Due Process
    b.   Freedom of Speech
    c.   Freedom of Press
    d.   Self-Incrimination

7. When a state regulation encroaches on interstate commerce, the courts will balance the state's interest in the merits and purposes of the regulation against the _____.

    a.   enumerated powers provision
    b.   burden on interstate commerce
    c.   necessary and proper clause
    d.   ability of the government to enforce the law

8. State law enacted to promote the health, safety, and welfare of local citizens is presumed by the courts to be:

    a.   protectionist.
    b.   invalid.
    c.   unconstitutional.
    d.   valid.

9. Congress passed the Federal Waste Disposal Act. The Act
    states the federal government intended to exclusively
    regulate the disposal of nuclear waste. The Act created
    a federal agency to regulate, administer, and enforce the
    statute. If the State of Arizona enacts legislation con-
    cerning the disposal of nuclear waste sites in the state,
    the state law will most likely be held unconstitutional
    as a violation of the:

    a. Supremacy Clause.
    b. Due Process Clause.
    c. Federalism Clause.
    d. Commerce Clause.

10. The _____ Clause of the U.S. Constitution requires
    the state government to treat similarly situated individ-
    uals in a similar manner.

    a. Search and Seizure
    b. Police Power
    c. Equal Protection
    d. Self-Incrimination

11. Victor is caught robbing a federally insured savings and
    loan by federal agents. The Justice Department prose-
    cutes Victor under federal criminal law. The jury
    decides the government has failed to prove their case
    beyond a reasonable doubt and returns a verdict of not
    guilty. The State of California, where the savings and
    loan was located, now wants to prosecute Victor under
    state criminal law for the same crime. Victor may have
    the state's case dismissed under the:

    a. Double Jeopardy Clause.
    b. Self-Incrimination Provision.
    c. prohibition against cruel and unusual punishment.
    d. none of the above. The state may prosecute the case.

12. Refer to question 11. Federal prosecutors called Victor
    to the stand in an attempt to coerce him into testifying
    against himself. Victor refused to answer the prosecu-
    tors' questions and was held in contempt of court by the
    judge. Which of Victor's constitutional rights have been
    violated?

    a. privileges and immunities
    b. full faith and credit
    c. equal protection
    d. freedom from compelled self-incrimination

13.   Refer to question 11. Federal agents go to the home of
      Linda Schmidt (Victor's wife) in order to gather evidence
      against Victor. Federal agents enter Violet's home by
      breaking down the rear door without a search warrant.
      After a thorough search, agents find and seize the weapon
      Victor used in the robbery. During the trial, Victor may
      have the weapon excluded because the search violated the:

      a.   Fourth Amendment.
      b.   Fifth Amendment.
      c.   Fourteenth Amendment.
      d.   none of the above.

14.   Commercial speech is protected by the First Amendment.
      Business has the right to advertise its products, subject
      to some limitations. The First Amendment does not pro-
      tect commercial speech which:

      a.   is profit motivated.
      b.   also promotes a political cause.
      c.   is made by a private utility company.
      d.   is deceptive.

15.   Public officials seeking to recover damages in a defama-
      tion case must prove _____ of the person making
      the untrue statement.

      a.   the negligence
      b.   actual malice
      c.   slight malice
      d.   the specific intent

16.   The State of Texas forbids retail automobile outlets to
      be open on Sunday. The Automobile Association of Texas
      believes the law advances religion and is a violation of
      the constitution. Which, if any, constitutional provi-
      sion has been violated?

      a.   the Free Exercise Clause
      b.   the Establishment Clause
      c.   the Equal Protection Clause
      d.   no constitutional provisions have been violated

17.   The Commerce Clause of the U.S. Constitution confers the
      power on the federal government to regulate:

      I.   business activity between two or more states.

      II. business activity in only one state which has a
           substantial effect on commerce.

III. business activity with foreign nations.

a. I only
b. I and II only
c. I, II, and III
d. II and III only

18. The State of Alaska passed a statute requiring Alaskan employers to hire only residents of Alaska. The state was attempting to reduce unemployment among its citizens. John Smith was refused employment because he was not a resident of Alaska. John sues in federal court, alleging his constitutional rights have been violated. What is his best argument?

a. The state has violated the Due Process Clause.
b. The state has treated him unequally.
c. The state has violated the Privileges and Immunities Clause.
d. The state has done nothing wrong.

19. Jeff Jacobs left his new Ford Mustang on the shoulder of the highway due to a malfunction of the transmission. Jeff returned the next day to find a bright orange sticker on the window of the car, stating the car would be towed unless it was moved within 24 hours. Jeff returned the next day to find his automobile had been towed away by the city. Jeff telephoned the police department and was informed that his car had been destroyed by the city and was at the junkyard. Jeff claims his constitutional rights have been violated by the city. What is Jeff's best argument against the city if a lawsuit is brought?

a. The city did not treat him equally.
b. The city does not have the police power to tow automobiles off the highway.
c. The city violated Jeff's procedural due process rights.
d. The city violated Jeff's substantive due process rights.

20. Refer to question 19. The city has deprived Jeff of:

a. a liberty interest.
b. a property interest.
c. privacy.
d. the right to travel.

21. Which of the following are checks and balances which
     limit the amount of power any one branch of the federal
     government can obtain?

       I.   presidential veto of Congressional Acts.
      II.   judicial review of Congressional Act.
     III.   power of eminent domain.

     a.   I only
     b.   II only
     c.   I and II only
     d.   I, II, and III

22. The Necessary and Proper Clause of Article I section 8
     gives which branch(es) of the government implied powers?

       I.   legislative
      II.   executive
     III.   judicial

     a.   I only
     b.   II only
     c.   III only
     d.   I and III only

23. The power of the federal government to tax includes which
     of the following activities?

       I.   transfer of firearms
      II.   income
     III.   gambling

     a.   I only
     b.   II only
     c.   III only
     d.   I, II, and III

24. The major obstacle to a taxpayer challenging specific
     governmental spending of funds collected through taxes
     is:

     a.   the police power.
     b.   separation of powers.
     c.   selective incorporation.
     d.   standing to sue.

25. The state of Montana enacts legislation which forbids the
     use of nonreturnable plastic milk containers. The stat-
     ute permits glass and paperboard milk containers to be
     used in the sale of milk. The state is attempting to

relieve the problem of waste disposal by prohibiting the use of plastic milk containers. The Borden Milk Company, a producer of milk in plastic containers, believes this statute violates the Equal Protection Clause. The court will use which test to analyze the case?

a. rational basis test
b. reasonable test
c. strict scrutiny test
d. presumption of invalidity test

Essay Question

1. The State of Indiana, through passage of a statute, pro-hibited trains that were longer than one-hundred cars from entering the state. The Indiana legislature be-lieved the longer trains were unsafe and created long delays at railroad crossings for motorists. Any train with over one-hundred cars coming from another state would have to leave the excess railroad cars at the border. Several freight companies that were affected have challenged the statute as being unconstitutional. Is the Indiana statute unconstitutional?

Answers to Study Questions

Fill-in-the-Blank Questions

The advertisement is a form of commercial speech. (p. 111)

The advertisement is protected by the First Amendment if it is true. (p. 111)

The New York State Bar Association does not have the right to prohibit all forms of attorney advertising. (p. 111)

The firm of Able, Barker and Carlson is required to disclose all material information concerning the costs of litigation in the advertisement. (p. 112)

True-False Questions

1. False. The Supremacy Clause does not require preemption in all cases. (p. 104)

2. False. The three branches were created to reduce the
    power of the federal government. (p. 104)

3. False. The state governments may regulate interstate
    commerce. (p. 107)

4. True (p. 107)

5. False. The police power is the government's power to
    promote health, safety, welfare, and morals of citizens.
    (p. 107)

6. True (p. 110)

7. True (p. 109)

8. False. Corporations are protected under the Bill of
    Rights. (p. 111)

9. False. The Due Process Clause is found in the Fifth and
    Fourteenth Amendments. (p. 109)

10. True (p. 115)

Multiple-Choice Questions

1. d (p. 120)
2. b (p. 104)
3. a (p. 107)
4. b (p. 120)
5. a (p. 107)
6. d (p. 118)
7. b (p. 107)
8. d (p. 107)
9. a (p. 104)
10. c (p. 120)
11. a (p. 109)
12. d (p. 118)
13. a (p. 109)
14. d (p. 111)
15. b (p. 111)
16. d (p. 113)
17. c (p. 107)
18. c (p. 121)
19. c (p. 120)
20. b (p. 120)
21. c (p. 104)
22. a (p. 106)
23. d (p. 108)
24. d (p. 108)
25. a (p. 120)

Essay Question

1. The State of Indiana through the police powers may regu-
    late interstate commerce. The state must be able to sub-
    stantiate the rationale underlying the statute prohibit-
    ing trains with over one-hundred cars in length. If it
    can be proven that trains over one-hundred cars long are
    more hazardous and cause unreasonable delays to motor-
    ists, the statute may be upheld.

The statute will not be upheld under the Commerce Clause if it places an undue burden on interstate commerce. If the free flow of commerce between the states is substantially impaired, the court will declare the statute void.

The court will balance the interests of the state against the burden placed on commerce. In <u>Southern Pacific Railroad v. Arizona</u>, 325 U.S. 761 (1945), a similar statute was declared unconstitutional. (p. 107)

Chapter 6
Administrative Agencies and the Regulation of Business

Major Concepts

Administrative agencies have been called the fourth branch of government. The administrative agency is a nonlegislative, nonjudicial governmental entity which creates rules and adjudicates cases. An agency may be created by Congress or a state legislature.

Many administrative agencies have been given the authority to perform legislative, judicial, and executive functions. The agency must attempt to perform these functions independently of each other as to preserve the separation of powers.

The administrative agency can create rules according to the informal or formal rulemaking process. Agency rules have the force and effect of law and and can be enforced by the agency. Informal rulemaking is known as "notice and comment," whereas formal rulemaking is known as "on the record."

The administrative agency also performs the judicial function which is known as adjudication. In an adjudication, an administrative law judge (ALJ) presides over the hearing of an alleged wrongdoer. The ALJ decides the case issuing an order with findings of fact.

A court may review the decisions of an administrative agency, overturning them if a violation of the Constitution occurred or proper procedures were not followed.

Chapter Outline

I. <u>Areas of Regulation</u>--Administrative agencies regulate
    two primary areas: Economic and Public Welfare. Eco-
    nomic regulation covers the entry of businesses into an
    industry and the operation of those businesses.

    Public Welfare regulation refers to the administration
    of programs which benefit the public at large. Public
    welfare regulation may ensure the safety of factory
    workers or distribute social security disability bene-
    fits. The benefits under these programs are called
    entitlements.

II. <u>Delegation of Power to Administrative Agencies</u>

    A. <u>Types of Administrative Agencies</u>--The first type of
        administrative agency is a line agency which is
        headed by a single person appointed by the President
        with confirmation of the Senate. The members of the
        President's cabinet are heads of line agencies. For
        example, the Attorney General heads the Department
        of Justice, responsible to enforce federal law.

        The second type of administrative agency is known as
        an independent agency. Independent agencies are
        created by Congress and run by a commission ap-
        pointed by the President. Independent agencies are
        separate and distinct from the executive branch.

        The third type of administrative agency is the gov-
        ernment agency which functions as a business entity.
        Government agencies conduct business to produce
        revenue. The Federal Deposit Insurance Corporation
        and the U.S. Post Office are both government agen-
        cies.

        The fourth type of administrative agency is called
        quasi-official. The quasi-official agency has
        limited authority and is created by Congressional
        enactment.

    B. <u>Federal Legislation</u>

        1. <u>Enabling Legislation</u>--Congress creates an admin-
            istrative agency through the passage of an en-
            abling act. The enabling act creates the
            agency, setting forth its structure and defining
            its powers. Congress decides if the agency will
            be independent or under the executive branch.

Congress and the executive branch exert control over the agency once it is created. Congress controls the appropriations to the agency and must confirm Presidential appointments to the agency. Congress may abolish an agency through Congressional enactment. The agency will establish a statement of general policy to broadly describe agency philosophy.

2. <u>Administrative Procedures Act (APA) of 1946</u>--The APA regulates all federal administrative agencies. The APA sets guidelines for the agency to follow when making rules, performing investigations, and adjudicating cases.

3. <u>Freedom of Information Act (FOIA)</u>--The FOIA amends the APA and makes information held by a federal administrative agency available to the public, subject to some exceptions. Any person may request a record held by an administrative agency. Some agency information is published in the Federal Register and some may be available for public inspection and copying at the agency. When a person cannot locate the information, each agency has established reasonable procedures for the public to follow when requesting information. The administrative agency may refuse to release information falling into one of the following exempt categories:

a. relating to national defense or foreign policy.

b. internal personnel rules.

c. information protected by other statutes that prohibit disclosure.

d. trade secrets, privileges, or confidential information.

e. any information which is private and protected.

An administrative agency must disclose information requested unless an exemption applies. An agency may at its discretion disclose exempt information.

4. Privacy Act--The Privacy Act is an amendment to
    the APA which protects citizens and legal aliens
    from unwanted intrusions into private facts. An
    agency is not allowed to disclose information
    about an individual unless certain conditions
    are met. The Act requires the information to be
    accurate, complete, and up-to-date. An individ-
    ual may inspect his/her own record and correct
    any inaccurate information.

5. Sunshine Act--Most administrative agencies fall
    under the Sunshine Act and are required to hold
    open meetings. The public must receive notice
    of the time and place of an agency meeting. If
    the agency votes to hold a closed meeting, no-
    tice must be given along with an explanation for
    excluding the public. An agency may close its
    meetings if the subject matter to be discussed
    falls into an exception (e.g., national secu-
    rity, internal personal rules, and trade
    secrets).

6. Regulatory Flexibility Act--Congress passed the
    Regulatory Flexibility Act to minimize the ad-
    verse impact created by imposing the same
    standards on small firms that is expected of
    large firms. Agencies must attempt to reach
    their goals by rules that consider the economic
    size of the business to be regulated. The Act
    requires a special regulatory flexibility agenda
    to be printed in the Federal Register twice a
    year, which lists the proposed rules which may
    have a significant economic impact on large
    numbers of small businesses.

7. Sunset Acts--A sunset act designates a specific
    date for the automatic termination of an agency.
    Congress must intervene for the agency to con-
    tinue after the expiration date has been
    reached. Congress may require the agency to
    provide justification for its continued exis-
    tence.

8. Equal Access to Justice Act--The Equal Access to
    Justice Act attempts to allow ordinary individ-
    uals and small businesses to challenge an
    incorrect legal position held by the government.
    The Act applies to individuals with a net worth
    no more than $2 million and businesses with no

more than 500 employees and a net worth no more
than $7 million.

The Act allows an administrative law judge or a
court to award legal fees (up to $75/hour),
expert witness fees, or costs of studies to
individuals or small businesses. The ALJ or the
court will not award such fees if the administrative agency was substantially justified in
bringing charges.

III. <u>Functions of Administrative Agencies</u>--The administrative
agency may be authorized to perform legislative, judicial, and executive functions. Agencies may possess all
three powers but do not have the same power as the legislative, judicial, or executive branches of the federal
government.

A. <u>Rulemaking</u>--The purpose of rulemaking is to implement, interpret, or proscribe a law, policy, or
practice of an agency. A rule adopted by an agency
has the force and effect of law. There are various
methods for rulemaking and different types of rules.

The three types of rules are procedural rules,
interpretive rules, and substantive rules. Procedural rules specify the internal practices of an
agency. The agency is required to follow its own
procedural rules.

Interpretive rules define the terms of the statute
the agency is administering. The agency may adopt
an interpretive rule without public input but must
publish the adopted rule in the Federal Register.

Substantive rules are created through specific statutory authority and regulate the relationships
between government and private entities for the
protection of society. The agency may create a
substantive rule by the informal or formal rulemaking process.

1. <u>Informal Rulemaking (Notice and Comment)</u>--In
informal rulemaking, the agency must first publish notice of the proposed rule in the Federal
Register. The agency notifies the public of the
opportunity to send written comments concerning
the proposed rule to the agency for consideration. When the deadline for written comments
has lapsed, the agency will decide to promulgate

(publish) the rule as originally proposed, modify the proposed rule, or withdraw the rule entirely. If the proposed rule is promulgated, the agency must publish it in the Federal Register along with a concise general statement of its basis and purpose. This form of rulemaking is quick and efficient.

Rules made informally may be reviewed by a court. If the party challenging the rule can prove the rule is arbitrary, capricious, an abuse of discretion or not in accord with the law, the court will invalidate the rule. The agency, when creating a rule informally, must base their action on rational explanations after a reasoned and good faith effort to consider alternative means of advancing the agency's purpose.

2. Formal Rulemaking--In formal rulemaking, the agency must publish the proposed rule in the Federal Register. The agency must hold public hearings after the proposed rule has been published. Interested parties may participate in the hearing by submitting oral and written evidence, presenting witnesses, and examining witnesses who testify at the hearing. The hearing is similar to a trial in many respects. Most parties are represented by attorneys, and the agency heads preside over the hearing.

Rules created through the formal process may be reviewed by a court. The formal rulemaking method requires the agency to base its action on substantial evidence from the record as a whole. In other words, the evidence presented at the public hearing must be considered as a whole by the agency before a rule is promulgated. If the rule fails to conform to the evidence, the court may invalidate the rule (i.e., Substantial Evidence Test).

B. Adjudication--Agency adjudication is the process of conducting a trial within the agency to determine if an individual or business has violated an agency rule or a statute. Adjudication is a judicial function of an agency which considers the past conduct of an individual or business. The Administrative Law Judge (ALJ) has the authority to issue subpoenas, administer oaths to witnesses, conduct hearings, rule on the admissibility of evidence, and rule on the issues presented at the hearing. The ALJ issues a decision with findings of fact and conclusions.

Adjudication commences with a complaint and requires the alleged wrongdoer to provide an answer. The case is heard by the ALJ who decides the issues of fact and the issues of law. No right to a jury exists in an adjudication. The ALJ will issue an order which may be reviewed by the head of the agency.

C. <u>Investigation and Enforcement</u>--The administrative agency is able to ensure the compliance of their rules and standards through the executive function. Business is required by agency rules to keep accurate records and make periodic reports. The agency may acquire information through voluntary submissions or legal order. The agency may enforce its orders by imposing penalties for noncompliance.

IV. <u>Limitations on Administrative Agency Powers</u>

A. <u>Fourth Amendment</u>--The Fourth Amendment of the U.S. Constitution protects businesses and individuals from unreasonable searches and seizures. This has been interpreted by the courts to require enforcement agents to secure a warrant based upon probable cause before conducting a search and seizure. The search warrant requirement is subject to some exceptions.

Administrative agency inspectors must secure a search warrant if the business refuses to consent to a search. The requirement of probable cause is de-emphasized for administrative investigations.

B. <u>Fifth Amendment</u>--The Fifth Amendment of the U.S. Constitution protects an individual from being forced to testify against himself or herself in a criminal case. Corporations are not protected under this provision of the Fifth Amendment. Administrative agencies may compel the production of business records for prosecution purposes. The agency has a right to inspect and use the records in its investigations.

C. <u>Other Statutes</u>--In addition to the constitutional limitations on agency authority, various other federal statutes exist. The Freedom of Information Act (FOIA), Privacy Act, Sunshine Act, Regulatory Flexibility Act, and Sunset Acts previously discussed limit the power of administrative agency.

D.   <u>Judicial Review</u>--The court has the authority to review agency action. The court may reverse the agency action if the agency violated the U.S. Constitution, the APA, the agency's enabling act, or failed to provide a reasonable basis for an informal rule or a formal rule.

Courts generally give judicial deference to an agency decision and will refuse to hear a case unless the party has first exhausted his or her administrative remedies. In other words, a party must follow the appeals procedures of the agency before resorting to the court.

Study Questions

Fill-in-the-Blank Questions

Administrative agencies have the power to create law; this process is known as _____.
                    (adjudication/rulemaking)

The authority of an administrative agency is outlined in _____.
    (its enabling act/the APA)

An independent federal agency is one that _____ established by Congress.   (is/is not)

The _____ permits an individual to re-
     (FOIA/Sunshine Act)
quest information held by an agency.

True-False Questions

1.   The power of the courts to review agency decisions is known as judicial review and is specifically stated in the U.S. Constitution. _____

2.   Congress has delegated part of its legislative powers to administrative agencies. _____

3. A federal administrative agency need only follow the pro-
    cedural rules it has adopted. _____

4. The administrative agency is constrained by the U.S. Con-
    stitution when dealing with citizens. _____

5. A party to an administrative adjudication has a right to
    a jury. _____

6. The APA provides procedural guidelines for federal admin-
    istrative agencies. _____

7. There are hundreds of federal administrative agencies,
    but state administrative agencies are prohibited. _____

8. A line agency is under the direct control of the Presi-
    dent. _____

9. An example of a government agency is the U.S. Postal Ser-
    vice. _____

10. The Federal Register is the method the federal adminis-
    trative agency uses to notify the public of a proposed
    rule. _____

Multiple-Choice Questions

1. An administrative agency may have the authority to do
    which of the following?

    a. adjudications
    b. rulemaking
    c. investigations
    d. all of the above

2. Which of the following is not an advantage of administra-
    tive agencies?

    a. limitation on the power of elected officials to
        effect change
    b. expertise
    c. well-developed hierarchy
    d. flexibility

3. Which of the following types of agencies is freestanding
    from the President and Congress?

    a. line agency
    b. independent agency

     c.   government agency
     d.   quasi-official agency

4. Which of the following creates an administrative agency?

     a.   APA
     b.   FOIA
     c.   enabling act
     d.   Privacy Act

5. The power of an administrative agency to create law through its legislative authority is known as:

     a.   quasi-legislative function.
     b.   judicial review.
     c.   adjudication.
     d.   subpoena power.

6. The type of agency rules that govern the internal practices of the agency are called:

     a.   the APA.
     b.   interpretive rules.
     c.   procedural rules.
     d.   substantive rules.

7. When a federal agency begins the informal rulemaking process, it must publish the proposed rule in:

     a.   the United States Code.
     b.   the Federal Register.
     c.   the Federal Reserve Board.
     d.   none of the above.

8. A final order issued by an administrative law judge which is violated by a wrongdoer may be enforced by imposing:

     a.   treble damages.
     b.   punitive damages.
     c.   imprisonment.
     d.   penalties.

9. Which provision of the U.S. Constitution protects individuals and business from an agency conducting a search without a warrant?

     a.   Thirteenth Amendment
     b.   First Amendment
     c.   Fourth Amendment
     d.   Fifth Amendment

10. Which provision of the U.S. Constitution protects an individual against self-incrimination?

    a. Thirteenth Amendment
    b. First Amendment
    c. Fourth Amendment
    d. Fifth Amendment

11. Which federal statute requires an agency to keep accurate and current information on an individual who has a record with the agency?

    a. Privacy Act
    b. FOIA
    c. APA
    d. enabling act

12. Fidel, a foreign citizen, sent a Freedom of Information Act request to the U.S. Department of Defense asking for the design drawings of the new stealth bomber. The Department denied the request without giving any explanation. Fidel may:

    a. request an appeal of the decision to the agency.
    b. file in federal court.
    c. appeal to the U.S. Supreme Court.
    d. none of the above.

13. Under the Freedom of Information Act, an agency must release information requests unless an exemption applies. Which of the following is not an exemption?

    a. sensitive information
    b. internal personnel rules
    c. confidential information
    d. trade secrets

14. The Federal Trade Commission (FTC) promulgates a rule prohibiting used car dealerships from selling used automobiles without fully disclosing all major defects to the buyer in written form. The FTC published the proposed rule in the Federal Register and gave interested parties 90 days to submit written comments. After the expiration of the 90-day period, the FTC promulgated the rule. This form of rulemaking is known as:

    a. formal.
    b. informal.
    c. adjudication.
    d. exhaustion of remedies.

15. Refer to question 14. The rule created by the FTC is an example of a(n):

   a. interpretive rule.
   b. procedural rule.
   c. substantive rule.
   d. ordinance.

16. Refer to question 14. According to the Administrative Procedures Act, the FTC is required to follow which of the following procedures in the promulgation of the rule?

   a. give notice of the proposed rule
   b. publish the promulgated rule
   c. publish a statement of findings and conclusions with the promulgated rule
   d. all of the above

17. Refer to question 14. Acme Auto Inc. has been in business for over 25 years as a dealer of antique automobiles. Acme submitted a written comment to the FTC during the 90-day comment period. Acme's letter requested the FTC to amend the proposed rule to exclude the sales of antique automobiles. The FTC, after the 90-day comment period, has the option of:

   a. publishing the proposed rule.
   b. modifying the rule.
   c. withdrawing the rule.
   d. all of the above.

18. Refer to question 17. Assume the rule is promulgated by the FTC without amendment. Acme Auto Inc. refuses to comply with the FTC rule. Acme is found in violation of the FTC rule by an administrative law judge and fined $500. Acme appeals the case directly to the U.S. Court of Appeals. The court will:

   a. dismiss the case because of the exhaustion of remedies doctrine.
   b. dismiss the case because Acme has violated the rule.
   c. hold in favor of Acme because Acme made a written comment.
   d. issue a cease and desist order.

19. Refer to question 18. Assume the U.S. Court of Appeals hears Acme's case and reviews the administrative law judge's decision. Acme contends the administrative law judge failed to consider all the evidence. The court will decide the case according to which standard of review?

    a.   arbitrary and capricious
    b.   reasonableness
    c.   substantial evidence in the record
    d.   exhaustion of remedies

20.   The Securities and Exchange Commission (SEC) proposed a new rule to define insider trading and prohibit all forms of securities transactions based upon the use of material nonpublic information. The SEC held public hearings allowing interested parties to participate. Which of the following is not permitted by a participant during the hearing?

    a.   examine witnesses
    b.   present oral testimony
    c.   to be appointed an attorney if he/she can't afford one
    d.   present documentary evidence

21.   Refer to question 20. If the rule is later properly challenged in the U.S. Court of Appeals by a group of investment bankers, the court may invalidate the rule if:

    a.   it violates the FTC's enabling act.
    b.   the court disagrees with the findings of fact.
    c.   it violates the APA.
    d.   it is based on the record adduced from the public hearing.

22.   Bard Inc., a manufacturer of household products, employs two-hundred factory workers at their Chicago plant. The plant manager at the Chicago facility allows the OSHA inspector to search the facility for hazardous working conditions. The inspector issues a citation for a dangerous machine at the facility. The attorney for Bard Inc. seeks to challenge the search as a violation of the U.S. Constitution. If the search is challenged, the likely outcome will be:

    a.   the evidence is held inadmissible.
    b.   a violation of the U.S. Constitution.
    c.   no violation of the U.S. Constitution.
    d.   Bard Inc. will win the case.

23.   OSHA may obtain a warrant from a federal judge based upon:

    a.   probable cause.
    b.   specific evidence of a violation.

c.   a general administrative plan for inspections.
d.   all of the above.

24. Which of the following statutes have opened up adminis-
     trative agency decisions and activities to public exami-
     nation?

       I. Freedom of Information Act
      II. sunset acts
     III. Sunshine Act

     a.   I only
     b.   I and II
     c.   I, II, and III
     d.   I and III

25. The Federal Communication Commission promulgated a rule
     which prohibited advertisers from exploiting children
     through the use of television commercials which exag-
     gerated the performance of children's products. A major
     advertiser and manufacturer of children's toys was caught
     by the FCC violating the rule. The Commission found the
     manufacturer in violation of the rule and issued a cease
     and desist order. The manufacturer followed all the
     proper channels for appeal and now requests an appeal
     with the U.S. Court of Appeals. The court will:

     a.   not hear the case because the appellant did not
          exhaust administrative remedies.
     b.   not hear the case because any delegation of authority
          to an agency is unconstitutional.
     c.   substitute its judgment for the agency's.
     d.   give judicial deference to the agency's findings.

Essay Question

  1. Eldridge, a disabled worker, received social security
     benefits. The Social Security Administration (S.S.A.)
     determined Eldridge was no longer disabled and not en-
     titled to benefits under the Social Security Act. The
     S.S.A. made the determination based upon information
     gathered from Eldridge's family doctor. Eldridge was
     informed by letter that the S.S.A. had discontinued his
     benefits and that Eldridge had the right to appeal the
     decision. Eldridge believes his constitutional rights
     have been violated and appeals the S.S.A. decision. What
     is the result?

Answers to Study Questions

Fill-in-the-Blank Questions

Administrative agencies have the power to create law; this process is known as <u>rulemaking</u>. (p. 135)

The authority of an administrative agency is outlined in <u>its enabling act</u>. (p. 133)

An independent federal agency is one that <u>is</u> established by Congress. (p. 131)

The <u>FOIA</u> permits an individual to request information held by an agency. (p. 135)

True-False Questions

1. False. The concept of judicial review is not stated in the U.S. Constitution. (p. 150)

2. False. Congress cannot delegate its legislative power to an administrative agency. (p. 135)

3. False. The federal administrative agency must follow the APA. (p. 133)

4. True (p. 144)

5. False. In an adjudication, no right to a jury exists. (p. 139)

6. True (p. 133)

7. False. Most states have created administrative agencies. (p. 128)

8. True (p. 131)

9. True (p. 131)

10. True (p. 136)

Multiple-Choice Questions

1.	d (p. 135)		14.	b	(p. 136)
2.	a (p. 130)		15.	c	(p. 136)
3.	b (p. 133)		16.	d	(p. 136)
4.	c (p. 133)		17.	d	(p. 136)
5.	a (p. 135)		18.	a	(p. 150)
6.	c (p. 136)		19.	c	(p. 139)
7.	b (p. 136)		20.	c	(p. 144)
8.	d (p. 142)		21.	c	(p. 133)
9.	c (p. 144)		22.	c	(p. 144)
10.	d (p. 146)		23.	d	(p. 144)
11.	a (p. 149)		24.	d	(p. 149)
12.	a (p. 146)		25.	d	(p. 144)
13.	a (p. 146)				

Essay Question

1. Eldridge should argue that his due process rights have been violated under the Fifth Amendment. The Due Process Clause states, "no person shall be deprived of life, liberty or property without due process of law." The courts have interpreted the clause to require notice and an opportunity to be heard.

    The court will weigh the private interest affected against the possibility of an erroneous deprivation and the amount of administrative burden on the agency, to determine if a hearing is required before the deprivation occurs.

    In <u>Mathews vs. Eldridge</u>, the Supreme Court held that a hearing was not required prior to the termination of disability benefits. Due process was not violated.
    (p. 144)

Chapter 7
The Regulation of Business Through Criminal Law

Major Concepts

The corporation is increasingly being prosecuted for the criminal acts of its employees and its own criminal acts. Crime may be broadly classified as either a felony, misdemeanor, or a petty offense. The most serious crimes are classified as felonies and the least serious as petty offenses.

Today, the criminal law is embodied in state and federal statutes. Historically, the criminal law came from the common law which required proof of a criminal intent (mens rea) and a criminal act (actus reus). Under the Model Penal Code, an individual in some cases can be convicted of a crime for committing only the criminal act. Modern statutes state the essential elements of a crime. The prosecution must prove each element of the crime beyond a reasonable doubt in order to obtain a conviction of the accused. The accused is presumed innocent until proven guilty by the prosecution.

The Constitution protects the rights of the accused by ensuring the process is fair. The Fourth and Fifth Amendments attempt to prohibit unreasonable searches and seizures and require the defendant to be formally charged and given an opportunity to be heard.

A wide variety of crimes affect the efficient operation of business. Many federal statutes have been passed to protect consumers, competition, and stop corruption. The corporation involved in criminal activity may be fined, and the corporate employees may be fined and sent to prison.

<u>Chapter Outline</u>

I.   <u>The Criminal Law</u>--Criminal law is the body of law which attempts to protect society from wrongful acts. The criminal law is punitive in nature, whereas the civil law is compensatory. A criminal action is commenced by the government and brought in the name of the state or United States. A civil action is brought by a private party to redress harm committed by the defendant. Under the criminal law, a party may be incarcerated, fined, or both.

The criminal act may also be a civil wrong in which the wrongdoer is required to compensate the injured party for damages. In a criminal action, the prosecution must prove every element of the crime beyond a reasonable doubt. In a civil action, the plaintiff must prove the case by a preponderance of the evidence, which is a lessor standard than required in criminal prosecutions.

A.   <u>Classification of Crimes</u>--A crime is classified as either a felony, misdemeanor, or petty offense. Criminal law is defined by state statute and may differ from state to state.

     1.   A felony is punishable by imprisonment in a penitentiary for more than a year or by death. The Model Penal Code divides felonies into four categories: capital offenses punishable by death, first-degree felonies punishable by up to life imprisonment, second-degree felonies punishable up to ten years imprisonment, and third-degree felonies punishable up to five years imprisonment.

     2.   A misdemeanor is a crime of lessor seriousness than a felony and punishable up to a maximum of one year confinement. The convicted party is usually confined at a city or county jail (e.g., disorderly conduct).

     3.   A petty offense is punishable by a few days in jail, a fine, or both (e.g., traffic violation).

B.   <u>Criminal Statutory Law</u>--Historically, the criminal law has been defined by the courts. The common law required proof of two elements: criminal intent (mens rea) and criminal conduct (actus reus). The defendant must have had both a guilty mind and committed a criminal act to be convicted. The mental state of the wrongdoer is important to determine the degree of guilt (e.g., premeditated murder is a first-degree felony, whereas killing someone in an auto accident is involuntary manslaughter). The greater degree of guilt or wrongfulness, the more reprehensible the crime and greater the punishment.

Criminal law today is defined by state and federal statute. Courts still defer to the original common law when interpreting criminal statutes. The criminal code defines a crime as comprised of specific elements.

1. <u>Categories of Criminal Intent</u>--Contrary to the common law, some criminal statutes do not require proof of criminal intent to be convicted of certain crimes. However, most crimes require some level of criminal intent for the wrongdoer to be convicted.

    The Model Penal Code sets forth four levels of criminal intent or mens rea:

    a. The first level is the <u>purpose</u> of the accused. Did the accused consciously set out to accomplish an objective?

    b. The second level of intent is the <u>knowledge</u> of the accused. Did the accused know what he or she was doing, and did he or she know the result?

    c. The third level of intent is <u>recklessness</u>. Did the accused act with knowledge of a considerable risk to others from his or her actions and consciously disregard such risk?

    d. The fourth level of intent is <u>negligence</u>. Did the accused deviate from the standard of care a reasonable person would have exercised under the same circumstances? Depending on the crime, the statute may require from the highest level of intent "purpose" to the lowest level of "negligence."

II. <u>Constitutional Safeguards</u>--In a criminal case, the accused is presumed innocent until proven guilty. Unless the prosecution proves every element of the crime beyond a reasonable doubt, the presumption requires the court to acquit the accused. The U.S. system of criminal justice is premised on the axiom that it is better to allow a guilty person to go free than to put an innocent person in prison. Requiring the prosecution to prove each case beyond a reasonable doubt may allow a guilty person to be acquitted.

A. Criminal Procedure--The criminal safeguards in the Constitution apply to federal prosecutions and state prosecutions through the Fifth and Fourteenth Amendment's Due Process clause. The Fourth Amendment protects individuals from unreasonable searches and seizures. A search warrant for arrest cannot be issued unless probable cause exists that a crime has been committed.

In Arizona v. Miranda, the U.S. Supreme Court established that when a person is arrested, he or she must be informed of their rights. Enforcement officers are required to warn the accused that they have a right to remain silent and the right to an attorney even if they cannot afford one.

The Fifth Amendment requires an individual be formally charged with the specific crime before being brought to trial. The charge may be an indictment issued by a grand jury or a bill of information issued by a magistrate. The charges must be based upon sufficient evidence to justify the trial.

Courts are required to follow the rules of evidence. The rules allow the parties to exclude evidence that is irrelevant, unreliable, and unfairly prejudicial to one of the parties.

III. Crimes Affecting Business

A. Offenses Against Property--Corporations usually own extensive amounts of intangible and tangible property. Business must attempt to protect itself against crimes involving property. There are eight basic criminal offenses against property.

1. Burglary--Burglary is the breaking and entering into the building of another, usually at nighttime, with the intent to commit a felony. Burglary is aggravated if the burglar uses a deadly weapon while in the process of committing a felony.

2. <u>Larceny</u>--Larceny is the taking and carrying away of personal property of another with the intent to permanently deprive the person of his or her interest in the property. In some states, the stealing of computer programs, trade secrets, natural gas, and electricity are subject to larceny statutes.

3. <u>Robbery</u>--The taking of personal property of another in the presence of a person by force or intimidation with the intent to permanently deprive him or her of it is robbery. Aggravated robbery is robbery with the use of a deadly weapon.

4. <u>Receiving Stolen Goods</u>--Receiving stolen goods is the receiving and taking possession of personal property with knowledge that the goods were stolen with the intent to permanently deprive the owner of his or her interest in the property. A party has knowledge if he or she should have known the goods were stolen.

5. <u>Arson</u>--Arson is the willful and malicious burning of a building owned by another. If a person dies in the building after the fire is set, the act is felony murder.

6. <u>Forgery</u>--Forgery is the fraudulent making or altering of a writing that changes the legal liability of another. Changing or altering a trademark, public record, or any legal document is considered forgery.

7. <u>Obtaining Money or Goods by False Pretenses</u>--Obtaining title to the property of another by an intentional false statement of past or existing fact with the intent to defraud the other is the crime of obtaining goods by false pretenses. The majority of the states have statutes prohibiting the transfer of an insufficient funds check with the intent to defraud.

    The Trademark Counterfeiting Act makes it a crime to sell goods or services with a counterfeit trademark.

    The False Statement Act prohibits making an intentional false statement to the United States government to obtain a monetary return.

8.   Embezzlement--Embezzlement is the fraudulent conversion of property of another by a person in lawful possession of that property. When a bank officer transfers the bank's money into a personal account, he or she is guilty of embezzlement. Embezzlement does not involve the physical taking of property by force from another.

Misapplication of trust funds is a special type of embezzlement where a trusted person is given money for a specific use and he fails to use the money for its intended purpose.

B.   White-Collar Crime--White-collar crime can be divided into two categories: occupational and corporate. Occupational crime consists of those illegal activities committed by a person through his or her work. Committing a crime in the course of doing a person's job is occupational crime (e.g., insider trading, tax evasion, check kiting, kickbacks, and bribes).

Corporate crime is committed by the corporation in general. No one person is responsible for the crime, but the entire organization has contributed to the illegal activity.

Five areas of white-collar crime will be discussed in the rest of this chapter.

1.   Computer Crimes--A computer can be a tool to commit a wide variety of crimes. An electronic theft can occur by programming a computer to write extra paychecks, transfer large sums of money, or skim cents off interest accounts and place it in a personal account.

Congress enacted two federal statutes to combat computer crime: the Counterfeit Access Device and Computer Fraud and Abuse Act of 1985 and the Electronic Communications Privacy Act of 1986. Both statutes prohibit the entrance of anyone into a computer system without proper authorization. The act covers governmental computers, computers of federally insured institutions, cellular car telephones, and computer access that crosses state lines. The penalties can be up to ten years imprisonment, $100,000 fine, or both.

2. Mail Fraud--Use of the mails or telegram to
    defraud the public is a federal crime. The
    prosecution must prove the mailing of a writing
    to execute a scheme to defraud and an organized
    scheme to defraud by false pretenses.

3. Racketeering--Congress enacted the Racketeer
    Influenced and Corrupt Organizations Act of 1970
    (RICO) to stop organized crime from being in-
    volved in legitimate businesses. RICO has both
    criminal and civil sections.

    a. Criminal RICO--The statute requires proof
        that a person has committed two or more
        racketeering acts within ten years of each
        other to show a pattern of racketeering
        activity. The Act specifies racketeering
        acts as mail fraud, wire fraud, fraud in the
        sale of securities, extortion, arson,
        murder, gambling, drug dealing, and others.

        A criminal conviction under RICO allows the
        court to access a fine up to $25,000, order
        imprisonment up to twenty years, and forfeit
        the property obtained through criminal
        activity.

    b. Civil RICO--The Act allows a private indi-
        vidual to bring a lawsuit to recover treble
        damages from a defendant who has violated
        RICO. The plaintiff does not have to prove
        the defendant has been convicted or prose-
        cuted to show a racketeering injury.

4. Bribery--Three separate offenses are considered
    under the classification of bribery.

    a. Bribery of Foreign Officials--The Foreign
        Corrupt Practices Act of 1977 (FCPA) pro-
        hibits American companies from offering
        something of value to foreign government
        officials to obtain or retain business. The
        FCPA requires all companies registered with
        the Securities and Exchange Commission to
        keep detailed records that "accurately and
        fairly" reflect the company's financial ac-
        tivities and an accounting system which
        provides "reasonable assurance" that trans-
        actions of the company are accounted for and
        are legal.

A corporation violating the FCPA can be fined up to $1 million. Officers and directors violating the FCPA can be imprisoned up to five years and personally fined up to $10,000.

b. Bribery of Public Officials--Offering a public official a thing of value with the intent to influence the public official to act in a way to serve a private interest is a crime.

c. Commercial Bribery--Giving kickbacks or payoffs to an employee of one company with the intent to obtain proprietary information, cover up an inferior product, or secure new business is a crime.

5. Bankruptcy Fraud--When a person has filed for relief under the Bankruptcy Reform Act of 1978 and is not honest with the court, he or she may have committed a Bankruptcy Fraud.

False claims of creditors, transfer of property to defraud creditors, and scam bankruptcies are examples of bankruptcy fraud.

IV. Corporate Crime--Corporate crime is a generic term which covers crimes that are related to corporations. The following are examples of crimes a corporation may commit.

A. Regulatory Offenses--Congress has enacted a wide variety of statutes that regulate the way businesses operate (e.g., Environmental Protection Act, Securities and Exchange Act of 1934, Sherman, and Clayton Acts). Most violations of such acts are prosecuted through an administrative agency which may impose civil and administrative penalties against the corporation. An administrative law judge decides if a violation has occurred and what the fine will be.

B. Breach of Fiduciary Duty--The federal mail fraud statute allows a prosecutor to bring a case against an executive who has failed to disclose material information he or she had a duty to disclose by use of the mails.

C. Obstruction of Justice--Corporate employees may not destroy or hide corporate records from the court or

an administrative agency. If the business records
are necessary for an investigation, the corporation
must turn over the business records according to a
court order.

D. <u>Conspiracy or Aiding and Abetting</u>--If a corporation
aids, abets, counsels, commands, induces, procures,
or conspires to commit a crime, it has committed a
crime.

Study Questions

Fill-in-the-Blank Questions

Allen Johnson was employed by Memco, Inc. as the treasurer and
chief financial officer. Memco was a very prosperous company
with 5,000 employees shipping computer equipment around the
world. Allen has cleverly devised a scheme in which company
funds are transferred into his personal account. The books
reflect these transfers as consulting fees.

The president of Memco, Inc. discovers the payments and orders
an audit of the financial records. The president believes
Allen is guilty of _____.
                          (robbery/embezzlement)

Under the old common law, a crime required proof of a mens rea
and _____.
              (an actus reus/premeditation)

A magistrate may issue a(n) _____
                                    (bill of information/
_____ which formally charges Allen with the commission
  indictment)
of a crime.

During Allen's trial, the prosecutors must prove every element of the crime _____
                            (by a preponderance of the evidence/
_____.
    beyond a reasonable doubt)

True-False Questions

1. Crime is classified into two categories: felony and mis-
    demeanor. _____

2. A misdemeanor is a crime punishable by a fine or confinement up to one year. _____

3. Today, all crimes are based on statutes. _____

4. Most white-collar crimes are prosecuted in federal courts. _____

5. The Constitution protects only those accused of committing federal crimes. _____

6. In a criminal trial, all the evidence is admissible even if it is prejudicial to the defendant. _____

7. For a warrant for arrest to be issued, probable cause must exist to believe the accused committed a crime. _____

8. An indictment is issued by a grand jury. _____

9. The killing of another person with premeditation is first-degree murder. _____

10. Criminal statutes always require proof of criminal intent. _____

Multiple-Choice Questions

1. Which of the following include a traffic violation?

   a. felony
   b. petty offense
   c. misdemeanor
   d. second-degree felony

2. Which of the following is punishable by imprisonment in a federal or state penitentiary for more than a year?

   a. felony
   b. petty offense
   c. misdemeanor
   d. none of the above

3. Which of the following can be classified as a crime against property?

   a. burglary
   b. assault

    c.   murder
    d.   rape

4. Which of the following is <u>not</u> a premise of the criminal justice system?

     I.   It is worse to punish an innocent person than to let a guilty person go free.

    II.   In a criminal case, the prosecution must prove the crime beyond all doubt.

   III.   The accused is guilty until proven innocent.

    a.   I only
    b.   I and II
    c.   I, II, and III
    d.   II and III

5. Adam Smith was arrested by police officers after robbing the First National Bank. Adam was captured after a high speed chase through downtown Dallas. Adam was handcuffed and taken to the city jail. The officers did not talk to Adam before, during, or after the arrest. Which of the following is true?

     I.   Adam is guilty of misapplication of trust funds.
    II.   Adam's constitutional rights have been violated.
   III.   The police must have a warrant for a crime they witness.

    a.   I only
    b.   II only
    c.   I, II, and III
    d.   II and III

6. Which of the following is not a recognized category of mens rea under the Model Penal Code?

    a.   premeditation
    b.   purpose
    c.   negligence
    d.   knowledge

7. Ford Motor Co. designed the Pinto in such a way that if the car was in a rear end collision it would burst into flames. The company was aware of the defect but decided not to install a safety device at a cost of $11 for each automobile. Indiana prosecutors brought a criminal action against Ford for which of the following crimes?

    a.   first-degree murder
    b.   embezzlement
    c.   reckless homicide
    d.   conspiracy

8. Which of the following crimes requires the use of force or intimidation?

      I. Burglary
     II. Larceny
   III. Robbery

    a.   I only
    b.   I and II
    c.   III only
    d.   I and III

9. Dan Walker is a college student at State University. Dan sells his stereo system to Fred Fredericks for $400. Dan sold the stereo to have enough money to vacation in Florida over spring break. Fred sets up the stereo in his room at the dormitory. The police, two weeks later, knock on Fred's door and ask if they can search Fred's room. Fred agrees to the search, and the police confiscate the stereo as stolen goods. Fred is charged with receiving stolen goods. Fred's best defense is:

    a.   he didn't really know the thief.
    b.   he paid for the stereo with a bad check.
    c.   he did not know and should not have known the stereo was stolen.
    d.   the stereo did not work.

10. Refer to question 9. The police officers arrest Fred and take him to the station. Fred asks to use the telephone to call his lawyer but is denied. The police interrogate Fred and obtain a confession of his guilt. During Fred's trial, the prosecution asks to have the confession admitted into the evidence. Fred may object on the ground that:

    a.   the police officers violated Fred's constitutional right to an attorney.
    b.   Fred did not steal the stereo.
    c.   Fred only knew Dan for one month before the sale.
    d.   Fred did not have the requisite criminal conduct.

11. Sandy Hawkins purchases a new video recorder from Audio World Inc. for $500, paying with a personal check. Sandy

knows the check will bounce because she has $20 in her account. Sandy may be prosecuted for:

a. forgery.
b. misappropriation.
c. robbery.
d. obtaining goods by false pretenses.

12. Which of the following is not classified as a white-collar crime?

a. computer crime
b. embezzlement
c. mail fraud
d. robbery

13. Which of the following statutes make(s) it a crime to enter a computer system without proper authorization?

  I. Securities and Exchange Act of 1934
 II. Electronic Communications Privacy Act
III. Counterfeit Access Device and Computer Fraud and Abuse Act

a. I only
b. I and II
c. II and III
d. I, II, and III

14. Dave Weber sends a letter by mail offering to sell stock in a nonexistent company. Dave collects $100,000 from offerees through the mail. Dave is guilty of:

a. RICO.
b. mail fraud.
c. wire fraud.
d. robbery.

15. A person convicted under RICO may be:

a. fined $25,000 and imprisoned up to 20 years.
b. fined $50,000 and imprisoned up to 20 years.
c. fined $25,000 and imprisoned up to 25 years.
d. fined $100,000.

16. Criminal RICO requires proof of:

  I. robbery and burglary.
 II. a pattern of racketeering activity.
III. drug usage and gambling.

a. I only
b. II only
c. I and II
d. I, II, and III

17. In a civil RICO case, a private party may seek
    _____ for the actual damages resulting from a
    violation.

    a. treble damages
    b. double damages
    c. penalties.
    d. punitive damages

18. Under RICO, a list of federal and state crimes constitute
    racketeering acts. Which of the following is/are listed?

      I. bankruptcy fraud
     II. extortion
    III. arson

    a. I only
    b. II only
    c. I, II, and III
    d. I and III

19. Harold Houser is the vice president of a large exporting
    manufacturing company called Tronix Inc. Tronix manu-
    factures very sophisticated radar equipment for use on
    commercial airliners. Harold obtains a large contract by
    bribing a foreign company president. Harold is guilty of
    violating:

    a. the Securities and Exchange Act of 1934.
    b. the Foreign Corrupt Practices Act.
    c. the Bankruptcy Act.
    d. none of the above.

20. A violation of the Foreign Corrupt Practices Act may
    result in:

      I. up to a $1 million fine.
     II. up to 5 years in prison.
    III. up to a $10,000 fine for directors and officers.

    a. I only
    b. I and II
    c. I, II, and III
    d. I and III

21. Which of the following is considered a bankruptcy fraud?

    I.   A creditor files a false claim against the debtor.
   II.   A debtor wants his or her debts discharged.
 III.   A debtor has debts greatly in excess of their assets.

    a.   I only
    b.   I and II
    c.   I, II, and III
    d.   III only

22. Which of the following is considered a regulatory offense?

    a.   hazardous working conditions for employees in violation of OSHA
    b.   embezzlement of corporate funds
    c.   theft of company property
    d.   none of the above

23. An executive who destroys company records that are about to be subpoenaed by a grand jury is guilty of:

    I.   a regulatory offense.
   II.   conspiracy.
 III.   obstruction of justice.

    a.   I only
    b.   I and II
    c.   I, II, and III
    d.   III only

24. A criminal action is brought in the name of:

    a.   the state.
    b.   the victim of the crime.
    c.   the prosecutor.
    d.   none of the above.

25. Which of the following statutes requires a company to keep accurate financial records?

    a.   RICO
    b.   FCPA
    c.   OSHA
    d.   none of the above

Essay Question

1. Clarence Clark is a successful real estate salesperson
    working on straight commission. Clarence believes in
    impressing his clients. Clarence leases a very expensive
    office and automobile for company business. Clarence
    lands a deal on one of the more expensive homes he is
    brokering, taking a $25,000 deposit on behalf of the
    client. Clarence knows the house will close next week,
    and he will be paid a $42,000 commission. Clarence uses
    the $25,000 deposit to pay his personal bills. Has
    Clarence committed a crime?

Answers to Study Questions

Fill-in-the-Blank Questions

The president of Memco, Inc. discovers the payments and orders
an audit of the financial records. The president believes
Allen is guilty of embezzlement. (p. 165)

Under the old common law, a crime required proof of a mens rea
and actus reus. (p. 162)

A magistrate may issue a bill of information which formally
charges Allen with the commission of a crime. (p. 161)

During Allen's trial, the prosecutors must prove every element
of the crime beyond a reasonable doubt. (p. 158)

True-False Questions

1. False. Crime is classified as either a felony,
    misdemeanor, or petty offense. (p. 158)

2. True (p. 158)

3. True (p. 159)

4. True (p. 167)

5. False. The Constitution protects state and federal
    offenders. (p. 161)

6. False. The rules of evidence exclude some types of
    evidence. (p. 161)

7.   True (p. 161)

8.   True (p. 161)

9.   True (p. 162)

10. False. Some criminal statutes require proof of only a
     criminal act. (p. 163)

Multiple-Choice Questions

1.	b (p. 158)		14.	b (p. 168)
2.	a (p. 158)		15.	a (p. 170)
3.	a (p. 164)		16.	b (p. 171)
4.	d (p. 158)		17.	a (p. 171)
5.	b (p. 161)		18.	c (p. 171)
6.	a (p. 162)		19.	d (p. 171)
7.	c (p. 165)		20.	c (p. 173)
8.	c (p. 164)		21.	a (p. 174)
9.	c (p. 165)		22.	a (p. 175)
10.	a (p. 161)		23.	d (p. 175)
11.	d (p. 165)		24.	a (p. 159)
12.	d (p. 167)		25.	b (p. 173)
13.	c (p. 168)			

Essay Question

1.   Clarence is guilty of a form of embezzlement called mis-
     application of trust funds. When a real estate broker
     holds earnest money for a client, a trust relationship is
     created. The broker is the trustee responsible for
     acting honestly and in good faith toward the parties
     involved. Clarence has fraudulently appropriated the
     funds to his own account. Clarence has used the money in
     a way inconsistent with the terms of the contract with
     the intent to defraud the buyer. (p. 167)

PART II
BUSINESS AND PRIVATE LAW

Part Summary

Part II involves areas which deal primarily with commercial law. The basis of commercial law is the contract. The legal rights and responsibilities of contracting parties under the common law and the Uniform Commercial Code are essential to understanding the chapters which follow. Contract law is covered in Chapter 9.

Contract law is deeply rooted in the common law and is the foundation for understanding consumer rights, product liability, and property law. An overview of contract law is provided for the student along with an introduction to the Uniform Commercial Code. Article II of the Uniform Commercial Code governs the sale of goods.

The torts and product liability areas involve the liability of a business when a civil wrong has been committed. Business's liability for defective products and services has expanded by substantial proportions in the last two decades. Computer law involves a newly developed branch of the law which will be increasingly more important as technology advances.

Chapter 8
Torts

Major Concepts

This chapter deals with tort law. Tort law can be divided
into intentional torts, negligence, and strict liability.

Intentional torts can be further divided into torts against
the person and torts against property. Torts against the person include assault and battery, false imprisonment, infliction of mental distress, defamation, disparagement of goods,
slander of title, defamation by computer, and fraud. Torts
against property include trespass to land, conversion, and
nuisance. The commission of an intentional tort requires the
plaintiff to prove a wrongful act done with specific or general intent.

Negligence is considered an unintentional tort and requires
proof of three elements. The plaintiff in a negligence case
must prove a duty of care, breach of the duty of care, and
causation.

Strict liability is a tort which holds the defendant liable
when a plaintiff is injured from the defendant's abnormally
dangerous activities. Strict liability does not require the
plaintiff to prove the defendant was at fault.

Some torts are directly related to business activity. The
torts of wrongful interferences with a contractual or business
relationship, infringement of trademark, trade names, patents
and copyrights, and the theft of trade secrets all involve the
assets of the business entity. The largest judgment ever

rendered in the United States came from a case where a corporation interfered with the merger between two other corporations.

Chapter Outline

I. <u>Torts</u>--A tort is a civil wrong. Torts can be classified as intentional, unintentional (negligence), or strict liability. These classifications are related to the degree of intent of the wrongdoer.

A. <u>Intentional Torts</u>--The party who commits an intentional tort must have the requisite intent to do a specific act. The wrongdoer must consciously intend to harm another (specific intent) or intend the consequences of his conduct if he knows with substantial certainty that certain consequences will result (general intent). The elements necessary for the commission of an intentional tort are: an act by the wrongdoer, intent, and causation. Intentional torts can be divided into two categories: intentional torts to the person and intentional torts against property.

1. <u>Intentional Torts to the Person</u>

a. <u>Assault and Battery</u>--The commission of an assault and battery requires placing a person in reasonable apprehension or fear of bodily harm (assault) and physical contact that results in an injury (battery). The plaintiff must be aware of the defendant's act to be put in fear of harm. A battery may be any harmful or offensive contact with the plaintiff. Words alone do not constitute an assault.

b. <u>False Imprisonment</u>--False imprisonment is an act or omission by the wrongdoer which confines or restrains a person to a bounded area with the intent to confine or restrain. The plaintiff must not consent to the confinement.

Most states have adopted merchant protection legislation which permits a shopkeeper who suspects someone of shoplifting to detain the person without fear of a civil lawsuit for false imprisonment. The merchant must have a reasonable belief that the party has shoplifted. The merchant may reasonably detain the alleged shoplifter to conduct an investigation.

c. <u>Infliction of Mental Distress</u>--An act which amounts to extreme and outrageous conduct with the intent to cause severe emotional distress is an intentional tort. Outrageous conduct is conduct which goes beyond the bounds of decency tolerated by society. If the wrongdoer knows a person is more sensitive and more susceptible to emotional distress than an average person and takes advantage of this person, an intentional tort has been committed (e.g., children, pregnant women, and elderly people).

d. <u>Defamation</u>--Defamation is considered a quasi-intentional tort because intent is not always a necessary element. Defamation is publishing defamatory language about another person which damages the reputation of the person and was the defendant's fault. Defamation comes in either of two forms: libel, which is written or recorded, or slander, which is spoken.

The law requires a person to refrain from communicating language which would adversely affect another person's reputation. Some examples of defamation are impeaching one's honesty, integrity, virtue, or sanity. Pictures, satire, or drama may be actionable defamation.

A person may have several defenses to a defamation action, such as truth, absolute privilege, or a qualified privilege. If the statement is true, this normally is a complete defense.

Some individuals are privileged to make defamatory statements. Judges, executive officials, and legislators have an absolute privilege to make defamatory statements during governmental proceedings.

A qualified privilege may exist for a person to make a defamatory statement. Usually, a

person will not be held liable in a qualified privilege situation if the person has
acted in good faith and the statement is
limited to those who have a legitimate
interest in the communication (e.g., statement made by a credit bureau to customer or
a statement made by a former employer to a
prospective employer).

e. <u>Disparagement of Goods, Slander of Title,
    and Defamation by Computer</u>--Disparagement of
    goods is the communication of false state-
    ments about a business's products. Slander
    of title is the communication of statements
    that may prevent a person from selling his
    or her property. Defamation by computer is
    the communication of false information by
    computer about a person or business.

f. <u>Fraud or Deceit</u>--Fraud is comprised of five
    elements.   The injured party must prove:

    (1) a misrepresentation of material fact,

    (2) made with the intent to deceive or with
        reckless disregard of the truth,

    (3) made with knowledge of the falsity,

    (4) the victim has justifiably relied on the
        falsity, and

    (5) damages resulted.

    Fraud is most commonly found in contract
    situations. If a party has a duty to speak
    and fails to, a case of fraud may be
    brought.

2. <u>Intentional Torts against Property</u>--Intentional
    torts perpetrated against the property of
    another are trespass, conversion, and nuisance.

    a. <u>Trespass to Land</u>--An act of physical inva-
        sion of another's real property with the
        intent to bring about a physical invasion is
        a trespass. Examples of a physical invasion
        are: the defendant personally coming on the
        land of another, the defendant flooding the
        plaintiff's land, or throwing rocks on the
        plaintiff's property.

The trespasser may be liable for any damage caused to the property. The landowner can remove the trespasser with reasonable force.

b. <u>Conversion</u>--Conversion is the act of interfering with the property of another with the intent to interfere. The interference must be serious enough to warrant the defendant paying for its full value (e.g., theft, embezzlement, wrongful selling, wrongful refusing to return to owner, wrongful destruction).

c. <u>Nuisance</u>--A nuisance is a substantial, unreasonable interference with a private individual's use or enjoyment of property which he or she possesses. A nuisance may be public or private. A public nuisance disturbs or interferes with the health, safety, or property rights of the community and is usually also a crime. Private nuisance interferes with the property of a limited number of individuals.

B. <u>Negligence</u>--Negligence is an unintentional tort. The plaintiff need not prove the wrongdoer acted with specific or general intent.

1. <u>Essential Elements of Negligence</u>--Negligence requires the proof of three elements: breach of a duty of care, injury, and causation.

a. <u>Breach of a Duty of Care</u>--A duty of care must first be proven by the plaintiff. A duty of care is created by an objective standard or imposed by statute. The objective standard determines if a duty of care exists by asking the question: How would a reasonable person in the same circumstances have acted? The actions of a reasonable person create a duty of care on others to act in the same manner.

Federal and state statutes may impose a duty of care on individuals or business. Failure to act in accordance with the duty of care is a breach.

b. <u>Injury</u>--The plaintiff must prove an injury occurred. Personal injury to the plaintiff or damage to the plaintiff's property must be shown.

c.   Causation--Causation is the link between the breach of the duty of care and the injury. Causation is divided into causation in fact and proximate cause. The plaintiff must prove both types of causation.

Causation in fact asks the question: Would the injury have occurred without the wrongful act? If the answer is no, the wrongful act was a cause in fact or a cause of the injury. The injury would not have occurred but for the breach of a duty of care.

Proximate cause must also be proven by the plaintiff. Proximate cause limits the potential liability of the defendant. Proximate cause is tested by foreseeability. If the consequences of the harm done or the victim are foreseeable, there is proximate cause. Would a reasonably thoughtful person have foreseen the potential for injury from his or her actions?

2. Defenses to Negligence--A defendant may assert a wide variety of defenses to a negligence lawsuit. Three such defenses are: superseding intervening forces, assumption of risk, and contributory or comparative negligence.

a.   Superseding Intervening Forces--A superseding or intervening force breaks the connection between a breach of duty and an injury, therefore, negating causation.

b.   Assumption of Risk--A party who knowingly and voluntarily enters a risky situation is responsible for his or her own injury.

c.   Contributory Negligence--The defense of contributory negligence bans the plaintiff from any recovery from the defendant because the plaintiff's own negligence contributed to the injury. The modern trend in most states is to adopt the theory of comparative negligence over contributory negligence. Comparative negligence requires the plaintiff to reduce the amount recovered by the percen-

tage he or she was at fault in causing their own injury.

C. Strict Liability--Strict liability is a no fault theory of recovery. Under strict liability, a defendant may be held liable for the injury of another without being at fault.

Strict liability holds defendants liable for damages caused from abnormally dangerous activities. An abnormally dangerous activity involves potential harm of a serious nature to persons or property, a high degree of risk that cannot be completely guarded against by exercising reasonable care and is not commonly performed in the community (e.g., blasting with dynamite).

The strict liability doctrine has expanded into the landlord-tenant, workers compensation, and product liability areas. One court has concluded that a landlord engaged in leasing dwellings is strictly liable in tort for injuries resulting from a latent defect which existed in the premises at the time the dwellings were let.

The public policy behind the strict liability doctrine is twofold. The first reason is that an employer and manufacturer are in a better position to bear the cost of injury than the injured person. And the second, the employer and manufacturer should bear the cost of injury as an operating expense.

II. Specific Torts Related to Business--Torts that are directly related to business are wrongful interference with a contractual or business relationship, infringement of trademarks, trade names, patents and copyrights and theft of trade secrets.

A. Wrongful Interference with a Contractual or Business Relationship--A party may be liable for intentionally causing the breach of a valid contract or business relationship. The plaintiff must prove a valid contract existed, the defendant knew the contract existed, and the defendant intentionally induced a breach of contract.

B. Infringement of Trademarks, Trade Names, Patents, and Copyrights--A business who has designed a trade mark or service mark will usually obtain the right to exclusive use through government registration.

If the trademark or service mark is copied to a substantial degree, intentionally or unintentionally, the mark has been infringed. The trademark does not have to be registered to obtain protection from infringement.

A patent infringement occurs when a party has secured a patent from the federal government on a device and another party uses a substantially similar or the same device. The patent grants the owner the exclusive right to make, use, and sell the invention for seventeen years.

A copyright is granted by the government to an author of literary or artistic productions. The author has exclusive rights to the work for the author's life plus fifty years.

C.   <u>Theft of Trade Secrets</u>--A trade secret is information or a process which a business owns and desires it to be kept confidential. Employers require employees to agree to not divulge trade secrets to third parties. If an employee communicates a trade secret to a competitor, the employee has misappropriated the employer's assets and breached his or her employment contract. If confidential information is stolen from an employer, it is considered theft of trade secrets.

Study Questions

Fill-in-the-Blank Questions

Harriet Baker and Harry Wade were travelling on the interstate when their automobiles collided. Harriet changed lanes to get to the inside lane, and Harry ran into the rear end of Harriet's automobile. Both Harriet and Harry are not injured and pull over to the side of the road. Harriet and Harry exchange words when Harriet punches Harry in the nose. Harry does nothing.

Harriet may bring a lawsuit against Harry for the damage to her car under _____.
                    (strict liability/negligence)

Harriet has committed a(n) _____ by punching Harry in the nose.   (assault/battery)

If Harriet is found negligent as a plaintiff, she will be barred from any recovery under _____ _____ negligence.   (contributory/ comparative)

Words usually _____ enough apprehension (do not create/create) sion in another party to give rise to an assault.

True-False Questions

1. Battery is the act which puts another person in reasonable apprehension of bodily harm. _F_

2. The loss to business for shoplifting is estimated in excess of $10 billion a year. _T_

3. Slander is the injuring of a person's reputation by spoken word. _T_

4. An absolute privilege applies to judges during judicial proceedings for defamatory language. _T_

5. Trespass to land always requires a person to invade real *or tangible object* property. _T_   F

6. Negligence is a no fault theory. _F_ (Strict Liability)

7. Nuisance may be classified as public or private. _T_

8. A duty of care may be created only by an objective standard. _T_   F   *and statute.*

9. A defense to negligence is assumption of risk. _T_

10. Strict liability applies only to abnormally dangerous activities. _T_   F

Multiple-Choice Questions

1. Which of the following is an offense against a person?

   a. trespass
   b. infliction of mental distress
   c. conversion
   d. nuisance

2. In order to prove a case of false imprisonment, the plaintiff must have:

    a. been arrested.
    b. put in jail.
    c. confined to a bounded area.
    d. handcuffed.

3. Which of the following is/are provisions of merchant protection legislation concerning shopkeepers adopted by most states?

    I.   The merchant must have reasonable cause for suspicion.
    II. Confinement is carried out in a reasonable way.
    III. The police are called immediately.

    a. I only
    b. I and II
    c. I, II, and III
    d. II and III

4. Which of the following is <u>not</u> an element of the tort of intentional infliction of mental distress?

    a. defamatory statements
    b. outrageous conduct
    c. severe emotional distress
    d. trespass

5. Joseph Jackson walks across the neighbor's property in an effort to catch a runaway dog. Joseph has committed the tort of:

    a. nuisance.
    b. defamation.
    c. trespass.
    d. deceit.

6. The objective standard under the theory of negligence requires the court to consider:

    a. state statutes.
    b. common law.
    c. cause in fact.
    d. what a reasonable person would do.

7. In order to prove the negligence of the defendant, the plaintiff must prove proximate cause. The best term to describe proximate cause is:

a.   reasonableness.
b.   foreseeability.
c.   substantial.
d.   none of the above.

8. Walter Wallace attends the opening day of the local base-
    ball team. Walter sits in an area where foul balls
    usually land. Walter hopes to catch a foul ball to take
    home to his ten-year-old son. While Walter is at the
    game, a ball hits him on the head, causing severe injury.
    Walter sues the ball park under which theory of recovery?

    a.   strict liability
    b.   negligence
    c.   trespass
    d.   slander.

9. Refer to question 8. The ball park's best defense
    against Walter's lawsuit is:

    a.   assumption of risk.
    b.   misuse.
    c.   qualified privilege.
    d.   none of the above.

10. In order for a person to claim a qualified privilege
    after using defamatory language against another person,
    he or she must prove:

    a.   disparagement.
    b.   the statements were made in good faith.
    c.   the party assumed the risk.
    d.   libel.

11. Tom Slick owns a home he wants to sell. Tom places a for
    sale sign in the front yard and advertises an open house
    on weekends. Harvey Ruben reads the advertisement and
    attends the open house. Tom fails to tell Harvey that
    every spring the basement fills up with water from the
    heavy rains. Harvey purchases the house. The following
    spring the basement floods, and Harvey wants to bring a
    lawsuit against Tom. What is Harvey's best theory of
    recovery?

    a.   trespass to land
    b.   infliction of mental distress
    c.   interference with contractual relations
    d.   fraud

12. Refer to question 11. Assume that Harvey's neighbor has
     a swimming pool which leaks. Harvey discovers that his
     basement is flooding not because of heavy rains but be-
     cause the neighbor's pool is flowing onto his land and
     running into the basement over the top of the foundation.
     Harvey's neighbor knows the pool water is flowing onto
     Harvey's land. Harvey may sue the neighbor for:

     a. fraud.
     b. trespass to land.
     c. public nuisance.
     d. none of the above.

13. Which of the following is most closely associated with
     the but for test?

     a. proximate cause
     b. causation in fact
     c. duty of care
     d. injury

14. Which of the following is <u>not</u> a defense to negligence?

     a. contributory negligence
     b. assumption of risk
     c. superseding intervening forces
     d. good faith

15. Which of the following is considered an abnormally dan-
     gerous activity under strict liability theory?

     a. manufacture of a product
     b. defamation
     c. construction of a building
     d. blasting with dynamite

16. The purpose of strict liability in tort is:

     a. to create large monetary judgments for plaintiffs.
     b. to protect sellers from liability.
     c. to insure that the cost of injuries is borne by manu-
         facturers.
     d. all of the above.

17. Pennzoil and Getty Oil had agreed to merge together. The
     management of Texaco attempted to persuade Getty Oil Co.
     to breach the merger agreement. Texaco may be found
     liable for:

a.   infringement of trademark.
b.   theft of trade secrets.
c.   fraud.
d.   interference with a contractual relationship.

18.   Which of the following is granted by the federal govern-
      ment to the inventor of a device to make use and sell
      such device exclusively?

      a.   copyright
      b.   trade secret
      c.   patent
      d.   all of the above

19.   The author has exclusive rights to a work for the au-
      thor's life plus fifty years under a:

      a.   copyright.
      b.   patent.
      c.   trademark.
      d.   tradename.

20.   Steve works for one of the largest manufacturers of com-
      puter software called BMI. Steve is working on a top
      secret project which will revolutionize the industry.
      Steve is fired from his job for insubordination and goes
      to work for a competitor of BMI. Steve divulges the
      specifics of the BMI project to his new supervisor. The
      supervisor immediately utilizes the information to invent
      a new software package. Steve's actions are considered:

      a.   a trespass.
      b.   a private nuisance.
      c.   a public nuisance.
      d.   theft of trade secret.

21.   Edith and Judy live in the dormitory next to each other
      at State University. Edith and Judy are friends, but
      Judy distrusts Edith because Edith gossips behind Judy's
      back. Edith needs transportation to her new job down-
      town, so she goes into Judy's room and secretly takes the
      key to her moped. Judy did not consent to Edith using
      her moped. Edith uses the moped as if it were her own
      the entire week. Judy can hold Edith liable for:

      a.   negligence.
      b.   trespass to land.
      c.   strict liability.
      d.   conversion.

22.   The local newspaper has written a defamatory article on a local politician accusing him of dishonesty and bribery. The accusations are false. The newspaper may be liable to the politician for:

→   a.   libel.
     b.   slander.
→   c.   defamation.
     d.   two of the above.

23.   Which of the following defenses can be used in a slander case by the defendant?

     a.   truth
     b.   absolute privilege
     c.   qualified privilege
     d.   all of the above

24.   The tort of fraud is also known as deceit. Fraud is:

     a.   intentional tort.
     b.   unintentional tort.
     c.   always a crime.
     d.   abnormally dangerous.

25.   Strict liability holds a defendant liable even if he or she was not at fault. Strict liability does not apply to which of the following areas?

     a.   product liability
     b.   conversion
     c.   workmen's compensation
     d.   landlord-tenant

Essay Question

1.   John Jacoby was driving his 1967 Ford Falcon across town to visit some friends. As John proceeded through an intersection, he was broadsided by Fred Farely. Fred was driving his Chevy Blazer 4X4 at 50 mph. Fred failed to see the red light and John's car. John was seriously injured and his car was destroyed. If John Jacoby sues Fred Farely under the theory of negligence, what will he have to prove?

breach of duty of care

injury

causation

Answers to Study Questions

Fill-in-the-Blank Questions

Harriet may bring a lawsuit against Harry for the damage to her car under <u>negligence</u>. (p. 189)

Harriet has committed a <u>battery</u> by punching Harry in the nose. (p. 184)

If Harriet is found negligent as a plaintiff, she will be barred from any recovery under <u>contributory</u> negligence. (p. 195)

Words usually <u>do not create</u> enough apprehension in another party to give rise to an assault. (p. 185)

True-False Questions

1. False. A battery is the harmful or offensive contact with another person. (p. 184)

2. True (p. 185)

3. True (p. 187)

4. True (p. 188)

5. False. Trespass to land may be committed if a tangible object invades the property. (p. 189)

6. False. Negligence is a fault theory. (p. 189)

7. True (p. 189)

8. False. A duty of care may be created by an objective standard and statute. (p. 190)

9. True (p. 194)

10. False. Strict liability applies to abnormally dangerous activities, product liability, and other areas. (p. 196)

Multiple-Choice

1. b (p. 187)   4. a (p. 187)
2. c (p. 185)   5. c (p. 189)
3. b (p. 186)   6. d (p. 190)

7. b (p. 193)	17. d (p. 198)
8. b (p. 189)	18. c (p. 199)
9. a (p. 195)	19. a (p. 200)
10. b (p. 188)	20. d (p. 202)
11. d (p. 189)	21. d (p. 189)
12. b (p. 189)	22. d (p. 187)
13. b (p. 192)	23. d (p. 187)
14. d (p. 194)	24. a (p. 188)
15. d (p. 196)	25. b (p. 196)
16. c (p. 196)	

Essay Question

1. John will have to prove every element of negligence by a preponderance of the evidence. The three elements John must prove are: (1) breach of the duty of care, (2) injury, and (3) causation.

    The duty of care can be proven through the motor vehicle code. Fred had a statutory duty of care to stop at the red light. The duty of care was created by state statute. The duty of care was breached when Fred failed to stop at the red light.

    John has suffered personal injury and property injury as a result of the accident.

    The injury occurred because Fred failed to yield to the red light. The injury would not have occurred but for the breach of the duty of care.

    In addition, the breach of the duty was the proximate cause of the injury. It was foreseeable that if Fred ran a red light someone could be seriously injured and property damaged. (pp. 189-195)

Chapter 9
Contract Formation

Major Concepts

Contract law has evolved primarily through the common law.
The Uniform Commercial Code (UCC) was drafted to provide uni-
formity in the law of sales contracts. The UCC has been
adopted in 49 states and governs the sales of goods
(i.e., tangible personal property) and many other types of
business transactions. The UCC Article 2 has modified many of
the common law rules of contract.

The common law applies primarily to contracts for services and
real estate, whereas the UCC Article 2 applies to contracts
for the sale of goods. A contract is a legally binding agreement between two or more parties, where a meeting of the minds
has occurred. All the elements of a contract must be fulfilled in order for the contract to be enforceable.

Chapter Outline

I. Source of Commercial Law

A. Commercial Law--Business law has developed over the
   centuries through custom and usage in business
   transactions. The law of merchant was created in
   England through mercantile courts which unified
   business custom across the country. The law of
   merchant eventually became part of American law.

1. Uniform Commercial Code--The uniform commercial code was a uniformly drafted code adopted in all states, the District of Columbia, and the Virgin Islands. The code creates a uniform body of law covering most commercial transactions.

    The code encourages the execution of business transactions by providing clarity and standardized rules.

II. Contract Terms--A contract is a legally binding agreement between two or more parties. Legally enforceable means that if one of the parties fails to perform his or her obligations under the contract, the nonbreaching party may seek legal or equitable relief.

A. Unilateral and Bilateral Contracts--A unilateral contract is one where the offeror makes a promise to perform if the offeree completes an act. The contract does not come into existence until the act is fully completed by the offeree (i.e., promise for an act).

    A bilateral contract is created where the offeror makes a promise to perform and the offeree also makes a promise to perform. It is characterized as "a promise for a promise." The offeror is inducing the offeree to make a return promise. The contract comes into existence when the offeree makes the promise asked for by the offeror.

B. Express and Implied Contracts--An express contract is one in which the parties have specifically stated the terms of the contract in writing or orally.

    An implied contract is implied by the conduct of the parties which evidences a contract. No words are spoken or writings created, but the parties act as if a contract exists.

C. Quasi Contract--The court will impose an obligation to perform where unjust enrichment has occurred under the quasi contract doctrine. In a quasi contract, one party transfers a benefit to another party inadvertently. The party who received the benefit is required to pay the reasonable value of what was received. The party receiving the benefit will not have to pay unless he or she had an opportunity to stop the other party from performing.

D. <u>Formal and Informal Contracts</u>--A formal contract must meet specific statutory requirements and be in writing (e.g., checks and letters of credit). Most contracts do not require a particular form to be valid and therefore are classified as informal. The requirement of the Statute of Frauds that certain contracts be written does not make them formal contracts.

E. <u>Void and Voidable Contracts</u>--A void contract is not a contract at all. A void contract is unenforceable.

A voidable contract is one which may be avoided by one or both of the parties. Usually only one of the parties has the right to disaffirm the contract.

F. <u>Valid and Unenforceable Contracts</u>--A valid contract is one which is binding on the parties and enforceable by a court.

An unenforceable contract is one that may meet all the requirements of a contract but fails to be enforceable against a party due to a legal defense (e.g., statute of frauds).

G. <u>Executed or Executory Contracts</u>--An executed contract is one which has been fully performed by all the parties involved.

An executory contract has not been performed by one or more of the parties.

III. <u>Elements of a Contract</u>--Traditional contract law has defined the essential elements of a contract as mutual assent, consideration, capacity, and legality. Mutual assent is comprised of an offer and acceptance. The writing requirement is an important factor but not traditionally considered an element of a contract. For a contract to exist, all four elements must be present. If the contract is required to be evidenced by a writing and is not, the contract is unenforceable. If the agreement lacks one of the four traditional elements, no contract exists.

A. <u>Mutual Assent</u>--This is composed of two parts: an offer and an acceptance. A valid offer and acceptance is a manifestation of the intent to be legally bound. Where the parties have a meeting of the minds, mutual assent is present. The offeror and offeree must agree on the material terms of the contract.

1. Offer--An offer is made by the offeror to the offeree or offerees.

    a. The essential elements of an offer are:

        (1) objective intent by the offeror to be bound.

        (2) the terms reasonably definite.

        (3) the offer communicated to the offeree.

    The objective intent to be bound is determined by the words and conduct of the offeror as interpreted by a reasonable offeree. Communications which are made in jest, or as a joke, are not made with serious intent to be bound.

    Reasonably definite means the offeror must state all the material terms of a contract. The parties must agree on the price, time of performance, time of payment, and quantity being sold. Under the common law, a contract cannot be enforced if material terms are missing.

    Under the UCC, the requirement of definiteness has been relaxed. The UCC will supply the missing terms if the parties have failed to provide them. UCC Rules are as follows for missing terms: price--a reasonable price at delivery (UCC 2-305); place of delivery--seller's place (UCC 2-308(a)); time of shipment--reasonable time (UCC 2-309); and time of payment--due at time and place of delivery (UCC 2-310(a)).

    The third element of an offer is communication to the offeree. The offeree receives the power of acceptance when the offer is communicated. Only parties who have the power of acceptance may accept an offer.

    b. Termination of the Offer--An offer may be terminated by either the offeror, offeree, or by operation of law.

(1) **By the Parties**

    (a) Revocation--The offeror may revoke the offer any time up until the offeree makes a valid acceptance subject to three exceptions. Even if the offeror promises to keep the offer open for a specified period of time, he or she may revoke the offer before the expiration of the time period. The revocation is not effective until it is received by the offeree.

        Option contracts, firm offers, and gratuitous promises under promissory estoppel are situations where the offeror does not have the right to revoke his or her offer. An option contract is a contract where the offeror promises to keep the offer open for a specified period of time in exchange for payment of consideration by the offeree.

        A firm offer is created when a merchant makes a written offer giving assurances the offer will be held open and signs the offer. The merchant under the UCC must keep the offer open for the specified period up to a maximum of three months (UCC 2-205).

        Promissory estoppel may be applied when a promisor makes a promise which a promisee relies on and acts upon to his or her detriment. No contract exists, but the court will enforce the promise.

    (b) Rejection--The offeree may reject the offer which causes a termination. The offeree may affirmatively reject the offer or make a counteroffer. A counteroffer acts as a rejection to terminate the original offer. The rejection

must be communicated to the
offeror and is not effective until
received.

(2) By Operation of Law

(a) The offer will terminate if the
subject matter of the contract is
destroyed, with the death of a
party, or by lapse of time. An
offer automatically expires if a
specified date has passed. Otherwise, if no date for expiration is
stated, the offer is open for a
reasonable period of time.

2. Acceptance--The acceptance of an offer must be
unequivocal and communicated to the offeror.
The common law, mirror-image rule requires the
acceptance to conform to the exact terms of the
offer. The term unequivocal means the acceptance must clearly indicate the offeree's intent
to enter a contract. Silence generally does not
operate an an acceptance.

a. Communication of Acceptance--In a bilateral
contract, the offeree must communicate
acceptance of the offer to the offeror.
Under the mailbox rule, an acceptance that
is properly dispatched is effective when released into the mode of communication. The
term properly dispatched means the acceptance is correctly addressed and the mode of
communication is as efficient as the one
used by the offeror (e.g., offer sent by
mail, acceptance sent by telegram is proper
dispatch, but offer sent by telegram and
acceptance sent by mail is improper dispatch). If an improper dispatch is made,
the acceptance is not effective until received. The offeror may specify the mode of
communication to be used since the offeror
is "master over the offer."

The UCC relaxes the previously stated common
law rules. Parties may add terms to the
acceptance without creating a counteroffer.
If the contract is between merchants, the
additional terms automatically become part
of the contract subject to some exceptions.

If a nonmerchant is a party, then additional terms are proposals to be accepted by the offeror (UCC 2-207).

B.   Genuineness of Mutual Assent--In some cases, the parties may have signed a written agreement but no mutual assent existed. When mutual assent is genuine, the parties have come to an agreement, or what is known as a meeting of the minds. When the parties are not acting voluntarily, under a deception, or mistaken, mutual assent is lacking. The following theories test the genuineness of mutual assent.

1.   Fraud or Misrepresentation--When one party misrepresents a material fact with the intent to deceive the other party into the contract, a fraud has occurred. If the innocent party proves the wrongdoer made a materially false statement of fact with knowledge of its falsity, intending to deceive and the innocent party justifiably relies on the falsity which causes damages, the innocent party may avoid the contract. The contract is voidable by the innocent party.

2.   Unilateral Mistake--If one party makes a mistake, and the other party has no reason to know of the mistake and has no actual knowledge of it, a contract still exists (e.g., a salesman quotes a price as $450 when it should be $550 and the other party does not know of the mistake).

3.   Mutual Mistake--When the parties are mistaken as to the identity of the subject matter or the existence of the subject matter, no contract exists. Mutual mistakes as to the value of an item do not effect the contract.

4.   Duress--When a party is forced by physical or mental coercion to enter a contract, the contract is voidable by the innocent party under the theory of duress. The innocent party's free will must be overcome by the stronger party to avoid the transaction.

5.   Undue Influence--Undue influence is when a party uses his or her influence wrongfully to take advantage of another by having them enter a contract. The weaker party is being taken advan-

tage by the influencing party through a special relationship of trust, such as doctor-patient or attorney-client. The contract is voidable by the weaker party.

C.   <u>Consideration</u>--Consideration is an essential element of a contract. Consideration can be broken down into two elements: legal value exchanged and bargained for exchanged.

The legal value exchanged may take the form of a promise to do or not to do something. The parties are called promisor and promisee when consideration is the issue. The promisor makes a promise, and the promisee receives a promise. A promise to not do an act can serve as legal value as long as the promisor has a legal right to do the act.

Bargained for exchanged is the inducement to enter into a contract. A party enters into a contract because of what the other party promises to do or not to do.

A court will not ordinarily question the adequacy of consideration exchanged. The inequality of the values being exchanged does not effect the consideration. Past consideration is not consideration at all.

Study Questions

Fill-in-the-Blank Questions

Harold Watts purchased a complete stereo system from Audio Inc., a local retailer of stereo equipment. Harold signed a written agreement which described the stereo and warranty provided. Harold's stereo had to be specially ordered from the manufacturer and was scheduled to be delivered in two weeks.

The contract between Harold and Audio Inc. is governed primarily by _____.
          (common law/the UCC)

If Audio Inc. fails to deliver the stereo to Harold, Audio Inc. has _____ the contract.   (breached/not breached)

The agreement entered into by Harold and Audio Inc. is a

_____, _____
    (bilateral/unilateral)   (express/implied)
contract.

True-False Questions

1. An implied contract is created by the conduct of the parties. _____

2. When one of the parties has not yet performed, the contract is executed. _____

3. The offeror and the promisor are always the same party.

   _____

4. A bail bond is an example of a formal contract. _____

5. A contract that is void may be enforced by the innocent
   party. _____

6. A voidable contract is one which the contracting parties
   have the right to equitable relief. _____

7. Bill made a date with Ann for dinner and the opera, which
   Ann cancelled. Bill entered a contract with Ann and may
   sue for damages. _____

8. Many principles of business law were developed from the
   law of merchant. _____

9. One of the essential elements of an offer is definite-
   ness. _____

10. An offer, unless otherwise stated, will lapse in a rea-
    sonable time. _____

Multiple-Choice Questions

1. Which of the following common law rules requires the
   acceptance to conform to the terms of the offer?

   a. mailbox rule
   b. undue influence rule
   c. UCC
   d. mirror-image rule

2. The Uniform Commercial Code Article 3 applies to which of the following?

    a. sales of goods
    b. secured transactions
    c. chattel paper
    d. commercial paper

3. Sam, after work, stops off at the local grocery store. Sam steps up to the counter, puts down his groceries, and pays the checker without a word. This is an example of a(n):

    a. quasi contract.
    b. formal contract.
    c. implied-in-fact contract.
    d. express contract.

4. Sally's uncle has promised to give her $10,000 at the end of the year so she can go in business for herself. Sally rents a storefront shop, buys inventory, and hires a salesclerk, relying on her uncle's promise. At the end of the year, the uncle refused to pay and Sally takes him to court. What theory of recovery should Sally argue?

    a. firm offer
    b. promissory estoppel
    c. option contract
    d. counteroffer

5. Refer to question 4. Assume Sally's uncle promises to pay Sally $10,000 if she will go into the home interiors business within the next 12 months. If uncle fails to pay after Sally establishes a home interiors business within the one year time period, Sally will most likely sue her uncle under what theory?

    a. promissory estoppel
    b. mirror-image rule
    c. breach of contract
    d. quasi contract

6. Jim hires Tom to paint the exterior of his home. Tom arrives on Tuesday when Jim is at work. Tom mistakenly paints the neighbor's house. The neighbor was not home at the time. Tom may collect from the neighbor under which of the following?

    a. quasi contract
    b. definiteness

c. consideration
d. none of the above

7. Which of the following is not an essential element for
    the creation of a contract for the sale of goods?

    a. mutual assent
    b. definiteness
    c. consideration
    d. contractual capacity

8. Barnes offers to sell his brand new Mercedes Benz to
    Treece for $50. Barnes makes the offer several times and
    even takes Treece for a test drive. Treece knows the car
    is really worth about $45,000. Treece, believing Barnes
    is serious, pulls $50 out of his wallet and pays Barnes.
    Barnes gives Treece the title and the keys and asks for a
    ride home. Barnes may later challenge the sale on which
    of the following legal grounds?

    a. adequacy of consideration
    b. duress
    c. statute of frauds
    d. none of the above

9. Refer to question 8. Assume Treece is the medical doctor
    of Barnes and he purchases the car for $500. Which of
    the following theories may Barnes use to avoid the agree-
    ment?

    a. duress
    b. fraud
    c. mistake
    d. undue influence

10. Which of the following is not an element of an offer
    under the common law?

    a. objective intent
    b. definiteness
    c. communicated to offeror
    d. communicated to offeree

11. Which of the following terminates the original offer
    created by the offeror?

    a. acceptance
    b. counteroffer
    c. firm offer
    d. option

12. Carl owns a small bicycle shop in a small rural town.
     Carl sends a letter to several of his customers, offering
     new 12-speed mountain bikes at 20% off the list price.
     Carl signed the letter and assured the customers the
     offer would be open for the next 120 days. Carl has
     created:

     a. an option.
     b. an executory contract.
     c. an assignment.
     d. a firm offer.

13. Refer to question 12. Fourteen weeks later Carl decides
     to revoke his letter offering the discount on mountain
     bikes. Carl writes a letter to each customer officially
     retracting his offer. Carl's letter becomes effective:

     a. when it was sent.
     b. when the letter was at the post office.
     c. when received by the customers.
     d. never since Carl may not revoke his offer.

14. Refer to question 12. One of Carl's customers, Abbey,
     put a letter in the mail accepting the offer to buy a
     mountain bike at 20% off list price the morning of
     April 26. That afternoon the postman delivered Carl's
     letter to Abbey retracting the offer. Was a contract
     created?

     a. No, because of the statute of frauds.
     b. No, because of fraud.
     c. Yes, because the letter of acceptance was effective
         when sent.
     d. Yes, because Carl cannot retract his offer.

15. Bob offers to sell his mountain ranch to Fred for a small
     fortune. Bob agrees to hold his offer open for three
     weeks if Fred will give him $500. Fred pays the $500 and
     puts the agreement in writing and signs it himself. Fred
     gives a copy of the agreement to Bob. Bob and Fred have
     entered into a:

     a. firm offer.
     b. option contract.
     c. confirmation agreement.
     d. executed contract.

16. Refer to question 15. Bob realizes the price for the
     ranch was much too low and wants to get out of the deal.

Fred attempts to force Bob to sell the ranch at the original price. Bob's best defense would be:

a. statute of frauds.
b. fraud.
c. duress.
d. mistake.

17. Justin offers to mow Mr. Smith's lawn for $20. Mr. Smith responds to Justin by stating, "That price is too much. I'll pay you $15 to mow my lawn." Mr. Smith's response is a:

a. counteroffer.
b. revocation.
c. acceptance.
d. none of the above.

18. Herb, the president of a large real estate development company, has made several offers to buy Arthur's home. Herb wants to demolish Arthur's home and build a fifty-story high rise on the property. Herb has already acquired all the adjoining properties and needs Arthur's to begin excavation of the property. Arthur refuses to sell, and Herb threatens him with a handgun. Arthur agrees to sell his property after the threat was made. Arthur may avoid the contract on which of the following grounds?

a. fraud
b. mistake
c. duress
d. undue influence

19. Refer to question 18. The contract entered into by Herb and Arthur is:

a. voidable.
b. void.
c. valid.
d. none of the above.

20. Bertha placed an advertisement in the local newspaper in hopes of selling her Ford Falcon for $1,000. Bertha received several calls on the car and finally sold it to Harold. Bertha gave Harold the title and a bill of sale specifically describing the car. On the way home, Harold inadvertently put his foot through the floorboard. After an examination, Harold discovered someone had covered the hole in the floorboard by gluing a new piece of carpet

over the hole. Harold wants to sue Bertha to recover his money. The best theory of recovery for Harold to assert is:

a. duress.
b. fraud.
c. undue influence.
d. mutual mistake.

21. Refer to question 20. Bertha's advertisement in the newspaper was a(n):

a. option.
b. offer.
c. counteroffer.
d. none of the above.

22. Which of the following is <u>not</u> an element of fraud?

a. negligence
b. intent to deceive
c. justifiable reliance
d. material misrepresentation

23. Terry sells an old violin he found in the attic of his home to his neighbor, John, for $50. Both Terry and John knew nothing about violins. The violin turned out to be a Stradivarius worth $10,000. Terry wants to avoid the contract. Which is his best theory to attempt to avoid the agreement?

a. mutual mistake
b. unilateral mistake
c. duress
d. fraud

24. A contract based upon a mutual mistake of fact is:

a. void.
b. voidable.
c. valid.
d. none of the above

25. Uncle Ned promised to pay nephew Bob (22 years old) $10,000 if he would refrain from smoking and drinking for the next year. At the end of the year, Ned refused to pay even though Bob did not smoke or drink for one full year. Can Bob collect from Uncle Ned?

a.   Yes, because a unilateral contract existed.
b.   Yes, because a bilateral contract existed.
c.   No, because the agreement lacked consideration.
d.   none of the above.

Essay Question

1.   Marge buys a brand new microwave oven from Appliance
     World, Inc. The saleswoman tells Marge the oven is
     entirely safe and has been approved by Underwriters
     Laboratories (U.L.). Marge paid cash for the oven and
     receives a written bill of sale which describes the oven
     and indicates it has been U.L. approved. The saleswoman
     failed to read the microwave oven literature carefully,
     which indicated the oven purchased by Marge was not U.L.
     approved. Marge, after the oven is delivered to her
     home, discovers the microwave was not U.L. approved and
     wants to return the oven. Appliance World, Inc. refuses
     to take the oven back. If Marge sues Appliance World,
     what is her best theory of recovery?

Answers to Study Questions

Fill-in-the-Blank Questions

The contract between Harold and Audio Inc. is governed primarily by the UCC. (p. 209)

If Audio Inc. fails to deliver the stereo to Harold, Audio
Inc. has breached the contract. (p. 210)

The agreement entered into by Harold and Audio Inc. is a
bilateral, express contract. (p. 210)

True-False Questions

1.   True (p. 210)

2.   False. An executed contract is one where both parties
     have performed their obligations. (p. 212)

3.   False. The offeror may be the promisee. (p. 213)

4.   True (p. 211)

5. False. A void contract is not enforceable by either party. (p. 211)

6. False. A voidable contract allows one or both of the parties to avoid the contract. (p. 211)

7. False. A promise to go on a date is unenforceable. (p. 226)

8. True (p. 208)

9. True (p. 213)

10. True (p. 213)

Multiple-Choice Questions

1.	d (p. 218)	14.	c (p. 219)
2.	d (p. 209)	15.	b (p. 216)
3.	c (p. 210)	16.	d (p. 220)
4.	b (p. 217)	17.	a (p. 217)
5.	c (p. 210)	18.	c (p. 224)
6.	d (p. 210)	19.	a (p. 224)
7.	b (p. 215)	20.	b (p. 220)
8.	d (p. 224)	21.	d (p. 213)
9.	d (p. 224)	22.	a (p. 220)
10.	c (p. 213)	23.	a (p. 223)
11.	b (p. 216)	24.	a (p. 223)
12.	d (p. 216)	25.	a (p. 225)
13.	c (p. 216)		

Essay Question

1. Marge should sue Appliance World, Inc., asking the court to order a rescission of the contract and the return of Marge's money. Marge should argue the contract was based upon innocent misrepresentation and therefore voidable. Innocent misrepresentation requires the plaintiff to prove a material false representation of fact, which was relied on by the plaintiff and intended to induce the plaintiff into a contract. The theory of fraud is similar to innocent misrepresentation except the seller makes the statement not knowing it was false. Here, the saleswoman innocently made a false statement which Marge relied on. Marge may avoid the contract and get her money back. (p. 225)

Chapter 10
Contract Defenses and Remedies

<u>Major Concepts</u>

This chapter completes the material on contract law. The elements of contract known as mutual assent and consideration were discussed in Chapter 9. The elements of capacity and legality along with the statute of frauds are outlined and explained in this chapter.

Contractual capacity is the requirement that a party to a contract must have the mental ability to understand the material terms of the agreement entered into. Generally, minors, mental incompetents, and intoxicated individuals do not have contractual capacity.

Legality is the contractual requirement that the contract is legal in its purpose and subject matter. Courts will refuse to enforce an agreement that is illegal.

The statute of frauds requires that certain contracts be evidenced by a writing to be enforceable. There are four major types of contracts which come under the statute of frauds.

In addition, the chapter discusses assignment, delegation, third-party beneficiaries, discharge, and legal remedies.

<u>Major Concepts</u>

I.   <u>Contractual Capacity</u>--The parties to a contract must have contractual capacity. When both parties have contractual capacity, the contract can be enforced against either of them if the other elements of a contract exist.

Minors, intoxicated parties, and mental incompetents may in some cases avoid a contract. A person who has not reached the age of majority (usually eighteen years old) is called a minor.

A minor can disaffirm a contract up until he or she reaches the age of majority, or within a reasonable time thereafter. The minor must return what he or she re- ceived. A contract for necessaries (i.e., food, cloth- ing, and shelter) may be disaffirmed by the minor, but the minor can be held for the reasonable value of what was received under quasi-contract liability. If the minor fails to disaffirm after he or she reaches major- ity, an implied ratification will occur. The minor may ratify the contract expressly after reaching the age of majority.

A.   <u>Legality</u>--The subject matter and the purpose of the contract must be legal. A contract to perform a crime, tort, or an act against public policy is illegal and void.

   1.   <u>Types of Illegal Agreements</u>

       a.   <u>Doing Business without a License</u>--State law may require a business to have a license to do business. If the law requires a business to have a license under a regulatory licens- ing statute and a business fails to obtain a license to do business, any contract entered into by the business is void. Revenue rais- ing licensing statutes, if not complied with, do not affect the contracts a business enters into.

       b.   <u>Usury</u>--A state may by statute set a maximum rate of interest that may be charged on loans. A contract which charges an interest rate above the maximum allowable is usurious and illegal.

       c.   <u>Blue Sky Laws</u>--Blue Sky Laws are state statutes which require a seller of stocks or bonds to register with the state before selling any stock or bond to the public.

d. <u>Restraints of Trade</u>--An agreement to restrain trade is illegal and violates federal antitrust law. Examples of restraints of trade are: price fixing agreements, group boycotts, and horizontal division of markets.

e. <u>Unconscionable Bargain</u>--An unconscionable contract is one which is unreasonably favorable to the stronger party to the contract and lacking a meaningful choice for the weaker party. Unconscionable contract provisions and unconscionable contracts are illegal and not enforceable.

B. <u>A Writing</u>--The Statute of Frauds requires certain contracts to be in writing and signed by the party charged to be enforceable. The four primary types of contracts which must be in writing are:

1. interests in land.

2. cannot be performed in one year.

3. collateral promise to pay the debt of another.

4. sale of goods for $500 or more.

The Statute of Frauds requires some contracts to be in writing for the protection of the parties against fraud. Oral contracts not within the Statute of Frauds are just as enforceable as written contracts.

The UCC creates several exceptions to the writing requirement. Oral contracts admitted to in court by a party and partially performed oral contracts will be enforced to the extent admitted to in court or performed.

II. <u>Third Party Contracts</u>

A. <u>Assignment</u>--A party to a contract may assign (transfer) their right to receive a benefit to a third party. The party transferring the contract right is the assignor and the party receiving the right is the assignee. The assignee steps into the shoes of the assignor. The assignee gets no better rights than the assignor.

The transfer of a duty under a contract is called a delegation. If the duty is a personal one, it cannot be delegated.

B.   Third-Party Beneficiary Contract--A third-party beneficiary contract is one where a third person, outside of the buyer or seller, receives a benefit under the contract. The third-party beneficiary must be an intended beneficiary to have legal rights to enforce the contract.

Intended beneficiaries are either creditor or donee beneficiaries. A party to the contract owes a creditor beneficiary a duty to perform. A donee beneficiary is a third party who receives a benefit under the contract as a gift.

III. Remedies and Damages--Failure to perform a contract according to its terms subjects the nonperforming party to a lawsuit. The nonbreaching party may sue the breaching party for damages or other equitable relief.

A.   Equitable Remedies

1.   Rescission and Restitution--If the contract is voidable, the injured party may ask the court to rescind the contract or bring the contract to an end. Restitution is the action of restoring the parties to their position before the contract was entered into. The parties must give back all money and items received.

2.   Reformation--The court may rewrite the contract in accordance with the intentions of the parties.

3.   Specific Performance--A contract may be specifically enforced by the court if it involves a unique item. The court requires the breaching party to do what they promised to do under the contract. Specific performance is only granted if money damages are inadequate.

B.   Legal Remedies--Money damages are available for injury caused to the nonbreaching party.

1.   Compensatory Damages--Compensatory damages attempt to place the nonbreaching party in the position he or she would have been if the contract had been performed.

2. Consequential Damages--Consequential damages are
    damages which are foreseeable by the parties at
    the time the contract is entered into. Conse-
    quential damages occur as a consequence of a
    breach of contract and payable by the breaching
    party.

IV. Discharge--Discharge of a contract occurs when the
parties have no further obligations under the contract.

A. Discharge by Agreement--The parties may agree to
    discharge the agreement.

    1. Accord and Satisfaction--An accord and satisfac-
        tion involves a contract in which an unliqui-
        dated claim exists, and the party with an un-
        satisfied claim agrees to accept a lesser
        amount. The accord is an offer to accept a
        lesser amount, and the satisfaction is the ac-
        ceptance of that amount.

    2. Release or Covenant Not to Sue--A release is an
        agreement to settle a claim for a breach of con-
        tract. A release and a covenant not to sue
        forecloses the parties from later bringing a
        lawsuit for breach of contract.

    3. Novation--A novation is an entirely new contract
        which substitutes a new party for an original
        party. The discharged party is released from
        the original contract.

    4. Discharge by Operation of Law

        a. The statute of limitations may bar a party
            from bringing a lawsuit after a specified
            period of time has lapsed.

        b. A discharge in bankruptcy of a debtor bars
            the creditors from collecting damages for a
            breach of contract.

        c. Objective impossibility is when the contract
            is impossible to perform due to the destruc-
            tion of the subject matter.

Study Questions

Fill-in-the-Blank Questions

Jennifer Jones and Harrold Smith entered into an agreement for the sale of Jennifer's 50-acre ranch. Jennifer and Harrold negotiated with each other for weeks before they actually came to an agreement. Both parties felt they received most of what they wanted.

The contract between Jennifer and Harrold _____
                                             (does/does not)
need to be evidenced by a writing to be enforceable.

The statute of _____ is a state law requiring
                 (evidence/frauds)
certain contracts to be evidenced by a writing to be enforceable.

If Jennifer decides not to sell the ranch to Harrold after a valid contract has been entered into, Harrold may sue for

_____.
    (specific performance/a cease and desist order)

True-False Questions

1. The age of majority for contractual purposes is exactly the same in all states. _____

2. A minor is never liable on the contracts he or she enters into. _____

3. Minors, mental incompetents, and intoxicated individuals generally lack contractual capacity. _____

4. The general effect of an illegal agreement is that it is void. _____

5. Blue Sky Laws prohibit certain businesses from being open on Sunday. _____

6. Restraints of trade may be illegal under state law as well as federal law. _____

7. There are no exceptions to the UCC writing requirement. _____

8. A party to a contract may transfer his or her right to receive a benefit to another individual called an assignee. _____

9. All contractual duties can be delegated to someone else. _____

10. A "covenant not to sue" is a contract where one party gives up the right to sue. _____

Multiple-Choice Questions

1. Which of the following persons does not have contractual capacity?

    a. a 50-year-old used car salesman
    b. a 22-year-old stock boy at a toy store
    c. an elderly gas station attendant
    d. a 17-year-old college student

2. Which of the following limits the contractual competence of an individual?

      I. intoxication
     II. ratification
    III. insanity

    a. I only
    b. I and II
    c. I and III
    d. I, II, and III

3. In most states, the age of majority is:

    a. 18 years old.
    b. 21 years old.
    c. 17 years old.
    d. 16 years old.

4. Generally, minors can enter into the same contracts adults enter into. However, minors have the right to:

    a. ratify their contracts.
    b. disaffirm all contracts.
    c. disaffirm some contracts.
    d. disaffirm contracts for necessaries.

5. Jerod is 16 years old and lives at home with his parents. Jerod receives an allowance every week for cutting the

grass. Jerod has been saving his allowance for six months to purchase a new rare coin to add to his collection. Jerod takes $500 in cash to Carl's Coins and buys a rare vintage silver quarter. The coin is one of a kind. Which of the following is (are) permitted under contract law?

    I.   Jerod can disaffirm the contract for the coin.
   II.   Jerod can demand all his money returned.
  III.   Carl's Coins can disaffirm the contract for the coin.

    a. I only
    b. I and II
    c. I and III
    d. I, II, and III

6. Refer to question 5. Jerod after purchasing the rare quarter from Carl's Coins accidentally put the quarter into a Coke machine to get a can of Diet Coke. Jerod didn't realize he spent the quarter until 3 days later. Jerod now decides to avoid the contract with Carl's Coins. Jerod's best argument to avoid the contract is:

    a. lack of consideration.
    b. fraud.
    c. unconscionability.
    d. lack of contractual capacity.

7. Refer to question 5. Jerod paid cash for the rare coin, but Carl's Coins' salesman told him to come back tomorrow to take possession of the coin. Jerod came back the next day, but Carl's refused to give him the coin. Jerod wants the coin to add to his coin collection. Which of the following remedies should Jerod pursue?

    a. compensatory damages
    b. injunction
    c. liquidated damages
    d. specific performance

8. Refer to question 5. The contract entered into between Jerod and Carl's Coins is:

    a. voidable.
    b. void.
    c. unenforceable against Carl's Coins.
    d. all of the above.

9. A minor is legally responsible for the reasonable value of which of the following?

a.   nonnecessary goods
b.   nonnecessary services
c.   necessary goods
d.   all of the above

10.   Justin purchased a brand new 20-inch color television for his room. Justin works at the local fast food restaurant which enabled him to save enough money to buy the television with cash. Justin is 17 years old and lives with his parents. Justin bought the new TV set from TV World, Inc. Justin uses the television for two weeks before he sells it to Ray, a college student at State University, for $100.

The television at the time it was purchased by Justin from TV World, Inc. is a:

a.   necessary item.
b.   nonnecessary item.
c.   illegal.
d.   none of the above.

11.   Refer to question 10. Justin decided to disaffirm his contract with TV World, Inc. Justin demands TV World return his $250 he paid for the television. In order for Justin to get his money back, he must:

a.   return the television.
b.   return the value of the television.
c.   vow to never buy another television.
d.   return the television if he has it; otherwise, he need not return anything.

12.   Refer to question 10. Ray sells the television to Mary Ann, a college student at State University. Mary Ann buys the television not knowing Ray bought it from a minor. Justin now disaffirms his contract with Ray and demands the return of the television.

a.   Justin will be able to get the set back.
b.   Justin will not be able to get the set back.
c.   Justin can force Ray to buy the set back from Mary Ann.
d.   Justin cannot disaffirm the contract.

13.   Rick purchased a used refrigerator from Ron's Appliance Store on credit. Rick agreed to make twelve equal monthly payments. The contract charged Rick 22% interest on the unpaid balance. State law set the maximum interest rate

at 18% on consumer items. The contract between Ron's Appliance Store and Rick is:

a. legal and enforceable.
b. legal but void.
c. lacking consideration.
d. illegal with a usurious rate of interest.

14. Jamie, after graduating from business school at State University, opens a construction company. Jamie has several employees including three office staff. The Jamie Construction Company specializes in building custom homes. What type of license will Jamie's company need to obtain?

a. regulatory
b. revenue raising
c. usurious
d. none of the above

15. Which of the following has been adopted by the Uniform Commercial Code?

a. restraints of trade
b. Blue Sky Laws
c. unconscionable contracts
d. usury

16. Which of the following contracts is (are) required to be in writing under the statute of frauds?

I. a contract to install 2,000 yards of carpet
II. an actor's contract to screen a movie over the next six months
III. a contract to buy a 3,000 square foot house

a. I only
b. I and II
c. I and III
d. III only

17. The Uniform Commercial Code (UCC) Article II applies to the sale of goods. The UCC requires contracts for the sale of goods for a price of $_____ or more to be in writing.

a. 500
b. 600
c. 1,000
d. 1,500

18. Which of the following is not an exception to the UCC
     writing requirement?

     a. an oral contract for goods already paid for
     b. an oral contract for a computer at a price of $1,500
         not yet delivered or paid for
     c. an oral contract admitted to in court
     d. none of the above are exceptions

19. Rodney contracts to purchase furniture for his new house
     from ABC Furniture. Rodney buys the furniture on credit,
     agreeing to pay $300 per month. ABC Furniture transfers
     the right to receive $300 a month to Western Financial.
     The arrangement between ABC Furniture and Western Finan-
     cial is:

     a. an assignment.
     b. a delegation.
     c. mortgage.
     d. third-party beneficiary contract.

20. Refer to question 19. Rodney sells the furniture to his
     cousin, Rhonda. Rhonda agrees to make the payments to
     Western Financial. Rodney is completely discharged from
     the original contract. The arrangement substituting
     Rhonda for Rodney is:

     a. novation.
     b. covenant not to sue.
     c. accord and satisfaction.
     d. none of the above.

21. Which of the following is an equitable remedy?

     a. compensatory damages
     b. liquidated damages
     c. rescission
     d. consequential damages

22. When a contract has substantial errors, the parties may
     ask the court to rewrite the contract. The rewriting of
     the contract to conform to the true intentions of the
     parties is called:

     a. rescission.
     b. reformation.
     c. specific performance.
     d. compensatory damages.

23. Becky is involved in an auto accident with Robert. Robert is at fault causing substantial damage to Becky's car. Robert offers to pay Becky for all of the damage done to her car. Becky agrees to not sue Robert if he pays to have her car repaired. Robert has Becky's car fixed, and Becky agrees in writing to give up her right to sue. Becky has entered into which of the following?

    a. accord and satisfaction
    b. liquidated damages
    c. novation
    d. covenant not to sue

24. A collateral contract must be in writing to be enforceable. A collateral contract can be defined as:

    a. the substitution of one party for a new party.
    b. a contract involving the sale of land.
    c. a contract involving the sale of goods.
    d. a promise to pay the debt of someone else.

25. Illegal contracts are generally not enforceable by the parties. Which of the following, if made part of an agreement, does not meet the legality requirement?

      I. a tortious act
     II. opposed to public policy
    III. restraint of trade

    a. I only
    b. I and II
    c. I and III
    d. I, II, and III

Essay Question

1. Mike, a minor, purchased a 1990 pick-up truck from Trucks America, Inc. for $12,000. Mike paid cash for the truck the day he took delivery. Mike drove the truck to school for several months. While driving on an off-the-road trail, Mike rolled the truck causing several thousand dollars of damage to the truck. Mike was not physically injured but is very disappointed about the damage to the truck. Mike calls Trucks America, Inc. and disaffirms the contract demanding they take the truck back. Trucks America had the truck towed to the dealership but refuse to return the $12,000 to Mike. Mike decides to file a lawsuit against Trucks America, Inc. for the $12,000. Who will win the lawsuit and why?

Answers to Study Questions

Fill-in-the-Blank Questions

The contract between Jennifer and Harrold <u>does</u> need to be evidenced by a writing to be enforceable. (p. 240)

The statute of <u>frauds</u> is a state law requiring certain contracts to be evidenced by a writing to be enforceable. (p. 239)

If Jennifer decides not to sell the ranch to Harrold after a valid contract has been entered into, Harrold may sue for <u>specific performance</u>. (p. 246)

True-False Questions

1. False. The age of majority differs from state to state. (p. 234)

2. False. A minor may be liable on some contracts for necessary items. (p. 234)

3. True (p. 234)

4. True (p. 237)

5. False. Blue sky laws apply to the sale of securities. (p. 238)

6. True (p. 238)

7. False. There are several exceptions to the UCC writing requirement. (p. 240)

8. True (p. 242)

9. False. Not all contractual duties can be delegated to a third party. (p. 242)

10. True (p. 245)

Multiple-Choice Questions

1.	d (p. 234)	5.	b (p. 235)
2.	c (p. 234)	6.	d (p. 234)
3.	a (p. 234)	7.	d (p. 246)
4.	c (p. 234)	8.	a (p. 234)

9. c (p. 234)
10. b (p. 234)
11. d (p. 235)
12. b (p. 234)
13. d (p. 237)
14. a (p. 237)
15. c (p. 238)
16. d (p. 239)
17. a (p. 239)

18. b (p. 240)
19. a (p. 242)
20. a (p. 246)
21. c (p. 246)
22. b (p. 246)
23. d (p. 246)
24. d (p. 240)
25. d (p. 237)

Essay Question

1. Mike will win the lawsuit against Trucks America. Mike, as a minor, has the right to disaffirm contracts for nonnecessaries. The truck would be considered a nonnecessary item. Mike is entitled to the return of his $12,000. Adults entering into contracts with minors must return any money received from the minor. The minor must return whatever he or she received. The minor is only required to restore the goods if the minor still has the goods. (pp. 234-236)

Chapter 11
Sales Law and Product Liability

Major Concepts

The area of sales is primarily governed by the provisions of
the Uniform Commercial Code (UCC) Article 2. Article 2 of the
UCC defines and regulates sales contracts involving goods.
Goods are defined as things that are movable at the time they
are identified. The UCC has made it easier for business
people to carry out their agreements. The UCC Article 2 and
the common law differ in several aspects concerning contract
formation.

In addition, the chapter discusses title, risk of loss, performance, remedies, and product liability. The concepts of
title and risk of loss involve the sales transaction and when
the buyer receives ownership and risk of loss. Title to the
goods and risk of loss in the event the goods are destroyed in
transit do not necessarily pass to the buyer at the same time.

The concept of performance involves the buyer's and seller's
legal obligations to carry out their promises under the
contract. In the event one of the parties fail to fulfill his
or her obligations, the other party may have a legal remedy
for breach of contract.

Product liability is the area of law concerning defective
products which may cause injury to a purchaser or the user of
a product. The chapter discusses various theories of product
liability.

Chapter Outline

I.   <u>Uniform Commercial Code (UCC)</u>--The UCC Article 2 governs the sales of goods. The UCC gives guidance to contracting parties when they are executing an agreement. The UCC attempts to promote the freedom of the contracting parties to enter into and design an agreement. The UCC makes it easier for a contract to come into existence.

The UCC can fill in the gaps when the parties have failed to specify all the terms. The UCC allows the parties to rely on the usage of trade to fill gaps or customs of the industry. In addition, the parties' course of dealing in previous transactions may guide the court in determining the provisions of the contract.

A.   <u>Goods</u>--Under UCC § 2-105, goods are defined as items which are movable at the time they are identified. Crops, animals, automobiles, stereos, furniture, and equipment are considered goods. Services, real estate, and investment securities are not goods.

B.   <u>Identification</u>--Goods which have been set apart for the purchaser by the seller are identified to the contract. Goods must be in existence before identification can take place.

II. <u>Title</u>--Title is defined in terms of ownership. In a sales transaction, the buyer may be concerned as to when he will receive title. In addition, the buyer needs to make sure that the seller passes good title.

A.   <u>Warranty of Title</u>--UCC § 2-312 implies a warranty of good title into the contract for the sale of goods. Under the warranty, the seller guarantees that he or she has good title to the goods being sold. The seller must also state the type of interest being transferred and if any liens exist against the goods.

B.   <u>Passage of Title</u>--The title to goods is in the seller until it passes to the buyer at some time during the sales transaction. The buyer and seller can agree to a specific time for the passing of title. Title cannot pass to the seller until the goods have been identified to the contract (UCC § 2-401(1)).

1.   <u>Shipping Contracts</u>--F.O.B. point of shipment is a shipping contract designation which requires

title to pass at the time the seller completes
his duty to deliver the goods. In a shipment
contract, the seller is obligated to transport
the goods to the shipper. Upon delivery to the
shipper, title passes to the buyer.

2. <u>Destination Contracts</u>--F.O.B. destination is a
contract which obligates the seller to transport
the goods to the buyer's place of business.
Upon delivery to the buyer's place of business,
title passes. The seller will tender the goods
or offer the goods to the buyer at the buyer's
place of business.

3. <u>Documents of Title</u>--A document of title is a
document which indicates ownership of the goods.
If the goods are transported by common carrier,
a bill of sale is used as a document of title.
If the goods are stored in a warehouse, then a
warehouse receipt is used as a document of
title. Generally, when the seller gives the
document of title to the buyer, title passes
(UCC § 2-401(3)(a)).

If no document of title is involved, title
passes at the time and place of contracting,
assuming the goods are identified (UC § 2-401(3)
(b)). If the buyer rejects nonconforming goods,
title reverts back to the seller if it has
already passed (UCC § 2-401 (4)).

4. <u>Voidable Title</u>--A person with a voidable title
can transfer good title to a buyer who purchases
an item in good faith without knowledge of possible problems with the title. The buyer has
good title to the item, meaning the original
owner does not have the right to get the item
back.

III. <u>Risk of Loss</u>--The concept of risk of loss concerns who
will be responsible for the goods in the event the goods
are destroyed. Risk of loss passes to the buyer some
time after the contract is entered into. If the goods
are destroyed during shipment, the party with risk of
loss will incur the loss. The parties may agree as to
when risk of loss will pass to the buyer.

A. <u>Shipment Contract</u>--In a shipment contract, the risk
of loss passes to the buyer when the seller delivers
the goods to the shipper. The buyer has the risk of
loss during shipment.

B. <u>Destination Contract</u>--In a destination contract, the risk of loss passes to the buyer when the goods are tendered at the destination specified (UCC § 2-319).

C. <u>Document of Title</u>--If the transaction involves a document of title, the risk of loss passes to the buyer when he or she receives the document of title.

D. <u>No Document of Title</u>--If the goods are to be picked up at the seller's place of business and the seller is a merchant, risk of loss passes when the goods are received by the buyer. If the seller is a nonmerchant, risk of loss passes when the goods are tendered to the buyer (UCC § 2-509(3)).

E. <u>Seller Sends Nonconforming Goods</u>--When the seller sends nonconforming goods, the seller has breached the contract. The risk of loss remains with the seller. If the buyer accepts nonconforming goods but later revokes his acceptance, the seller will have the risk of loss to the extent the buyer does not have insurance coverage.

F. <u>Buyer Wrongfully Rejects Goods</u>--When the buyer refuses to accept conforming goods, the risk of loss is in the buyer to the extent the seller does not have insurance coverage (UCC § 2-501(3)).

IV. <u>Performance</u>--The terms require the parties to carry out the contract.

A. <u>Right to Inspect</u>--The buyer has the right to inspect the goods before they are accepted to ensure their conformity to the contract, unless the goods are sent C.O.D. (UCC § 2-513).

B. <u>Right to Adequate Assurances</u>--The parties have the right to feel secure that the contract will be performed. Either party may request the other party to provide assurances that they will perform their obligations under the contract. The party must present sufficient evidence proving they will perform the contract.

V. <u>Remedies</u>--When a party breaches a contract, the other party may be able to sue for damages. The nonbreaching party will have several remedies available.

A. <u>Remedies of Buyers</u>--When the seller has breached the contract, the buyer has several options to attempt to recover his or her losses.

    1. <u>Cover</u>--The buyer can go into the market and buy substitute goods or cover. The buyer will be entitled to recover the difference between the cover price and the contract price plus incidental or consequential damages (UCC § 2-712).

    2. <u>Specific Performance</u>--In some cases, the buyer can legally force the seller to go through with the contract. The subject matter of the contract must be unique or rare. The court will not order specific performance if the party can obtain cover.

B. <u>Remedies of Sellers</u>--When the buyer breaches the contract, the seller may have several options to recover his or her losses.

    1. <u>Damages</u>--The seller may be entitled to money damages if the buyer has refused to accept the goods and repudiates the contract. The seller will be able to collect the difference between the market price and the contract price together with incidental damages less expenses saved. The seller may be able to collect his profits, including overhead, if the ordinary damage amount would fail to compensate the seller (UCC § 2-708).

    2. <u>Contract Price</u>--If the seller is not able to resell the goods at a reasonable price, he may collect the contract price from the buyer (UCC § 2-709).

VI. <u>Product Liability</u>--When a product is sold in a defective condition, the buyer and user of the product may have several remedies available under the product liability law. A defective product is one that malfunctions, usually causing an injury. A product may be defective because it is manufactured improperly, designed poorly, packaged incorrectly, fails to warn users of potential dangers, or provides faulty installation instructions. An injured party may sue the retailer or manufacturer under a variety of different legal theories of recovery.

A. <u>Negligence</u>--Negligence is a tort or civil wrong which allows an injured party to collect all foreseeable damages. The plaintiff in a negligence cause of action must prove four elements: (1) Duty of Care, (2) Breach of the Duty of Care, (3) Proximate Cause, and (4) Damages. The plaintiff must show that the defendant/manufacturer failed to exercise due care which caused the injury. Negligence is a fault theory.

The defendant/manufacturer is liable if he failed to design the product properly or failed to assemble the product correctly.

The defendant may assert several defenses to a negligence cause of action. Such defenses are assumption of risk, contributory negligence, misuse, or modification of the product.

B.   Strict Liability--The strict liability theory of product liability is not dependent on proving the culpability of the manufacturer or other party in the distribution line. An injured consumer does not have to prove how the product became defective but only that the defective product caused injury. A bystander who is injured by a defective product may recover under strict liability. The defendant may be liable for property damage and personal injury.

1.   Essential Elements of Strict Product Liability Cause of Action

a.   The defendant sold the product in a defective condition.

b.   The defendant is in the business of selling the product (i.e., merchant).

c.   The defect makes the product unreasonably dangerous.

d.   The defective product was the proximate cause of the injury or damage.

e.   The product was not substantially changed from the date sold to the date of injury.

2.   Defenses to Strict Product Liability--The major defense a manufacturer has to liability is assumption of risk. The defendant must prove the plaintiff voluntarily proceeded while recognizing the risk, that the plaintiff knew

and appreciated the risk, and the plaintiff's decision to undertake the risk was unreasonable.

C. Contract Theories--The contract theories of product liability are the express and implied warranties. The warranty is based upon the seller's assurances or implied assurances to the buyer that the goods will meet certain standards. If the warranty is breached, the defendant may be held liable for damages. The Uniform Commercial Code defines several types of warranties in the sale of goods (tangible personal property).

1. Express Warranties--Any seller of goods can create an express warranty by making oral or written representations about the quality, condition, description, or performance of a product. An express warranty may have one of three forms. A warranty may be an affirmation of fact or a promise, a description, or a sample or model. The warranty must become part of the basis of the bargain.

2. Implied Warranties--Implied warranties are implied by the law into a sales contract under certain circumstances.

   a. Implied Warranty of Merchantability--The implied warranty of merchantability is created whenever a merchant sells goods. A merchant is a seller who normally sells the type of goods in question. The implied warranty requires the goods sold to be merchantable or reasonably fit for the ordinary purpose for which the goods are used (i.e., at least average, fair, or medium grade). The goods must also be adequately packaged and labeled to be merchantable.

   If a consumer is injured from unmerchantable goods, the implied warranty has been breached.

   b. Implied Warranty of Fitness for a Particular Purpose--The implied warranty of fitness for a particular purpose is created when the buyer expresses a specific purpose to the seller and the buyer relies on the seller's skill or judgment to select a suitable product for the buyer. The buyer purchases

the item, relying on the seller. A breach
of the implied warranty occurs when the
product does not perform according to the
buyer's particular purpose.

3. Disclaimers Against Implied Warranty Liability--
The Uniform Commercial Code allows a seller to
disclaim liability for implied warranties. The
seller may disclaim both the implied warranty of
fitness and merchantability. The implied warranty of fitness must be disclaimed in writing
and only by specific language indicating no
implied warranty exists and done conspicuously
(UCC § 2-316(2)).

The implied warranty of merchantability may be
disclaimed orally or in writing. Expressions
such as "with all faults" or "as is" disclaim
all implied warranties (UCC § 2-316(3)(a)). The
implied warranty of merchantability may be also
disclaimed by using the word merchantability.

The implied warranty of merchantability does not
exist as to obvious defects a consumer would
have discovered from an examination of the goods
(UCC § 2-316(3)(b)).

Implied warranties may be excluded or modified
by usage of trade or course of performance
between the parties (UCC § 2-316(3)(c)).

VII. Magnuson-Moss Warranty Act--The federal Magnuson-Moss
Warranty Act is primarily a disclosure statute. The Act
does not require a merchant to give a warranty. If the
merchant does provide a written express warranty on a
consumer item costing more than ten dollars, the Act
requires the warranty must be labeled "full" or
"limited." A full warranty requires the seller to
replace or refund the buyer's money for a defective good
if it cannot be repaired within a reasonable time.

If the goods cost more than fifteen dollars, the warran-
tor must make disclosures in a single document in "read-
ily understood language." The disclosures must be
conspicuous and range from disclosing the seller's name
and address to the process for enforcing the warranty.

Under the Magnuson-Moss Warranty Act, a seller may not
disclaim or modify the implied warranty of merchantability or fitness in the sale of a consumer item,

although the seller may limit the duration of implied warranties. The Federal Trade Commission has the authority to enforce the Act.

Study Questions

Fill-in-the-Blank Questions

Joshua has been accepted at a well-known private university. Joshua has decided to major in business. In anticipation of his first year writing courses, Joshua purchases a business computer at Pacific Computer near the campus. The salesman tells Joshua that the computer has a one-year warranty.

The sale of the computer is considered the purchase of a
_____.
   (service/good)

Pacific Computer has given Joshua a one-year _____
_____ warranty.   (express/
  implied)

Since Pacific Computer is a merchant of computers, the computers they sell to consumers will have warranties of _____ implied into the sales contract.
  (merchantability/fitness)

True-False Questions

1. The Uniform Commercial Code Article 3 covers the sales of goods. _____

2. The goods must be in existence before they can be identified. _____

3. A contract can be made for goods that do not exist but will exist in the future. _____

4. Sellers of goods warrant they have good title under the UCC. _____

5. The concept of title and risk of loss are exactly the same. _____

6. The term F.O.B. means free on board. _____

7. A bill of lading is a document of title, but a warehouse receipt is not. _____

8. The buyer, when purchasing goods C.O.D., does not have the right to inspect the goods prior to payment. _____

9. One of the major remedies of the seller when the buyer breaches the contract is cover. _____

10. The plaintiff in a product liability cause of action has several legal theories of recovery he or she can use to win a damages award. _____

Multiple-Choice Questions

1. The previous conduct between the parties which may help the court to interpret a contract is called:

    a. usage of trade.
    b. implied warranty.
    c. identification.
    d. course of dealing.

2. When a seller gives a warranty of good title under the UCC, which of the following guarantees are included?

    I.   The seller has good title.
    II. The seller owns the entire property.
    III. The seller's property is of good quality.

    a. I only
    b. I and II
    c. I and III
    d. I, II, and III

3. Realtech, Inc. manufactures computer chips for the latest edition of Virtual Reality. Realtech is located in Austin, Texas. Realtech purchases most of its supplies from Silicon, Inc. in San Jose, California. Realtech placed an order for $10,000 of plastic with Silicon to be delivered F.O.B. When will the title to the plastic pass to Realtech?

    a. when the contract is signed
    b. when the goods are tendered at San Jose
    c. when the goods are delivered to the shipper
    d. when the goods are delivered halfway to Austin

4. Refer to Question 3. Assuming neither party is at fault and the goods are destroyed while being shipped, who has the risk of loss?

    a. Realtech
    b. Silicon
    c. each company has equal responsibility
    d. none of the above

5. Refer to Question 3. Assume the contract contains no shipping terms but instead a bill of lading has been issued to Silicon. Silicon has the goods shipped by common carrier to Realtech. When does the risk of loss pass to Realtech?

    a. upon delivery of the goods to the common carrier
    b. upon delivery of the goods to Realtech
    c. upon the signing of the contract
    d. upon receipt of the bill of lading by Realtech

6. Which of the following cannot be bargained over by the parties to a contract involving goods?

    a. when title passes to the buyer
    b. when risk of loss passes to the buyer
    c. express warranty
    d. all of the above can be negotiated

7. John Smith is the purchasing manager for European Auto Equipment, Inc. John, as agent for European, has ordered $100,000 worth of leather from J. M. Leather Products. European purchases leather for use in manufacturing leather seats for custom luxury foreign cars. John recently heard that J. M. Leather is having financial difficulties. John is concerned because European needs the $100,000 worth of leather to fill a big order they just signed. What is European's most appropriate course of action?

    a. sue J. M. Leather immediately
    b. go into the market and cover
    c. demand adequate assurances from J. M. Leather
    d. cancel the contract

8. Refer to Question 7. John receives a letter from J. M. Leather stating that they will not be able to perform the contract. In addition, J. M. Leather refuses to return European's $20,000 deposit. Which of the following options should European pursue?

    a. cover
    b. strict liability
    c. demand adequate assurances
    d. none of the above

9. Refer to Questions 7 and 8. European decides to sue
    J. M. Leather for money damages. European did go into
    the market and buy substitute goods. What is the measure
    of European's damages?

    a. the contract price
    b. profits plus overhead
    c. profits only
    d. the difference between the cover price and the
        contract price plus incidentals or consequential
        damages

10. Which of the following is not a remedy available to the
    buyer?

      I. cover
     II. action for contract price
    III. profits plus overhead

    a. I only
    b. I and II
    c. II and III
    d. I, II, and III

11. Which of the following is not a theory used in product
    liability litigation?

    a. conversion
    b. negligence
    c. strict liability
    d. warranty

12. Which of the following are considered elements the plain-
    tiff must prove in a negligence case?

      I. The product was unreasonably dangerous.

     II. The product has not been substantially changed
          since purchased.

    III. The defendant had a duty of care.

    a. I only
    b. I and II

c.   I and III
d.   III only

13.   Which of the following can make a product defective?

a.   failure to place warnings on the product
b.   designing the product poorly
c.   improper installation instructions for a product
     which is installed
d.   all of the above

14.   In a negligence action, the plaintiff must prove the
      defendant failed to use due care. Due care is defined
      as:

a.   according to industry standard.
b.   what a reasonably prudent person would have done
     under similar circumstances.
c.   what the average American would have done in similar
     circumstances.
d.   what a lawyer would have done in similar circum-
     stances.

15.   Under strict liability theory, the plaintiff must prove
      the product is unreasonably dangerous to the user. Which
      of the following products would be considered unreason-
      ably dangerous?

a.   an automobile that leaks gas when hit from the rear
     at a speed of over 30 mph
b.   a very sharp pocket knife
c.   a color television
d.   two of the above

16.   Which of the following defenses can be used by the
      defendant in a strict liability case?

a.   assumption of risk
b.   contributory fault
c.   negligence
d.   all of the above can be used

17.   Which of the following theories of product liability
      proved inadequate to compensate parties injured by
      defective products?

a.   strict liability
b.   negligence
c.   warranty
d.   two of the above

18. Which of the following can be held liable for a defective product under strict liability?

      I.   a retailer, normally selling the product
     II.   a manufacturer selling the product manufactured
    III.   a university professor selling his lawn mower

    a.   I only
    b.   I and II
    c.   I, II, and III
    d.   I and III

19. Susan Strickland purchases a toaster from Sears Department Store. The toaster has the capacity to toast six pieces of bread at the same time. The first time Susan attempted to toast an English muffin, the toaster shot the muffin right into Susan's eye. Susan's eye was severely injured as a result. If Susan sues the manufacturer for a defective product, which theory should she use?

    a.   negligence
    b.   implied warranty of fitness
    c.   strict liability
    d.   conversion

20. Refer to question 19. Assume the toaster was sold as a demonstrator model, and the contract of sale clearly stated "This toaster sold AS IS." Which, if any, of the following warranties is disclaimed under the UCC?

      I.   express warranty
     II.   implied warranty of merchantability
    III.   implied warranty of fitness

    a.   I only
    b.   II only
    c.   I and II
    d.   II and III

21. An express warranty under the UCC can be created in which of the following ways?

      I.   affirmation
     II.   sales puffing
    III.   a sample

    a.   I only
    b.   I and II
    c.   I and III
    d.   I, II, and III

22. The implied warranty of merchantability is implied into contracts for the sale of goods by a merchant. Merchantability means the goods are:

    a. fit for all purposes.
    b. reasonably fit for a specific purpose.
    c. reasonably fit for ordinary purposes.
    d. fit for almost every purpose.

23. Steve of Steve's Preowned Autos, Inc. made several statements to Ed, a prospective buyer. Ed purchased an automobile from Steve for $450 under an oral agreement. Ed paid cash for the used automobile. Which of the following statements made by Steve during the sale to Ed constitutes an express warranty?

    I.   The car is a first-class one and the best I've seen at this lot.

    II. The car has 200 horsepower.

    III. The car has a 24,000 mile or 24-month guarantee, whichever comes first.

    a. I only
    b. I and II
    c. II and III
    d. I, II, and III

24. Sean sold his five-year-old all-terrain vehicle (ATV) to his neighbor, Shea. Shea paid $350 in cash to Sean and drove the ATV home. Shea is injured one day while driving the ATV. Shea contends the ATV is defective and the defect caused his injury. Which of the following is (are) true?

    I.   Shea can sue Sean under the implied warranty of merchantability.

    II. Shea can sue Sean under strict liability.

    III. Shea can sue Sean for breach of express warranty, if one was given by Sean.

    a. I only
    b. I and II
    c. I, II, and III
    d. III only

25. Decker Manufacturing Company produces electric devices
     for household and industrial use. Decker sold to A&M
     Retail Outlet electric lawn mowers and hedge trimmers.
     Mike purchases a Decker lawn mower from A&M Retail
     Outlet. Mike paid cash for the mower and received no
     express warranty. A&M is in the business of selling lawn
     mowers. Mike plugged the lawn mower into an electrical
     outlet for the first time, and the cutting blade flew out
     from under the mower and hit Mike in the leg. Mike was
     severely injured and wants to sue A&M. Under what
     theories of recovery can Mike bring his case against A&M?

       I. implied warranty of merchantability
      II. implied warranty of fitness
     III. strict liability

     a. I only
     b. I and II
     c. I, II, and III
     d. I and III

Essay Question

1. John Jacoby purchased a brand new forklift from a local
    forklift retailer called F & F Forklift Inc. The fork-
    lift's original cost was $18,000, but John got it for
    just over $15,000. The written contract for sale stated
    in large bold print "SOLD AS IS" and was signed by both
    parties.

    John asked the salesman to supply him with a forklift
    that could lift at least 5 tons and go up a 45% incline.
    The salesman showed John the demonstrator model John
    later purchased.

    One of John's employees, Jack, was using the forklift to
    move a 4-ton crate. Jack was seriously injured when the
    rear wheels of the forklift raised up off the ground and
    caused the forklift to crash into a cement wall. Jack
    wants to sue F & F and the manufacturer of the forklift.
    What theories of recovery are available to Jack?

Answers to Study Questions

Fill-in-the-Blank Questions

The sale of the computer is considered the purchase of a good.
(p. 255)

Pacific Computer has given Joshua a one-year _express_ warranty. (p. 270)

Since Pacific Computer is a merchant of computers, the computers they sell to consumers will have warranties of _merchantability_ implied into the sales contract. (p. 270)

True-False Questions

1. False. Article 2 covers the sale of goods. (p. 254)

2. True (p. 255)

3. True (p. 255)

4. True (p. 255)

5. False. Title and risk of loss differ substantially. (p. 257)

6. True (p. 257)

7. False. A warehouse receipt is also a document of title. (p. 257)

8. True (p. 263)

9. False. Cover is a buyer's remedy. (p. 265)

10. True (p. 266)

Multiple-Choice Questions

1. d (p. 254)
2. a (p. 255)
3. c (p. 257)
4. a (p. 259)
5. d (p. 259)
6. d (p. 259)
7. c (p. 263)
8. a (p. 265)
9. d (p. 265)
10. c (p. 265)
11. a (pp. 266-271)
12. d (p. 266)
13. d (p. 266)
14. b (p. 266)
15. a (p. 267)
16. a (p. 270)
17. d (p. 266)
18. b (p. 267)
19. c (p. 267)
20. d (p. 271)
21. c (p. 270)
22. c (p. 270)
23. c (p. 270)
24. d (p. 270)
25. d (pp. 267-271)

Essay Question

1. Jack may use the tort theories to recover damages. Jack
    may sue the manufacturer for negligently designing a
    forklift which was unsafe for lifting heavy loads. Jack
    will have to prove the manufacturer had a duty of care to
    make the forklift safe for operation and the duty of care
    was breached, causing injury to Jack.

    Jack may also sue under strict liability. Jack must
    prove the forklift was defective when sold, unreasonably
    dangerous in its defective condition, and the defect
    caused the injury. Jack may sue F & F or the manufac-
    turer under strict liability.

    Jack will not be able to sue under the contract theories.
    First, no express warranty was given by the manufacturer
    or the retailer. Second, the implied warranties have
    been disclaimed by the disclaimer in the contract, "SOLD
    AS IS." The disclaimer is conspicuous and in writing.
    As such, the implied warranty of fitness and the implied
    warranty of merchantability have been disclaimed.
    (pp. 267-271)

Chapter 12
Commercial Paper and Secured Transactions

Major Concepts

This chapter covers two major areas of business law: commercial paper and secured transactions. Commercial paper involves the transfer of negotiable instruments as a substitute for money. There are various types of instruments used to accomplish this purpose. The check is the most common type of commercial paper. Other types are drafts, trade acceptances, promissory notes, and certificates of deposit.

In order to qualify as a negotiable instrument, the instrument must meet six requirements. A negotiable instrument may be negotiated to a holder. If the holder qualifies as a holder in due course, he or she receives special rights under the instrument.

The holder in due course is free from all personal defenses of payment subject to only real defenses. In other words, if the maker or drawer of an instrument has a real defense to justify nonpayment of the instrument, a holder in due course cannot force the party to pay.

The bank is considered the drawee on a check. The relationship between the bank and the customer is one of debtor-creditor. The bank has the contractual obligation to execute the orders of the customer. The bank can be held liable for failing to execute an order or paying on an unauthorized signature.

Secured transactions involves the relationship between a debtor and creditor where the creditor has received a security interest in the debtor's property (i.e., collateral). The creation of a security interest requires a security agreement, the creditor giving value, and the debtor obtaining rights in the collateral. Creation and attachment of a security interest occur at the same time.

The creditor (i.e., secured party) may protect his or her interest from third party claims by perfecting the security interest. Perfection of a security interest may occur by possession, filing a financing statement, or attachment. If the debtor defaults, the secured party with a perfected security interest usually has priority to the collateral. Two secured parties may have perfected security interests in the same collateral. In cases of conflicting security interests, the rules of priority apply.

A secured party may peacefully repossess the collateral if the debtor has defaulted. The secured party may keep or sell the collateral to satisfy the unpaid balance owed by the debtor.

Chapter Outline

I.   Commercial Paper--The law of commercial paper is codified in Article 3 of the Uniform Commercial Code (UCC). Commercial paper serves as a substitute for money and as a credit device.

   A.   Types of Commercial Paper--Two types of commercial paper exist. Commercial paper may be classified as either two-party or three-party paper. The most common type of two-party paper is a promissory note, and the most common type of three-party paper is a check.

   In UCC § 3-104, four types of commercial paper have been listed.

   1.   Promissory Notes--A promissory note is a promise to pay a certain sum by the maker to the payee. The party issuing the promissory note is considered the maker. The maker may promise to pay to a specific payee, such as "I the undersigned promise to pay to the order of John Smith," or the maker may issue the note to the "order of cash" or "to bearer." Notes issued to cash or bearer are called bearer paper and collectible by anyone in possession of the note.

Many types of notes are commonly used in business. A mortgage note is a promissory note
issued by the buyer of real property promising
to repay the lending institution the money
loaned.

A collateral note is a promissory note issued by
the buyer of personal property promising to repay the loan amount which was used to buy the
item. The collateral note is secured by the
item purchased. If the maker fails to pay on
the note, the payee, usually a bank, can repossess the collateral.

An installment note is a promissory note payable
in installments over a certain period of time.
Automobiles are usually purchased on collateral
installment notes (e.g., the buyer is required
to pay $250 per month for the next 48 months).

2.   Certificate of Deposit--A certificate of deposit
     (CD) is an obligation issued by a bank to repay
     a certain amount with interest in a number of
     months or years. A party deposits a specified
     amount with a bank receiving back a CD guaran-
     teeing repayment with interest.

3.   Drafts--A draft is three-party paper and repre-
     sents a debt owed. The drawer issues the draft
     payable to a payee or to cash or bearer. The
     drawer is ordering the drawee to pay the payee a
     sum specified in the draft.

     The draft may be a time or sight draft. A time
     draft is payable in the future. A sight draft
     is payable upon proper presentment to the
     drawee.

4.   Checks--A check is a draft where the drawee is a
     bank or financial institution. Checks are drawn
     on a bank from the account of the drawer. If
     Jack opens a checking account at First State
     Bank by depositing $1,000 into his account and
     subsequently issues a check to State University
     to pay tuition, First State Bank is the drawee,
     Jack is the drawer, and State University is the
     payee. Jack is ordering the bank to pay a cer-
     tain amount out of his account to the University
     when the University presents the check to Jack's
     bank.

B. <u>Negotiation of Commercial Paper</u>--Both two- and
    three-party paper can be transferred to another
    party. For example, Jack issues a check to Joan for
    $20 as payment for her used legal environment text-
    book. Joan may transfer Jack's check to her friend,
    Steve. Steve can now take the check to Jack's bank
    and collect the $20. Transfer of an instrument is
    made differently depending on the type of instrument
    that is being negotiated.

    1. <u>Order Paper</u>--Order paper is commercial paper
        that has been issued to a specific person or
        entity (UCC § 3-110). A check made "payable to
        the order of Jack Smith" is order paper. To
        properly transfer or negotiate order paper, the
        payee (Jack Smith) must indorse the instrument
        and deliver it to the new transferee. When Jack
        signs his name on the back of the check, it con-
        stitutes a blank indorsement. A blank indorse-
        ment makes the instrument payable to whoever has
        possession of the instrument. The payee may
        indorse the instrument to a new payee and sign
        his name. This is known as a special indorse-
        ment which preserves the instrument as order
        paper (e.g., Pay to Joan Jacobs, Jack Smith).

    2. <u>Bearer Paper</u>--Bearer paper is commercial paper
        payable to the order of cash or to bearer (UCC
        § 3-111). To negotiate bearer paper, the
        transferor must deliver the instrument to the
        transferee. No indorsements are required to
        properly transfer a bearer instrument. Any per-
        son in possession of a bearer instrument has the
        right to collect from the maker or drawer. A
        bearer instrument can be turned into an order
        instrument by a special indorsement.

C. <u>Requirements for a Negotiable Instrument</u>--Commercial
    paper may be either negotiable or nonnegotiable. In
    order for an instrument to be negotiable, it must
    meet certain criteria. Six criteria must be ful-
    filled under UCC § 3-104(1) for an instrument to be
    negotiable.

    1. <u>In Writing</u>--The instrument must be in writing on
        something of permanence. Since the instrument
        serves as a substitute for money, the document
        must be durable.

2. <u>Signed by the Maker or the Drawer</u>--The instru-
    ment must be signed by the maker in the case of
    a note or CD or by the drawer of a draft. The
    party may sign with whatever symbol they have
    adopted as their signature. A party's signature
    must appear on an instrument for the party to be
    legally obligated to pay.

3. <u>Unconditional Promise or Order to Pay</u>--The in-
    strument cannot be conditional or contingent on
    the happening of some event. The promise or
    order to pay must be definite and unequivocal.
    The instrument must promise to pay or order
    someone to pay on the obligation (UCC § 3-
    104(1)(b) & § 3-105). A mere acknowledgment of
    a debt is insufficient.

4. <u>To Pay a Specific Sum of Money</u>--A specific sum
    of money must be stated or such that the holder
    of the instrument can calculate the amount due
    and payable (UCC § 3-106) (e.g., an installment
    note payable in 90 days at 10% interest for
    $1,000 meets the criteria of a specific sum of
    money). The amount must be denominated in money
    (UCC § 3-106).

5. <u>Payable on Demand or at a Definite Time</u>--The
    instrument must be payable on demand or at a
    definite time. Instruments payable on demand
    are payable when properly presented to the pay-
    or, such as a check (UCC § 3-104(2)(b)). Other
    instruments not payable on demand must state
    when payment is to be made (UCC § 3-109).

6. <u>Payable to Order or to Bearer</u>--The instrument
    must state it is payable to order or to bearer
    to be negotiable (UCC § 3-104 (1)(d)).

II. <u>Holders and Holders in Due Course</u>--Commercial paper may
    be transferred to holders who may become holders in due
    course. A holder is a person who takes possession of an
    instrument drawn, issued, or indorsed to his or her
    order or to bearer or in blank (UCC § 1-201(20)). If a
    negotiable instrument is negotiated to a transferee, the
    transferee is considered a holder (UCC § 3-202(1)). The
    holder who fails to qualify as a holder in due course
    receives only the rights of the transferor. The trans-
    fer of a nonnegotiable instrument is an assignment. In
    an assignment, the assignor transfers or assigns a con-
    tract to an assignee. The assignee receives no better

rights than the assignor.

A. <u>Holder in Due Course (HDC)</u>--A holder in due course
    may acquire a negotiable instrument and gain better
    rights than the previous party. The holder in due
    course rule states: "if a negotiable instrument is
    negotiated to a HDC, the holder takes the instrument
    free of all personal defenses subject to only real
    defenses." To become a HDC, three requirements must
    be met.

    1. <u>Requirements of Holder in Due Course</u>

        a. <u>Value</u>--The holder in due course must give
            value for the instrument (UCC § 3-303). A
            holder gives value if the consideration has
            been performed. An executory promise to
            perform in the future is not considered
            value, although taking a instrument in
            payment of a prior debt is considered the
            giving of value.

        b. <u>Good Faith</u>--A holder in due course must take
            the instrument in good faith (UCC § 3-302
            (1)(b)). Good faith is defined as "honesty
            in fact" in the transfer of the instrument.

        c. <u>Without Notice</u>--The holder in due course
            must have received the instrument without
            notice that it had been dishonored, a de-
            fense existed against it, or another claim
            to it existed (UCC § 3-302(1)(c)).

    2. <u>Defenses</u>--Defenses are used by the drawer,
        maker, or indorser to avoid making payment on an
        instrument. (e.g., Fred purchases a used car
        from Bill. Fred gives Bill a check for the pur-
        chase price. Bill guarantees the car is in
        excellent operating condition. The car in
        reality does not run. Fred stops payment on his
        check. Fred may assert the defense of fraud or
        breach of contract against Bill to avoid making
        payment.)

        Defenses can be classified as either real or
        personal. A holder in due course is not subject
        to personal defenses.

        a. <u>Real Defenses</u>--A real defense is valid
            against a holder of an instrument, even a

holder in due course. If a maker or drawer
has a real defense, the holder of the instrument cannot force the maker or drawer to
pay. The following are real defenses:

(1) <u>Forgery</u>--Forgery of a maker's or a
    drawer's signature is a real defense
    and does not bind the person whose name
    is forged (UCC § 3-401 & § 3-404(1)).

(2) <u>Fraud in Execution</u>--If a person is
    tricked into signing a negotiable
    instrument believing it to be something
    else, fraud in execution has occurred.
    The party who signed may assert fraud
    in execution as a real defense.

(3) <u>Material Alteration</u>--Material altera-
    tion is a real defense which precludes
    the holder from collecting anything.
    If the holder is a HDC, he or she may
    collect only according to the original
    terms of the instrument before it was
    altered (UCC § 3-407). For example,
    completing an instrument in an unautho-
    rized manner, changing the amount, and
    removing something from the writing are
    material alterations.

(4) <u>Bankruptcy</u>--When a debtor has received
    a discharge by the Bankruptcy court,
    any instrument representing a dis-
    charged debt is not collectible. The
    discharge is a real defense usable
    against the holder of an instrument
    issued or indorsed by the debtor (UCC
    § 3-305(2)(d)).

(5) <u>Operation of Law</u>--If an instrument is
    rendered void by operation of law, a
    holder or a holder in due course cannot
    require payment. Instruments issued by
    persons adjudicated insane and illegal
    instruments are void (UCC § 3-305(2)
    (a)).

b. <u>Personal Defenses</u>--Personal defenses consti-
    tute all other defenses that are not real
    defenses. Examples of personal defenses are
    breach of contract, breach of warranty, mis-

representation, mistake, undue influence, and duress.

3. <u>The Shelter Principle</u>--The shelter principle allows a person not a HDC to have the rights of a HDC. If a person takes a negotiable instrument from a HDC but does not qualify as a HDC himself, he receives the rights of a HDC (UCC § 3-201). (e.g., Sally, a HDC, gives a $500 check to her nephew as a birthday gift. Nephew is not a HDC but has the rights of a HDC under the shelter principle.)

4. <u>The Federal Trade Commission Rule (FTC Rule)</u>-- The FTC Rule applies to consumer credit transactions where a consumer has purchased a consumer item on credit and issued a negotiable instrument to pay for the item purchased. The FTC Rule requires the promissory note to contain a legend stating any holder of the instrument is subject to all contract defenses of the original purchaser. This legend forecloses any subsequent holder of the instrument from becoming a HDC.

III. <u>Indorsements</u>

A. <u>Liability of Indorser</u>--The indorser by placing his or her signature on an instrument becomes obligated to pay if certain events occur.

1. <u>Secondary Liability</u>--The blank and special indorser agree to pay on the instrument if the instrument is dishonored and timely notice is received of the dishonor (UCC § 3-414). This type of liability is called secondary because the indorser is not liable until the instrument is presented for payment by the holder and the instrument is dishonored or the maker or drawee refuses to pay.

Proper presentment is necessary to hold an indorser liable. Proper presentment requires the holder to present the instrument to the party responsible to make payment on or before the instrument is due (UCC § 3-503 & § 3-504).

The holder must present a check within seven days of the indorsement to hold the indorser liable (UCC § 3-503(2)). If the instrument is dishonored, the holder must notify the secondary party in a reasonable manner by midnight of the next banking day if a bank and before midnight of the third business day for other holders. Written notice of dishonor is effective when sent (UCC § 3-308). If the holder fails to make proper presentment or does not properly notify the indorser, the indorser is discharged from liability.

2. <u>Transfer Warranty Liability</u>--A transferor who receives consideration for an instrument makes five warranties of transfer to subsequent holders. The transfer warranties are:

   a. The transferor has good title to the instrument or is authorized to obtain payment or acceptance on behalf of one who does have good title.

   b. All signatures are genuine and authorized.

   c. The instrument has not been materially altered.

   d. No defense of any party is good against the transferor.

   e. The transferor has no knowledge of any insolvency proceedings against the maker, the acceptor, or the drawer of an unaccepted instrument.

   If any warranty is breached at the time of transfer, the transferor may be liable to subsequent holders. A nonindorser also gives the transfer warranties but only to his or her immediate transferee.

3. <u>Disclaimer of Secondary Liability</u>--A qualified indorsement is used to disclaim secondary liability of an indorser or drawer on an instrument. If a party signs an instrument "without recourse," he or she has created a qualified indorsement. The indorser or drawer is not guaranteeing payment if the instrument is dishonored.

   The qualified indorsement also alters the fifth transfer warranty. The qualified indorser warrants only that he or she has no knowledge of a defense good against the transferor (UCC § 3-417(2)(3)). The other four transfer warranties remain unchanged.

4. <u>Restrictive Indorsements</u>--A restrictive indorsement requires a future holder to follow the restriction. Restrictive indorsements do not prevent further transfer or negotiation of the instrument (e.g., For Deposit Only).

IV. <u>Liability of Makers, Acceptors, and Drawers</u>--Makers and acceptors have primary liability on an instrument. The maker or acceptor is required to pay on the instrument according to its terms.

A drawer has secondary liability on an instrument. The drawer agrees to pay on the instrument if proper presentment, dishonor, and notice of dishonor have been made (UCC § 3-413(2)). Failure to make a proper presentment does not excuse the drawer, unless the drawee bank is insolvent and the drawer suffered a loss (UCC § 3-502(1)(b)).

V. <u>Discharge</u>--Discharge is the termination of any further obligation on an instrument. Discharge can occur in the following ways:

A. <u>Payment</u>--Payment on the instrument discharges the instrument (UCC § 3-603).

B. <u>Cancellation</u>--The payee or holder has the right to cancel an instrument by marking it paid or destroying it (UCC § 3-605).

C. <u>Material Alteration</u>--If a party has materially altered the instrument, such alteration may cause total discharge (UCC § 3-407).

VI. <u>The Banking System</u>

A. <u>Bank-Customer Relationship</u>--The bank-customer relationship is a debtor-creditor relationship. The bank (debtor) is obligated to repay money deposited by the customer (creditor). Article 4 of the UCC governs the deposit and collection procedures of banks.

The bank has several major responsibilities to the customer of a checking account. The bank is required to honor checks on funds deposited, accept deposits in United States currency, and collect on checks written to or indorsed over to its customers drawn on other banks.

1. The Bank's Duties

    a. <u>Honoring Checks</u>--The bank has a contract with the customer to honor checks written by the customer if sufficient funds exist in the customer's account. If the bank wrongfully fails to honor a check, it may be liable to the customer for damages (UCC § 4-402). The bank may agree with the customer to honor overdrafts. The bank will consider the overdraft as a loan (UCC § 4-401(1)).

    b. <u>Stop-Payment Orders</u>--A customer may issue an order to his or her bank to stop payment on a check. A stop-payment order can be oral or in writing. An oral stop-payment order is effective for fourteen calendar days, whereas a written stop-payment order is effective for six months (UCC § 4-403(2)). The bank must be provided a reasonable amount of time to execute the order. If the bank pays a check after a customer has issued a proper stop-payment order, the bank is liable for any actual loss suffered by the customer, which is not necessarily the amount of the check. A bank is required to inform customers of the requirements necessary for stop-payment orders.

    c. <u>Bank's Duty to Know the Customer's Signature</u>--If a bank fails to recognize a forged drawer's signature and pays on the check, the customer is not liable. Unless the customer's negligence substantially contributed to the forgery, the bank must recredit the customer's account (UCC § 3-406).

2. <u>Customer Duties</u>--The customer is responsible to examine the monthly statements and cancelled checks, promptly reporting any forgeries or mistakes to the bank. The customer may be held for a loss resulting from failure to examine his or her statements and cancelled checks or carelessness.

B. Electronic Funds Transfer Systems (EFT)--New tech-
    nology has allowed the banking industry to make
    customer transfers through electronic funds transfer
    systems. The EFT system helps reduce the use of
    paper documentation in the collection process. An
    EFT system may consist of letter machines, point-of-
    sale systems, automatic payments and direct depos-
    its, telecommunications systems, and automatic
    clearinghouses. All of these computer systems may
    be directly connected to various banks and allow
    customers to transfer funds quickly.

    1. A Bank's Liability in EFTs--The bank's EFT sys-
        tem is governed by the Electronic Fund Transfer
        Act (EFTA) if the transfer is operated by tele-
        phone or debit cards to merchants. A monthly
        statement must be issued by the bank for any
        month a transfer is made and must specifically
        describe the transfers made.

VII. Secured Transactions--The area of law called secured
      transactions involves the creation of a security inter-
      est for the protection of a creditor. The creditor who
      loans money to a debtor may receive a security interest
      in the item purchased. The security interest gives the
      creditor greater rights in the event that the debtor
      defaults on the loan. Article 9 of the UCC governs the
      creation of a security interest in personal property.

      A. Creation of a Security Interest--Three requirements
          must be fulfilled before a security interest is
          created.

          1. A written security agreement executed unless
              creditor is in possession of the collateral
              (i.e., usually the property purchased).

          2. The creditor must give value to the debtor.

          3. The debtor must have rights in the collateral.

          When all three requirements have been met, a secu-
          rity interest is created and attaches to the col-
          lateral. The attachment of the security interest
          gives the secured party an ownership interest in the
          collateral and establishes the rights and liabili-
          ties of the debtor and creditor (UCC § 9-203).

      B. Perfection--Perfection is the process a creditor
          uses to protect his or her security interest against

third parties. A secured party with a perfected security interest will have priority to the collateral in the event of a default.

The general rule of priority is the first in time of perfection or purchase is the first in priority to the collateral. A buyer in the ordinary course of business will take goods free of any security interest in inventory a secured party may have (UCC § 9-307 (1)). The three methods of perfection are:

1. <u>Automatic Perfection or Upon Attachment</u>--Perfection occurs automatically upon attachment when consumer goods are sold on credit under a purchase money security interest. A purchase money security interest involves the sale of an item where the funds used to purchase the item come from a lending institution or the secured party seller and the creditor take a security interest in the collateral.

2. <u>Possession</u>--Possession of the collateral by the secured party creates a perfected security interest in the collateral. Perfection lasts as long as the collateral is in the possession of the secured party.

3. <u>Filing</u>--A secured party may file a financing statement with the recorder's office in order to obtain perfection.

C. <u>Default</u>--When the debtor fails to make payments according to an agreed payment schedule, the secured party may exercise his or her legal right to pursue a remedy (UCC § 9-501).

1. <u>Secured Party's Remedies</u>--The secured party may pursue a judgment against the debtor or repossession of the collateral. The secured party may take the debtor to court and obtain a judgment for the amount of the unpaid debt. The secured party may then attempt to collect the amount through the judgment.

The secured party has the right under the security agreement to repossess the collateral from the debtor. The secured party may keep the collateral or resell the goods in a commercially reasonable manner (UCC § 9-503, § 9-505(2) & § 9-504).

The secured party must peacefully repossess the collateral. The secured party does not have the right to break and enter or assault and batter the debtor. Upon the sale of the collateral by the secured party, the proceeds will be used to pay off the amount owed by the debtor. The reasonable expenses from retaking the collateral and the costs of the sale are first deducted from the proceeds. Second, the unpaid balance of the debt is satisfied. Third, other subordinate security interests balances are paid. Any surplus is paid to the debtor (UCC § 9-504 (1)).

D.   Termination--The total payment of a debt requires the secured party to terminate the security interest. The secured party must send a termination statement to the debtor or may be required to file a statement with the state. The secured party may be liable for any loss caused to the debtor for failing to file the proper documents. In consumer cases, the secured party may be liable to the debtor for $100 if no termination statement was filed within 30 days.

Study Questions

Fill-in-the-Blank Questions

Sue Applewood bought a new four-wheel drive pick-up truck at Trucks Unlimited, Inc. Sue paid $1,000 by check and agreed to pay the balance in 36 monthly installments. The dealership had Sue sign an instrument promising to repay the amount owed and giving Trucks Unlimited a security interest.

The $1,000 instrument Sue issued to Trucks Unlimited as a deposit is called a _____.
                    (check/trade acceptance)

The instrument Sue issued to Trucks Unlimited for the balance is called a _____.
                    (check/promissory note)

The truck Sue purchased from Trucks Unlimited is called the

_____.
        (proceeds/collateral)

Sue is the _____ on the instrument she issued
                 (drawer/drawee)
to make the down payment.

True-False Questions

1. Commercial paper serves as a substitute for money and a credit device. _____

2. Commercial paper may be negotiable and nonnegotiable. _____

3. A certificate of deposit is not considered commercial paper. _____

4. A draft is three-party commercial paper. _____

5. The payee on a check is the party responsible for making payment. _____

6. A restrictive indorsement prohibits further transfer of the instrument. _____

7. Indorsers who sign a check with an unqualified indorsement have secondary liability. _____

8. A blank indorsement is made by the signature of the indorser. _____

9. All holders of an instrument are considered holders in due course. _____

10. A promissory note to repay money lent to purchase real property is called a mortgage note. _____

Multiple-Choice Questions

1. Which of the following is two-party commercial paper?

   a. a check
   b. a draft
   c. a trade acceptance
   d. a promissory note

2. Which of the following instruments is an obligation usually owed by a bank where the bank is considered the maker?

    a.   a trade acceptance
    b.   a certificate of deposit
    c.   a promissory note
    d.   a draft

3.   Acme Inc. manufactures household products and sells them through independent distributors. Acme sells $25,000 of inventory to ABC Distribution on credit. Acme issues a document as maker to ABC, the drawee of the goods. ABC accepts by signing the instrument and returning it to Acme. Acme then negotiates the document to a local bank. The document created by Acme is a:

    a.   draft.
    b.   check.
    c.   trade acceptance.
    d.   none of the above.

4.   Emily Emerson issues a check "payable to the order of Betty Johnson" for $500. The check is considered which of the following?

     I. a draft
   II. order paper
 III. bearer paper

    a.   I only
    b.   I and II
    c.   I, II, and III
    d.   I and III

5.   Refer to question 4. Betty receives the check and signs her name to the back of it, along with the words, "For Deposit Only." What type of indorsement has Betty made?

    a.   blank, restrictive
    b.   special, restrictive
    c.   blank, qualified
    d.   special, unqualified

6.   Refer to question 4. Betty signs the back of the check with her name and transfers it to Bob. Bob is considered a:

    a.   holder.
    b.   debtor.
    c.   drawee.
    d.   secured party.

7. Which of the following is a requirement of becoming a holder in due course (HDC)?

    a. transferor gives value
    b. transferor transfers in good faith
    c. HDC takes in good faith
    d. HDC takes with notice of dishonor

8. Joshua Jones transfers an instrument to Jerry Johnson. The check is "payable to the order of Joshua Jones" for $1,200. Joshua signs the back of the instrument "pay to Jerry Johnson; signed, Joshua Jones."

    Jerry receives the check from Joshua as payment for a previous debt. Jerry gives the check to his son, Jack, age 12, by signing the back with his name. Has Joshua properly transferred the instrument?

    a. Yes, because it was order paper.
    b. Yes, because it was bearer paper.
    c. No, because it was order paper.
    d. No, because it was bearer paper.

9. Refer to question 8. Does Jerry Johnson qualify as a holder in due course?

    a. Yes, because he took with notice.
    b. Yes, because he gave value.
    c. No, because he did not give value.
    d. No, because he had notice.

10. Refer to question 8. Does Jack Jones qualify as a holder in due course?

    a. Yes, because all the requirements were met.
    b. Yes, because he is a holder.
    c. No, because no value was given.
    d. No, because he is a minor.

11. Refer to question 8. The instrument was originally issued by Jackie to Joshua Jones. Jackie has drawn the check on the First National Bank. Jackie believes she was defrauded by Joshua in the original transaction and orders the bank to stop payment. Jack attempts to collect on the check from First National Bank and is refused payment. Jack then approaches Jackie and demands payment. Will Jack be able to collect from Jackie?

    a. Yes, because Jack is a HDC.
    b. Yes, because Jack has the rights of a HDC.

c. No, because Jack is not a HDC.
d. No, because Jackie has a defense.

12. Refer to question 11. Jackie has which of the following defenses?

a. fraud, a real defense
b. breach of contract, a real defense
c. fraud, a personal defense
d. none of the above

13. Which of the following is a requirement of a negotiable instrument?

I.   signed by the maker or drawer
II. on a preprinted form
III. payable to order or to bearer

a. I only
b. I and II
c. I, II, and III
d. I and III

14. Dave Wall issued a promissory note for $50,000, to be paid in 90 days with 10% interest payable to the order of City Bank. The note referred to the original contract of purchase and allowed the bank to recover attorney fees if Dave defaulted. Is the note negotiable?

a. Yes, because all the requirements are met.
b. No, because of no sum certain exists.
c. No, because it refers to another agreement.
d. No, because it allows for attorney fees.

15. Refer to question 14. Assume the promissory note is non-negotiable. City Bank transfers the note to Commercial Financial, Inc. for value. Commercial Financial, Inc. is a(n):

a. holder in due course.
b. holder.
c. assignee.
d. debtor.

16. The negotiation of an order instrument requires which of the following?

a. delivery and indorsement
b. delivery

c.   indorsement
d.   a restrictive indorsement

17.   Which of the following is considered a real defense?

a.   breach of contract
b.   mistake
c.   undue influence
d.   forgery of drawer's signature

18.   Which of the following limits the holder in due course rule in consumer credit transactions?

a.   The FTC Rule
b.   EFT system
c.   UCC Article 9
d.   UCC Article 2

19.   Andy Berg issued a check "payable to the order of Tom Johnson" for $500. Tom indorsed the check and transferred it to Sandy Hogan for value. Tom has which of the following liabilities?

   I.   secondary
  II.   transfer warranty
 III.   primary

a.   I only
b.   I and II
c.   I, II, and III
d.   I and III

20.   Which of the following is <u>not</u> necessary to create a security interest?

   I.   a written security agreement
  II.   creditor gives value to debtor
 III.   debtor has rights in the collateral

a.   I only
b.   II only
c.   I and III
d.   III only

21.   The attachment of a security interest in the collateral is sufficient to bind the debtor and _____.

a.   third parties
b.   the secured party

c.   general creditors
d.   trustee in bankruptcy

22. Tim purchased a stereo system from Pacific Stereo Inc. by
     giving $500 as a down payment and signing a promissory
     note and security agreement for the balance of $2,000
     payable to Pacific. Tim took the stereo home the same
     day. Does Pacific Stereo have a perfected security
     interest?

     a.   Yes, by possession.
     b.   Yes, by attachment.
     c.   Yes, by filing.
     d.   No, because Pacific did not file a financing state-
          ment.

23. General Electric (G.E.) manufactures appliances and gen-
     eral household durables. G.E. sold 500 refrigerators to
     American Appliance, a retail outlet store. G.E. sold the
     merchandise on credit and set up a warehousing arrange-
     ment at American Appliance. G.E. had strict control over
     all the refrigerators until American Appliance produced a
     voucher proving a sale. Does G.E. have a perfected secu-
     rity interest in the refrigerators?

     a.   Yes, by possession.
     b.   Yes, by attachment.
     c.   Yes, by filing.
     d.   No, because no written security was signed.

24. Which of the following is not a remedy available to a
     secured party when the debtor defaults?

     a.   secure a judgment
     b.   peaceful repossession
     c.   repossession by breaking and entering
     d.   all of the above

25. Once a debt is completely paid by the debtor, the secured
     party must:

     a.   repossess the collateral.
     b.   release the judgment.
     c.   execute a security agreement.
     d.   file a termination statement.

Essay Question

1. Dan Wells issued a check "payable to the order of Dave
    Adams" for $1,000. Dave negotiated the check to Stan

Flint for a previous debt Dave owed Stan. Stan cleverly altered the check from $1,000 to $10,000. Stan then transferred the check to Acme Inc. for value. Acme attempted to collect from the First National Bank, the drawee. The bank refused to pay on the instrument, and Acme attempted to collect from Dan Wells. Will Acme Inc. be able to collect from Dan Wells?

Answers to Study Questions

Fill-in-the-Blank Questions

The $1,000 instrument Sue issued Trucks Unlimited as a deposit is called a <u>check</u>. (p. 284)

The instrument Sue issued to Trucks Unlimited for the balance is called a <u>promissory note</u>. (p. 282)

The truck Sue purchased from Trucks Unlimited is called the <u>collateral</u>. (p. 306)

Sue is the <u>drawer</u> on the instrument she issued to make the down payment. (p. 283)

True-False Questions

1. True (p. 282)

2. True (p. 291)

3. False. A CD is commercial paper. (p. 283)

4. True (p. 283)

5. False. The payee receives payment on a check. (p. 283)

6. False. A restrictive indorsement does not limit further negotiation. (p. 297)

7. True (p. 297)

8. True (p. 296)

9. False. Not all holders qualify as holders in due course. (p. 285)

10. True (p. 290)

Multiple-Choice Questions

1.	d (p. 290)		14.	a (p. 291)
2.	b (p. 290)		15.	c (p. 292)
3.	c (p. 284)		16.	a (p. 292)
4.	b (p. 284)		17.	d (p. 295)
5.	a (p. 296)		18.	a (p. 296)
6.	a (p. 285)		19.	b (p. 297)
7.	c (p. 285)		20.	a (p. 306)
8.	a (p. 292)		21.	b (p. 306)
9.	b (pp. 286, 287)		22.	b (p. 306)
10.	c (pp. 286, 287)		23.	a (p. 306)
11.	b (p. 285)		24.	c (p. 307)
12.	c (p. 295)		25.	d (p. 311)
13.	d (p. 291)			

Essay Question

1. Yes, but only to the extent of the original terms of the instrument or $1,000. Acme qualifies as a holder in due course. Acme gave value for the instrument, took the instrument in good faith, and without notice of dishonor or a claim against it. Acme as a HDC is not subject to personal defenses. When a HDC receives a negotiable instrument through a negotiation, the HDC may collect, unless the drawer has a real defense. In this case, Dan Wells, the drawer, has the real defense of material alteration but only as to the amount altered. Dan must pay, according to his secondary liability, $1,000. (pp. 285-295)

Chapter 13
Rights of Consumers, Debtors, and Creditors

Major Concepts

The consumer credit market has surpassed the $500 billion mark. With the great expansion of the consumer credit market came the abuse of consumers. Congress has enacted a variety of federal statutes to help consumers make an informed decision before they make major purchases involving credit.

The Federal Truth-in-Lending Act is part of the Consumer Credit Protection Act and is the primary source of federal law regulating consumer credit transactions. The Truth-in-Lending Act requires certain disclosures to be made by the creditor to the consumer in credit transactions where a finance charge exists or more than four installments must be made. The disclosures help the consumer to shop for the best credit terms. Other provisions of the Truth-in-Lending Act cover real estate transactions, credit cards, billing errors, and credit reporting. The Consumer Credit Protection Act prohibits discrimination in credit and prohibits debt collectors from harassing or abusing debtors.

Once a debtor has failed to pay his or her bills, state law allows the creditor to pursue a legal remedy. The creditor may secure a judgment from the court for the amount owed. If the judgment is not satisfied, a writ of execution may be issued by the court. The writ directs the sheriff to seize and sell any of the debtor's nonexempt property.

The creditor may ask the court to garnish the wages of the debtor. Garnishment is a court order which seizes the debt-

or's property that is in the possession of a third party. All
money collected is used to satisfy the debt owed.

When a debtor fails to make payments on real property, the
lender can foreclose on the property. The property will be
seized and sold to pay off the debt.

In the event a debtor desires to be released of his or her
debt, a bankruptcy may be sought. Bankruptcy law allows a
debtor to start over. Federal bankruptcy courts have the authority over all bankruptcy matters. The Bankruptcy Code is
comprised of several Chapters dealing with different types of
debtors and relief. The most common form of bankruptcy is a
Chapter 7 Straight Bankruptcy, also called a Liquidation. The
debtor is discharged of all his or her dischargeable debts.

Chapter Outline

I.   Consumer Credit Protection Act (CCPA)--Congress passed
      the CCPA to alleviate consumer abuse in credit trans-
      actions. The escalation in credit availability over the
      past three decades has led to misrepresentation, harass-
      ment, and the lack of opportunity to correct inaccurate
      credit records. The CCPA is comprehensive federal leg-
      islation to protect consumer rights. The CCPA has many
      provisions dealing with credit transactions. Five of
      the major provisions of the Act will be discussed in
      this chapter.

      A.   Truth-in-Lending Act--Title I of the CCPA is known
           as the Federal Truth-in-Lending Act (TILA). The Act
           requires the creditor to make certain disclosures to
           the consumer.

           TILA applies to credit transactions with a finance
           charge or where the debtor is required to make more
           than four installments. The lender is required to
           clearly disclose the cash price, the down payment or
           trade-in allowance, the unpaid cash price which is
           financed, the finance charge, and the annual percen-
           tage rate of interest. The lender is also required
           to disclose other items to the consumer. The TILA
           applies to sales and leases of personal and real
           property for personal, family, household, or agri-
           cultural use where the amount financed is less than
           $25,000. Lenders in the ordinary course of their
           business who lend money, sell on credit, or arrange
           for the extension of credit to consumers must comply

with the Act. Individuals and not corporations are protected by the Act.

A consumer may sue for actual damages of twice the finance charge and attorney's fees up to $1,000 for a creditor violation of the TILA. A criminal violation of TILA carries a fine of up to $5,000 and/or imprisonment up to one year, if willfully and knowingly done.

1. <u>Real Estate Improvements</u>--A consumer home improvement loan falls under the TILA. The lender who loans money to a consumer for a home improvement in which the lender takes a security interest is required to disclose to the consumer the right to rescind by midnight of the third business day following the signing of the loan agreement, the annual percentage rate, the finance charge, the amount financed, the total of the payments, and the payment schedule. The consumer must notify the lender within the three-day period to have the transaction voided.

    Lenders need not give a three-day right of rescission to a consumer in an emergency situation in which the customer's home needs repairs or when a consumer purchases a house, granting a first mortgage.

2. <u>Credit Cards</u>--TILA applies to the issuance and use of credit cards. Credit cards cannot be sent to an individual or business unless requested. Cardholder liability for unauthorized uses when a card is lost or stolen is limited to $50.

3. <u>Fair Credit Billing Act (FCBA)</u>--The FCBA is an amendment to the TILA which requires creditors to correct billing errors promptly without damage to an individual's credit rating. An individual has the right to notify the creditor in writing of a perceived error. The creditor must acknowledge the receipt of the letter in 30 days and correct or explain the error in 90 days. The individual need not pay the disputed amount until the matter is corrected or explained.

4. <u>Fair Credit Reporting Act (FCRA)</u>--The FCRA has become part of the CCPA and has given consumers the right to know the type of credit investiga-

tions conducted, the information being compiled, and the persons who will receive a credit report. The credit reporting agency must ensure accuracy in credit reporting. A consumer may add to a credit report a 100-word statement describing an adverse item. Information over seven years old must be deleted, and a bankruptcy more than ten years old must be removed.

A consumer credit agency may be liable for actual damages, punitive damages, attorney's fees, and court costs for violating the FCRA.

5. <u>Equal Credit Opportunity Act (ECOA)</u>--The ECOA is part of the CCPA and prohibits discrimination in credit transactions based upon race, color, religion, national origin, sex, marital status, age, or a person's income being derived from public assistance.

A creditor may be held liable for actual damages and punitive damages up to $10,000 plus attorney's fees and court costs.

6. <u>Fair Debt Collection Practices Act (FDCPA)</u>--The FDCPA is part of the TILA and applies to collection agencies dealing with consumers. The Act prohibits the harassment or abuse of consumers in the debt collection process. A debt collector cannot call a consumer between 9 p.m. and 8 a.m., repeatedly call the consumer, contact the consumer at work if the employer prohibits it, threaten to use physical violence or harm the consumer, or use obscene or profane language. On the envelopes used by a debt collector, the return address cannot indicate a collection agency. The consumer has the right to demand a debt collector stop contacting him or her (i.e., the consumer must demand in writing).

A debt collector who violates the FDCPA is liable for actual damages, attorney's fees, and additional damages up to $1,000.

II. <u>Other Consumer-Oriented Laws</u>

A. <u>Uniform Consumer Credit Code (UCCC)</u>--The UCCC is a uniformly drafted statute which only a few states have adopted. The UCCC covers most sales of real and personal property. The UCCC comprehensively regulates installment loans, retail installment sales, and usury (i.e., interest rate ceilings).

B.   The Real Estate Settlement Procedures Act (RESPA)-- RESPA is a federal statute which requires all closing costs in the purchase of a home be specifically stated to the buyer. The lender is required to send a booklet prepared by the U.S. Department of Housing and Urban Development to each loan applicant within three days of the loan application. Once the loan is approved, the lender is required to provide a truth-in-lending statement that clearly shows the annual percentage rate.

C.   State Usury Laws--Usury laws prohibit the charging of interest above a stated maximum rate. Usury laws apply to loans made to individuals for cash. Many states have abolished usury laws altogether. Some states have adopted usury laws for credit card interest.

III. Creditor's Rights--The creditor has many legal courses of action when the debtor defaults on the obligation. The following are some remedies the creditor may pursue.

A.   Writ of Execution--Once the debtor has defaulted, the creditor may secure a judgment from the court. If the debtor fails to pay voluntarily, the creditor may go to court and obtain a writ of execution directing the sheriff to seize and sell any of the debtor's nonexempt real or personal property at a judicial sale. The proceeds from the sale will be used to satisfy the judgment and the expenses of the sale. The debtor has the right to pay the amount of the judgment and redeem the nonexempt property. Exempt property is property the debtor may keep which is not subject to a writ of execution.

B.   Attachment--Attachment is the seizure of property of a debtor by court order. Attachment usually occurs before a final judgment is rendered by the court.

The creditor must file with the court an affidavit alleging the facts of the default and post a bond to cover court costs, the value of the use of the debtor's goods, and the value of the property. The court will issue a writ of attachment which directs the sheriff to seize the nonexempt property of the debtor.   The property will not be sold until the creditor prevails at trial.

C.   <u>Garnishment</u>--Garnishment is the legal procedure of obtaining the debtor's property while in the possession of a third party.   The court, after a judgment is obtained by the creditor, may issue a writ of garnishment for the debtor's wages.   The employer will be required to deduct a specific portion from the wages of the debtor and remit it to the court to satisfy the judgment.

Congress has enacted legislation which provides the debtor with limited protection against overly harsh garnishments.   Federal law permits garnishment up to a stated maximum percentage of the debtor's disposable income.   An employer cannot discharge an employee because the employee's paycheck has been garnished.   The debtor has a right to a hearing before his or her wages can be garnished by court order.

D.   <u>Foreclosure on Real Property</u>

1.   <u>Mortgage</u>--A mortgage is a lien on real property to secure repayment of a loan given by a lender. A bank, savings and loan, or credit union may loan a buyer the necessary funds to purchase a home.   The lender will have the buyer sign a promissory note for the amount of the loan and a mortgage document giving the lender an interest in the real property.   If the debtor later fails to pay the monthly payment, the lender has the right to foreclose (i.e., repossess the property).

2.   <u>Default and Foreclosure</u>--The mortgage agreement allows the lender (mortgagee) to declare the entire balance due, once a default has occurred. The lender then may foreclose by seizing the property and having the court order the property sold.   The proceeds are used to pay off the balance owed and costs of the foreclosure.   Any surplus is paid to other subordinate interests and to the debtor.

The lender may obtain a deficiency judgment against the debtor if the proceeds from the sale are insufficient to cover the costs of the foreclosure and the balance owed.

The debtor has the right to redeem the property before the judicial sale by paying the full amount owed, plus interest and costs. Some state laws allow the debtor to redeem the property for a specified period after the judicial sale.

E.   Protection for the Debtor--State law may declare certain types of real and personal property exempt from creditor execution. The statute will specify which property of the debtor cannot be levied against by the creditor. A common exemption is the homestead exemption. The homestead exemption permits the debtor to keep the home entirely or up to a specified dollar amount, such as $30,000.

IV.   Bankruptcy and Reorganization--Article I, Section 8 of the United States Constitution gives Congress the authority to establish laws on the subject of bankruptcies. Congress has enacted a Bankruptcy Code to provide relief (a fresh start) and protection to debtors. The Bankruptcy Reform Act of 1978, 1984, and 1986 established federal bankruptcy courts as presiding over bankruptcy matters. The code provides for five types of debtor relief: Chapter 7 for liquidations, Chapter 9 for adjustment of debts of a municipality, Chapter 11 for reorganization of individuals and business debtors, Chapter 12 for relief of family farmers, and Chapter 13 for adjustment of debts of individuals with a regular income. Chapters 7, 11, 13, and 12 will be discussed below.

A.   Chapter 7: Liquidations--A Chapter 7 bankruptcy is called a straight bankruptcy. The debtor relinquishes all of his or her nonexempt assets to the trustee. The debtor provides a schedule of all the debts owed and all assets owned. The trustee liquidates the assets and distributes the proceeds to the creditors. The remaining debts of the debtor are discharged.

1.   Procedure--The debtor is required to file a petition with the bankruptcy court. The unsecured creditors of the debtor may force the debtor into bankruptcy if they are not being paid and their claims aggregate $5,000 or more. If the debtor has twelve or more creditors, three creditors must sign the petition. If the debtor has less then twelve creditors, only one creditor must sign the petition.

The debtor must completely fill out the petition with a list of secured and unsecured creditors, the amounts owed, a list of all property owned by the debtor, and a statement of financial affairs. Once the petition is filed, all civil actions against the debtor are suspended by an automatic stay.

2. Trustee--The bankruptcy court appoints an interim trustee until a permanent trustee is elected at the first meeting of the creditors. The trustee collects the debtor's property, liquidates it at a sale, distributes the proceeds to the creditors, and closes the estate.

    The trustee has the power to avoid transactions the debtor entered into based upon fraud, duress, or mutual mistake. The trustee may also avoid preferential transfers which attempt to defraud creditors prior to the filing of the petition.

3. Exemptions--The debtor may choose to keep exempt property. State and federal law enumerate the exemptions available. Examples of the exemptions are: one motor vehicle up to $1,200, jewelry up to $500, life insurance contracts and miscellaneous property up to $400.

4. Property Distribution--The trustee in bankruptcy will distribute the available funds to the unsecured creditors who have filed claims. The Bankruptcy Code sets forth classes of creditors in order of priority. All the members of a class must be fully paid before the next lower class receives a distribution. The order of priority is as follows:

    a. bankruptcy costs.

    b. unpaid wages, salaries, or commissions due employees earned within 90 days of the bankruptcy petition up to $2,000 per employee.

    c. claims for funds prepaid by creditors to the debtor for goods or services not delivered up to $900 each.

    d. certain taxes.

e.   general unsecured creditors.

5.   <u>Nondischargeable Debts</u>--The following debts are
     not dischargeable under the Bankruptcy Code:
     debts for back taxes, alimony and child support,
     student loans, judgments based upon the debtor's
     intoxication while driving.

6.   <u>Reaffirmation</u>--A debtor may reaffirm a debt dis-
     charged by entering a new agreement before the
     discharge. The agreement must be filed with the
     court, the debtor must be counseled by his or
     her attorney, a declaration must be filed stat-
     ing the debtor is aware of the consequences of
     the voluntary agreement, and no hardship must be
     imposed on the debtor as a result of the reaf-
     firmation. The debtor may rescind the agreement
     before the discharge or within sixty days of
     filing the agreement, whichever is later.

B.   <u>Chapter 11:   Reorganization</u>--Chapter 11 allows busi-
     nesses and individuals to submit a plan to the
     bankruptcy court. The plan outlines how the credi-
     tors will be paid. The debtor may continue to
     operate a business as long as the requirements of
     the plan are being fulfilled.

     The plan must be approved by each class of credi-
     tors. If the plan is in the best interests of the
     creditors and they confirm the plan, the debtor will
     receive a discharge. The creditors under the plan
     are usually partially paid according to the plan,
     and the remainder is discharged.

     The same rules that apply to a Chapter 7 petition
     apply to a Chapter 11 proceeding. The petition may
     be voluntary or involuntary. The court may appoint
     a trustee to manage the business if the debtor is
     grossly mismanaging or it is in the best interests
     of the debtor to do so.

C.   <u>Chapter 13:   Adjustment of Debts of an Individual
     with Regular Income</u>--Chapter 13 allows the wage
     earner to petition the bankruptcy court with a plan
     of adjustment. Individuals with a regular income
     who owe unsecured debts of less than $100,000 and
     secured debts of less than $350,000 may file under
     Chapter 13.

1. Procedure--The debtor will propose a plan to pay the creditors partial or full payment. The time for payment under a plan may not exceed five years with an extension, otherwise three years. The plan will be approved by the court if all the debtor's disposable income is applied to the plan.

   The debtor is required to make payments under the plan. Upon completion of all payments, the court will discharge the debts listed in the plan. Some debts are not dischargeable, such as taxes, alimony, and child support. The debtor may receive a hardship discharge if the plan was not completed due to circumstances beyond the debtor's control.

D. Chapter 12: Adjustment of Debts of a Family Farmer with Regular Income--The Family Farmer Bankruptcy Act of 1986 allows a farmer with 50% gross income from the farm and 80% debt from the farm to propose a plan for relief. The farmer debtor files a petition with the bankruptcy court and proposes a plan to repay creditors in partial or full payment. The process for a Chapter 13 is similar to a Chapter 12 proceeding.

   The plan must fully pay the secured debt up to the value of the collateral. As to unsecured debt, the plan will be approved if the value of the property to be distributed is equal to the claim or the plan requires all the debtor's disposable income over a three-year period to be applied to making payments.

   A farmer may convert from a Chapter 11 or Chapter 13 to a Chapter 12 or to a Chapter 7.

Study Questions

Fill-in-the-Blank Questions

Albert Joseph purchased a brand new washer and dryer from Applewood Appliance on credit. Albert agreed to pay a set amount for the next twelve months at a stated interest rate.

Under the Truth-in-Lending Act, Applewood Appliance must disclose the _____ in the
                    (finance charge/add-on interest rate)

loan contract for the washer and dryer.

The unpaid cash price under the Truth-in-Lending Act is defined as the cash price minus the _____
_____.
(sales tax/down
payment)

The provisions of the Truth-in-Lending Act apply to
_____ of personal and real
(sales and leases/only sales)
property.

The _____
(Federal Trade Commission/Federal Reserve Board)
issues the administrative rules that implement the Truth-in-
Lending Act.

True-False Questions

1. The Consumer Credit Protection Act is an amendment to the
    Truth-in-Lending Act. _____F

2. A violation of the Truth-in-Lending Act can be punished
    by a $5,000 fine. _____T

3. The Truth-in-Lending Act requires a lender to charge a
    specified interest rate. _____F   report?

4. The Equal Credit Opportunity Act prohibits discrimination
    in credit transactions based on race but not national
    origin. _____F

5. Under the Bankruptcy Code, a debtor may be put into bank-
    ruptcy by his or her creditors if certain criteria are
    fulfilled. _____T

6. A creditor may seize all the debtor's property under a
    writ of execution. _____F

7. An employer cannot fire an employee because the employ-
    ee's wages are garnished. _____T

8. In the financing of real property, the lender is known as
    the mortgagor. _____F

9. Chapter 7 of the Bankruptcy Code is the liquidation pro-
    vision. _____T

10. An automatic stay suspends all civil litigation against the debtor in a bankruptcy. ___T___

Multiple-Choice Questions

1. Which of the following must be disclosed under the Truth-in-Lending Act when a consumer makes a purchase on credit with a finance charge?

      I.   cash price
     II.   annual percentage rate
    III.   prepayment penalty, if any

    a.   I only
    b.   I and II
    c.   I, II, and III
    d.   I and III

2. Truth-in-Lending applies to which of the following transactions?

      I.   Sam sells his lawn mower to his neighbor on credit.

     II.   A G.M. dealership sells a truck to Acme, Inc. for use in the business.

    III.   Audio Inc. sells a stereo to a college student on credit for use at the dormitory.

    a.   I only
    b.   I and II
    c.   I, II, and III
    d.   III only

3. The real estate provisions of the Truth-in-Lending Act applies to which of the following transactions?

      I.   Emergency loan for a consumer to repair his home.

     II.   A consumer purchases a home and gives a first mortgage.

    III.   A consumer takes a second lien on their home to build a swimming pool.

    a.   I only
    b.   I and II
    c.   I, II, and III
    d.   III only

4. Under the Truth-in-Lending Act, a credit cardholder can be held liable for unauthorized uses up to _____?

   a. $50 per card
   b. $500 per card
   c. $500 for all cards
   d. $1,000 per card

5. Under the Fair Credit Reporting Act, any inaccurate material must be removed. Which of the following is a provision of the Act?

   a. annual percentage rate disclosure
   b. information over seven years old must be deleted from the records
   c. credit card limit
   d. none of the above

6. The Equal Credit Opportunity Act prohibits discrimination based upon which of the following?

     I. religion
    II. age
   III. marital status

   a. I only
   b. I and II
   c. I, II, and III
   d. I and III

7. The Fair Debt Collection Practices Act applies to which of the following?

   a. collection agencies
   b. attorneys
   c. creditors
   d. retail sellers

8. Henry Wallace exceeded his limit on his Master Charge credit card. Henry lost his job and could not pay his bill. After several months, Master Charge turned the bill over to a debt collector. The debt collector sent a letter threatening Henry with a lawsuit if he did not pay. The return address of the letter clearly indicates it was sent by a debt collector. Which of the following has been violated?

   a. Equal Credit Opportunity Act
   b. Fair Debt Collection Practices Act

    c.   Fair Credit Billing Act
    d.   all of the above

9. Refer to question 8. Henry hires an attorney to represent him and informs the debt collector of this. The debt collector must:

    a.   send a letter to both the attorney and Henry.
    b.   bring a lawsuit against the attorney and Henry.
    c.   not contact Henry again.
    d.   contact Henry only.

10. If the Fair Debt Collection Practices Act is violated, the violator may be required to pay:

    I.   actual damages.
   II.   attorney fees.
  III.   punitive damages.

    a.   I only
    b.   I and II
    c.   I, II, and III
    d.   I and III

11. William Long purchased a new home from Sunnyside Builders. William obtained a thirty-year loan from First Federal Savings and Loan. Which of the following requires the lender to outline all closing costs before the purchase of the home?

    a.   Uniform Consumer Credit Code
    b.   State Usury laws
    c.   Equal Credit Opportunity Act
    d.   Real Estate Settlement Procedures Act

12. Refer to question 11. William Long lived in his new home for five years before he had difficulty making the payments. William failed to make his payments for eight months. First Federal Savings and Loan notified William legal action would be taken if he did not get caught up on his payments. The lender may:

    a.   foreclose on the property.
    b.   obtain a deficiency judgment after foreclosure.
    c.   issue an automatic stay.
    d.   two of the above.

13. A creditor may obtain a writ of execution from the court against a debtor who has defaulted. Which of the following is exempt from seizure under the writ of execution?

         I.   debtor's home
        II.   furniture
       III.   family yacht

        a.   I only
        b.   I and II
        c.   I, II, and III
        d.   I and III

14. If a debtor is fired because his or her wages were gar-
     nished, the employer may be:

     p.329

     a.   fined up to $10,000.
     b.   fined up to $5,000.
     c.   fined $1,000 and imprisoned for one year, or both.
     d.   none of the above.

15. Before a debtor's wages are garnished, the Due Process
     Clause requires:

         I.   proper notice.
        II.   a hearing available to the debtor.
       III.   an opportunity to refinance the debt.

        a.   I only
        b.   I and II
        c.   I, II, and III
        d.   I and III

16. A real estate mortgage is defined as:

        a.   a lien against the realty to secure payment on the
             loan.
        b.   a lease.
        c.   a contract to purchase.
        d.   a settlement statement.

17. Under the Bankruptcy Code, which of the following may
     file a petition under Chapter 7?

         I.   individuals
        II.   partnership
       III.   corporation

     p.333

        a.   I only
        b.   I and II
        c.   I, II, and III
        d.   I and III

18. Unsecured creditors can file bankruptcy against a debtor if their claims aggregate:

    a. $500 or more.
    b. $5,000 or more.
    c. $50,000 or more.
    d.   none of the above.

19. Which of the following is/are not dischargeable under Chapter 7 of the Bankruptcy Code?

    a.   back taxes
    b.   credit card debts
    c.   car loans
    d.   none of the above

20. Which of the following is/are requirements for a reaffirmation agreement to be enforceable?

      I.   agreement made before the discharge granted
     II.   agreement notarized
    III.   agreement filed with the court

    a.   I only
    b.   I and II
    c.   I, II, and III
    d.   I and III

21. Chapter 11 of the Bankruptcy Code involves:

    a.   liquidation.
    b.   reorganization.
    c.   debt adjustment.
    d.   none of the above.

22. Jim Riley has gone through hard times. Jim lost his job two months ago and has accumulated a mountain of debt. Jim wants to file for a Chapter 13 bankruptcy. Will the bankruptcy court grant Jim relief under Chapter 13?

    a.   Yes, because he has debts.
    b.   Yes, because he can't make his payments.
    c.   No, because Jim intentionally got into debt.
    d.   No, because Jim does not have a regular income.

23. Which of the following is the most recently enacted Chapter of the Bankruptcy law?

    a.   Chapter 7
    b.   Chapter 12   farmers '86

c.   Chapter 13
d.   Chapter 11

24. Which of the following allows a consumer to ask a creditor to explain a perceived error?

a.   Fair Credit Reporting Act
b.   Usury laws
c.   Equal Opportunity Credit Act
d.   Fair Credit Billing Act

25. Which of the following is a state law adopted in only a
few states?

a.   Uniform Consumer Credit Code
b.   Truth-in-Lending Act
c.   Consumer Credit Protection Act
d.   Real Estate Settlement Procedures Act

Essay Question

1.   Frank Finn, a sole proprietor in the shoe repair business, has filed a petition in bankruptcy under Chapter 7.
Wilbur Inc. is Frank's supplier of materials and his
largest creditor. On the bankruptcy petition, Frank
failed to list Wilbur Inc. as a creditor or that anything
was owed to Wilbur Inc.

Frank has unsecured debts of $25,000, a secured debt on
his car of $10,000, and a student loan of $15,000. Which
of Frank's debts will be discharged by the bankruptcy
court? *not student loan*

unsecured $25k.

Answers to Study Questions

Fill-in-the-Blank Questions

Under the Truth-in-Lending Act, Applewood Appliance must disclose the <u>finance charge</u> in the loan contract for the washer
and dryer. (p. 316)

The unpaid cash price under the Truth-in-Lending Act is defined as the cash price minus the <u>down payment</u>. (p. 316)

The provisions of the Truth-in-Lending Act apply to <u>sales and
leases</u> of personal and real property. (p. 317)

The <u>Federal Reserve Board</u> issues the administrative rules that implement the Truth-in-Lending Act.   (p. 317)

True-False Questions

1.   False.   TILA is an amendment to CCPA.   (p. 316)

2.   True (p. 317)

3.   False.   TILA does not require a lender to charge a certain interest rate but does require the lender to make some disclosures.   (p. 316)

4.   False.   ECOA prohibits discrimination based upon race and national origin in credit transactions.   (p. 325)

5.   True (p. 333)

6.   False.   A creditor may not seize a debtor's exempt property.   (p. 333)

7.   True (p. 329)

8.   False.   The lender is known as the mortgagee in real property financing.   (p. 331)

9.   True (p. 333)

10.   True (p. 333)

Multiple-Choice Questions

1. c (p. 316)	14. c (p. 329)
2. d (p. 317)	15. b (p. 329)
3. d (p. 317)	16. a (p. 331)
4. a (p. 322)	17. c (p. 333)
5. b (p. 322)	18. b (p. 333)
6. c (p. 325)	19. a (p. 334)
7. a (p. 325)	20. d (p. 334)
8. b (p. 325)	21. b (p. 334)
9. c (p. 325)	22. d (p. 336)
10. b (p. 326)	23. b (p. 338)
11. d (p. 317)	24. d (p. 322)
12. d (p. 331)	25. a (p. 328)
13. b (p. 329)	

Essay Question

1. Frank will not have all of his debts discharged by the
    bankruptcy court. Any debt not listed on the bankruptcy
    petition is an exception to the discharge. If the debtor
    fails to list a creditor on the petition, the creditor
    will not receive notice of the bankruptcy and, as a re-
    sult, fail to file a proof of claim. Wilbur Inc. may
    still collect the amount owed from Frank after the bank-
    ruptcy.

    Frank's automobile will be repossessed by the lender and
    most likely sold. Frank may have an allowable exemption
    in his automobile under state statute. The federal
    exemptions allow $1,200 equity in one motor vehicle.

    Frank's unsecured debts of $25,000 will be discharged if
    they do not fall into any special nondischargeable cate-
    gory. Frank's student loan is not dischargeable under
    Chapter 7. (p. 334)

Chapter 14
Consumer Protection

Major Concepts

The law of Consumer Protection has greatly expanded in the last quarter of a century. The increase in consumerism and hazardous products has caused legislators to enact federal and state statutes for the protection of consumers.

The Federal Trade Commission (FTC), under the Wheeler-Lea Act and the Federal Trade Commission Act, has been given the responsibility of providing consumer protection. The FTC has broad discretion to promulgate rules and prosecute "unfair or deceptive acts or practices." The FTC has promulgated rules prohibiting bait and switch, deceptive price comparisons, and deceptive testimonials and endorsements.

The FTC has the authority to issue cease and desist orders and also require advertisers to correct misleading advertisements. Deceptive advertising may come in many forms. The advertisement may make outright false claims or fail to tell the whole truth about the product.

Congress has enacted a variety of statutes concerning consumer protection. Federal statutes requiring adequate and accurate packaging and labeling, warranty disclosures, the safe use of food, drugs, and cosmetics, and prohibiting the use of the mail service to defraud are just a few of the areas protected by law.

The Consumer Product Safety Act protects consumers from products which might be hazardous to their health. The Consumer

Product Safety Commission has been given wide authority over the production of consumer products and their use.

Chapter Outline

I. The Federal Trade Commission (FTC)--The FTC is a federal administrative agency established to regulate competitive activity and provide consumer protection. The Bureau of Competition is responsible for the regulation of competition, and the Bureau of Consumer Protection investigates and prosecutes consumer cases involving unfair or deceptive practices.

The Wheeler-Lea Act of 1938 amended the Federal Trade Commission Act and prohibited "unfair or deceptive acts or practices." The FTC has the responsibility to define unfair and deceptive activity through regulation. Industries regulated by local, state, or other federal authorities are exempt from FTC trade regulations (e.g., utilities, securities sales).

A. Trade Regulation Rules--A trade regulation is a rule promulgated by the FTC under its rulemaking authority. The regulations implement the FTC Act, policy, and practices of the FTC.

The FTC may investigate an entire industry to formulate rules for the protection of consumers. The FTC publishes the rules in the Federal Register to give the public and interested parties notice.

B. FTC Procedure--The FTC has the authority to bring charges against an alleged wrongdoer in either federal court or an administrative law court. The parties may attempt to settle with the FTC before the trial commences. Most businesses enter into a consent decree with the FTC, agreeing to an order restraining the unfair or deceptive activity.

1. Court Orders

a. Cease and Desist--If no consent decree is executed, the FTC may ask the administrative law judge to issue a cease and desist order requiring the defendant to stop violating the Act. The FTC may also obtain an injunction from a federal court to restrict a particular activity. The wrongdoer may be fined up to $10,000 per day.

b. Affirmative Disclosure--The FTC may issue an affirmative disclosure order to rectify past deceptive advertising. The affirmative disclosure order requires the defendant to make affirmative disclaimers in future advertisements.

c. Corrective Advertising--The FTC may order corrective advertising. Corrective advertising requires the defendant to make affirmative disclosures about the product and a statement that previous advertisements were deceptive or false (i.e., contrary to prior advertising).

d. Multiple Product--The multiple product order requires all future advertisements of a particular firm to be accurate. The FTC will only issue a multiple product order if the firm has a history of deceptive advertising.

C. Deceptive Advertising--The FTC defined deceptive advertising in 1983. Deceptive advertising is comprised of three elements: (1) a representation, omission, or practice, (2) likely to mislead consumers acting reasonably, and (3) which is material or significant. The FTC may bring an action against an advertiser if the advertisement could deceive consumers. Advertisements may deceive consumers, or have the potential to deceive consumers because false statements have been made, or the advertiser fails to disclose all the facts.

1. Methods of Deception

a. False Statements or Claims--Misrepresentations or false statements about a product's quality or performance are illegal. An advertisement which creates a false impression through explicit or implicit statements is considered deceptive.

b. Failure to Disclose Important Facts--Advertisements which make representations without disclosing important facts to consumers is deceptive. Consumers need to be apprised of the advantages and disadvantages of a product to make an informed decision.

    c.   <u>Statements That Are Less Than the Whole Truth</u>--Advertisements which take true statements out of context or are made in a way that is deliberately misleading are deceptive. The advertiser must be careful to explain statements which are subject to several interpretations. The advertiser has the responsibility to consider how a reasonable consumer will interpret the representations.

    d.   <u>Unsupported Claims</u>--Advertisements which make product claims must be supported by reasonable, scientific evidence. The claim must be one of fact and not opinion.

D.   <u>Other Deceptive Practices</u>--The broad language of the FTC Act allows the FTC to prosecute a wide range of deceptive acts.

   1.   <u>Bait and Switch</u>--Bait and switch is designed to lure a consumer into a retail outlet by advertising a very low price on an item. When the consumer arrives at the store, the sales personnel are instructed to switch the consumer to a higher-priced item. Bait advertising is illegal if the seller refuses to show the advertised item, does not have adequate quantities available, fails to promise or deliver the advertised item within a reasonable time, or discourages employees from selling the item.

   2.   <u>Deceptive Comparisons</u>--The Lanham Act of 1946 prohibits false descriptions about products or services. An advertisement which inaccurately compares the competitor's products to the defendant's products by making false statements about the quality or price is deceptive.

      Many forms of comparison are used by advertisers to generate sales of an item. Advertising the price in a way which leads a consumer to believe they are getting a bargain is deceptive, if the item is ordinarily sold at the same price.

      Sellers may not offer a product at a discount from the regular price if the product has not been sold at a higher regular price. If goods are offered "two for the price of one" or "buy one, get one free," the buyer must actually receive one item free. The seller cannot raise the price to cover the cost of the free item. The regular price of the item must be used for the sale.

The FTC Guidelines prohibit a seller from advertising a product as marked down from a higher price, unless the former price was genuine (e.g., was $7.95; now $5.95). The former price must have been offered for a substantial period of time as the regular price.

Clearance sales, introductory offers, close-outs, limited offers, a repossession sale, and a fire sale are all used to imply that a purchaser is getting a good deal. If the description of the sale is accurate, no deception exists. But, if for example, the seller has been going out of business since he or she opened the doors, the advertising is misleading.

3. Deceptive Testimonials and Endorsements--Deceptive testimonials and endorsements are illegal to promote products. The FTC requires the endorsement of a product by a celebrity to reflect the celebrity's honest opinion. Any implication that the U.S. government has endorsed a product is false, as the government does not endorse products.

II. Other Consumer Protection Laws

A. Fair Packaging and Labeling Act (FPLA)--The FPLA was enacted by Congress in 1966 and applies to anyone who packages or labels a consumer commodity. The Department of Commerce has been given the authority to enforce the Act with primary focus on items carried in supermarkets. The FPLA requires the label to contain the name of the manufacturer, address of the manufacturer, the name of the packer or distributor, net quantity, quantity in a specific manner, and size of servings.

The Department of Commerce, FTC, and the Food and Drug Administration all have the authority to promulgate rules under the FPLA.

B. Magnuson-Moss Warranty Act--The Magnuson-Moss Warranty Act was enacted in 1975 to protect consumers

purchasing items with warranties. The Act requires
a merchant to make certain disclosures if a written
express warranty is provided. The consumer, under
the Act, can bring legal action to compel the ful-
fillment of the warranty. The FTC or the U.S.
Attorney General may sue a violator to compel
adherence to the Act.

C. <u>Food, Drug, and Cosmetic Act (FDCA)</u>--The FDCA of
1938 prohibits the adulteration or misbranding of
various items. The Food and Drug Administration
(FDA) has the responsibility of enforcing the FDCA.
The FDA has the duty to notify the public of dangerous products through the press.

The FDA, as part of the Department of Health and
Human Services, establishes rules to ensure food,
drugs, and cosmetics are safe for use. The FDA can
impose fines which may result in imprisonment for
violations of the FDCA.

D. <u>Postal Fraud Statutes</u>--Congress has enacted two
statutes which prohibit mail fraud. One allows the
violator to be criminally prosecuted. The other
statute allows the postmaster to intercept, confiscate, or return mail used to defraud another.

E. <u>Mail-Order Houses</u>--The postal service and the FTC
regulate the operation of mail-order houses. A
negative option plan which requires a consumer to
respond negatively in order to not receive a product
is regulated by the FTC. The book, record, videotape, or compact disc club must disclose all the
terms of the agreement and allow enough time for a
member to accept or reject the item and include a
rejection form.

The FTC rule requires all items ordered from mail-
order houses to be shipped within 30 days or notify
the buyer of the right to cancel, receive a refund,
or accept the delay.

F. <u>Interstate Land Sales Full Disclosure Act (ILSFDA)</u>--
The ILSFDA is enforced by the Office of Interstate
Land Sales Registration within the Department of
Housing and Urban Development (HUD). Developers of
undeveloped land for homesites are required to fully
disclose their financial condition. The developer
must file a registration statement with the agency
and gain approval before soliciting any sales.

The Act requires purchasers to receive a copy of the property report before they sign a contract for sale or lease.

G. <u>Consumer Product Safety Act (CPSA)</u>--The CPSA was enacted in 1972 and is enforced by the Consumer Product Safety Commission (CPSC) to protect consumers from hazardous products. The CPSC has the responsibility to do research on product safety and assimilate data on injuries caused by consumer products. The CPSC has broad authority under the Act to establish construction standards and performance standards for finished products. The CPSC may ban a consumer product that is extremely hazardous to consumers.

H. <u>Door-to-Door Sales</u>--The FTC has promulgated a three-day cooling period for door-to-door sales, where the consumer has the right to rescind a transaction valued at over $25. The door-to-door salesperson must notify consumers of their right to cancel the sale within three days.

Study Questions

Fill-in-the-Blank Questions

Harold, the owner of a stereo outlet store, advertises Sony compact disc players at a price of $199, with the representation that the price is "one-third off of our regular price, under our list price, and $100 under comparable disc players in the area." Harold has never sold Sony compact disc players before, and dealers do not sell at the list price in the area.

Harold has violated the Federal Trade Commission Act by
_____.
      (deceptive advertising/unfair competitive methods)

The FTC may order Harold to cease and desist his advertising
through _____.
            (an administrative order/the federal court)

The FTC must prove the advertisement _____ deceive
consumers.   (did/could)

True-False Questions

1. The Federal Trade Commission has the authority to issue a trade regulation rule. ___T___

2. The FTC's Bureau of Competition protects consumers from anticompetitive activity. ___T___ F _protects competitors_

3. All industries fall under the authority of the Federal Trade Commission's authority. ___f___ _not heavily regulated industries_

4. Failure to disclose important facts may be deceptive advertising. ___T___

5. The Magnuson-Moss Warranty Act was enacted in 1975 and applies to consumer sales where the seller has given a written express warranty. ___T___

6. The Interstate Land Sales Full Disclosure Act applies to all residential sales. ___f___ _only residential sales which cross state line_

7. The consumer in a door-to-door sale has five business days to rescind the transaction. ___F___ _3_ _$25._

8. The Consumer Product Safety Commission has the authority to ban an extremely hazardous product. ___T___

9. The FTC can order an advertiser to correct deceptive advertising. ___T___

10. The FTC may bring charges against a business in federal court. ___T___

Multiple-Choice Questions

1. The Federal Trade Commission under the authority of the Wheeler-Lea Act has the power to prosecute which of the following?

   I.   unfair or deceptive acts
   II. deceptive advertising
   III. regulate anticompetitive activity

   a. I only
   b. I and II
   c. I, II, and III
   d. I and III

2. Which of the following divisions of the FTC monitors advertising and labeling practices?

    a. Bureau of Competition
    b. Bureau of Deception
    c. Bureau of Consumer Protection
    d. none of the above

3. Which of the following is exempt from FTC trade regulations? *heavily regulated firms*

    a. a used car dealership
    b. a new car dealership
    c. household consumer products retailer
    d. an investment banking firm

4. Which of the following FTC orders requires the seller to make all future advertisements accurate for all the firm's product?

p. 347

    a. multiple product
    b. corrective advertising
    c. affirmative disclosure
    d. cease and desist

5. The Federal Trade Commission is headed by:

    a. an executive director.
    b. a president.
    c. 6 commissioners.
    d. four commissioners and a chairperson.

6. Sears, Roebuck and Co. advertised the Lady Kenmore dishwasher as completely eliminating the need for prescraping and prerinsing, characterizing the machine as the "freedom maker." The FTC determined the claim to be false. Sears, Roebuck and Co. challenged the FTC judgment. Which of the following did the FTC order?

    a. cease and desist
    b. multiple product
    c. corrective advertising
    d. none of the above

7. When the United States Court of Appeals reviews a Federal Trade Commission order, the court will give the order:

    a. some consideration.
    b. due deference.

c. substantial respect.
d. no consideration.

8. If an advertiser challenges an FTC administrative court
    ruling in a judicial court, the FTC must prove which of
    the following to win the case?

    a. The advertisement deceived consumers.
    b. The advertisement reached 1 million consumers.
    c. The advertisement caused damages to the consumer.
    d. The advertisement could deceive consumers.

9. Which of the following is/are not an element(s) of decep-
    tive advertising?

    I.   a representation, omission, or practice

    II. the representation, omission, or practice is
         material

    III. the representation was grossly false

    a. I only
    b. I and II
    c. II only
    d. III only

10. Which of the following statements made in advertisements
    would most likely be considered deceptive or misleading
    by the FTC?

    I.   Parker pens are guaranteed for life.

    II. Cranberry Cocktail Juice has more food energy than
         orange juice or tomato juice.

    III. Cigarettes are just what the doctor ordered.

    a. I only
    b. I and II
    c. I, II, and III
    d. II and III

11. Warner-Lambert manufactured Listerine mouthwash and
    advertised that it prevented, cured, and alleviated the
    common cold. The FTC requires that product claims be
    supported by:

    a. reasonable, scientific evidence.
    b. reasonable evidence.

c. substantial evidence.
d. none of the above.

12. Valley Eye Wear, Inc. has advertised contact lenses at $19.95, including the eye examination. When customers come to the store to purchase the specially priced contact lenses, the salesperson is instructed to say the contact lenses are all sold out but a little more expensive brand is available. The FTC decides to prosecute Valley Eye Wear for which of the following offenses?

a. door-to-door sales
b. deceptive comparison
c. bait and switch
d. false labeling

13. World Sporting Goods Store advertises jogging suits on sale: "Buy one, get one free this week only." World decides to eliminate their entire stock of jogging suits and running apparel. The price of the sale item is the regular price of the suits. Which of the following FTC provisions has been violated?

a. bait and switch
b. deceptive comparisons
c. Lanham Act
d. none of the above

14. Mary Carter Paint Company sells interior and exterior paint in gallon cans. The paint is advertised as follows: "Buy one, get the second can free." The marketing program of the company has been to always sell paint in quantities of two. The company did not offer single gallon cans of paint. No regular price for a single can has ever been established by the company. Has the Mary Carter Paint Company violated the FTC Act?

a. Yes, because the second can is not really free.
b. Yes, because not all consumers need two cans of paint.
c. No, because the advertisement is true.
d. No, because the act does not apply.

15. Which of the following are FTC requirements placed on a celebrity when endorsing a product?

I. The endorser must be a user of the product.

II. Endorsement must reflect the celebrity's honest opinion.

III. The endorser can only be paid a specified amount.

a. I and II
b. II and III
c. I and III
d. I, II, and III

16. Stone Pizza Company produces frozen pizzas of all sizes for sale to independent grocery stores. Stone is required under the Fair Packaging and Labeling Act to do which of the following?

a. sell at a specified price published in the Federal Register
b. sell a specified quantity of pizzas
c. list their name and address
d. all of the above

17. The Consumer Product Safety Commission was charged by Congress to accomplish which of the following?

I. conduct research on product safety

II. analyze data on injuries related to consumer products

III. disseminate injury data about consumer products

a. I only
b. I and II
c. I, II, and III
d. I and III

18. Steve Walton calls the A to Z Residential Siding Company to obtain some prices on new siding for his home. The salesperson will not give a quote over the telephone but sets up an appointment to come to Steve's home. The salesperson quotes Steve what seems to be a reasonable price for siding. Steve signs the contract on Tuesday. Wednesday morning Steve decides he does not want siding after all but is going to build a new home instead. Steve calls to cancel the order with A to Z and is informed a "contract is a contract" and no cancellations are accepted. Steve brings his case to the FTC with what result?

    a.   Steve will win and be able to cancel the contract.

    b.   Steve will win, but under state law and not FTC rules.

    c.   Steve will lose because the sale was not a door-to-door sale.

    d.   none of the above.

p.364

19. The state of Florida has determined an advertisement to be legal, but the FTC claims the advertisement is misleading. If the FTC prosecutes the advertiser, what will be the result?

    a.   The advertiser will win because of state law.

    b.   The advertiser will lose because the FTC ruling will preempt the state determination.

    c.   The court will refuse to hear the case.

    d.   None of the above.

20. Which of the following agencies promulgate rules under the Fair Packaging and Labeling Act?

    I.   Department of Commerce
    II.   Federal Trade Commission
    III. Food and Drug Administration

    a.   I only
    b.   I and II
    c.   I, II, and III
    d.   III only

21. The Food and Drug Administration (FDA) is responsible to enforce the Food, Drug, and Cosmetic Act of 1938. The FDA is part of the _____.

    a.   Department of Health and Human Services
    b.   Department of Housing and Urban Development
    c.   Federal Trade Commission
    d.   Consumer Product Safety Commission

360

22. Which of the following is an unfair or deceptive act or practice prohibited by the Federal Trade Commission?

    I.   the mark-down of the price of a product from $9.95 to $4.95 when the regular price was $9.95

    II.   an advertisement which implies the U.S. government endorses the product

    III. an advertisement of a fire sale but no fire ever occurred

a. I only
b. I and II
c. II and III
d. I, II, and III

23. The Food and Drug Administration must approve a drug before it is marketed in the United States to consumers. The Commissioner of the FDA considers a drug safe when _____ .

    I. it has no adverse effects on the consumer

   II. no incidents of sickness have resulted from its use

 III. when the expected therapeutic gain justifies the risk entailed by its use

a. I only
b. II only
c. III only
d. II and III

24. Jim Suitor ordered a videotape from an out-of-state mail-order house. The company advertised on television and the radio. Jim has not received the tape after 45 days. What are Jim's rights under the FTC rule?

a. Jim may cancel and receive a refund.
b. Jim may cancel but must take a credit.
c. Jim has no rights.
d. Jim must wait to receive the item, then bring a legal action.

25. Under postal fraud statutes, the Postmaster General may do which of the following when a fraudulent seller's mail is involved?

    I. intercept the mail
  II. confiscate the mail
 III. return it

a. I only
b. I and II
c. I, II, and III
d. II and III

Essay Question

1. Wonder Bread was advertised as building strong bodies
    twelve ways. The company made several other statements
    which implied the product was responsible for the growth
    of children. The television advertisement actually
    showed a child growing into an adult. The bread con-
    tained only the usual ingredients, and no proof existed
    that Wonder Bread caused growth in children. Does the
    advertisement violate the Federal Trade Commission Act?

Answers to Study Questions

Fill-in-the-Blank Questions

Harold has violated the Federal Trade Commission Act by <u>decep-
tive advertising</u>. (p. 347)

The FTC may order Harold to cease and desist his advertising
through <u>an</u> <u>administrative order</u>. (p. 347)

The FTC must prove the advertisement <u>could</u> deceive consumers.
(p. 350)

True-False Questions

1. True (p. 344)

2. False. The FTC Bureau of Competition protects competi-
    tors. (p. 344)

3. False. Heavily regulated industries are not under the
    authority of the FTC. (p. 350)

4. True (p. 351)

5. True (p. 360)

6. False. The Act only applies to residential sales which
    cross state lines. (p. 362)

7. False. The FTC rule allows the consumer 3 days to re-
    scind a transaction valued at more than $25. (p. 364)

8. True (p. 364)

9. True (p. 347)

10.   True (p. 347)

Multiple-Choice Questions

1.	c (p. 344)		14.	a (p. 357)
2.	c (p. 344)		15.	a (p. 359)
3.	d (p. 350)		16.	c (p. 359)
4.	a (p. 347)		17.	c (p. 363)
5.	d (p. 346)		18.	c (p. 364)
6.	b (p. 350)		19.	b (p. 351)
7.	b (p. 348)		20.	c (p. 360)
8.	d (p. 350)		21.	a (p. 360)
9.	d (p. 350)		22.	c (p. 355)
10.	c (p. 350)		23.	c (p. 360)
11.	a (p. 353)		24.	a (p. 362)
12.	c (p. 356)		25.	c (p. 362)
13.	d (pp. 355-359)			

Essay Question

1.   Yes, the FTC held the advertisement falsely portrayed
     Wonder Bread as an extraordinary food for children's
     growth.   The case was appealed to the Second Circuit of
     Appeals.   The Second Circuit affirmed the decision of the
     FTC with some modification.

     The FTC reasoned that the advertisement had the capacity
     to deceive children and parents.   (pp. 350, 351)

Chapter 15
Property Law and Computer Law

12 Q.

Major Concepts

The protection of property is deeply rooted in our American culture. The United States Constitution in the Fifth and Fourteenth Amendments protects individuals from having their property taken away by the government without Due Process of Law. The government may take real property for a public use as long as just compensation is paid.

Property can be classified as real, personal, tangible, and intangible. Real property is considered land and anything permanently affixed to the land, including fixtures. Personal property is any item which is moveable and not considered real property. Tangible property has a physical presence.

Ownership of real property is called an estate in land. Estates in land may be possessory or nonpossessory. Possessory estates in land can be divided into freehold and nonfreehold. Freehold estates are normally associated with the fee simple absolute which gives the landowner the total bundle of rights. Nonfreehold estates are associated with leases and the land-lord-tenant relationship. Nonpossessory estates are where a party has rights to use but not possess the property, such as an easement or covenant.

Real and personal property can be owned by two or more parties as concurrent owners. These types of ownership interests provide each party with full use of the property, subject only to the other parties' usage. Four types of concurrent interests are tenancy in common, joint tenancy, tenancy by the entirety, and community property.

Personal property may be acquired in a variety of ways.   In some cases, the mere possession of personal property gives the possessor ownership. Most acquisitions of personal property are by purchase. Personal property may be transferred by a valid will or through inheritance.

The protection of computer property has required the enactment of new statutes. The sale of the hardware and software together comes under Article 2 of the Uniform Commercial Code (UCC). The sale of only the software has created questions of whether the UCC or general contract law applies. The UCC generally provides greater protection for buyers. With the proliferation of computer technology, the body of law regulating computer usage will continue to expand.

Chapter Outline

I.   Real Property--Real property is the land, air space, materials underneath the surface, and anything permanently attached to the land. All other property is classified as personal.

Personal property can become real property by permanent affixation of the personal property to the real property. This type of real property is known as a fixture. Fixtures are transferred along with the sale of the land. For example, the sale of a house will include the garage, kitchen cabinets, plumbing, windows, built-in dishwasher, central air conditioner, and electric lights. To determine if an item is a fixture, the court will consider the following six factors: (1) the nature of the property; (2) the manner in which the property is annexed to the realty; (3) the purpose for which the annexation is made; (4) the intention of the annexing party to make the property a part of the realty; (5) the degree of difficulty and extent of any loss involved in removing the property from the realty; and (6) the damage to the severed property which such removal would cause.

A.   Real Property Rights--Ownership of real property consists of a bundle of rights. The owner may transfer the full bundle or only a portion of the bundle. The two most important rights of property ownership are the right of possession and the right of disposition by sale, gift, lease, or will.

1.   Air and Subsurface Rights--The owner of real
     property historically owned unlimited air space
     above the property. Since the invention of the
     airplane and commercial air travel, the property
     owner's rights have been cut back.

     The owner of property may divide the surface
     rights from the subsurface rights. An owner may
     transfer to buyers the air space, surface space,
     or the subsurface.

B.   Estates in Land--Ownership rights in real property
     are called estates and are classified as either
     freehold or nonfreehold.

     1.   Freehold Estates--A freehold estate allows the
          owner to possess the property for an undeter-
          mined time period.

          a.   Estates in Fee--There are three major types
               of estates in fee: fee simple absolute, fee
               simple defeasible, and fee simple subject to
               a condition subsequent.

               (1) Fee Simple Absolute--The fee simple
                    absolute is the highest estate in land
                    an individual can obtain. The fee
                    simple absolute owner may use the land
                    for any legal purpose as long as the
                    use does not interfere with another
                    property owner, violate zoning regula-
                    tion, or building codes. The owner may
                    transfer the property by deed, will,
                    gift, or sale.

               (2) Fee Simple Defeasible--The fee simple
                    defeasible is an estate in land which
                    can be terminated by the happening of
                    an event. The transferor may reserve
                    the right to reacquire the property if
                    a specified event occurs. The trans-
                    feror (grantor) retains a future
                    interest which may come into being at a
                    future date (e.g., To Robert Smith and
                    his heirs so long as the land is used
                    for a school). Upon the happening of
                    the stated event, the land automati-
                    cally reverts back to the transferor.
                    This is called the possibility of
                    reverter. The words "so long as,"

"until," or "during" are used to create the fee simple defeasible.

    (3)   <u>Fee Simple Subject to a Condition Subsequent</u>--A fee simple subject to a condition subsequent is an interest in land which may be terminated if a stated event occurs and the grantor takes affirmative steps to reacquire the land.

The fee simple subject to a condition subsequent is usually created by the words "on condition that," "but if," "on the express condition that," or "provided that." (e.g., "To John Jackson and his heirs, but if intoxicating beverages are ever sold on the property, the grantor has the right to reenter and repossess the land.") The grantor has the right of reentry if the condition occurs. This right is called the power of termination.

    b.   <u>Life Estate</u>--A life estate is an estate in land for the duration of the life of one or more human beings. At the termination of the life estate, the land either goes back to the grantor or to another person (e.g., "to John Jackson for life"). The life tenant has the same rights as a fee simple except he or she may not waste the property. Most life estates are measured by the life of the life tenant. During the life estate, the life tenant may transfer his or her interest. The life tenant must repair the property if necessary.

    2.   <u>Nonfreehold Estates</u>--A nonfreehold estate is defined as a possessory interest in the land without ownership. Nonfreehold estates are called leaseholds or tenancies. Most tenancies involve a landlord-tenant relationship.

The landlord is the owner of real property who enters into a contract called a lease with the tenant for use and possession of the premises. The tenant is required to pay rent and return the premises in good condition at the termination of the lease. The tenant has the right to

possess the property and to quiet enjoyment.
The landlord is required to make major repairs
of the property, while the tenant is obligated
to maintain and make minor repairs of the
premises.

a.   Types of Tenancies--There are four different
     types of tenancies giving the tenant the
     exclusive right of possession.

     (1)   Tenancy for Years--A tenancy for years
           can be oral or in writing, in which the
           property is leased for a specified pe-
           riod of time, such as one month,
           6 months, or one year. The tenancy
           automatically terminates at the end of
           the specified period time.

     (2)   Tenancy from Period to Period--A ten-
           ancy from period to period is for a
           fixed period of time but is automati-
           cally renewed, unless properly termi-
           nated. The parties are usually
           required to give 30-days notice before
           the end of the period if they desire to
           end the lease; otherwise, the lease
           continues for another period of time.

     (3)   Tenancy at Will--Under the tenancy at
           will, either party may terminate the
           lease at any time. The tenancy con-
           tinues only as long as the parties both
           agree to the arrangement.

     (4)   Tenancy by Sufferance--A tenancy by
           sufferance is created when a tenant
           wrongfully holds over on the premises
           after the lease has expired. The ten-
           ant is retaining possession of the
           property without the permission of the
           landlord. The landlord may demand
           immediate eviction of the tenant. The
           landlord may seek legal recourse to
           have the tenant ejected and obtain dam-
           ages.

C.   Transfer of Ownership--The owner of real property
     has the power to convey it through a number of mech-
     anisms.

1. Transfer by Inheritance or Will--If the owner of
    property has a valid will which covers the real
    property, the real property will transfer
    through the probate court according to the will.
    If the will does not include the real property
    or no will exists, the real property will be
    inherited by the heirs.

2. Eminent Domain--The government has the authority
    to take private property for a public use
    through condemnation proceedings. This is known
    as the power of eminent domain. If the govern-
    ment takes private property for a public use
    (e.g., highways, post office), the Fifth Amend-
    ment of the U.S. Constitution requires the gov-
    ernment to pay just compensation to the property
    owner. The taking by the government need not be
    for an indefinite period of time for the prop-
    erty owner to receive just compensation.

3. Adverse Possession--Adverse possession is the
    process of obtaining legal title to land by pos-
    sessing it over the objection of the true owner
    for a specified period of time. A party must
    take control of property of another in an open,
    hostile, notorious manner for a continuous peri-
    od of time. The specific period of time is
    stated in the state statute and ranges from
    three to thirty years. Once the period of time
    has lapsed, the adverse possessor must file an
    action to quiet title to the property. The
    court will convey the property to the adverse
    possessor if all the requirements have been ful-
    filled.

4. Conveyance by Deed--The title to real property
    is known as a deed. A deed is used to transfer
    ownership. Deeds must be written and signed by
    the grantor(s) (seller, owner), delivered to the
    grantee (buyer), and contain a legal description
    of the property.

    a. Types of Deeds

        (1) General Warranty Deeds--The general
            warranty deed provides three warran-
            ties: that the seller has the right
            and power to convey the property, that
            no liens or encumbrances exist which
            are not known to the buyer, and that

the buyer will have quiet enjoyment of
the property.

The general warranty deed gives the
buyer the most protection in the purchase of real property.

> (2) <u>Special Warranty Deed</u>--A special war-
> ranty deed provides less protection
> than a general warranty deed. The
> grantor warrants that he or she has not
> done anything to encumber the property.
> The seller does not give any assurances
> that previous owners have kept the
> title free of defects.

> (3) <u>Quitclaim Deed</u>--The quitclaim deed con-
> veys only what the grantor's interest
> in the property is at the time of the
> conveyance. The grantor makes no as-
> surances that the grantee is receiving
> anything at all.

> (4) <u>Recording Statutes</u>--A recording statute
> is a state law allowing property owners
> to make their title part of the public
> record and puts all third parties on
> notice of the owner's interest. Deeds,
> mortgages, liens, and judgments are
> recorded by a government official for a
> nominal fee.

> The record allows other parties inter-
> ested in a parcel of real property to
> search the records for defects of title
> (i.e., clouds on the title). A bank,
> before lending money to a home buyer,
> will make sure the title to the prop-
> erty is free of defects. The bank
> wants to be assured first priority in
> the event the buyer defaults (by re-
> cording a mortgage).

D. <u>Other Real Property Interests</u>

1. <u>Easement</u>--An easement is the right to use
   another's property. The easement is considered
   a nonpossessory interest. Utility companies
   usually have an easement for the placing of
   water pipes, electric wires, sewage pipes, and

telephone wires. Private parties may create an easement by deed, will, or contract. If John's driveway is partially on Fred's property, Fred may grant John an easement. Otherwise, Fred has the right to demand John remove the driveway from Fred's property. The easement is usually recorded and continues to run with the land.

2. Covenants--A covenant is an agreement or promise to do or not to do something. A covenant is attached to the land and usually places some restrictions on the land. The restrictions are binding on all subsequent owners of the property. A covenant is usually recorded.

E. Zoning--Local government has the authority to restrict land use in its jurisdiction through zoning laws. Zoning laws attempt to allow the development of land in an orderly and planned manner. Local governments have wide discretion to restrict land use under their police powers. The police power may be exercised to advance public health, safety, and the welfare of citizens. A city zoning board may designate certain areas for residential use, industrial use, or recreational use.

II. Concurrent Real and Personal Property Ownership--Concurrent ownership is the simultaneous ownership by two or more persons of a parcel of land or personal property. There are four types of concurrent interests: tenancy in common, joint tenancy, tenancy by the entirety, and community property.

A. Tenancy in Common--Each owner has a distinct proportional undivided interest in the property which is freely transferable and subject to the claims of creditors. Two or more persons own an interest in the property, which upon the death of a tenant the interest passes to his or her heirs. The heirs become tenants in common with the original owners. The tenants are not required to own equal interests in the property. The tenants have the right to use the whole property, subject to the equal right of a co-tenant (e.g., Able and Baker own a farm as co-tenants).

B. Joint Tenancy--In a joint tenancy, two or more people own an undivided interest in the property. The joint tenants must have received their interest at the same time, through the same instrument which transferred identical rights to possession and enjoyment to each joint tenant. The conveyance must specify the parties will receive the property as joint tenants; otherwise, a tenancy in common will result.

A joint tenancy carries the distinguishing characteristic of the right of survivorship. The right of survivorship requires that when one joint tenant dies the other joint tenants automatically succeed to the descendant's interest equally. The heirs do not receive the joint tenant's interest at his or her death because it passes to the other surviving joint tenants. The interest passes outside of the descendant's will, if any. If a joint tenant transfers his or her interest before death to another party, the party becomes a tenant in common with the original parties.

C.   Tenancy by the Entirety--A tenancy by the entirety can only be held by a husband and wife. Neither spouse can sell or transfer their interest without the other spouse's consent. The tenancy by the entirety has the right of survivorship. The tenancy by the entirety can be terminated by death of either spouse, divorce, or mutual agreement.

D.   Community Property--Community property laws have been enacted in Arizona, California, Idaho, Louisiana, Nevada, New Mexico, Texas, Washington, and Wisconsin. Community property laws apply only to married couples. All property acquired during the marriage is owned by each spouse in an undivided one-half interest. A spouse can transfer his or her one-half interest to another person by will. Property owned by a spouse prior to the marriage is considered separate property and the sole possession of that spouse.

III.   Personal Property--Personal property is property which is moveable and capable of being possessed. Personal property may be tangible (has physical presence, such as a car or boat) or intangible (no physical presence, such as stocks and bonds). Personal property is everything that is not considered real property.

A.   Ownership of Personal Property--Personal property can be acquired by possession, purchase, production, gift, will or inheritance, accession, and confusion.

1. <u>Possession</u>--Possession of personal property usually means the possessor is the owner with superior rights to the property. In cases like wildlife, lost or mislaid property, and abandoned property, possession is very important.

   a. <u>Mislaid, Lost, and Abandoned Property</u>--Mislaid property is property the owner has inadvertently forgotten. The owner of the place where the property was mislaid is the caretaker of the property until the owner comes to claim it.

      Lost property is property the owner involuntarily has left somewhere by neglect, carelessness, or inadvertence. A finder of lost property may claim title to the property against anyone except the true owner. The true owner may demand the property returned.

      Abandoned property has been discarded by the owner with no intention of keeping title. The finder of abandoned property has good title as against all the world, even the original owner.

2. <u>Purchase</u>--The transfer of personal property by the terms of a contract.

3. <u>Production</u>--The production of an item by invention or manufacture gives the producer ownership of the item.

4. <u>Gifts</u>--A gift is a voluntary transfer of personal property delivered to the recipient with the intent to make a gift. Upon delivery, the recipient obtains title to the property.

5. <u>Will or Inheritance</u>--A party may transfer personal property through a valid will upon death. The bequests will be carried out by the probate court. If a party dies without a will, they die intestate, and state law will determine how the property of the decedent is distributed.

6. <u>Accession</u>--When a party adds value to another party's personal property, accession occurs. The owner of the personal property gains the improvement.

7.   Confusion--The mixing of fungible goods is known
     as confusion. When confusion occurs, the par-
     ties become tenants in common of the personal
     property mixed.

B.   Bailments--A bailment is created when a bailor
     (usually the owner) delivers personal property over
     to a bailee under an agreement for a specific
     purpose (e.g., valet service at a fine restaurant).
     The bailee does not receive title to the property.
     A bailee is obligated to take reasonable care of the
     personal property and return it to the bailor as
     directed. Both the bailee and the bailor have du-
     ties and rights in the relationship.

IV. Computer Law--Laws dealing with the use and transfer of
     computers is of recent origin. Congress and the states
     have attempted to protect the legal user of computer
     materials from theft and misappropriation.

     Computer law can be divided into the laws which protect
     the software and those that protect the hardware. The
     software is the programming involved with a computer
     system. Software may coordinate the operation of the
     computer or solve particular user problems (e.g., word
     processing, spreadsheet).

     The hardware is the equipment, such as the printer,
     screen, and central processing unit.

A.   Uniform Commercial Code Application--Article 2 of
     the UCC applies to the sale of goods (tangible per-
     sonal property). If only the hardware is sold, the
     UCC applies to the sale. If the software is sold or
     provided with the hardware, a sale of goods has
     occurred and Article 2 applies. A question exists
     that if only the software is sold, does the UCC
     apply? Is the software a good or a service? Most
     courts consider it a sale of goods when a store
     sells the software under a sales contract. If a
     program is specifically written for a buyer, the
     courts are divided on whether it is a sale of goods
     or a service. If considered a service, the UCC does
     not apply, and the court will apply general contract
     law, which tends to favor the seller.

     If the transfer of a computer program is done by a
     lease or license, the UCC does not apply because a
     sale has not occurred. The court may utilize a
     variety of legal theories to grant UCC protection of
     licenses and leases.

1. <u>Software Warranties</u>--If the sale of the software is considered a sale of goods, then the UCC warranty provisions apply. The seller of software may give an express warranty, implied warranty of merchantability, or an implied warranty of fitness for a particular purpose.

B. <u>Protection of Property Rights in Computer Programs</u>-- A developer of a new software program may seek protection through patents, trademarks, copyrights, and the doctrine of trade secrets.

1. <u>Patent Law</u>--Computer software may receive patent protection from the U.S. Patent and Trademark Office. An inventor of software can apply to the U.S. Patent Office for protection. The patent gives the inventor the exclusive right to use, make, and market the software for seventeen years.

2. <u>Copyright Law</u>--A copyright provides the owner with protection for the life of the author plus fifty years. Computer programs may receive copyright protection under the Federal Copyright Act of 1976.

3. <u>Trademark Law</u>--The Trademark Revision Act allows trademark holders to receive protection. A trademark holder may register under the act prior to use.

<u>Study Questions</u>

<u>Fill-in-the-Blank Questions</u>

Burt Lund purchased a new hot water heater for his home from Harrison Heating and Supply. Burt paid an extra fee to have it installed. The hot water heater was delivered and installed by the Harrison serviceman. The hot water heater was bolted to the basement floor.

The hot water heater at the time of Burt's purchase was _____ property.
   (real/personal)

Burt's residence and anything permanently affixed to it is considered _____ property.
       (real/personal)

Personal property which becomes part of the real property is known as a(n) _____.
(fixture/easement)

Burt sells his home to Barney. If Barney received the highest estate possible, Burt must have conveyed a _____
_____.   (life estate/
fee simple absolute)

True-False Questions

1. Property may be classified as real or personal, tangible or intangible, and fixtures. ___T___

2. Once property is classified as personal, it must always be classified as such. ___f___

3. Examples of intangible property are copyrights, patents, and stocks. ___T___

4. Two or more persons may own the same real property. ___T___

5. A tenancy by the entirety may be created only if the owners of the property are husband and wife. ___T___

6. A tenancy in common is a co-ownership of property with the right of survivorship. ___f___   joint tenancy

7. The surface and subsurface rights for a parcel of real property may be sold separately. ___t___

8. A life estate may be granted only for the life of the grantor. ___f___

9. The hardware of a computer when sold is considered the sale of goods under Article 2 of the Uniform Commercial Code. ___T___

10. The law does not provide copyright protection for newly invented software programs. ___f___

Multiple-Choice Questions

1. Property rights are protected by the United States Constitution under which of the following amendments?

    a. First
    b. Second
    c. Fourth
    d. Fifth

2. Which of the following powers of government regulate the use of property?

    a. police power   *Zoning*
    b. Uniform Commercial Code
    c. enumerated
    d. none of the above

3. Real property is defined as which of the following?

    I. land surface and items attached
   II. air space
  III. materials underneath the land

    a. I only
    b. I and II
    c. I, II, and III
    d. I and III

4. A tree which has been cut down and sold to a lumber company is:

    a. real property.
    b. personal property.
    c. intangible property.
    d. a fixture.

5. Which of the following is not intangible property?

    a. stocks
    b. bonds
    c. annuities
    d. cattle

6. Patrick Ritzsel purchased a ten-year-old home from John Johnson, the owner. Patrick signed the contract and gave John $10,000 earnest money. The seller, John Johnson, promised to convey the real property to Patrick Ritzsel on the closing date. Which of the following will be transferred as part of the real estate?

    I. gas furnace to heat the home
   II. draperies in the kitchen
   III. throw rugs in the bedrooms

a. I only
b. I and II
c. I, II, and III
d. I and III

7. Which of the following is <u>not</u> a consideration in deter-
    mining whether an item is a fixture?

    a. nature of the property
    b. manner in which the property is annexed to the realty
    c. the cost of the item
    d. intention of the annexing party

8. Which of the following types of concurrent ownership does
    <u>not</u> give a co-owner the rights of survivorship?

      I. Tenancy in Common
     II. Joint Tenancy
    III. Tenancy by the Entirety

    a. I only
    b. I and II
    c. I, II, and III
    d. II and III

9. Dick and Jennifer purchased a new house in Atlanta after
    Dick was transferred by his company. Dick and Jennifer
    received the deed as joint tenants from the grantor.
    Dick has a valid will which gives all his real and per-
    sonal property to his younger sister, Karen. Jennifer's
    will gives all her real and personal property to her
    younger brother, Dave. Two years after moving to
    Atlanta, Dick is killed in an auto accident. Who will
    receive Dick's interest in the house?

    a. Karen
    b. Dave
    c. Jennifer
    d. none of the above

10. Which of the following type(s) of concurrent ownership
     does not allow a co-owner to sell his or her interest in
     the property?

      I. Tenancy in Common
     II. Joint Tenancy
    III. Tenancy by the Entirety

    a. I only
    b. II only

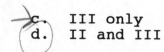

c.   III only
d.   II and III

11. Tom Klag conveys Blackacre to Sherry Smith by the follow-
     ing language: "To Sherry Smith for life and then to Dan
     Jarvis." What type of estate has Sherry Smith obtained?

     a.   fee simple absolute
     b.   life estate
     c.   fee simple defeasible
     d.   periodic tenancy

12. Refer to question 11. Upon the death of Sherry Smith,
     Blackacre goes to Dan Jarvis. Dan has obtained:

     a.   a life estate.
     b.   a fee simple defeasible.
     c.   a periodic tenancy.
     d.   a fee simple absolute.

13. Rex is a wealthy oil man from Texas who has acquired hun-
     dreds of acres of prime land in Dallas. Rex has no need
     for a ten-acre parcel located in a residential area of
     Dallas. Rex deeds the ten-acre parcel to the school
     district by the following language: "To the Dallas
     School District as long as the land is used as an
     elementary school." What type of estate has the Dallas
     School District received?

     a.   nonfreehold
     b.   fee simple defeasible
     c.   fee simple subject to a condition subsequent
     d.   fee simple absolute

14. Refer to question 13. Rex, as the grantor, retains which
     of the following?

     a.   future interest
     b.   fee simple absolute
     c.   life estate
     d.   none of the above

15. Refer to question 13. Assume the Dallas School District
     closes the school due to a lack of enrollments. The
     school district sells the building to a real estate
     developer who uses the building as a warehouse. What are
     Rex's rights?

     I.   Rex has no rights to the property.
     II. The property automatically reverts to Rex.

III. The property escheats to the state, but Rex may redeem it.

a. I only
b. II only
c. III only
d. II and III

16. Laura conveys Blackacre to Linsey Parker, using the following language: "To Linsey Parker and her heirs on the condition that the property is used as a flower shop, and if used for any other business, the grantor has the right to reenter and repossess the land." Linsey Parker has obtained:

a. fee simple subject to a condition subsequent
b. fee simple defeasible
c. life estate
d. fee simple absolute

17. Refer to question 16. Linsey Parker runs into financial difficulties in the floral business. Linsey remodels the shop into a restaurant with a 50s decor. The restaurant proves to be very successful for Linsey. Laura may do which of the following?

a. reenter and retake the property from Linsey
b. reenter and obtain all the profits Linsey made from the restaurant
c. Laura has no rights to the property
d. the property automatically is reverted back to Laura at the time it was remodeled into a restaurant

18. Which of the following is a nonfreehold estate?

a. tenancy in common
b. life estate
c. tenancy at will
d. tenancy by the entirety

19. Daniel owns a cabin in the mountains with twenty acres of wooded property. Daniel has not been able to visit the property for several years. One weekend, Daniel drives to his mountain cabin only to find Jim and Carla occupying the premises. Jim refuses to allow Daniel on the property, stating he and Carla are the new owners. Jim files a lawsuit the next day to quiet the title. Jim is attempting to gain possession of Daniel's property through:

    a.   conveyance.
    b.   quitclaim deed.
    c.   eviction.
    d.   adverse possession.

20. Peter owns twenty-five acres of wooded property located
    on a large lake. Peter has a fishing boat docked on the
    lake in front of his cabin. Peter's neighbor, Ron, de-
    sires to cross over Peter's property occasionally to get
    to the lake. Peter grants Ron a right-of-way to drive
    across the property to the lake. Peter has given Ron:

    a.   a covenant.
    b.   a life estate.
    c.   an easement.
    d.   a quitclaim.

21. During their lunch hour, Steve and Jack ate lunch at a
    local restaurant. Steve left his hat on the coat rack at
    the restaurant. The restaurant owner decided to keep the
    hat for himself. Steve, one day while walking down the
    sidewalk, sees the restaurant owner wearing his hat.
    Steve takes the hat away from the restaurant owner and a
    fight ensues. Who has superior rights to the hat?

    a.   Steve   *misplaced, not abandoned*
    b.   Jack
    c.   the restaurant owner
    d.   the city

22. Refer to question 21. The hat, after Steve left it at
    the restaurant, is considered which of the following?

    a.   mislaid property
    b.   lost property
    c.   abandoned property
    d.   none of the above

23. Which Article of the Uniform Commercial Code applies to
    the sale of computer software along with the hardware?

    a.   2
    b.   3
    c.   4
    d.   8

24. Which of the following is/are aspects of a copyright?

      I.   an original work
     II.   protection for life of author plus fifty years
    III.   computer program can be protected

  a. I only
  b. I and II
  c. I, II, and III
  d. I and III

25. The Franklin Computer Corporation copied the operating
    system of an Apple II Computer. Apple Computer, Inc.
    brought a suit against Franklin to enjoin the use of
    Apple's operating system. Franklin argued the operating
    system was not protected. The court held:

    a. computer software programs may be protected by copy-
        right laws.
    b. computer software is not protected.
    c. computer software is a matter of public property.
    d. none of the above.

Essay Question

1. Stuart Seagrove owns several apartment buildings in
   Denver, Colorado. The Colorado Department of Transportation has proposed building a new eight-lane expressway.
   One of Stuart's apartment buildings is in the path of the
   expressway. The state has commenced condemnation proceedings to acquire the building. Stuart does not want
   to sell the building since it is his most profitable one.
   What are Stuart's legal rights?

Answers to Study Questions

Fill-in-the-Blank Questions

The hot water heater at the time of Burt's purchase was **personal** property. (p. 370)

Burt's residence and anything permanently affixed to it is
considered **real** property. (p. 370)

Personal property which becomes part of the real property is
known as a **fixture**. (p. 370)

If Barney received the highest estate possible, Burt must have
conveyed a **fee simple absolute**. (p. 373)

True-False Questions

1. True (p. 370)

2. False. Personal property may become real property. (p. 370)

3. True (p. 370)

4. True (p. 372)

5. True (p. 372)

6. False. A tenancy in common is a co-ownership of property without the rights of survivorship. (p. 372)

7. True (p. 373)

8. False. A life estate may be granted for other than the life of the grantor. (p. 375)

9. True (p. 382)

10. False. The federal copyright law protects software programs if a copyright is obtained. (p. 385)

Multiple-Choice Questions

1. d (p. 370)	14. a (p. 373)
2. a (p. 370)	15. b (p. 373)
3. c (p. 370)	16. a (p. 373)
4. b (p. 370)	17. a (p. 373)
5. d (p. 370)	18. c (p. 375)
6. a (p. 371)	19. d (p. 379)
7. c (p. 371)	20. c (p. 380)
8. a (p. 372)	21. a (pp. 380-381)
9. c (p. 372)	22. a (pp. 380-381)
10. c (p. 372)	23. a (p. 382)
11. b (p. 375)	24. c (p. 385)
12. d (p. 375)	25. a (p. 385)
13. b (p. 373)	

Essay Question

1. The government may take Stuart's property under the police power. This is called eminent domain. The government may take private property for a public use.

Stuart does have the constitutional right to receive just compensation for the value of his property from the state. Under the Fifth Amendment, private property may not be taken for a public use, unless just compensation is given. (p. 370)

PART III
BUSINESS FORMATION

Part Summary

Part III deals primarily with the law of agency, partnership, and corporations. Agency and private employment law are studied first to provide a foundation for the areas of sole proprietorship, partnership, limited partnership, and corporations. Agency relationships are essential to the operation of a business. Agency law categorizes the different types of agency relationships and defines the rights and responsibilities of the parties involved.

The most common types of business enterprises are the sole proprietorship, partnership, and the corporation. The sole proprietorship is the least formal type of business enterprise in formation and operation. The partnership involves greater formality than the sole proprietorship but less than the corporation. Each type of business enterprise has advantages and disadvantages that must be carefully considered by an individual starting a new business. The corporate form is the most widely used by large businesses.

Chapter 16
Agency and Private Employment Law

Major Concepts

Agency law defines the rights and responsibilities of parties involved in agency relationships. Agency relationships may be categorized into three groups: principal/agent, master/servant, and employer/independent contractor.

The principal/agent relationship is the most common. The principal authorizes the agent to enter contracts on the principal's behalf. The agent acts as the representative of the principal. Contracts the agent enters into for the principal are binding only on the principal if the agent acted within his or her authority. The principal is liable for the actions of the agent.

The master/servant or employer/employee relationship is characterized by the amount of control the master has over the servant. In this type of relationship, the master controls how the job is performed, and the servant does not have the authority to bind the master in contract. The master is responsible for the torts committed by the servant within the scope of employment. If the servant injures someone while on the job, the master is held responsible under the theory of respondeat superior.

The employer/independent contractor relationship is one which the employer has minimal control over the independent contractor. The independent contractor performs the job independently and is not under the control of the employer. The employer may only control the result of the independent contractor's work. As such, the employer is not responsible for the contracts or torts of the independent contractor. The employer has no vicarious liability for the actions of the independent contractor, unless ultrahazardous activities are being performed.

The principal/agent and master/servant are usually employment relationships. Most employment arrangements are created by oral or written contracts. The contract defines the responsibilities of the parties. The relationship may be classified as "at-will" or one requiring "just cause" to terminate. An "at-will" relationship may be terminated by either party for any reason, whereas the "just cause" relationship can only be terminated if facts exist which justify a termination.

Chapter Outline

I.   Formation of the Agency Relationship--The agency relationship can be created formally through written agreement or informally by the conduct of the parties.

   A.   Agency by Agreement--An individual may be appointed as an agent through a written or an oral contract. In most instances, the agreement between the parties is called an employment contract. Some agency agreements must be in writing, according to the Statute of Frauds, to be enforceable. Agency agreements which give the agent the authority to buy and sell an interest in real property and agreements which cannot be performed in one year must be in writing (e.g., an agency contract for the life of the agent is enforceable even if oral), according to the Equal Dignity Statute.

   B.   Agency by Ratification--Agency by ratification occurs when the principal affirms a contract that the agent had no authority to enter into. The agent must have been acting on behalf of the principal at the time of the contract, and the principal must know all the material terms before affirming the entire contract. The principal may expressly or impliedly ratify the contract.

   Express ratification occurs when the principal agrees to be bound to the contract. Implied ratification occurs when the principal fails to repudiate the contract and accepts the benefits of it. The principal may ratify a contract entered into by a party who is not an agent of the princi-

pal. Once ratification occurs, the principal is
solely responsible on the contract.

C.   Apparent Agency--Apparent agency exists when the
     principal represents to a third party that a person
     is an agent with the authority to act and such per-
     son has no actual authority to bind the principal.
     If a reasonable third party believes the alleged
     agent has actual authority, the principal is
     responsible for the contract created. The principal
     may create an apparent agency by express statements,
     conduct, or by failing to disclaim an individual as
     an agent.

II.   Types of Agency Relationships

A.   The Principal Agent Relationship--An agent has the
     authority to bind the principal on contracts with
     third parties. The principal directs the agent to
     act as his or her representative. The principal
     controls how the agent performs his or her duties.

     The agent acts on behalf of the principal. The
     agent has the responsibility of carrying out the
     interests of the principal. If the agent enters
     into a contract on behalf of the principal with
     actual or apparent authority, the principal is bound
     to the contract.

     1.   Types of Authority

          a.   Actual Authority--Actual authority is the
               authority delegated to the agent by the
               principal. Actual authority may be express
               or implied. Express authority is granted to
               the agent in writing or orally by the prin-
               cipal. Implied authority is not specific-
               ally stated but is necessary for the agent
               to carry out his or her express authority.
               A power of attorney is an example of a
               written document which grants an agent
               express authority to act on the principal's
               behalf (e.g., to sell a parcel of real prop-
               erty), whereas implied authority bolsters
               the express authority and is intended by the
               principal but not stated (e.g., the author-
               ity to advertise the sale a parcel of real
               property the agent was instructed to sell).

agree or ratify

b. Apparent Authority--Apparent authority is
    created by the principal leading a third
    party to reasonably believe a person is an
    agent of the principal with actual author-
    ity. If the third party believes the
    representation and enters into a contract
    with the person, the principal is bound to
    the contract. The principal may not assert
    the person lacked the authority to act for
    the principal. In cases of apparent author-
    ity, courts have asserted an agency by
    estoppel which stops the principal from
    denying the agent's authority.

    Customary business practices have associated
    a person's business title with a sphere of
    actual authority. A person who is a general
    manager ordinarily has the authority to pur-
    chase materials and supplies for use in the
    business. If the general manager's author-
    ity has been limited to the purchase of
    office supplies, he or she will have
    apparent authority to purchase materials,
    unless the principal makes third parties
    aware of the limitation. This is known as
    title authority or the authority that comes
    with the position.

c. Employer/Employee Relationship--The employ-
    ment of an employee is a type of agency
    relationship. The employer has the right to
    control how the employee performs the job.
    In most employment relationships, the em-
    ployee is paid either a salary or a wage per
    hour.

    The employer/employee relationship is also
    called a master/servant relationship. The
    employee/servant does not have the authority
    to enter contracts on behalf of the employ-
    er/master. The employee/servant ordinarily
    performs various types of mechanical func-
    tions.

d. Independent Contractors--An independent con-
    tractor is employed by an employer but is
    not an employee. The employer hires an
    independent contractor to perform special
    tasks which the employer usually does not
    have the skill or knowledge to perform. The

employer controls the result of the work performed by the independent contractor but does not have the right to control the method of performance.

The crucial factor for determining if a person is an independent contractor is the extent of control the employer may exercise over the method of performance. If the employer has extensive control over the details of the job, the person is not an independent contractor. Other factors the courts consider when determining if a person is an independent contractor are: the type of job, business or occupation, who supplies the tools or equipment, length of employment, method of payment, and tax returns filed.

The employer is not responsible for the actions of the independent contractor. If the independent contractor negligently causes an injury to a bystander, the independent contractor is solely liable for the injury. Employers may be held liable for the acts of an independent contractor if the independent contractor is performing a duty required by law of the employer or if the independent contractor is performing ultrahazardous activities.

III. Duties of Agents and Principals--The principal-agent relationship is one of trust. Both parties are obligated to each other in several respects.

A. The Agent's Duties to the Principal

1. Duty of Performance--The agent is required to use reasonable diligence and skill in the performance of the job. The standard of care the agent must exhibit is that of a reasonable person under similar circumstances. If the agent fails to perform as a reasonable person, he or she has breached the duty of performance and can be held responsible for any damages that result.

2. Duty of Notification--The agent must notify the principal of all matters concerning the subject matter of the agency. The common law imputes the agent's knowledge to the principal.

3. <u>Duty of Loyalty</u>--The agent is required to act only in the interests of the principal. The agent may not represent two principals in the same transaction unless full disclosure is made to all the parties involved of the dual capacity.

An agent may not deal with himself concerning the subject matter of the agency, and the agent may not buy or sell to the principal. The agent may not profit at the expense of the principal.

4. <u>Duty of Obedience</u>--The agent must follow all lawful instructions of the principal, whether or not they are reasonable.

5. <u>Duty of Accounting</u>--The agent is required to keep accurate records of the principal's money and property and return such items to the principal. The agent may not commingle the principal's assets with his or her own assets. The agent must keep the principal's funds in a separate and identifiable account.

B. <u>Principal's Duties to the Agent</u>

1. <u>Duty of Compensation</u>--The principal must pay the agent for services performed unless the parties have specifically agreed to a gratuitous agency relationship. If the parties fail to agree on the amount of compensation, the agent is entitled to a reasonable or customary amount.

2. <u>Duty of Reimbursement and Indemnification</u>--The principal must reimburse the agent for expenses paid in the course of carrying out his or her duties as an agent. The agent must be acting on behalf of the principal at the time the expense was paid.

The principal is required to indemnify the agent for losses incurred while the agent was performing his or her duties (e.g., the agent's watch is destroyed while helping the principal move some equipment).

3. <u>Duty of Cooperation</u>--The principal must assist and cooperate with the agent as the agent performs his or her job. The principal cannot interfere with the agent performing his or her duties.

4. <u>Duty to Provide Safe Working Conditions</u>--The principal must inspect the work premises and warn agents of any unsafe or hazardous areas.

IV. <u>Liability of Principals and Agents to Third Parties</u>

A. <u>Contract Liability</u>--In some cases, both the principal and the agent may be liable for a breach of contract to a third party. If the agent has actual authority, the principal is contractually bound. When the agent has neither actual nor apparent authority, then only the agent is liable for having breached the implied warranty of authority. If the agent has apparent authority, the principal is bound, but the agent can be held responsible to the principal for breaching the duty of obedience. Liability is determined in accordance with how the principal is classified.

1. <u>Disclosed Principal</u>--In a disclosed principal relationship, the third party knows an agency relationship exists and the identity of the principal. The <u>principal has sole liability</u> on the contracts entered into by the agent within his or her scope of authority.

2. <u>Partially Disclosed Principal</u>--In a partially disclosed principal relationship, the third party knows the agent is acting for a principal but the identity of the principal is not known. The third party may hold either the agent or the principal to the contract.

3. <u>Undisclosed Principal</u>--In an undisclosed principal relationship, the third party believes he or she is dealing only with the agent. The third party has no knowledge of the agency or the identity of the principal. The third party may hold the agent or the principal to the contract.

Disclosed, partially disclosed, and undisclosed principals have the right to enforce a contract against a third party.

B. <u>Tort Liability</u>--When the employee/servant commits a tort (civil wrong), the employer/master can be held responsible. The employee is always responsible for his or her own torts.

car crash?

1. <u>The Doctrine of Respondeat Superior/Negligence</u>--The term means "let the master respond" for the

actions of the employee/servant. The employer/master is liable for the negligent acts committed by the employee/servant within the scope of employment. The court will consider various factors to determine if the tort occurred in the scope of employment. Some of the factors to consider are: was the act authorized, what was the purpose of the act, was the act commonly performed by other employees, and was the employee acting in the employer's interests.

Ordinarily, if the employee/servant was on the job, acting on behalf of the employer/master, and commits a tort, the employer/master will be held liable. If the employee/servant substantially departs from the employer's business, the employer is not responsible because the employee is outside the scope of employment. An employee can be disobeying the employer's instructions and still be within the scope of employment. (e.g., Employee/delivery truck driver picks up a hitchhiker when instructed not to pick up riders; on the way to make a delivery, he runs a red light and injures the hitchhiker; the employer is liable.)

2. Liability for Misrepresentation--The principal is liable when an agent misrepresents the facts to a third party, and the principal placed the agent in the position to defraud the third party. If it appears the agent is acting within the scope of the agency, the principal is liable.

3. Liability for Other Intentional Torts--The employer is liable for other torts such as assault and battery and false imprisonment if the employee acted within the scope of employment.

V. Termination of the Agency Relationship--The agency relationship can be ended by either the voluntary acts of the parties or by operation of law.

A. Termination by Acts of the Parties

1. Lapse of Agreement--The agency will terminate when the agreement specifies a time period and the time period has expired. If no time period has been set, the agency continues for a reasonable time period.

2. <u>Accomplishment of Purpose</u>--An agency may have been set up to accomplish a specific objective. When the objective is completed, the agency is terminated.

3. <u>By Agreement</u>--The parties may mutually agree to terminate the agency relationship. Each individual party may withdraw from the agency relationship. The principal may revoke the agent's authority or the agent may renounce his or her authority.

B. <u>Termination by Operation of Law</u>--If either the principal or the agent dies, is declared insane, or goes bankrupt, the agency relationship is terminated automatically by law. The agency is also terminated if the subject matter of the agency is destroyed. If the agency is terminated by operation of law, no notice is required to third parties.

C. <u>Notice Required for Termination</u>--When the agency is terminated by an act of the parties, the principal must notify third parties of the termination. <u>Third parties who dealt with the agent must receive actual notice and all other parties must be constructively notified</u> (i.e., by publication in a newspaper or trade journal).

is not, still bound by contracts

VI. <u>Regulation of the Employer-Employee Relationship</u>

A. <u>Employment Contracts</u>--Most employment relationships are created by oral or written contracts. The contract defines the parameters of the relationship between employer and employee. The contract may specify the employee's authority and the scope of employment.

In most written employment contracts, an employer cannot terminate an employee unless "just cause" exists. In cases where no written contract has been executed, the parties must rely on the oral agreement which, in most cases, creates an "at-will" relationship. In "at-will" employment, the employer may terminate the employee at any time, for any reason.

The modern trend of the law is to narrow the "at-will" doctrine by creating three exceptions. The exceptions are:

1.   employer's conduct undermined some important public policy.

2.   proof of an implied-in-fact promise of employment.

3.   proof of an implied-in-fact covenant of "good faith and fair dealing."

> If the employer breaches any one of the three exceptions, the employee may be entitled to damages and reinstatement.

Study Questions

Fill-in-the-Blank Questions

Steve owns a sporting goods store in downtown Houston, Texas called "Steve's Sports." Steve hires Dave as the general manager of the store. Steve specifically tells Dave he may purchase inventory for the store, hire employees, and manage the business.

If Dave hires Fred as a sales clerk, this is an example of Dave exercising his _____ authority.
(express/implied)

If Dave advertises in the local newspaper for a sales clerk, Dave is exercising his _____ authority.
(express/implied)

The relationship between Steve's Sports and Dave is that of a
_____.
(principal-agent/employer-independent contractor)

If Dave hires an electrician to install an electric sign on the roof of the building, the electrician is an
_____.
(employee/independent contractor)

True-False Questions

1.   The principal-agent relationship can only be created by a written contract.   _F_

2.   An agency to sell real property may be oral.   _F_

3. An agent is responsible for torts he or she commits while on the job. ___T___

4. An agent may choose to disobey unreasonable instructions of the principal. ___F___

5. The agent is entitled to be compensated for his or her services unless otherwise stated. ___T___

6. The principal is obligated to tell the agent of any hazardous conditions of performing the job. ___(___

7. It is assumed that any information possessed by the agent is also known by the principal. ___T___

8. An agent can be held liable on a contract entered into for the principal. ___T___ *partially or undisclosed principle.*

9. Actual authority of an agent may be express or implied. ___T___

10. Generally, the principal is responsible for the crimes committed by an agent. ___F___ *agent — Duty of Performance* → *within scope of duty?*

Multiple-Choice Questions

1. Which of the following is a written document given by the principal to the agent that is usually notarized and appoints a person to be "an attorney-in-fact"?

   a. facit per se
   b. employment contract
   c. apparent authority
   d. power of attorney

2. Which of the following is not a method of creating an agency relationship?

   a. ratification
   b. facit per se
   c. agreement
   d. apparent agency

3. In order for ratification to occur, which of the following requirements must be met?

   I. principal affirms the contract
   II. principal signs a new contract
   III. principal is aware of all material facts

a. I only
b. I and II
c. I and III
d. I, II, and III

4. Christopher is employed at a local department store as a
    sales clerk. Christopher is responsible to wait on cus-
    tomers in the housewares department. Christopher sells
    some merchandise to a customer. The department store
    owner is bound to the contract if Christopher:

      I. had actual authority.
     II. had apparent authority.
    III. had express authority.

    a. I only
    b. I and II
    c. I and III
    d. I, II, and III

5. Curt hired a local real estate broker to sell his home.
    The sales agent is considered a(n):

    a. subagent.
    b. employee.
    c. gratuitous agent.
    d. none of the above.

    Curt — Principle
    who's agent?

6. Harvey is hired by Acme Co. to pave the employee parking
    lot with asphalt. Harvey has ten of his own employees
    run the machinery which Harvey owns. Which of the fol-
    lowing factors are considered by the courts to determine
    if Harvey is an independent contractor?

      I. who owns the equipment
     II. the method of payment
    III. the type of job being performed

    a. I
    b. I and II
    c. I and III
    d. I, II, and III

7. Refer to question 6. Harvey and his employees begin to
    do work preparing the site. One of Harvey's bulldozer
    drivers accidentally crashes into a car driving on the
    road in front of Acme Co. The driver of the car was
    seriously injured and decides to sue Acme Co. The court
    will decide:

a.   in favor of the plaintiff due to Acme's negligence.
b.   in favor of the plaintiff because of respondeat superior.
c.   against the plaintiff because Acme is not responsible.
d.   none of the above.

8.   The major distinction between an employer-employee relationship and the employer-independent contractor relationship is:

a.   type of work performed.
b.   amount of control the employer possesses.
c.   amount of compensation paid.
d.   the duty of care owed.

9.   Jack is employed by IBM as a sales representative. Jack has the authority to sell office machines, receive payments, and make deliveries. Jack received payment on two office typewriters and deposited the checks in his own personal account. Jack has breached the duty:

a.   to account.
b.   to notify.
c.   of reasonable care.
d.   of reimbursement.

10. Mark was employed as the president of Texatron Oil Co. Mark was approached one day by a Texas oil man who wanted to sell several acres of property believed to have oil underground. Mark purchases the property for himself without telling the corporation. Mark has breached the duty:

a.   to account.
b.   of loyalty.   *agent can't benefit at*
c.   reasonable care.   *expense of principle.*
d.   none of the above.

11. The <u>fiduciary duty</u> of an agency relationship is defined as:

  I.   loyalty to the principal.
 II.   good faith to the principal.
III.   integrity.

a.   I
b.   I and II
c.   I, II, and III
d.   I and III

12. Jeff drives a delivery truck for U.P.S. Jeff, on the way to make the day's deliveries, realizes he is almost out of gas. Jeff stops at a gas station and spends his own money to fill up the tank. Jeff is most likely entitled to receive back the amount paid under the principal's duty of:

    a. indemnification.
    b. reimbursement. — *for expenses*
    c. compensation.
    d. notification.

13. Refer to question 12. While out making deliveries one day, Jeff's U.P.S. truck blows a head gasket and is no longer drivable. Jeff calls the office and receives instructions from his supervisor. The supervisor asked Jeff to make the rest of the deliveries with his own personal automobile. Jeff agrees, but while making a delivery his car was damaged by a hit-and-run driver who negligently ran a red light. Jeff most likely will be able to collect the amount of the damages from his employer under the principal's duty of:

    a. indemnification. — *for losses*
    b. reimbursement.
    c. compensation.
    d. notification.

14. Walmart Co. hires an agent to buy a 25-acre parcel for development of a shopping center. The vice president of Walmart instructs the agent to pay no more than $2 million dollars and not reveal that an agency exists. The parties have created a(n):

    a. apparent agency.
    b. disclosed principal relationship.
    c. partially disclosed principal relationship.
    d. undisclosed principal relationship.

15. Refer to question 14. The agent purchases the property for $2.5 million dollars. Walmart refuses to go through with the deal. The property owner can hold which of the following liable?

    a. Walmart
    b. the agent   *outside his authority*
    c. Walmart's president
    d. all of the above

16. Refer to question 14. The agent enters into a contract to purchase the property for $1.75 million dollars. Walmart's president decides they no longer want to build the shopping center. The agent notifies the seller that the contract will not be performed. The seller of the property may hold which of the following parties liable for the breach of contract?

    I. Walmart
   II. Walmart's president
  III. the agent

can hold both responsible because of undisclosed principle.

   a. I only
   b. I and II
   c. I, II, and III
   d. I and III

17. Refer to question 16. If the agent is ordered by the court to pay damages for breach of contract of $50,000, the agent may require Walmart to:

   a. reimburse the loss.
   b. indemnify the loss. —
   c. justify the breach.
   d. compensate the loss.

18. Sam the salesman is required to sell the company's product by calling on clients around the country. Sam is authorized to entertain clients if there is the potential for a sale. Sam, while taking a client out to dinner, is involved in an auto accident. The client was injured, and it was determined that Sam was negligent. The client sues Sam and the company, and if he wins, the court will order:

   a. both Sam and the company to pay.
   b. only Sam to pay.
   c. only the company to pay.
   d. Sam to pay half and the company to pay half.

agent always liable for own torts. Principle also liable if in the line of duty.

19. Apparent authority exists when a person:

    I. has no actual authority.
   II. is a general manager.
  III. does not know the principal.

→ lead third party to believe actual authority exists

   a. I only
   b. I and II
   c. I, II, and III
   d. I and III

20. When an agent acts outside the scope of authority, he or she may be held liable for:

    a. breach of the original contract with the third party.
    b. commission of a tort.
    c. commission of a crime.
    d. breach of implied warranty of authority.

21. The concept which makes the employer responsible for the negligence of the employee is called:

    a. respondeat superior.
    b. facit per se.
    c. qui facit per alium.
    d. apparent authority.

    "let the master respond"

22. Generally, the employer can be held responsible for which of the following activities of the employee, if done while on the job?

       I. a truck driver accidentally injures a third party
      II. a bouncer in a tavern assaults a third party
     III. a sales clerk commits a crime ✓

    a. I only
    b. I and II
    c. I, II, and III
    d. I and III

23. Termination of the agency relationship may occur by which of the following methods?

    a. mutual rescission
    b. bankruptcy of the principal
    c. destruction of the subject matter of the agency
    d. all of the above

24. If the agency is terminated by the agent renouncing his or her authority, the principal must:

       I. give actual notice to all parties.
      II. give constructive notice to all parties.
     III. give actual notice to parties the agent previously dealt with.

    a. I
    b. I and II
    c. I, II, and III
    d. III only

    *II + III
    p. 269*

25. Which of the following is/are considered a termination by
     operation of law?

     death, insane, bankrupt

     a. death of the agent
     b. insanity of the principal
     c. principal revocation of agent's authority
     d. two of the above

Essay Question

1. Russ Grams was employed by Superior Sporting Goods Manu-
    facturing Co. as the sales manager for the midwestern
    states. Russ was expected to work from 8:00 a.m. to
    5:00 p.m. Monday through Friday, unless with a customer.
    The company vice-president instructed Russ to accommodate
    customers at all costs. The customers were department
    stores, sporting goods stores, and athletic clubs.

    One afternoon, while making a sales call at the Kohman
    Department Store, the director of purchasing told Russ he
    was planning to watch a basketball game on the other side
    of town but his car would not start. Russ said, "If you
    need a ride, I'd be happy to give you one." On the way
    to the game, Russ ran a red light and collided with
    another car. Neither Russ nor the director of purchasing
    was injured, but the other driver was severely injured
    and her car was damaged. What is the liability of
    Superior to the owner of the other car?

Answers to Study Questions

Fill-in-the-Blank Questions

If Dave hires Fred as a sales clerk, this is an example of
Dave exercising his express authority. (p. 401)

If Dave advertises in the local newspaper for a sales clerk,
Dave is exercising his implied authority. (p. 401)

The relationship between Steve's Sports and Dave is that of a
principal-agent. (p. 400)

If Dave hires an electrician to install an electric sign on
the roof of the building, the electrician is an independent
contractor. (p. 404)

True-False Questions

1. False. The principal-agent relationship need not be created by a contract. (p. 399)

2. False. An agency to sell real property for the owner must be in writing to be enforceable. (p. 399)

3. True (p. 407)

4. False. An agent has the duty to obey reasonable and unreasonable instructions. (p. 408)

5. True (p. 408)

6. True (p. 409)

7. True (p. 407)

8. True (p. 409)

9. True (p. 401)

10. False. Generally, a principal is not responsible for the crimes committed by the agent. (p. 410)

Multiple-Choice Questions

1.	d (p. 399)		14.	d (p. 409)
2.	b (pp. 398-400)		15.	b (p. 409)
3.	c (p. 399)		16.	d (p. 409)
4.	d (p. 401)		17.	b (p. 408)
5.	a (p. 403)		18.	a (p. 410)
6.	d (p. 404)		19.	a (p. 401)
7.	c (p. 405)		20.	d (p. 410)
8.	b (p. 404)		21.	a (p. 410)
9.	a (p. 408)		22.	b (p. 410)
10.	b (p. 407)		23.	d (p. 414)
11.	c (p. 407)		24.	d (p. 414)
12.	b (p. 408)		25.	d (p. 413)
13.	a (p. 408)			

Essay Question

1. Superior Sporting Goods Manufacturing Co. is liable for the personal injury and property damages to the other driver. Under the theory of respondeat superior, the master is responsible for the torts committed by the

servant within the scope of employment. Russ was within
the scope of employment at the time of the accident.
Russ was attempting to carry out the instructions of the
vice-president to accommodate customers at all costs.
Superior is liable for the negligence of its employee,
Russ Grams. (p. 410)

Chapter 17

Business Enterprises: Sole Proprietorships and Partnerships

Major Concepts

This chapter looks at four common forms of businesses: the sole proprietorship, partnership, limited partnership, and the corporation. The corporate form will be discussed in more detail in a later chapter. The businessperson must carefully consider which form of business entity best fits his or her business operation. Each form has its advantages and disadvantages. The sole proprietorship and the partnership are the easiest to create. Both forms allow the owners to have complete control of the business and directly receive the profits without federal income tax liability.

The owners of the sole proprietorship and the partnership have unlimited liability to creditors. Partners and a sole proprietor may have their personal assets executed against by creditors if the business goes bankrupt.

The limited partnership and the corporation are more difficult to form as some statutory requirements must be fulfilled. Both types of entities are creatures of statute and have no existence outside of state approval. The limited partnership is taxed as a general partnership, but the corporation is considered a taxable entity under federal tax law. The corporation must pay federal income taxes, and shareholders must pay income tax on dividends distributed by the corporation. The limited partnership and the corporation may generate capital from the sale of securities.

The Uniform Partnership Act (UPA) regulates the formation and operation of a general partnership. The UPA attempts to fill in the gaps in the partnership agreement.

The Uniform Limited Partnership Act (ULPA) and the Revised Uniform Limited Partnership Act (RULPA) govern the creation and operation of a limited partnership. Limited partners have limited liability.

The Uniform Commercial Code (UCC) Article 6 deals with Bulk Transfers. A bulk transfer is when a transfer of a major part of material, supplies, merchandise, or inventory is made outside the ordinary course of business. Bulk transfers occur when a businessperson sells his or her business and the assets go along as part of the sale.

Chapter Outline

I.   Comparing Sole Proprietorship, Partnership, Limited Partnership, and Corporation--These four types of business entities may be compared with each other on several factors. Before starting in business, an individual should carefully consider which business form best fits his or her business operation.

   A.   Difficulty of Formation--The sole proprietorship is the easiest to form because state laws place relatively few restrictions on this type of entity. The sole proprietorship is owned by a single person who usually employs a small number of employees. Most businesses start as sole proprietorships. An entity may use a fictitious name, such as Acme or Superior, but state law requires the owner of the business to file the fictitious name with the state. The filing notifies the public that the owner is doing business under the fictitious name.

   A general partnership (i.e., partnership) is a business owned by two or more persons to a make profit. A partnership can also be easily formed with few restrictions. The limited partnership requires some formality in its creation. The limited partnership must file with the state a certificate of limited partnership and execute an agreement between limited and general partners. The limited partnership is regulated by state law and more difficult to organize than an ordinary partnership.

The laws governing the formation of a corporation require articles of incorporation to be filed with the state and approved before the corporation comes into existence.

B.   Liability of the Owner--The sole proprietor and the general partner in a partnership and limited partnership have unlimited liability. Unlimited liability subjects the owner to the potential loss of all his or her personal assets. A creditor may execute against the assets of the business and the personal assets of the sole proprietor and the general partner. The limited partner has liability only to the extent of his or her investment.

The shareholders (i.e., owners) of a corporation have limited liability to the extent of their investment. Creditors in most situations cannot reach the personal assets of the shareholder.

C.   Tax Considerations--The sole proprietorship, partnership, and limited partnership are not taxed by the federal government on income produced. The income or loss flows through to the owners as personal income or loss. The partnership and the limited partnership must file informational returns with the government.

A corporation as a legal entity in and of itself is required to pay federal income tax. The corporation is subject to a special income tax rate. Any cash dividends distributed to shareholders are taxable as income on the shareholders' personal return. The corporation experiences double taxation because the profits of the corporation are taxed once and then again when distributed to shareholders. A corporation which meets certain Internal Revenue Service guidelines may qualify as an S corporation, which permits the corporation to be taxed as if it were a partnership.   < 35 shareholders, domestic...

The state may tax the income of any business located within the state.

D.   Continuity of Existence--The sole proprietorship, partnership, and limited partnership have a limited duration. These types of business forms are dependent on the owners to exist. A partnership goes through a dissolution every time a partner withdraws or is added. Dissolution of the partnership does

not require the business to cease. The partnership
may continue as before without an old partner or
with a new partner. The addition or subtraction of
a partner technically creates a new partnership even
though business may seem as usual. The addition of
a new partner requires the unanimous consent of all
the partners.

The corporation is a legal entity which is not dependent on particular owners for its existence. The
corporation has an indefinite duration.

E.   Transfer of Ownership--The sole proprietor may sell
      his or her business to another party. The buyer may
      purchase all the assets of the sole proprietorship
      without continuing the business under the same name.

      A partner may sell his interest in the partnership.
      The purchase of the partnership does not give the
      buyer the right to participate in management. The
      buyer is entitled to a percentage of the profits of
      the partnership. Unless the other partners agree to
      admit the buyer as a partner, the buyer has no part
      in running the partnership business.

      The limited partnership is similar to the general
      partnership in the sale of a partner's interest,
      except the limited partner may freely sell his or
      her interest in the partnership with no effect on
      the limited partnership business.

      The shareholders of a corporation may freely trans-
      fer their shares. The sale of stock in a corpora-
      tion does not effect the corporate existence. The
      ownership of the corporation may be shifted to a
      buyer who purchases large percentages of the out-
      standing stock. The stockholder who owns the major-
      ity of stock may control the management of the
      corporation. Stockholders commonly have one vote
      per share of common stock they own. Stockholders
      vote to elect the board of directors.

F.   Management and Control--The sole proprietor is the
      single owner of the business and has complete con-
      trol over its operation.

      The partnership and the limited partnership is man-
      aged by the general partners. Depending on the
      partnership agreement, each partner has some respon-
      sibility of assisting in the operation of the busi-

ness. If the management of the partnership has been
left out of the partnership agreement, each partner
has equal right to manage and control the partnership business.

In the corporation, the board of directors direct
the corporation as to major management policy, and
the officers manage the day-to-day business. The
shareholders elect the board of directors, and the
board appoints the officers of the corporation.

G.   Financing--The sole proprietorship and partnership
     raise funds through obtaining loans from financial
     institutions. The sole proprietor and the partner
     may be required to personally sign for a loan to
     purchase operating assets. The partners are com-
     monly required to make capital contributions into
     the partnership at the initial formation. The
     capital contributions are used to purchase assets
     necessary for the operation of the business.
     Partners from time to time may make loans to the
     partnership.

     The limited partnership raises capital through the
     sale of limited partnership interests to investors.
     A limited partnership interest entitles the limited
     partner to share in the profits and losses of the
     partnership business. The funds generated from the
     sale of limited partnership interests is used to
     purchase assets.

     The corporation raises capital through the selling
     of shares of stock. The stock may be sold privately
     or on a national exchange. The shareholders gain
     the right to receive dividends from the corporation
     once the board of directors has declared them. The
     corporation from time to time raises additional cap-
     ital through new stock issuances. Otherwise, a
     corporation may borrow money from a financial insti-
     tution.

H.   Licensing--Whether the business is a sole proprie-
     torship, partnership, limited partnership, or corpo-
     ration, state law may require the businessperson to
     obtain a license before conducting business. Li-
     censes are usually required for insurance agents,
     real estate brokers, sellers of guns or explosives,
     funeral homes, and day-care centers. In addition, a
     business may have to obtain a sales or use tax li-
     cense.

Two types of licensing statutes are common: the
regulatory licensing statute and the revenue raising
statute. A person who does business without a license under a regulatory statute is not allowed to
collect a fee. A regulatory statute requires licensing of an individual to protect the public from
abuse or deception. A revenue raising statute requires an individual to purchase a license merely as
a means of generating revenue for the state or local
government. A party not licensed under a revenue
raising statute may collect a fee for his or her
services.

I.   Location--Location of a new business is important to
     its success. The businessperson must consider the
     zoning restrictions when purchasing property to
     build on. Zoning restrictions may not permit cer-
     tain types of businesses in some areas. In some
     cases, a use permit or a variance may be obtained to
     operate a business in an area.

II. Partnership--A partnership is defined as "an association
     of two or more persons to carry on as co-owners in a
     business for profit" under the Uniform Partnership Act
     (UPA) Section 6. The UPA attempts to fill in the gaps
     when the parties have failed to include all terms in the
     partnership agreement. A written partnership agreement
     is not essential to the existence of a partnership un-
     less the partnership agreement cannot be performed in
     one year. The sharing of profits between individuals
     raises a presumption that a partnership exists (UPA Sec-
     tion 7(4)). The presumption may be refuted by evidence
     which proves the parties did not co-own business assets
     with the intent to make a profit.

     If the parties lead a third person to believe a partner-
     ship exists, the court may recognize a partnership by
     estoppel (UPA Section 16). In a partnership by estop-
     pel, the parties are foreclosed from asserting that a
     partnership did not exist. The parties making the
     representations are held liable as if partners.

     A partnership is considered the aggregate of the indi-
     vidual partners involved. The partnership is comprised
     of the partners who run the business. Under the UPA, a
     partnership may be treated as a legal entity for certain
     purposes. The partnership may own real property in the
     partnership name and sue and be sued in the partnership
     name.

A. <u>Partnership Management and Control</u>--Partners have an
    equal right to manage the partnership business un-
    less altered by the partnership agreement (UPA Sec-
    tion 18(e)). The partner is an agent of the part-
    nership. A partner has the authority to enter into
    contracts to carry out a business purpose on behalf
    of the partnership (UPA Section 9). A contract
    entered into by a partner within the scope of the
    partnership business binds the partnership to per-
    form according to the contract terms.

    A partner has a <u>fiduciary duty</u> to the other partners
    <u>to act in good faith for the benefit of the partner-
    ship</u> with utmost loyalty and diligence. The partner
    may not act in his or her own interests to the
    detriment of the other partners.

    A partner is entitled to a percentage of the busi-
    ness profits according to the partnership agreement,
    and if no agreement, then equally. Partners are
    obligated to share in the losses according to the
    partnership agreement. If the agreement fails to
    account for losses, losses are shared in the same
    proportions as profits (UPA Section 18(a)). Part-
    ners are not entitled to a salary unless stipulated
    in the partnership agreement.

    Partners have one vote each in management decisions.
    A majority vote is required for most partnership
    decisions (UPA Section 18 (b)). In some circum-
    stances, a unanimous consent is required by the
    partners. Any action which significantly alters the
    partnership business or a disposition of the good-
    will and submission of a dispute to arbitration
    requires a unanimous consent.

B. <u>Liability of the Partners</u>--Partners have unlimited
    liability. Each partner is liable for the partner-
    ship's debts. Partners are liable for the torts and
    contracts of other partners.

    The partners have joint liability for partnership
    contracts. A judgment creditor attempting to col-
    lect on a partnership debt created by a breach of
    contract must first exhaust the assets of the part-
    nership before looking to the personal assets of the
    partners. <u>Partners have joint and several liability
    for debts created through the commission of a tort.</u>
    Joint and several liability allows the creditor to
    proceed directly against the personal assets of a
    partner or the partners.

A new partner admitted to a partnership is not personally liable for prior debts of the partnership,
but his or her capital contribution in the event of
a dissolution may be used to satisfy prior claims
(UPA Section 17).

C.   Duration of the Partnership--The partnership has a
limited duration, unless the partnership agreement
provides for the continuance of the business despite
the withdrawal of a partner. The partnership agreement may set a fixed term for the existence of the
partnership. A partnership which dissolves after a
fixed period of time is considered a partnership for
a term. A partnership may last only as long as it
takes to complete a particular project.

A partnership at will has no fixed duration, and any
partner can dissolve it at any time without violating the partnership agreement. The closing of a
partnership business requires the completion of
three steps: dissolution, winding up, and termination.

1.   Dissolution--A dissolution may be caused by the
withdrawal of a partner, the adding of a partner, mutual agreement of the partners, or bankruptcy (UPA Section 31, 32). Dissolution does
not necessarily cause the partnership to cease
doing business (UPA Section 30). The business
may continue but is considered a new partnership. The old partnership ceases to exist.

2.   Winding Up--If the partnership business is going
to cease, the partnership will then proceed to
winding up. During the winding up period, the
partners must all be notified and no new business can be taken on. The partners are obligated to finish the transactions already begun,
collect all debts owed to the partnership, and
pay all the partnership debts.

The assets of the partnership will be liquidated
and an accounting will be made of the partners'
accounts. The partners will be paid the value
of their partnership interest. This means that
a partner's capital contribution will be returned along with any surplus or loans the partner made to the partnership.

Creditors of the partnership have priority to the partnership assets, and personal creditors of the individual partners have priority as to personal assets. This apportioning is called the marshalling of assets.

3. Termination--Termination involves the distribution of assets or the proceeds from the sale of the assets to partners and creditors.

The order of priority is as follows:

a. Debts owed to creditors other than partners;

b. Debts owed to partners for loans to the partnership;

c. Return of capital contribution; and

d. Debts owed to partners for profits (surplus).

III. Limited Partnership--A limited partnership is created under state statute. The Uniform Limited Partnership Act (ULPA) or the Revised Uniform Limited Partnership Act (RULPA) have been adopted in all states except Louisiana. The limited partnership must file a certificate containing general information about the limited partnership business with the state.

A limited partnership must have at least one general partner to manage the business and at least one limited partner. Limited partners make capital contributions to the partnership but do not participate in management. A limited partner who actively participates in the management of the limited partnership may be held as a general partner with unlimited liability.

limited give capital; not mgmt

The partners enter into a partnership agreement which specifies the essential terms of the limited partnership. The partnership agreement usually states how the partners will share in profits and losses.

A. Funding of a Limited Partnership--A limited partnership sells interests to limited partners which are considered securities. Under the Securities Act of 1933, all interests where a person pays money to another person, the money is invested in a common enterprise with the expectation of profit, and the profits are primarily from the efforts of other than

the limited partner are considered investment contracts which are classified as securities. The
transfer of a security subjects the limited partnership to federal and state securities laws.

The funds generated by the sale of limited partnership interests are used to purchase assets for the
business. The general partners may obtain loans if
additional capital is needed.

B. Liability of the Limited Partner--The liability of
the limited partner is limited to his or her capital
contribution. This means that if the limited partnership goes bankrupt, the limited partner will lose
his or her capital contributions but will not be required to make any additional payments if the liabilities of the limited partnership exceed the
assets.

C. Control of the Limited Partnership--The general
partners have been given the authority to manage the
limited partnership. General partners are not
required to make capital contributions. The general
partner must abide by the partnership agreement.

A limited partner has the right to gain access to
the partnership books and records, to receive a
share of the profits as stipulated in the partnership certificate, and to have his or her capital
contribution returned upon dissolution and distribution.

D. Tax Consequences for a Limited Partnership--The
limited partnership is not taxed as a legal entity
by the federal government. The partnership must
file an informational report of the allocation of
profits and losses to the partners. The profits and
losses flow through to the general and limited partners' personal income tax returns.

General partners must have substantial personal
assets. This is required by tax regulations such
that the unlimited liability of the general partner
is not just a sham. The general partners must be
careful to operate the business as a limited partnership and not a corporation. Operating as a
corporation may subject the limited partnership to
federal income tax liability.

[handwritten margin note: mgr?? don't contribute capital.]

*[handwritten margin note: * have to have assets to have unlimited liability of limited partnership]*

E. Priority in Distribution--The limited partnership
    may go through a dissolution, winding up, and termi-
    nation just like the general partnership. In the
    event of a termination of the limited partnership,
    the ULPA and the RULPA designate the priority of
    claims to partnership assets. The RULPA priorities
    are as follows:

    1. outside creditors and partner creditors.

    2. amounts before withdrawal to which partners are
        entitled.

    3. capital contributions, limited and general part-
        ners.

    4. profits, limited and general partners.

IV. Bulk Transfers--A bulk transfer is any transfer of a
    major part of the material, supplies, merchandise, or
    inventory not in the ordinary course of the transferor's
    business under the UCC Article 6. If a person sells his
    or her business along with the inventory, Article 6 of
    the UCC must be complied with.

    The seller and buyer are required to make certain dis-
    closures under the UCC. If the UCC is not followed, the
    creditors of the seller may have rights in the assets
    transferred to the buyer.

    A. Statutory Requirements under the UCC for Bulk Trans-
        fers--The following requirements are necessary to
        protect the buyer from the creditors of the seller:

        1. The seller must provide a sworn list of the
            existing creditors to the transferee (buyer)
            (UCC 6-104(1)(a)).

        2. The buyer and the seller must prepare a schedule
            of the property being transferred (UCC 6-104(1)
            (b)).

        3. The buyer must keep the list of creditors and
            the schedule of property for at least six
            months. Creditors may inspect the list (UCC
            6-104(1)(c)).

        4. The buyer must give the creditors notice of the
            transfer at least ten days before the buyer
            takes possession of the goods or pays for them
            (UCC 6-105).

If the requirements are fulfilled, the buyer acquires good title to the goods free of all claims of the seller's creditors.

Even if the requirements are not met, a bona fide purchaser of the goods from the transferee will receive good title free of any claim of creditors. If the seller failed to list a creditor and that creditor did not receive notice, the seller is liable for any damages the buyer incurs.

Study Questions

Fill-in-the-Blank Questions

Terry Tilton is considering going into the computer repair business. Terry believes he can be very successful without having to raise large sums of capital initially. Terry has a service truck and some equipment.

If Terry decides to go into business alone, the easiest form of business entity for Terry to create is the _____. (partnership/ sole proprietorship)

The owners of a corporation have _____ (unlimited/limited) liability for the debts of the business.

A partner in a partnership has _____ liability (personal/no) for torts committed by employees within the scope of partnership business.

A sole proprietor is _____ to file (not required/required) with the state a certificate of operation.

True-False Questions

1. The sole proprietorship is the easiest type of business entity to create. ___T___

2. A sole proprietorship is ^not a taxable entity for federal income tax purposes. ___F___

3. A partnership may not do business under a fictitious name. ___F___
   → unless it is properly filed.

4. The partnership is managed by the general partners. ___T___

5. The general partners in a partnership have limited lia-
    bility. ___F___

6. In a limited partnership, there must be at least one gen-
    eral partner. ___T___

7. A limited partnership can only be created if state stat-
    ute allows. ___T___

8. A corporation is managed by the board of directors. ___T___

9. The Uniform Partnership Act supersedes _fill gaps of_ the partnership
    agreement in all cases. ___F___

10. A bulk transfer is the sale of large amounts of fungible
    goods. ___F___ ↳ all assets of a business

Multiple-Choice Questions

1. Sarah Gaines desires to start an interior decorating
    business. Sarah rents office space, purchases office
    equipment, and hires three employees. Sarah calls her
    business "Exquisite Interiors" and has business cards
    printed with such name. Sarah has created which of the
    following forms of organizations?

    a. sole proprietorship
    b. partnership
    c. limited partnership
    d. corporation

2. Refer to question 1. Sarah is required by state law to
    do which of the following?

    a. file articles of incorporation
    b. file a certificate of limited partnership
    c. file a fictitious name
    d. record the partnership agreement

3. Refer to question 1. Sarah is very successful in her new
    business. At the end of the year, her accountant an-
    nounces the business made a profit of $150,000. Sarah is
    required to:

a. file a tax return for the business.
b. report and pay income tax on the income earned.
c. distribute the income equally among the employees.
d. file an informational return.

4. Refer to question 1. During the second year Sarah is in business, she is sued by a client. The client slipped and fell in Sarah's office because the janitor had waxed the floor, making it dangerously slippery. The client was awarded a judgment for $350,000. Sarah does not have insurance to cover the entire amount. The extent of Sarah's liability is:

a. limited.
b. unlimited.
c. none at all.
d. only personal.

5. Jack, Joseph, and Jim have all agreed to sell real estate together. Jack will be responsible for finding and purchasing the properties. Joseph will be responsible for the construction of mid-sized houses on the properties, and Jim will act as the financial manager of the entire operation. Jack contributed $10,000 to the business, Joseph contributed $20,000, and Jim contributed $25,000.

The three have agreed to share the profits from the sales of houses in the following percentages: Jack 30%, Joseph 30%, and Jim 40%. The parties do not have any written agreement concerning their business relationship. Which of the following type of organization has been created?

a. sole proprietorship
b. partnership
c. limited partnership
d. corporation

6. Refer to question 5. If Jack, Joseph, and Jim never agreed on how profits would be shared, the law would impose which of the following?

a. profit sharing according to capital contribution
b. equal sharing among the parties
c. profit sharing according to amount of responsibilities in the business
d. none of the above

7. Refer to question 5. In the first year of the operation of the business, Jim reports to the others that the business had a loss of $10,000. How will the parties share in the loss?

a.   equally
b.   according to capital contributions
c.   according to the profit sharing ratios
d.   none of the above

8.   Refer to question 5. Jack, Joseph, and Jim are required
     to do which of the following at the end of the tax year?

     a.   file an informational return with the government
     b.   pay income taxes for the business
     c.   declare dividends
     d.   elect directors

9.   Refer to question 5. Assume Jack, Joseph, and Jim failed
     to specify how profits or losses were to be shared. If
     the business experiences a loss the second year of opera-
     tion, how will the loss be shared by Jack, Joseph, and
     Jim?

     a.   according to capital contributions
     b.   equally
     c.   Jack 25%, Joseph 25%, and Jim 50% because Jim is the
          financial manager
     d.   Jack 30%, Joseph 30%, and Jim 30%

10. In a partnership, if the partners failed to divide up
     management responsibilities, each of the partners has:

     a.   one vote in management decisions.
     b.   very little authority to manage the business.
     c.   no authority to enter contracts on behalf of the
          partnership.
     d.   none of the above.

11. Andy is an apprentice electrician working for Richard, an
     experienced electrician. Andy, not yet licensed, agrees
     to wire the house of a friend for $750. Andy performs
     the services but is not paid by his friend. If Andy sues
     to collect the $750 fee, who will win?

     a.   Andy will win because the friend breached the con-
          tract.
     b.   Andy will win if the licensing statute for electri-
          cians is a revenue raising statute.
     c.   Andy will lose because the licensing statute for
          electricians is a revenue raising statute.
     d.   Andy will win because the licensing statute for
          electricians is a regulatory statute.

12. Which of the following is/are necessary for the formation
     of a partnership?

I.   two or more persons
II.   co-ownership of partnership property
III. a written partnership agreement

a. I only
b. I and II
c. I, II, and III
d. I and III

13. A partnership is treated as a legal entity for which of the following?

I.   tax purposes
II.   to hold partnership property
III. to sell partnership property

a. I only
b. I and II
c. I, II, and III
d. II and III

14. The Uniform Partnership Act (UPA) is a state statute adopted in most states. The UPA attempts to do which of the following?

a. govern the creation of limited partnerships
b. limit the liability of partners
c. supply missing provisions in partnership agreements
d. license partnership activities

15. A partnership agreement is required to be in writing if:

a. more than three persons are partners.
b. the partnership is to last longer than one year.
c. the partnership sells merchandise.
d. none of the above.

16. The Able, Baker and Carlson partnership has been in the business of providing accounting services for the past three years. Able has decided to withdraw from the partnership due to a conflict with Baker. The result of Able's withdrawal is:

a. a dissolution only.
b. a dissolution and winding up.
c. a dissolution, winding up, and termination.
d. bankruptcy of the partnership.

17. Refer to question 16. Assume the Able, Baker and Carlson partnership ceases to do business. In the event the

partnership goes through a termination, who will have first priority to the assets?

a. partners for capital contribution
b. partners for loans
c. partners for profits
d. creditors for debts owed by the partnership

18. During the winding up period, a partner may <u>not</u> do which of the following?

a. complete transactions already begun at the time of dissolution
b. pay debts owed to creditors   *p. 430 book*
c. create new liabilities on behalf of the partnership
d. two of the above   *p. 288 WB.*

19. The creation of a limited partnership requires which of the following?

    I. filing of a certificate of limited partnership
   II. at least one general partner
 III. at least one limited partner

a. I only
b. I and II
c. I, II, and III
d. I and III

20. A certificate of limited partnership contains basic information about the limited partnership. Which of the following is <u>not</u> information required to be in the certificate?

a. name of the business   *p. 433*
b. number of employees
c. location of the business
d. initial contributions of limited partners

21. Which of the following statements is/are true about a limited partnership?

    I. All partners in a limited partnership have unlimited liability.

   II. Limited partners have unlimited liability.

 III. Limited partners' liability is limited to their capital contributions.

a. I only
b. I and II
c. III only
d. II only

22. Which of the following characteristics distinguish a corporation from a partnership for tax purposes?

   I. continuity of life
  II. number of managers
 III. limited liability

a. I only
b. I and II
c. I and III
d. I, II, and III

23. Mark Jensen has organized a limited partnership known as
M. J. Properties. Mark is the only general partner. The
limited partnership buys and sells commercial real estate. The partnership will buy an old building which
needs some work. Mark will then hire contractors to re-
model the building. Once the building is in good shape,
the property will be sold at a profit. The limited
partnership received capital contributions from forty-
five limited partners initially. Mark must have:

a. sufficient net worth as a general partner.
b. at least one other general partner by law.
c. all the profits from the business distributed to
    limited partners.
d. filed a registration statement under federal securi-
    ties laws.

24. Refer to question 23. Rick Hansen purchased a limited
partnership interest in Mark's business. Rick visits
Mark's office on a regular basis to help with the books.
Rick, as a result, begins to help Mark in determining
which properties to purchase. Rick is given an equal
vote on most management decisions. Which of the following is true?

a. Mark must allow Rick to participate in the business.
b. Rick will have unlimited liability for partnership
    debts.
c. Mark's liability has been limited.
d. All of the above.

25. The sale of a business along with merchandise and supplies is considered a bulk transfer under the Uniform

Commercial Code (UCC). If the seller and buyer comply with all the requirements of the UCC, the buyer acquires which of the following?

a. a successful business
b. rights to sell to prior customers of the seller
c. goods free of claims of creditors of the seller
d. all of the above

Essay Question

1. The partnership of Brad, Burt, and Betty was created as an accounting firm. The partnership operated for several years at a profit due to the low overhead and hard work of the partners. Two years ago, the partners decided to move their office to a more affluent part of town. Along with the move came many unexpected expenses. The partnership is now being dissolved. The liquid assets of the partnership are $300,000 and the liabilities are $280,000. Of the total liabilities, $50,000 is owed to Brad for a loan to the partnership. The other $230,000 is owed to outside creditors. The capital contributions were: Brad $20,000, Burt $20,000, and Betty $15,000. Profits and losses were to be shared as follows: Brad 50%, Burt 30%, and Betty 20%. How should the assets be distributed?

Answers to Study Questions

Fill-in-the-Blank Questions

If Terry decides to go into business alone, the easiest form of business entity for Terry to create is the <u>sole proprietorship</u>. (p. 424)

The owners of a corporation have <u>limited</u> liability for the debts of the business. (p. 425)

A partner in a partnership has <u>personal</u> liability for torts committed by employees within the scope of the partnership business. (p. 430)

A sole proprietor is <u>not required</u> to file with the state a certificate of operation. (p. 424)

True-False Questions

1. True (p. 424)

2. False. A sole proprietorship is not considered a taxable entity. (p. 425)

3. False. A partnership may operate under a fictitious name if proper filings are made. (p. 424)

4. True (p. 425)

5. False. General partners in partnership or limited partnership have unlimited liability. (p. 430)

6. True (p. 433)

7. True (p. 433)

8. True (p. 425)

9. False. The UPA does not supersede the partnership agreement but attempts to fill the gaps. (p. 429)

10. False. A bulk transfer is the sale of substantially all the assets including supplies, merchandise, and inventory of a business. (p. 439)

Multiple-Choice Questions

1.	a (p. 424)	
2.	c (p. 424)	
3.	b (p. 425)	
4.	b (p. 425)	
5.	b (p. 428)	
6.	b (p. 429)	
7.	c (p. 429)	
8.	a (p. 425)	
9.	b (p. 429)	
10.	a (p. 428)	
11.	b (p. 426)	
12.	b (p. 428)	
13.	d (p. 428)	

14. c (p. 429)
15. b (p. 428)
16. a (p. 430)
17. d (p. 430)
18. c (p. 430)
19. c (p. 433)
20. b (p. 433)
21. c (p. 433)
22. c (p. 425)
23. a (p. 433)
24. b (p. 433)
25. c (p. 440)

Essay Question

1. The priorities in the termination of a partnership are as follows:

1. debts owed to outside creditors;
2. debts owed to partners;
3. return of capital contribution; and
4. profits to partners.

Each class must be paid fully before the next class receives anything.

The partnership has incurred a loss as a result of the termination. The total liabilities of the partnership are $335,000 ($230,000 + 50,000 + 20,000 + 20,000 + 15,000), which is subtracted from the total liquid assets of $300,000, leaving a deficit of $35,000.

The partners must contribute to the deficit according to their loss sharing ratios. Brad will have to contribute $17,500 (35,000 x .50), Burt $10,500 (35,000 x .30), and Betty $7,000 (35,000 x .20).

The outside creditors are paid off first. The partners will receive back any funds loaned to the partnership, capital contributions, less amount contributed to the deficit. The partners will receive as follows: Brad $52,500 (50,000 loan + 20,000 - 17,500), Burt $9,500 (20,000 - 10,500), and Betty $8,000 (15,000 - 7,000). (p. 430)

Chapter 18
Corporate Law and
Franchising Law

Major Concepts

This chapter discusses the important aspects of corporation
law and franchising. The corporation is the most formal type
of business organization in its creation and operation. The
corporation can only be created through state statute. The
incorporators of a business must file articles of incorporation with the appropriate state office. Upon approval of the
articles of incorporation, the state will issue the corporate
charter which brings the corporation into existence. The
corporation is considered a legal entity by the law.

The corporation, as a fictitious person, acquires almost all
the protections in the United States Constitution. The corporation may buy and sell, sue, and be sued in its own name.
The powers of the corporation are listed in the articles of
incorporation and the bylaws. The corporation has only the
powers given it by state and federal Constitutions, statutes,
the articles of incorporation, and the bylaws.

The Model Business Corporation Act (MBCA) and the revised version have been adopted in over two-thirds of the states. Both
Acts help guide the formation and operation of the corporation.

A corporation may be incorporated in a state where it does not
have an office or do business. A corporation which does business in the state where incorporated is called a domestic
corporation. A corporation that is doing business in a state
where it is not incorporated is called a foreign corporation.

Foreign corporations must file with the state, or they can be fined or penalized.

The corporation is owned by the stockholders but managed by the board of directors and officers. The board of directors are elected by the shareholders. The board can only make resolutions when a board meeting has been called, directors properly notified, and a quorum (i.e., a majority) is present. All resolutions are voted on by the directors present.

The officers are appointed by the board of directors and required to manage the business operation on a day-to-day basis. Directors are responsible for making major management decisions and creating policy.

The corporation has a perpetual existence, limited liability of shareholders, ease of transfer of ownership, and is a taxable entity.

The business of franchising has been rapidly growing in recent years. The franchise is an arrangement where the franchisor transfers to the franchisee the right to use a trade name, trademark, or copyright. The franchise agreement is governed by contract law. The franchisor has the authority to require the franchisee to maintain the quality of the product or service being provided. The franchised organization is a particularly appealing form of enterprise to many individuals pursuing business ownership. The franchisee may incorporate or operate under another form of business entity.

Chapter Outline

I. Formation of the Corporation--The formation of a corporation requires state approval. The corporation is considered a separate legal entity owned by the shareholders. Most states have adopted the Model Business Corporation Act which sets the parameters for the creation and operation of the corporate entity. The process of forming a corporation is called incorporation.

Incorporators and promoters work together in creating the business and its legal status. The promoter usually enters into contracts for inventory, office space, supplies, and equipment for use in the business operation. These agreements are called pre-incorporation contracts because the corporation is not yet in existence at the time of their making. Once the corporation comes into existence, the board of directors will decide whether or not to adopt the pre-incorporation contracts. If the corporation fails to adopt the pre-incorporation contracts, the promoter is personally liable, unless the original parties agreed to look only to the corporation. If the corporation adopts the pre-incorporation contracts, both the corporation and the promoter are liable if a breach occurs.

The corporation may issue an entirely new contract called a novation for a pre-incorporation contract. A novation releases the promoter from contractual liability. The corporation has the sole responsibility on the contract, if a novation is issued.

The incorporator has the responsibility of obtaining state approval by filing articles of incorporation.

A.   Articles of Incorporation--An incorporator may choose to incorporate in any state, even if the corporation will not do business in the state. The articles of incorporation contain basic information about the corporation and must be filed with the proper state office, usually the secretary of state. States may differ as to the information required. Most states require the incorporator to state the corporate name, purpose of the corporation, duration, address, number of directors, and the name and address of the corporation's registered agent in the state. The company name must indicate the corporate entity by using the word "corporation," "incorporated," "company," "limited," or an abbreviation of such words.

If the articles of incorporation are in proper order and all the requirements have been fulfilled, the state will issue a charter bringing the corporation into existence. The corporation does not exist until the charter has been issued. A corporation that is validly formed is called a de jure corporation.

If the incorporator fails to fulfill the requirements of the statute for incorporation, the corporation does not come into existence, although the business may be considered a de facto corporation if the incorporator has made a good faith effort to file the articles of incorporation and started doing business as a corporation. A de facto corporation is not a properly formed corporation, but the shareholders will have limited liability.

B. Bylaws--Subsequent to the approval of the articles
of incorporation, the first board of directors meeting will be called and the board of directors will
adopt bylaws. The bylaws are the internal guidelines for managing the corporation. The specific
procedures for running the corporation are set out
in the bylaws.

C. Funding of the Corporation--The corporation raises
money by issuing stock to the public. The corporation may raise funds by issuing equity securities or
debt securities.

1. Equity Securities--The corporation has the power
to sell ownership interests called equity securities (i.e., shares of stock). The stockholders are the owners of the corporation. The
corporation issues a stock certificate in
exchange for a stated value or the market value
of a share to the shareholder. The shareholder
of common stock generally has the right to one
vote per share owned.

Common stockholders have the right to vote in
the election of the board of directors, on
amendments to the articles and bylaws, on
mergers, and other major corporate events.
Common stockholders are entitled to receive
dividends which have been declared by the board
of directors. The amount of the dividend is in
the discretion of the board. In the event the
corporation is dissolved, common stockholders
are entitled to receive a proportionate share of
the assets after creditors have been paid.

2. Debt Securities--The corporation may raise money
by issuing bonds (i.e., long-term secured debt)
or debentures (i.e., unsecured debt). The bond
is a commitment to repay the principal amount
borrowed to the corporation with a stated interest rate over a period of several years. Upon
the maturity of the bond, the corporation is
required to repay the principal amount. The
corporation will pay the bondholder (i.e., creditor) interest earned at least once a year. The
bond is secured by the assets of the corporation. Upon default by the corporation on a
bond, the bondholders have priority to the
assets of the business.

A debenture is similar to a bond but is not secured by the assets of the corporation. The
debenture earns interest at a fixed rate which
is paid at least annually. Once the debenture
reaches maturity, the corporation must repay the
principal amount.

3. Preferred Stock--Preferred stock has the characteristics of equity and debt securities. Preferred stockholders receive a preference as to
   dividends over common stockholders. A preferred
   stockholder usually receives a fixed rate annually. Preferred stockholders, in most cases, do
   not have any voting rights.

   If the corporation is dissolved and liquidated,
   the preferred stockholders have priority to payment over common stockholders.

II. Corporate Liability--The major advantage to the corpo-
    rate form is the limited liability of shareholders.
    Many businesses start out as sole proprietorships and
    progress to the corporate form to limit the personal
    liability of the owner(s).

    A. Shareholder Liability--Shareholders in a corporation
       have limited liability. The extent of the share-
       holders' liability is the amount invested in the
       shares of stock owned. Creditors must satisfy
       claims from the assets of the corporation.

       1. Pierce the Corporate Veil--In some cases, a
          creditor may be able to satisfy a claim from the
          personal assets of the shareholders (pierce the
          corporate veil). The veil is the corporate
          shell which protects the shareholder from
          attacking creditors. The veil may be removed if
          certain conditions are met. The following are
          factors used by a court to allow the corporate
          veil to be pierced.

          a. A shareholder ignores corporate formalities
             and existence.

          b. A shareholder commingles personal and corpo-
             rate assets such that the corporation is the
             alter ego of the shareholder.

          c. The corporation is grossly undercapitalized.

d. The corporation was used to defraud, circumvent the law, or accomplish some illegal objective.

Piercing the corporate veil is an extraordinary remedy which is rarely applied.

B. Director and Officer Liability--The board of directors are elected by the shareholders to make major management decisions and policy. The officers are elected by the board of directors to manage day-to-day affairs. Both directors and officers are considered fiduciaries of the corporation. This means directors and officers owe the corporation and the shareholders a duty of loyalty, trust, and honesty. The directors and officers must perform only in the interests of the corporation.

fiduciary, loyalty, trust & honesty

Directors are required to act with due care and investigate when the circumstances warrant. Directors may rely on the opinions and records of experts within the corporation. Directors and officers will not be personally liable for honest errors if good faith was exercised (i.e., business judgment rule). Directors or officers are required to exercise the same degree of care that a reasonably prudent person would have in the conduct of their own business affairs.

Directors have a duty of loyalty to the corporation and the shareholders. Directors and officers as fiduciaries must act only in the interests of the corporation. A director or officer who has taken advantage of a corporate opportunity without first making full disclosure has violated the duty of loyalty.

III. Control--The corporation is controlled by several groups of individuals. Shareholders, directors, and officers share in guiding the corporation in its business activities. Shareholders elect directors, directors appoint officers, and officers hire the employees of the corporation. Corporate officers, such as the president, vice-president, secretary, and the treasurer, can be removed by the board of directors at any time with or without cause.

A. Shareholders--Shareholders have the right to vote on all major corporate matters. An individual or group who own(s) a majority of the shares of stock in a corporation will be able to control the corporation. The majority shareholders have a fiduciary duty to the corporation and to the minority shareholders when selling or transferring their controlling interest. Minority shareholders are vulnerable to the majority interest. The court may restrict the sale of the majority shareholders' interest if it would be a detriment to the corporation or fraud is involved.

B. <u>Directors</u>--The board of directors are elected by the shareholders either by a straight vote or by cumulative voting. A straight vote exists where each shareholder receives one vote per share per director to be elected. This type of voting allows the majority shareholders to elect all the directors. Cumulative voting allows each stockholder to multiply the number of shares owned by the number of directors to be elected and cast all his or her votes for any director. Cumulative voting allows the minority interest an opportunity to be represented on the board.

The board of directors does not have the authority to delegate total control of the corporation to an individual officer. The board may delegate the responsibility for day-to-day management to the officers. The board cannot delegate broad authority to the officers which would allow extraordinary commitments, significantly encumber the business assets, or hinder the functioning of the corporation.

C. <u>Close Corporation</u>--A close corporation is one in which the shares of stock are held by family members or by a small number of persons. Usually, the shares are not traded on the open market.

In a close corporation, the majority shareholders have almost complete control of the corporation. The majority shareholders may elect all the directors which appoint all the officers and establish the budget, salaries, and fringe benefits.

IV. <u>Transferability of Interest</u>--The shares of stock in a corporation are usually freely transferable. The transfer of shares may be restricted by the federal securities laws, state blue sky laws, the articles of incorporation, or the bylaws.

In a close corporation, the shareholders commonly desire to keep the stock of the company in the family or owned by other close relationships. The incorporator of the close corporation generally includes a provision in the articles of incorporation which restricts the transfer of the shares issued. One such provision is called the "right of first refusal." The right of first refusal requires a shareholder who desires to sell, to first offer the shares to the corporation or the other shareholders. They may refuse to buy the shares, at which time the shareholder may sell to an outside party. The right of first refusal may also exist upon the death of a shareholder.

Restrictions on resale of a security must be printed on the stock certificate to give notice to sellers and buyers. The restriction must clearly indicate what type of transfer is being restricted. The courts will strictly construe any restriction on the transferability of shares.

V. Taxes--The corporation is considered a taxable entity. The corporation is required to pay federal income taxes on its earnings. The Internal Revenue Code provides a separate tax schedule for corporations. The corporation is taxed on a graduated rate structure.

Cash dividends distributed to shareholders are considered taxable income. The shareholder who attempts to avoid double taxation by the payment of excessive salaries or loans to the corporation may be challenged by the Internal Revenue Service.

Under the Internal Revenue Code, a corporation may petition for S corporation status. If the qualifications are met, the corporation will be taxed as a partnership yet maintain its legal status as a corporation. The major requirements are that the corporation only have thirty-five or less shareholders and no more than twenty-five percent of its income earned from passive investments. The corporation can issue only one class of stock and must be a domestic corporation. All other corporations are classified as C corporations under the Internal Revenue Code.

VI. Duration--The corporation has a perpetual existence. Because the corporation is a legal entity, its existence is not tied to the life of any individual. In some cases, the corporation may be dissolved.

A. Dissolution--A corporation may be dissolved upon approval of a resolution by the board of directors and majority vote of the shareholders. The corporation must file articles of dissolution with the state which brings the corporate existence to an end.

The corporation may liquidate all the assets or appoint a receiver to supervise a liquidation. The proceeds from the sale of the assets will be applied to the liabilities. If the debts of the corporation are not fully paid off, the creditors may not hold the directors, officers, or shareholders liable.

The corporation may be involuntarily dissolved if the corporate purpose becomes illegal or through an action of the state's attorney general which asserts fraudulent corporate activities or violations of state statute. The corporation may be also dissolved if a merger or consolidation occurs or the specified date in the charter has lapsed.

VII. Franchising--A franchise is a license transferred from the owner (franchisor) to the buyer (franchisee) to use the franchisor's trademark, trade name, or copyright. The franchisee operates as an independent business with the assistance of the franchisor in purchasing inventory, supplies, products, and advertising. The franchisor usually provides a complete business system to the franchisee.

A. Types of Franchises

1. Distributorship--In a distributorship, the franchisor, (i.e., manufacturer of a product) licenses a dealer, the franchisee to sell its products to the public. The dealer may have an exclusive territory which gives the dealer the exclusive right to sell the product in a designated geographic area. The franchisor may not issue a franchise to any dealer located within the exclusive territory. In some cases, the dealer may be required to sell only the products of the franchisor under an exclusive dealing contract.

2. Business Format--Under the business format franchise, the dealer purchases the right to use the trademark of the franchisor. The franchisee produces and sells the product on its own. The

franchisor may assist in the operation by setting standards to be followed and suggesting
product quality (e.g., McDonald's).

3. <u>Manufacturing or Processing Plant</u>--The franchisor sells to the franchisee the materials
necessary to produce the product. The product
is then sold by the franchisee (e.g., Coca-Cola
bottlers).

B. <u>Franchising Law</u>

1. <u>Disclosure Protection for Franchisee</u>--Some
states have enacted statutes which require the
franchisor to make certain disclosures to the
franchisee before the franchise agreement is
signed by the parties. Since the franchisee is
usually required to pay a substantial fee for
the license, the potential for a loss exists.
State statutes may require the franchisor to
disclose a recent financial statement, a statement of all fees the franchisee is required to
pay, and the business experience of the franchisor.

The Federal Trade Commission has promulgated the
Franchise Rule of 1978 which requires the seller
of a franchise to furnish a potential franchisee
the necessary information to make an informed
decision about purchasing the franchise. The
basic thrust of the rule is to require the franchisor to make full and fair disclosures concerning the franchise agreement to the franchisee.

C. <u>The Franchise Agreement</u>--The franchisor and franchisee enter into a contract defining the rights and
duties of the parties.

1. <u>Payment for Franchise</u>--The franchisee is purchasing the right to use the name, trademark, or
product of the franchisor. The franchisee is
usually required to pay a specified amount
initially and then some set percentage of the
annual sales thereafter. The franchisee may
also be required to contribute to the advertising and administrative costs of the franchisor
under the agreement.

2. Location--The franchisor, in many cases, will specify where the franchisee is to locate the business. The franchisor may place limitations on the location of dealers to restrain intra-branch competition. Some franchisors have very specific requirements for the exterior and interior of the building of the franchisee.

The franchisor may supply the training for personnel involved in the operation. The franchisor usually monitors the administration of each franchise, checking on the maintenance of standards and sales figures.

D. Price and Quality Controls--The franchisor may require the franchisee to purchase materials or supplies from the franchisor or some other approved merchant. A requirement that the franchisee purchase all materials and supplies from the franchisor is called an exclusive dealing contract which usually violates federal antitrust law as a restraint on trade. The franchisor may require the franchisee to purchase from approved outlets. The franchisor attempts to maintain the quality of the product through these types of requirements.

E. Termination of the Franchise Arrangement--The franchise agreement will specify the length of time the arrangement is to last. Most agreements only allow the arrangement to be terminated for cause (e.g., death, insolvency, breach of agreement). At the termination of the agreement, the franchisee forfeits the right to use the name or trademark of the franchisor.

F. Relationship Between Franchisor and Franchisee--The relationship between the parties may be principal/agent or that of an employer/independent contractor. An agency relationship between the franchisor (principal) and the franchisee (agent) is indicated if any of the following factors are present:

1. The agreement creates an agency.

2. The franchisor exercises a high degree of control over the franchisee's activities.

3. The appearance of the relationship from a reasonable person's point of view suggests an agency.

4. The franchisor receives a _great benefit_ from the franchisee's activities.

If the relationship indicates a high degree of independence between the parties, the franchisee will be considered an independent contractor. The distinction is important for determining the liability of the franchisor for the actions of the franchisee.

Study Questions

Fill-in-the-Blank Questions

Bob Burkhard owns a computer repair service business in central Kansas. The store is located near a university, and Bob services mostly students with malfunctioning personal computers. Bob is concerned about his potential liability as a business owner.

If Bob decides to incorporate his business, he must file
_____ with the state
    (articles of incorporation/a bond)
before the corporation can come into existence.

Bob will be known as the _____ if he
                    (president/incorporator)
makes all the arrangements for incorporation himself.

The corporation is the most _____ form of
business organization.   (informal/formal)

The _____ of a corporation are considered
        (articles/bylaws)
the internal rules for management.

articles → charter → bylaws.

True-False Questions

1. A domestic corporation can be created through the common law. ___F___ → _statutes_

2. The corporation is a legal entity. ___T___

3. Common stock is considered an equity security. ___T___
        sold ; not loan

4. Debentures are debt securities which are secured by the assets of the corporation. ___F___
        unsecured.
        bonds are secured debt securities

5. Preferred stock owners, in the event of a liquidation of
    the corporation, have priority over common stock owners.
    __T__

6. Shareholders in a corporation have unlimited liability
    for corporate debt. __F__

7. The board of directors are elected by the shareholders.
    __T__   Shareholders → b.o.d → officers.

8. The board of directors appoints the officers of the cor-
    poration. __T__

9. The president of the corporation is considered an
    officer. __T__

10. Generally, an officer of the corporation cannot be on the
    board of directors. __F__   can be both.

Multiple-Choice Questions

1. Which of the following items must be included in the
    articles of incorporation?

        I. duration of the corporation
       II. purpose of the corporation
      III. signature of the incorporator

        a. I only
        b. I and II
        c. I and III
        d. I, II, and III

2. A provision that the corporate directors will serve a
    two-year term if elected should be found in the:

        a. articles of incorporation.
        b. charter.
        c. bylaws.
        d. state law.

3. Before the Civil War, very few corporations existed. Not
    until the late 1800s did the corporation begin to become
    accepted. The reason the corporate form was limited in
    the nineteenth century was because people feared the cor-
    poration would cause:

        I. disastrous effects on economic life of the commu-
            nity.

     II.   enslave labor.
III.   dominate the state.

    a.   I only
    b.   I and II
    c.   I, II, and III
    d.   I and III

4. Stock which requires dividends not paid in a given year to be paid in later years before any common stock dividends are paid is called:

    a.   preferred stock.
    b.   cumulative preferred stock.
    c.   participating preferred stock.
    d.   convertible preferred stock.

5. Shares which may be issued under the articles of incorporation are called:

    a.   issued shares.
    b.   outstanding shares.
    c.   treasury stock.
    d.   authorized shares.

6. Tim purchased 100 shares of IBM stock two years ago for investment purposes. IBM recently repurchased Tim's shares at a substantial profit for Tim. IBM is holding the 100 shares. These shares are called:

    a.   treasury shares.
    b.   authorized shares.
    c.   outstanding shares.
    d.   none of the above.

7. Which of the following types of stock gives the shareholder the right to vote in the election of directors?

    a.   debentures
    b.   preferred stock
    c.   callable preferred stock
    d.   common stock

8. Ted Turk was an independent taxicab driver who owned his own taxi in Boston. Ted has been involved in many auto accidents. Fortunately for Ted, these accidents have been relatively minor. Ted was concerned about his personal liability if a major accident occurs. Ted decided to incorporate to avoid large liability lawsuits. Ted has violated which of the following?

a.   Model Business Corporation Act   *— guides formations*
b.   Revised Model Business Corporation Act
c.   the Internal Revenue Code
d.   Ted has not violated any law

9.   Refer to question 8. Ted is in a major auto accident
     which severely injures the other driver. Ted was found
     negligent, and the damages were assessed at $1,200,000.
     Ted's automobile insurance only covers $500,000 of the
     damages. The injured driver believes Ted should be re-
     quired to pay out of his personal assets. Ted's only
     business asset is his cab. The injured party may attempt
     to do which of the following?   *b/c → undercapitalized*
                                        p.457   the corporation
     a.   have Ted penalized
     b.   pierce the corporate veil
     c.   have Ted criminally prosecuted
     d.   all of the above

10. Refer to questions 8 and 9. The injured party may set
     aside the corporate shield if which of the following has
     occurred?

     all   a.   inadequate capitalization of the corporation
     rules b.   commingling of the personal and business assets
             c.   fraud in the operation of the business
             d.   all of the above

11. The relationship between the directors and the corpora-
     tion is one of trust and confidence. This is called:

     a.   the reasonable person rule.
     b.   a closely held corporation.
     c.   a fiduciary relationship.   *definition.*
     d.   none of the above.

12. The Semco Corporation is owned by the Semco family.
     There are six shareholders in the corporation. All six
     shareholders are involved in the management of the
     corporation. Semco is what type of corporation?

     a.   illegal
     b.   publicly held
     c.   franchise
     d.   close   *— definition*

13. Refer to question 12. In Semco's articles of incorpora-
     tion, the incorporators placed restrictions on the sale
     of the company's stock. The restriction requires a
     shareholder to offer his or her shares to the corporation

before selling to an outside third party. This provision is called:

a. preemptive rights.
b. right of first refusal.
c. cumulative voting.
d. none of the above

14. Refer to question 12. The bylaws of the Semco Corporation specify how directors will be elected. The bylaws allow each shareholder one vote per share times the number of directors to be elected. This provision is called:

a. preemptive right.
b. cumulative voting.
c. straight voting.
d. none of the above.

15. A provision in a company's articles of incorporation which allows a shareholder to always keep his or her percentage of ownership through the purchase of new issuances of stock is called:

a. cumulative voting.
b. straight voting.
c. preemptive rights.
d. business judgment rule.

16. Which of the following is a requirement of an S corporation?

a. not more than 35 shareholders
b. not more than 25 shareholders
c. no more than 35 percent of income
d. none of the above

17. The dissolution of a corporation may be voluntary or involuntary. Which of the following would cause an involuntary dissolution?

a. procurement of the charter by fraud
b. sale of corporate assets
c. a franchise
d. none of the above

18. Under the Federal Trade Commission (FTC) Franchise Rule, the franchisor is required to:

a. put up a bond.
b. make certain disclosures to the potential fran-
    chisees.
c. promote exclusive territories.
d. none of the above.

19. Greg Rubin has purchased a franchise from the fastest
    growing fast food chain in America. Greg entered a two-
    year franchise agreement. Under the agreement, the
    franchisee is required to purchase all its supplies and
    food products from the franchisor. The franchisor re-
    serves the right to inspect the quality of the product.
    The relationship between the franchisor and the fran-
    chisee is ordinarily called:

a. an agency.
b. that of an independent contractor.
c. an employment relationship.
d. all of the above.

20. Refer to question 19. The franchisor requires Greg to
    sell his products at a specified price. The franchisor
    will terminate the franchise if the prices are not fol-
    lowed. The franchisor has violated:

a. the antitrust law.
b. the FTC Franchise Rule.
c. the federal securities law.
d. two of the above.

21. Refer to question 19. The provision in the franchise
    agreement which requires Greg to buy all his supplies and
    food products from the franchisor is called:

a. preemptive rights.
b. an agency.
c. exclusive dealing.
d. none of the above.

22. Refer to question 21. Greg believes the provision vio-
    lates federal law and he is entitled to damages. Which
    federal law has been violated?

a. FTC Franchise Rule
b. the antitrust law
c. securities law
d. none of the above

23. In order for a franchise relationship to be classified as
    an agency, which of the following must be present?

    a.   a high degree of independence between franchisor and franchisee

    b.   a franchise contract

    c.   franchisor with a high degree of control over franchisee's activities

    d.   all of the above

24.   If the franchisor and franchisee are in an agency relationship, which party is considered the principal?

    a.   franchisor

    b.   franchisee

    c.   stockholders of the franchisor

    d.   stockholders of the franchisee

25.   A franchise is defined as the licensing of a franchisee to use the trade name, trademark, or _____ of the franchisor.

    a.   good will

    b.   copyright

    c.   employees

    d.   stock

Essay Question

1.   Les Woodson has a great idea for a new kind of consumer product. Les believes the product will have great success in the market. Les decides to incorporate and then start to manufacture the product. Les, before filing the articles of incorporation, leases a warehouse, purchases thousands of dollars of materials, and hires five employees. The articles of incorporation are filed with the state and subsequently approved. At the first meeting of the directors, the contracts are adopted by the board. Six months later, the corporation is insolvent. The creditors on the materials contracts are attempting to collect from Les. Is Les personally liable to the creditors?

Answers to Study Questions

Fill-in-the-Blank Questions

If Bob decides to incorporate his business, he must file articles of incorporation with the state before the corporation can come into existence. (p. 446)

Bob will be known as the <u>incorporator</u> if he makes all the arrangements for incorporation himself. (p. 446)

The corporation is the most <u>formal</u> form of business organization. (p. 446)

The <u>bylaws</u> of a corporation are considered the internal rules for management. (p. 447)

True-False Questions

1. False. A domestic corporation can only be created through the use of a state statute. (p. 446)

2. True (p. 446)

3. True (p. 449)

4. False. Debentures are not secured by the business assets. (p. 449)

5. True (p. 449)

6. False. Shareholders have limited liability for corporate debts. (p. 451)

7. True (p. 457)

8. True (p. 457)

9. True (p. 457)

10. False. Officers may also serve as directors if elected. (p. 458)

Multiple-Choice Questions

1.	d (p. 446)	11.	c (p. 454)
2.	c (p. 447)	12.	d (p. 458)
3.	c (p. 448)	13.	b (p. 459)
4.	b (p. 449)	14.	b (p. 458)
5.	d (p. 450)	15.	c (p. 446)
6.	a (p. 450)	16.	a (p. 460)
7.	d (p. 450)	17.	a (p. 461)
8.	d (p. 451)	18.	b (p. 462)
9.	b (p. 451)	19.	b (p. 461)
10.	d (p. 452)	20.	a (p. 464)

21. c (p. 464)   24. a (p. 465)
22. b (p. 464)   25. b (p. 461)
23. c (p. 465)

Essay Question

1.   Yes, Les, as a promoter, has personal liability on pre-
     incorporation contracts. Even if the corporation has
     adopted the pre-incorporation contracts, the promoter is
     still liable in the event the corporation breaches. The
     promoter may escape liability if a novation is issued or
     the parties agree to look only to the corporation for
     performance of the contract. (p. 446)

PART IV
BUSINESS AND GOVERNMENT REGULATION

Part Summary

Part IV deals primarily with government regulation of business. Congress, over the past 75 years, has attempted to regulate business activity which defrauded consumers, suppressed competition, discriminated against labor, and polluted the environment.

The Federal Securities Laws enacted in 1933 and 1934 require investors to receive important disclosures about companies issuing securities and prohibits fraud in the sale of a security. The Antitrust Laws have attempted to preserve the free enterprise system and protect competition. The Federal Labor Law gave employees the right to form unions and prohibited employers from discriminating against employees because of race, color, national origin, religion, and sex. The Federal Environment Laws placed some responsibility on business to abrogate pollution.

The final chapter of the Study Guide discusses International Business Law. The major sources of international law are customs, treaties, and international organizations. The increasing trend toward multinational organizations has made most aspects of international law significant.

Chapter 19
Securities Regulation

Major Concepts

The primary means of raising capital for a corporation is
through the sale of securities. Securities sold to the public
are regulated by the Securities and Exchange Commission (SEC).
The SEC is a federal administrative agency created by Congress
in 1934. The SEC has the responsibility of making sure investors are provided with accurate information concerning a company at the initial issuance of stock. The Securities Act of
1933 requires most issuers to file a registration statement
with the SEC before selling a security to the public. The
issuer must also provide potential buyers with a prospectus
which summarizes the information in the registration statement. Some issuers may avoid filing a registration statement
if an exemption can be claimed.

The Securities and Exchange Act of 1934 covers the sales of
securities in the secondary markets. Under the 1934 Act, the
SEC may prosecute a person involved with a fraudulent sale of
a security. The 1934 Act regulates brokers, dealers, and requires certain large companies to register. The SEC has the
authority to prosecute insider trading under the 1934 Act as a
violation of Rule 10b-5. All states have securities laws
which regulate the sale of securities. Most state securities
laws are similar to the 1933 and 1934 Acts. State securities
regulations are called Blue Sky Laws.

Chapter Outline

I. <u>The Securities Markets</u>--The corporation initially attempts to raise capital through the sale of securities. Traditionally, securities have been thought of as stocks and bonds. Stocks are traded in a variety of different markets. The most well-known securities markets are the New York Stock Exchange and the American Stock Exchange. Most major corporations in the United States have sold stock on one of these markets. A third market is called the Over-the-Counter market, which sells the securities of smaller companies.

A corporation will hire a company to underwrite an issuance of securities. The underwriter assists the issuing company in marketing and distributing the securities. The underwriter will line up brokers and dealers to sell the security to the public. An investor can purchase a security from a dealer at the prevailing market price. The price of a security will fluctuate, depending on the market, the economy, and the company. The stock exchange has the responsibility of maintaining an orderly market. The investor may freely sell and buy securities through a dealer.

II. <u>The Securities Act of 1933</u>--Congress enacted the Securities Act of 1933 in response to the collapse of 1929. The 1933 Act regulates the initial issuance of a security. The Act requires the issuer to make full and truthful disclosures before sales are executed. The Act does not guarantee the security being sold is a worthwhile investment. The 1933 Act requires that certain disclosures be made to the investor such that the investor can make an informed decision. The Act requires the issuer to file a registration statement with the SEC and provide potential investors with a prospectus.

A. <u>Registration</u>--Under Section 5 of the 1933 Act, an issuer of a security is required to file a registration statement with the SEC before offering it to the public. The definition of a security is very broad. A security is a stock, bond, note, debenture, evidence of indebtedness, transferable share, certificate of deposit, and an investment contract. An investment contract is comprised of the following four elements:

1. an investment of money or other consideration;

2. in a common enterprise;

3. with the investor expecting a profit; and

4. the profit is derived primarily through the ef-
    forts of others.

In an investment contract, the investor places his
or her money in a common enterprise, which usually
produces a profit. The investor is entitled to receive a percentage of the profits.

The common enterprise may be a real estate business,
citrus grove, or even a mink and chinchilla farm. A
sale of an investment contract is a sale of a security under the 1933 Act.

The issuer must compile extensive amounts of information about the corporation for inclusion in the
registration statement. The process of filing a
registration statement with the SEC is very time-
consuming and requires the issuer to incur great
expense.

The issuer must hire attorneys and accountants to
assist in assembling the information requested by
the SEC. The contents of the registration statement
include a description of the issuer's business over
the past five years, future plans of the business,
the issuer's products and/or services, the issuer's
principal plants and physical properties, any material legal proceedings the issuer is involved in,
and the certified financial statements. The preparation of the registration statement is a substantial undertaking most issuers would like to avoid.
The registration statement must be signed by the
corporation's principal executive officer, accounting officer, financial officer, and a majority of
the board of directors. The registration requirement applies only to issuers, underwriters, and
dealers.

1. Filing the Registration Statement--The registra-
    tion statement is filed with the SEC for ap-
    proval. The SEC has twenty days to notify the
    issuer of any necessary amendments. If the SEC
    fails to reject the registration statement or
    require amendments during the twenty-day waiting
    period, the statement automatically becomes ef-
    fective. The securities may not be sold until
    the registration statement becomes effective.

During the waiting period, oral offers may be
made, written advertisements called tombstone
ads may be published, and a red herring prospectus may be distributed to interested investors.
The red herring prospectus is a preliminary
prospectus which carries a legend in red ink,
which indicates that a filing has taken place
but is not effective.

2. The Prospectus--The prospectus is a pamphlet
    summarizing the most important information con-
    tained in the registration statement. The
    prospectus is filed along with the registration
    statement. The prospectus must be given to
    every purchaser of the security. The prospectus
    serves the purpose of informing the investor
    about the issuer such that a rational decision
    can be made on whether to purchase the security.

3. Misrepresentations in the Registration State-
    ment--The issuer and all the parties who signed
    the registration statement can be held liable
    for material misrepresentations or omissions in
    the registration statement. Under Section 11 of
    the Securities Act of 1933, the issuer, the
    issuer's auditor, the underwriter, lawyers, and
    the directors can be held liable for the damages
    to an investor from a decrease in price of the
    security. The omission or misrepresentation is
    material if the average prudent investor ought
    reasonably to be informed of the fact before
    purchasing the security.

4. Exemptions--An issuer is not required to file a
    registration statement if the security transac-
    tion or the security itself is exempt. An
    exemption allows the issuer to avoid the high
    cost and time delays of registration.

    a. Exempt Transactions--There are several types
        of exempt transactions under the 1933 Act.
        The exemption only covers the initial offer-
        ing of the security.

        (1) Small Offering Exemptions--Under SEC
             Regulations, certain small offerings of
             securities are exempt from filing a
             registration statement. The require-
             ments of Regulation A are as follows:

(a) $1.5 million of securities sold within twelve months, and

(b) proper notification and offering circular provided to SEC and potential buyers.

Under Regulation A, the issuer is not completely exempt because a simplified form of registration is required. The issuer must file an offering circular which is similar to a prospectus with the SEC.

(2) Regulation D--Regulation D is a regulation adopted by the SEC to provide exemptions for private offerings. Regulation D provides exemptions under three rules: Rule 504, 505, and 506.

(a) Rule 504--Rule 504 provides an exemption for sales of securities up to $500,000 in a twelve-month period without the use of any advertising or solicitation, and the issuer must notify the SEC within 15 days of the first sale of securities. A subsequent sale of the securities may require filing a registration statement.

(b) Rule 505--Rule 505 provides an exemption to the issuer of up to $5 million in securities during a twelve-month period if there are no more than 35 unaccredited investors (i.e., average unsophisticated investor). The issuer cannot advertise or solicit the sale of securities. The issuer may sell to an unlimited number of accredited investors. An accredited investor is an individual or a company which has a high level of sophistication in the securities markets. Examples of accredited investors are: an insurance company, directors and officers of the seller, an individual with an annual income of over $200,000 for three consecutive years, an individual with a net worth over $1 million, and an individual who purchases $150,000 of the securities and the purchase price does not exceed 20% of the person's net worth. The issuer must provide purchasers with material information about the corporation if unaccredited investors are involved and notify the SEC within 15 days of the first sale.

(c)   <u>Rule 506/Private Placement</u>-- Rule 506 provides an exemption to an issuer for an unlimited amount as long as no advertising or solicitation occurs and only 35 unaccredited investors are involved, but such investors must have some level of sophistication in the securities markets. The investor has a level of sophistication if he or she has knowledge and experience in financial matters.

The seller may sell to an unlimited number of accredited investors. If unaccredited investors are involved, the seller must supply all purchasers with material information regarding the issuer and its business. The seller must notify the SEC within 15 days of the first sale.

(d)   <u>Intrastate Offering</u>--The intrastate offering exemption allows the issuer to sell an unlimited amount of securities to purchasers that are residents of the state of the issuer. The issuer must be organized within the state and principally doing business there. No resale of the securities is allowed to nonresidents for nine months. No sales or offers can be made to a nonresident during the initial offering period. The seller must take precautions to prevent sales or resales to non-residents. Usually a legend is printed on the certificate stating the securities are not registered and that sales and resales are restricted to residents.

b. Exempt Securities--Some securities are exempt from registration under the 1933 Act. Securities issued by governments, banks, savings and loan associations, charitable organizations, and common carriers are exempt. In addition, securities provided as a stock dividend or stock split are exempt.

Unsolicited broker or dealer transactions are exempt from registration. The exemption applies to the broker's or dealer's part in the transactions, and the seller must establish he or she is not an issuer, underwriter, or dealer. A transaction by any person not an issuer, underwriter, or dealer is considered a "casual sale" and exempt from the registration requirements of the 1933 Act.

5. Liability for Failing to File a Registration Statement--Any person who offers or sells a security in violation of the Act's registration requirements can be held liable to purchasers of the security for the amount paid, plus interest.

III. The Securities Exchange Act of 1934--The Securities Exchange Act of 1934 regulates the secondary sales of securities on the securities markets. The 1934 Act attempts to preserve the fairness and integrity of the national exchanges.

A. Registration Requirements--The 1934 Act requires the participants in the market, excluding the investors, to register.

1. National Security Exchanges--The national security exchanges must register with the SEC. The security exchange must provide the SEC with extensive information about the organization, its operation, and membership. The exchange, once registered, is subject to the continued regulation by the SEC. More than a dozen national exchanges are registered with the SEC. The most

well-known exchanges are the New York Stock
Exchange (NYSE) and the American Stock Exchange
(AMEX).

2.   <u>Brokers and Dealers</u>--Brokers and dealers of securities engaged in interstate commerce must
register with the SEC. Any broker or dealer
violating the federal securities laws may have
his or her registration suspended.

3.   <u>A Company with Securities Traded on a National
Exchange or with More than $3 Million in Assets
and Held by 500 or More Persons</u>--A company which
has issued securities traded on a national exchange or that has $3 million in assets and 500
or more shareholders must register with the SEC.

B.   <u>Reporting Requirements</u>--Companies required to register under the 1934 Act must file periodic reports
with the SEC. The three principal types of reports
required are as follows:

1.   <u>10-Q/Quarterly Reports</u>--A registered company
must file quarterly financial reports with the
SEC.

2.   <u>10-K/Annual Reports</u>--A registered company must
file an annual financial report which has been
certified by an independent certified public
accountant with the SEC. The annual report must
be filed within 90 days after the end of the
company's fiscal year.

3.   <u>8-K/Current Reports</u>--A registered company must
file an 8-K form when material events occur
(such as a disposition of a significant amount
of the assets) with the SEC.

C.   <u>Proxy Requirements</u>--The SEC regulates the solicitation of proxies from shareholders. A proxy is a
written authorization to vote on behalf of the owner
of a share of stock. Proxy materials must be filed
with the SEC before solicitation occurs. The party
soliciting the proxy of another must disclose all
matters to be voted on by the stockholder.

D.   <u>Antifraud Provisions</u>--The 1934 Act has two major
antifraud provisions: Section 16 and Section 10(b).
These provisions protect investors from being defrauded in the sale of a security.

1. Section 16/Illegal Short-Swing Profits--Sec-
    tion 16 prohibits an officer, director, or 10%
    owner from trading shares of any class of the
    company within a six-month period for profit.
    If an officer, director, or 10% owner buy the
    company's securities and subsequently sell
    within six months at a profit, Section 16 re-
    quires the insider to forfeit the profit gained
    to the issuer.

    The SEC is not required to prove the profit was
    obtained through the use of inside information.
    The liability of the insider is automatic if an
    illegal short-swing profit is obtained.

2. Section 10(b) and Rule 10b-5/Insider Trading--
    Under the 1934 Act, it is unlawful "to use or
    employ, in connection with the purchase or sale
    of any security . . . any manipulative or decep-
    tive device or contrivance, in contravention of
    such rules and regulations as the SEC may pre-
    scribe . . . ." Rule 10b-5 declares all
    activity illegal which defrauds or misleads a
    person in connection with the sale or purchase
    of a security.

    The courts have expansively interpreted Rule
    10b-5 to allow prosecution of a wide variety of
    activities. Generally, violations of Rule 10b-5
    fit into two categories: insider trading and
    manipulation by brokers and dealers in the trad-
    ing of a security. Under Rule 10b-5, a private
    party or the SEC may bring a lawsuit against the
    violator. The plaintiff must prove several
    elements under Rule 10b-5 to prevail.

    a. Elements of Proof of a Rule 10b-5 Violation

        (1) a material misstatement or omission of
             fact,

        (2) the defendant acted with the intent to
             deceive or in reckless disregard of the
             truth (scienter),

        (3) the plaintiff relied on the defendant's
             deceptive device, manipulation, or con-
             duct in the sale or purchase of a se-
             curity, and

(4)   the plaintiff suffered damages caused
by the defendant's conduct (only for a
private party).

Any material omission or misrepresentation
of a material fact in connection with the
sale or purchase of a security can be prosecuted by the SEC as a violation of Rule
10b-5. The courts have defined what is a
material misstatement or omission. A fact
is material if there is a substantial like-
lihood that its disclosure would have been
considered significant by a reasonable investor at the time. The provision generally
prohibits fraudulent activity and not mere
negligence. The requirement of scienter is
defined as a mental state or knowledge of
the deception.

Insider trading has been described as the
use or possession of nonpublic material information to make a profit or avoid a loss
in the purchase or sale of a security by an
insider. An insider may not trade on material nonpublic information, unless the information has been disclosed and translated
to the investing public.

An insider is a corporate officer, director,
majority shareholder, or anyone who has access to nonpublic material information about
the issuer. When an insider communicates
inside information to another person, that
person is called a tippee. A person who
discovers nonpublic information or who receives it through a tip is not in violation
of Rule 10b-5, unless that person owes a
duty to disclose the information before
trading. Traditional insiders owe a duty to
disclose material nonpublic information
before trading on it.

b.   Liability for Violating Rule 10b-5--A violator of Section 10b and Rule 10b-5 may face
civil and criminal liability. A private
party may sue a violator to rescind the sale
or recover money damages. Damages are the
difference between the price received in a
sale of the security and the price he or she
should have received had there been no
fraud.

The SEC may bring suit against the violator to recover the loss avoided or the profit gained. Under the Insider Trading Sanctions Act of 1984, the SEC may recover up to three times the profit made or loss avoided.

In criminal actions, the Justice Department may seek to have an individual fined from $100,000 to $1 million. A corporation or partnership may be fined from $500,000 to $2.5 million. An individual may receive a prison sentence of up to a maximum of ten years. Securities firms are required to monitor insider trading and may be penalized for failing to do so.

IV.   State Securities Laws--The states and federal government regulate the sale of securities concurrently. State securities laws are similar to 1933 and 1934 Acts. Most state laws require some form of registration, prohibit fraud, and mandate certain disclosures. State securities laws are called Blue Sky Laws.

V.   The Securities Investor Protections Act of 1970 (SIPA)--SIPA is an amendment to the 1934 Securities and Exchange Act. The amendment created the Securities Investor Protection Corporation to manage a fund to protect investors from financial harm when stock brokerage houses fail.

VI.   Foreign Corrupt Practices Act (FCPA)--The FCPA amended the 1934 Securities and Exchange Act in 1977. The FCPA requires public corporations to maintain accurate records of their financial activity and to have an internal accounting system to ensure accurate records.

The Act attempts to require companies to disclose illegal activities. The FCPA also prohibits bribery of foreign government officials to obtain or retain business.

Study Questions

Fill-in-the-Blank Questions

The Amcan Company desires to raise capital through the sale of common stock. The Amcan Company is presently privately owned by the Schmidt family. The company's owners seek to sell $4.5 million of stock to a small number of commercial investors.

Amcan, before selling any shares of stock, must determine if a registration statement must be filed with the

_____.
(Federal Trade Commission/Securities and Exchange Commission)

The _____ Act requires an issuer to provide a
        (1933/1934)
prospectus to potential public purchasers before a sale is completed.

Amcan may attempt to claim a _____
                              (Rule 505/the savings and loan
_____exemption to avoid the registration process.
  association)

Section 11 of the 1933 Act applies to the _____
                                            (banker/
_____involved in the initial issu-
  chief financial officer)
ance of a security.

True-False Questions

1. The Securities Act of 1933 defines a security broadly.
    _____

2. The Securities and Exchange Act of 1934 primarily regu-
    lates the sale of securities in the secondary markets.
    _____

3. The Securities Act of 1933 is known as the "Truth in Se-
    curities" law. _____

4. The Securities and Exchange Commission was established by
    the Securities and Exchange Act of 1934. _____

5. All sellers of securities must file a registration state-
    ment before selling to the public. _____

6. The registration requirements under the 1933 Act are
    exactly the same as those under the 1934 Act. _____

7. An individual investor with an annual income of over
    $200,000 for three consecutive years is considered an
    accredited investor. _____

8. An issuer who is properly exempt from filing a registra-
    tion statement is also exempt from the antifraud provi-
    sions. _____

9. A company whose securities are traded on a national ex-
    change must register under the 1934 Act. _____

10. Rule 10b-5 is based upon Section 10b of the Securities
    and Exchange Act of 1934. _____

Multiple-Choice Questions

1. Which of the following is <u>not</u> a security as defined under
    the Securities Act of 1933?

    a. investment contract
    b. insurance policy
    c. debenture
    d. stock

2. The owner of hundreds of acres of orange groves in Flor-
    ida offers to the public interests in the business. A
    buyer can purchase a share in the orange groves which
    produce income from the efforts of the owner. One-
    hundred investors buy interests in the orange grove with
    the expectation of deriving a profit. None of the
    investors are involved in the business. The investors
    have purchased:

    a. an investment contract.
    b. a certificate of deposit.
    c. a debenture.
    d. a preferred stock.

3. Refer to question 2. The owner offering the shares must
    do which of the following to be in compliance with the
    Securities Act of 1933?

      I. file a registration statement if no exemption is
          claimed
     II. file a proxy statement
    III. file a 10-K form

    a. I only
    b. I and II
    c. I and III
    d. I, II, and III

4. The Foreign Corrupt Practices Act requires which of the
    following?

      I. proxy statements to be filed with the SEC

II. the corporation to maintain records which accurately reflect financial activities

III. the prospectus to be filed with the SEC

a. I only
b. II only
c. I and II
d. I and III

5. Bob Ivanic orchestrated a plan to obtain confidential information from Larry Dirk, a stockbroker, about takeover target companies. Bob would pay Larry 10% of his profits. Bob would invest in the takeover target before the acquiring company announced its intentions to make a tender offer. The price of the stock of the target would rise, and Bob would subsequently sell at a substantial profit. Which of the following has Bob violated?

a. Section 16 of the 1934 Act
b. Rule 10b-5 of the 1934 Act
c. Section 11 of the 1933 Act
d. none of the above

6. Refer to question 5. Assume Bob is being prosecuted by the SEC under the 1934 Act. The name of the offense committed by Bob is most likely:

a. bribery.
b. failure to file.
c. a corrupt practice.
d. insider trading.

7. Refer to question 5. If Bob is found in violation of the 1934 Act, the government may seek which of the following?

I. a criminal fine from $100,000 to $1 million
II. three times the profit gained by Bob
III. imprisonment of up to 10 years

a. I only
b. I and II
c. I, II, and III
d. I and III

8. Which of the following Acts allows the government to assess a fine against a corporation for insider trading from $500,000 to $2.5 million?

    a.   Insider Trading Sanctions Act
    b.   Insider Trading and Securities Fraud Enforcement Act
    c.   Foreign Corrupt Practices Act
    d.   Securities Investor Protection Act

9.   The Securities Act of 1933 requires some issuers to file a registration statement before selling their securities to the public. The registration statement must be signed by which of the following persons?

      I. principal executive officer
     II. principal financial officer
   III. principal accounting officer

    a.   I only
    b.   II only
    c.   I and III
    d.   I, II, and III

10.   After an issuer files a registration statement with the SEC, the SEC will examine the registration for accuracy and completeness. The time after the registration statement is filed but before it is approved is called the waiting period. The waiting period is usually:

    a.   30 days long.
    b.   20 days long
    c.   two weeks long.
    d.   10 days long.

11.   During the waiting period, which of the following is permitted?

      I. a sale of the security
     II. a tombstone advertisement
   III. a red herring prospectus distributed

    a.   I only
    b.   I and II
    c.   II and III
    d.   I, II, and III

12.   BarChris Corporation filed a registration statement under the 1933 Act with the SEC for the sale of debentures. The registration statement was approved by the SEC, and the debentures were sold to the public. The company subsequently went bankrupt. The purchasers of the debentures brought suit under the 1933 Act, alleging the registration statement contained material false statements and omissions. The purchasers are alleging a violation of which Section of the 1933 Act?

   a.   5
   b.   16
   c.   10b
   d.   11

13.   Refer to question 12. The purchasers are attempting to
      hold any party who signed the registration statement li-
      able for damages. In order to be exonerated from liabil-
      ity, the underwriters who signed BarChris's registration
      statement must prove:

      a.   a due diligence defense.
      b.   contributory negligence.
      c.   reasonableness.
      d.   all of the above.

14.   Refer to question 12. To determine if the misstatement
      or omission is material, the court will consider:

      a.   the total amount of securities sold.
      b.   the number of securities sold.
      c.   what the average prudent investor ought reasonably be
           informed about.
      d.   none of the above.

15.   Which of the following are exempt securities under the
      Securities Act of 1933?

        I.   sale of securities by the First National Bank
       II.   sale of bonds by a church
      III.   sale of interests in a limited partnership

      a.   II and III
      b.   I and II
      c.   I and III
      d.   I, II, and III

16.   Regulation D has been promulgated by the SEC to provide
      exemptions to private sales of securities. Which provi-
      sion of Regulation D allows the issuer to sell up to $5
      million securities within a twelve-month period without
      filing a registration statement?

      a.   Rule 504
      b.   Rule 505
      c.   Regulation A
      d.   all of the above

17.   Under Regulation D, the issuer is prohibited from doing
      which of the following activities in the sale of a secu-
      rity?

    I.   advertising
   II.   selling to nonresidents
 III.   selling to the public

   a.   I only
   b.   II only
   c.   I and II
   d.   II and III

18. The intrastate offering exemption allows an issuer to sell an unlimited amount of securities without having to file a registration statement. The major restriction placed on the sale to claim the exemption is:

   a.   the number of investors is 35.
   b.   only accredited investors may purchase.
   c.   the issuer is a nonresident.
   d.   all offerees and purchasers are residents of the state.

19. The director of the Delaware Corporation, Joseph Welby, purchased 10,000 shares of the company's stock on March 1. On April 15, Joseph sold the shares at a substantial gain. Joseph is required to automatically return the profits to the Delaware Corporation under what provision of the Securities and Exchange Act of 1934?

   a.   Section 10b
   b.   Rule 10b-5
   c.   Section 16
   d.   Section 11

20. The Securities and Exchange Act of 1934 requires which of the following to register with the SEC?

   I.   brokers and dealers
  II.   national exchanges
 III.   national security associations

   a.   I only
   b.   I and II
   c.   I, II, and III
   d.   II and III

21. The TGS Corporation discovered a major ore deposit on their land in Ontario. TGS attempted to purchase all the land near the valuable ore deposit. The company issued a press release which played down the discovery. Several officers, before any information about the discovery was released, purchased thousands of shares of the company's

stock. After the discovery had been fully disclosed to the public and the price of the stock increased, the officers sold their shares at a profit. The SEC charged the officers with violating Rule 10b-5. The SEC will be required to prove which of the following to win the case?

    I.   scienter of the defendants
   II.   material misstatement or omission of fact
 III.   the securities were registered

   a.   I only
   b.   I and II
   c.   I, II, and III
   d.   II and III

22.   Refer to question 21. If the officers purchased options on the company's stock, the court will order the option contracts:

   a.   valid and enforceable.
   b.   rescinded.
   c.   carried out.
   d.   none of the above.

23.   Rule 10b-5 requires proof that the violator acted with knowledge of the manipulation or deceptive device. The requirement of knowledge is also known as:

   a.   negligence.
   b.   materiality.
   c.   scienter.
   d.   none of the above.

24.   Chiarella was a printer in New York. Chiarella printed corporate takeover announcements. The announcements were delivered to Chiarella in code. Chiarella discovered the code and purchased shares of stock in the takeover target company. Chiarella realized over $30,000 by trading in target companies' stock. Chiarella is considered a:

   a.   tipper.
   b.   corporate insider.
   c.   fiduciary.
   d.   none of the above.

25.   Refer to question 24. The court should hold Chiarella in violation of which of the following?

   a.   Section 16
   b.   Section 10b

c.   Rule 10b-5
d.   none of the above

Essay Question

1.   A major business newspaper printed articles spotlighting
     particular corporations. The column had the effect of
     increasing the price of the company's stock if the
     article was favorable or decreasing the price if unfa-
     vorable. The author of the articles agrees with several
     friends to release the column to them before it is pub-
     lished. The friends make several purchases for them-
     selves and on behalf of the author. The SEC prosecutes
     the author for violating Rule 10b-5. What is the result?

Answers to Study Questions

Fill-in-the-Blank Questions

Amcan, before selling any shares of stock, must determine if a
registration statement must be filed with the Securities and
Exchange Commission. (p. 476)

The 1933 Act requires an issuer to provide a prospectus to
potential purchasers before a sale is completed. (p. 478)

Amcan may attempt to claim a Rule 505 exemption to avoid the
registration process. (p. 483)

Section 11 of the 1933 Act applies to the chief financial
officer involved in the initial issuance of a security.
(p. 479)

True-False Questions

1.   True (p. 474)

2.   True (p. 476)

3.   True (p. 476)

4.   True (p. 476)

5.   False. A seller of a security may be exempt from filing
     under the 1933 Act. (p. 482)

6. False. The 1933 Act requires a registration statement to be filed, whereas the 1934 Act requires some companies to register. (p. 476)

7. True (p. 483)

8. False. The antifraud provisions apply to all sales of securities whether or not exempt. (p. 486)

9. True (p. 484)

10. True (p. 486)

Multiple-Choice Questions

1.	b (p. 474)	
2.	a (p. 474)	
3.	a (p. 476)	
4.	b (p. 478)	
5.	b (p. 486)	
6.	d (p. 486)	
7.	c (p. 478)	
8.	b (p. 478)	
9.	d (p. 479)	
10.	b (p. 479)	
11.	c (p. 479)	
12.	d (p. 479)	
13.	a (p. 480)	
14.	c (p. 480)	
15.	b (p. 483)	
16.	b (p. 483)	
17.	a (p. 483)	
18.	d (p. 483)	
19.	c (p. 486)	
20.	c (p. 484)	
21.	b (p. 488)	
22.	b (p. 489)	
23.	c (p. 491)	
24.	d (p. 493)	
25.	d (p. 493)	

Essay Question

1. This case has not yet been conclusively decided by the United States Supreme Court. The facts describe the Carpenter v. United States case. The Court in Carpenter was equally divided on the issue of securities fraud. The Court refused to accept the SEC's misappropriation theory for Rule 10b-5 cases. The SEC argued that R. Foster Winans, The Wall Street Journal reporter, misappropriated confidential material information from his employer for his own benefit.

    Winans and his accomplices traded on the confidential information and the effect the column had on the stock price. (See Carpenter v. U.S., 108 S.Ct. 316 (1987).) (pp. 484-494)

Chapter 20
Antitrust Law

Major Concepts

The antitrust laws were developed to promote and protect competition in the United States. In 1890, the Sherman Act was enacted to alleviate the business environment from harmful monopolies and restraints. The government began to take on some of America's largest corporations, charging violations of the Sherman Act. Some corporations had combined with competitors through the use of a legal entity called a trust, for the purpose of reducing competition and stabilizing prices. The government sought to break up such trusts, and, thus, the name antitrust evolved. The Sherman Act, Section 1, prohibits unreasonable restraints of trade. The courts have developed two rules to determine whether an activity is unreasonable and in violation of Section 1 of the Act. The rule of reason applies to activities which may or may not be unreasonable restraints. Under the rule of reason, the court must carefully consider the circumstances and the effect on competition.

The per se rule applies to activities which have a pernicious effect on competition and are automatically considered unreasonable. The courts have determined certain activities, such as price fixing, under the per se rule. In addition, horizontal market divisions and group boycotts are considered per se violations.

A monopoly may violate Section 2 of the Sherman Act, if the firm has monopoly power and the intent to monopolize. A firm may violate Section 2 by monopolizing, attempting to monopolize, or conspiring to monopolize.

A merger may be declared illegal under the Clayton Act, Section 7, if it substantially lessens competition or tends to create a monopoly. The Federal Trade Commission and the Department of Justice may challenge a merger, if the probable effect of the merger is to substantially lessen competition. Three types of mergers may occur: horizontal, vertical, or conglomerate. A merger involving a failing company does not violate Section 7 of the Clayton Act.

In 1914, Congress enacted the Clayton Act to bolster antitrust enforcement. The Clayton Act prohibits price discrimination, exclusive dealing, and tying arrangements which substantially lessen competition. The Clayton Act restricted mergers which would tend to create a monopoly.

The Federal Trade Commission Act was passed in 1914 to prevent "unfair or deceptive acts or practices in commerce." The Federal Trade Commission was created from the Act as an independent administrative agency headed by five commissioners. The FTC has broad authority to investigate violations of the Clayton Act and the FTC Act.

The antitrust laws may be enforced by the FTC, Department of Justice, and private parties. A private party may sue for treble damages (three times) under the Sherman and Clayton Acts. The government may pursue civil and criminal remedies against violators.

Chapter Outline

I.   Sherman Act--Congress in 1890 enacted the Sherman Act to combat forces which were suppressing competition. Big business had attempted to avoid the competitive market by a variety of collusive activities. The effect of eliminating competition was felt by consumers who had to pay higher prices for less quality products and services.

The Sherman Act has two major provisions dealing with anticompetitive activity.

A.   Section 1 of the Sherman Act--Section 1 of the Act prohibits contracts, combinations, or conspiracies in restraint of trade or commerce. A violation of Section 1 is illegal and considered a felony punishable by fine and/or imprisonment. The literal interpretation of Section 1 might lead to some unintended results. The language alone prohibits all restraints of trade (e.g., a simple contract for the sale of goods restrains trade in some respects).

The courts determined that a literal reading was inappropriate and developed two rules to determine if a violation of Section 1 has occurred: the Rule of Reason and the Per Se Rule.

The U.S. Supreme Court has declared that only unreasonable restraints of trade are illegal under Section 1.

1. <u>The Rule of Reason</u>--The rule of reason requires the court to review all the circumstances of a case before deciding whether the activity was an unreasonable restraint on competition. The court in a rule of reason case will consider the purpose and intent of the restraint by the parties imposing it. If the parties have a legitimate purpose for the restriction, the court will further evaluate the effect on competition. Activities which have a substantial adverse effect on competition tend to be unreasonable.

    Some activities which are judged under the rule of reason are vertical territorial restrictions and exclusive dealing contracts.

2. <u>The Per Se Rule</u>--The per se rule is used for activities considered inherently anticompetitive and having a pernicious effect on competition. Activities which are labeled per se are automatically unreasonable restraints of trade and illegal under Section 1 of the Act. The court need only determine if a contract, combination, or conspiracy existed to declare the activity unreasonable. The courts have predetermined that certain activities should be judged under the per se rule, such as price fixing agreements. The court will not delve into the circumstances of the activity under the per se rule. Over the years, the courts have labeled several anticompetitive activities as per se.

3. <u>Essential Elements of a Section 1 Violation</u>--A Section 1 violation requires proof of three elements. The plaintiff must prove:

a.   an agreement,

b.   between two or more parties, which

c.   restrains trade unreasonably.

The plaintiff need not prove the agreement by producing a written contract.

Most agreements involving anticompetitive activities are not reduced to written form. Parties may act upon oral agreement or even through concerted action. Some agreements may never be expressed in conversations between two or more parties but are tacit understandings that specific practices will follow. For instance, when a retailer follows the price of his competitor in the market, has an agreement come into existence? The courts have stated that parallel business behavior does not conclusively establish an agreement, although consciously parallel behavior is circumstantial evidence of a possible agreement. If a party acts independently, no violation of Section 1 exists.

Once an agreement has been proven, the plaintiff must prove an unreasonable restraint of trade or competition. If the per se rule is applicable, the plaintiff need not prove the restraint affects competition.

4.   Prohibited Activities under Section 1--Three anticompetitive activities which violate Section 1 are: price fixing, horizontal market division, and group boycotts.

a.   Price Fixing--Price fixing can be either horizontal or vertical. If two or more competitors fix the price of an item, it is considered horizontal price fixing. If two or more persons in a products distribution line fix price, it is vertical price fixing. Either form of price fixing is considered a per se violation.

The courts have said that any combination which tampers with price structures is unlawful activity. An agreement which raises, depresses, fixes, pegs, or stabi-

lizes the price of a commodity is illegal
per se. The parties need not agree as to a
specific price but may merely agree on a
formula to derive a price. Since price is
composed of other factors, such as credit,
discounts, or rebates, any agreement to
stabilize these factors is also illegal.

Even the exchange of price information
between competitors has been held to violate Section 1. Trade associations must be
careful as to not exchange specific price
information to its member competitors.

The most common vertical price fixing
agreements are between manufacturer
(i.e., franchisor) and a retailer
(i.e., franchisee).

The manufacturer may legally suggest the
retailer sell at a specified price, but if
the retailer is required to sell at such
price the activity is illegal. This arrangement is known as a resale price
maintenance agreement.

b. Horizontal Division of Markets--Dividing up
    the market for a product between two or
    more competitors is a per se violation.
    Competitors may divide up the market by
    agreeing to sell in one territory, making
    sure they are not in competition with each
    other. If the competitors previously were
    competing in two geographic areas and sub-
    sequently agree that one competitor will
    sell in one area and the other competitor
    will sell in a different area, the Sherman
    Act, Section 1, has been violated.
    (e.g., A and B are competitors in Utah and
    Nevada. A agrees to sell only in Utah, and
    B agrees to sell only in Nevada.)

c. Group Boycott--When two or more parties
    agree to exclude a party from a market,
    competition is lessened and a violation of
    Section 1 exists. A group of distributors
    may agree to not sell to a retailer who
    discounts the product, and as such a
    violation occurs. The purpose underlying a
    group boycott is to drive a competitor from

the market. Group boycotts, also known as
joint boycotts, are per se violations.

A seller may refuse to sell to a buyer and
not violate Section 1. A unilateral refusal to deal with a party is not illegal,
even if the refusal is based upon the fact
that the buyer discounts the product.

II. <u>Monopolies</u>--The Sherman Act, Section 2, prohibits monopolizing, attempts to monopolize, and conspiracies to
monopolize. Not all monopolies are in violation of
Section 2. A monopoly may be sanctioned by the government, such as a patent or a copyright. If a monopoly
has developed through the innovation of management or
because the company is the only seller of a product or
service in a geographic area, no violation exists.

A. <u>Monopolizing</u>--A violation of Section 2 of the Sherman Act for monopolizing requires proof of two
elements: monopoly power and the intent to monopolize.

1. <u>Monopoly Power</u>--Monopoly power has been defined
as the power to control prices or exclude competition. A firm's monopoly power is determined from its market share of the relevant
markets. Market share is the percentage of the
market the firm's product holds. If a firm's
market share is above 90 percent, the court
will conclude monopoly power exists. If the
firm's market share is between 30 and 90 percent, the firm may or may not have monopoly
power, depending on the analysis of other
factors.

a. <u>Relevant Markets</u>--Before market share can
be determined, the market must be defined.
Two types of markets must be analyzed: the
relevant product market and the relevant
geographic market.

(1) <u>Relevant Product Market</u>--The relevant
product market is comprised of all the
products which are interchangeable
(i.e., substitutes) with the firm's
product. If consumers are willing to
substitute the firm's product with
another product, the two products are
substitutes. The U.S. Supreme Court

has ruled that substitutability will
be determined by the cross-elasticity
of demand. The cross-elasticity of
demand measures the responsiveness of
the sales of one product to price
changes of another product. If a
slight decrease in the price of the
firm's product causes a considerable
number of customers to switch to the
firm's product, a high cross-elasticity of demand exists. A high
cross-elasticity of demand indicates
the two products are substitutes for
one another and in the same relevant
market.

The greater number of products in the
relevant product market, the smaller
market share a firm will have. A firm
being prosecuted for violating Section 2 of the Sherman Act will attempt
to decrease market share by enlarging
the relevant product market.

(2) Relevant Geographic Market--The relevant geographic market may be local,
regional, national, or international.
The courts determine the relevant geographic market according to the extent
a consumer is willing to travel to buy
the firm's product. Large ticket
items tend to have broader geographic
markets. Consumers will travel longer
distances to purchase such items as
television sets, refrigerators,
washers, automobiles, and sailboats.

2. Intent to Monopolize--The firm must not only
have monopoly power but also the intent to monopolize. Under Section 2, the prosecution
need only prove the general intent to monopolize. The general intent to monopolize is
defined as the conscious intent to acquire
monopoly power. Any activity on the part of
the firm to raise entry barriers or exclude
competition is considered evidence of general
intent.

III. Clayton Act--The Clayton Act consists of several important sections. The Clayton Act was enacted by Congress

in 1914 to bolster the existing antitrust law. The
most utilized Sections of the Act are 2, 3, 7, and 8.

A.   Section 2/Robinson-Patman Act--Section 2 is known
      as the Robinson-Patman Act, which prohibits price
      discrimination. The Robinson-Patman Act, Sec-
      tion 2(a), prohibits a seller from selling a good
      or commodity of like grade or quality at different
      prices to different buyers in commerce which has
      the potential to injure competition or has injured
      competition. A buyer may be in violation of Sec-
      tion 2(f) of the Robinson-Patman Act for knowingly
      inducing the seller to commit a Section 2(a) viola-
      tion. The Act also prohibits discriminatory promo-
      tional payments, allowances, or services.

      The Robinson-Patman Act was enacted to protect the
      small competitor against the large competitor's
      ability to purchase goods at reduced prices due to
      the volume being purchased. Congress feared the
      small retailer could be put out of business by the
      large chain stores.

B.   Defenses to Price Discrimination

      1.   The Meeting Competition Defense--If the seller
            in good faith meets an equally low price of a
            competitor, no Section 2(a) violation has oc-
            curred. The seller may sell goods or commodi-
            ties of like grade or quality at different
            prices if only attempting to meet the price of
            a competitor in good faith. (e.g., Borden
            Dairy Co. sells milk to a large chain store and
            a small independent grocery store for $1.00 a
            gallon. The large chain store seeks other bids
            for milk, and the Dean Dairy Co. offers to sell
            gallons at $.95. Borden may sell milk at $.95
            to the chain store to meet the competition.)

      2.   The Cost-Justification Defense--A seller may
            discriminate in price if it costs less to sell
            to a particular buyer and the cost savings is
            merely being passed on. The seller has the
            burden to prove that it actually costs less to
            sell to a particular buyer. Such cost reduc-
            tions may be due to lower transportation costs.

      3.   The Changing-Market-Conditions Defense--The
            seller may sell the product at different prices
            if conditions have changed to demand a corre-

sponding change in the price. Examples of
changing conditions are: discontinuance of a
product, a fire sale, bankruptcy sale, or
perishable goods deteriorating.

C. <u>Section 3</u>--Section 3 of the Clayton Act prohibits
exclusive dealing contracts and tying arrangements
which substantially lessen competition or tend to
create a monopoly.

The exclusive dealing contract requires the buyer
to buy only the products or product of the seller.
The exclusive dealing contract is evaluated under
the rule of reason.

The tying arrangement requires the buyer to purchase two products. The buyer desires the tied
product, and a substantial demand exists for its
sale; the seller adds an additional product to the
sale, called the tying product. The buyer must buy
both items to get the product desired. Tying
arrangements are per se violations.

D. <u>Section 8/Interlocking Directorships</u>--Section 8
prohibits a person from being a director of two or
more competing businesses where one of them has
assets greater than $1 million.

IV. <u>Mergers</u>--A merger is the combination of two or more
corporations or businesses through stock purchase or
asset acquisition. Certain mergers are prohibited
under Section 7 of the Clayton Act. A company may
acquire another company through purchasing the company's stock from stockholders or purchasing substantially all of the assets. A merger which will substantially lessen competition or which will tend to
create a monopoly is illegal under Section 7. The Act
covers mergers and consolidations. A merger is the
combining of two or more companies where one company
survives and the others are dissolved, whereas a
consolidation is the combining of two or more companies
and a new company is created, with the prior companies
being dissolved. A merger may be either horizontal,
vertical, or conglomerate.

The Federal Trade Commission (FTC) and the Department
of Justice, Antitrust Division, determine if the merger
will substantially lessen competition or tend to create
a monopoly. The Department of Justice and the FTC follow a set of guidelines to determine if the merger will

increase market concentration. To make this determina-
tion, the Herfindahl-Hirschman Index is used. The
Justice Department will analyze the merger according to
the index. The Department of Justice will challenge
the merger, if a certain point total is reached under
the index.

A. <u>Horizontal Merger</u>--A horizontal merger is the com-
    bination of two competing companies. The hori-
    zontal merger has the greatest potential for harm
    to competition since a competitor is automatically
    eliminated from the market as a result of the
    merger. A merger which facilitates collusion and
    fails to increase productivity or market efficien-
    cies will be held illegal.

B. <u>Vertical Mergers</u>--A vertical merger is the combina-
    tion of two or more companies in the distribution
    line of a product (e.g., an automobile manufacturer
    acquires automobile dealership). The court will
    consider the area of effective competition and if
    the merger will substantially lessen competition or
    tend to create a monopoly.

    In a vertical merger, competition may be foreclosed
    from the market. If a large share of the market is
    foreclosed, the merger violates Section 7. If a de
    minimis share of the market is foreclosed, no sub-
    stantial lessening of competition exists and no
    violation has occurred. If the vertical merger
    exists between a large share and a de minimis
    share, the court will consider other economic and
    historical factors. A trend toward concentration
    in the industry will cause the merger to violate
    Section 7.

C. <u>Conglomerate Merger</u>--A pure conglomerate merger is
    the combination of two or more firms selling unre-
    lated products and operating in markets not hori-
    zontally or vertically related. The conglomerate
    company is usually a large corporation seeking to
    diversify into other industries.

V. <u>The Federal Trade Commission Act</u>--The Federal Trade
    Commission Act (FTCA) created the Federal Trade Commis-
    sion (FTC) in 1914. The FTCA prohibits "unfair methods
    of competition in commerce and unfair or deceptive acts
    or practices in commerce." The FTC has the authority
    to enforce the Clayton Act and the FTCA. Most activi-
    ties which violate the Sherman Act or the Clayton Act
    also violate the FTCA.

VI.   Exemptions from the Antitrust Laws--Several types of
      businesses and business activities have been exempted
      from the authority of the antitrust laws. The follow-
      ing are such exemptions:

      A.   Labor Organizations--The Norris-La Guardia Act of
           1932 and the National Labor Relations Act of 1935
           specifically gave employees the right to collec-
           tively organize a union to facilitate negotiations
           with employers.

      B.   Agricultural Organizations--The Clayton Act specif-
           ically exempts agricultural businesses from the
           authority of the Sherman Act.

      C.   Baseball--The U.S. Supreme Court held baseball is
           exempt from antitrust laws.

      D.   Insurance Business--The McCarron-Ferguson Act of
           1945 exempted all activities that are in the busi-
           ness of insurance.

      E.   Export Associations--The Webb-Pomerene Act exempts
           export trade associations from the antitrust laws.

      F.   Legislative Influencing--The Noen-Pennington Doc-
           trine allows two or more persons to act in concert
           to influence the legislature or the executive.

      G.   State and Local Governments--General actions by
           state and local governments are exempt from the
           antitrust law.

VII. Defenses to Alleged Antitrust Violations--The courts
      have accepted several defenses to charges of antitrust
      violations.

      A.   The Colgate Doctrine--In the U.S. v. Colgate & Co.,
           the U.S. Supreme Court created the Colgate Doc-
           trine. The court held that a seller may unilat-
           erally refuse to deal with retailers who fail to
           follow suggested retail price lists.

      B.   The Standing Defense--The standing defense may
           apply when a private party sues a defendant for an
           antitrust violation. The private party plaintiff
           does not have standing to sue, unless he or she was
           actually injured by the defendant's violation. The
           Sherman and Clayton Acts allow a private party to
           sue for treble damages.

C. The Thrust-Upon Defense--A company which has monop-
    oly power but lacks the intent to monopolize may
    use the thrust-upon defense. The company must show
    that the monopoly power was gained by a superior
    product, better business practices, or being the
    only business of its type in a particular market
    (e.g., a small rural town in Iowa has only one
    newspaper or one movie theater).

D. The Failing-Company Defense--The courts allow a
    company to merge with a failing company and not
    violate Section 7 of the Clayton Act. Since a
    failing company is not a competitor in the market,
    competition is not effected.

VIII. Enforcement of the Antitrust Laws--The FTC, Department
       of Justice, and private parties may bring lawsuits
       based upon the antitrust laws.

   A. FTC Enforcement--The FTC, a federal administrative
       agency, has several powerful bureaus involved in
       antitrust investigations. The Competition and Eco-
       nomics Bureaus have the authority to investigate
       FTCA and Clayton Act violations.

       The FTC will usually issue a cease and desist
       order, prohibiting the individual or the corpora-
       tion from future violations. A business that fails
       to obey a cease and desist order can be fined up to
       $10,000 per day. The Department of Justice may
       bring criminal charges if a cease and desist order
       is ignored.

   B. Department of Justice--The Department of Justice,
       Antitrust Division, may bring civil or criminal
       charges for a violation. The Department of Justice
       may ask the court to order confiscation of the
       goods, divestiture, or dissolution. The Department
       of Justice may seek criminal sanctions under the
       Sherman Act. A criminal conviction carries a fine
       of up to $100,000 for an individual and up to
       3 years imprisonment, or both.

       A corporation can be fined up to $1 million. A
       criminal conviction requires the prosecution to
       prove the violator knowingly intended to violate
       the Sherman Act.

       Most cases are settled out of court with the De-
       partment of Justice. In a civil case, the accused

may enter into a consent decree in which the
defendant allows the court to impose a remedy
without the defendant admitting any guilt. Similarly, in a criminal case, the accused may plead
nolo contendere, which is not an admission of guilt
but the court may impose sanctions.

C.   Private Party Enforcement--Private parties may sue
for treble damages (three times) under the Sherman
and Clayton Acts. The party seeking a recovery
must prove that an injury was actually suffered as
a result of the defendant's illegal activity. The
antitrust violation must be a direct cause or a
substantial factor in causing the injury in which
the plaintiff is protected by the antitrust laws.

Study Questions

Fill-in-the-Blank Questions

Amoco Oil Company has entered into contracts with service station owners which requires the owner to buy all its gasoline,
oil, and car parts from Amoco. The owners receive the right
to use the Amoco name and are assisted by the company in
setting up a station. Amoco seeks to maintain high quality
among their service stations through the requirement.

The service station owners and Amoco have entered into a(n)
_____ contract.
     (exclusive dealing/tying)

The contract may be in violation of the Clayton Act, Section
_____.
(three/seven)

The Sherman Act, Section 1, prohibits _____
                                        (restraints of
_____ which have an adverse effect on competi-
     trade/mergers)
tion.

If Amoco will only sell gasoline to the service station owners
if they also purchase motor oil, Amoco may have violated Section _____ of the Clayton Act.
     (two/three)

True-False Questions

1. The antitrust laws in the United States are primarily state laws. _____

2. The courts have interpreted Section 1 of the Sherman Act literally. _____

3. The Sherman Act, Section 2, contains three offenses. _____

4. The per se rule requires the court to consider the circumstances of the case to determine if the activity is illegal. _____

5. The Sherman Act, Section 1, requires action by two or more people for a conviction. _____

6. The Federal Trade Commission has the authority to enforce the Clayton Act. _____

7. The Department of Justice has the authority to bring criminal charges under the Clayton Act. _____

8. Baseball associations are exempt from antitrust laws. _____

9. The Federal Trade Commission is headed by five commissioners. _____

10. Section 2 of the Clayton Act is known as the Robinson-Patman Act. _____

Multiple-Choice Questions

1. Which of the following legal entities was used during the nineteenth century to monopolize certain industries?

    a. sole proprietorship
    b. limited partnership
    c. joint venture
    d. trust

2. The Sherman Act was enacted by Congress in:

    a. 1890.
    b. 1914.
    c. 1929.
    d. 1945.

3. The Sherman Act, Section 1, prohibits which of the fol-
    lowing that have the effect of restraining trade?

       I. contracts
      II. combination
     III. conspiracy

    a. I only
    b. I and II
    c. I, II, and III
    d. II and III

4. The Sherman Act, Section 2, prohibits which of the fol-
    lowing?

       I. attempt to monopolize
      II. restraint of trade
     III. monopolize

    a. I only
    b. I and II
    c. II and III
    d. I and III

5. The major difference(s) between Section 1 and Section 2
    of the Sherman Act is (are):

      I. Section 1 requires two or more people for a viola-
        tion.

     II. Only Section 2 has a criminal sanction.

    III. The FTC can prosecute only Section 1 violations.

    a. I only
    b. I and II
    c. II and III
    d. I, II, and III

6. Pacific Outfitters was in competition with Landslide
    Fashions. Both retailers sold the same brands of camping
    equipment and sportswear. The owners of both companies
    agreed to sell sportswear above a stated minimum price.
    The owners agreed the minimum price would not be vio-
    lated, and most of the time, prices would be well above
    the minimum. The retailers have violated which provision
    of the antitrust laws?

    a. Section 1 of the Sherman Act
    b. Section 2 of the Sherman Act

c.   Section 7 of the Clayton Act
d.   no antitrust law has been violated

7.   Refer to question 6. The Department of Justice investigates both Pacific and Landslide and discovered the
arrangement. The Department of Justice will call the
arrangement a(n):

a.   tying arrangement.
b.   exclusive dealing.
c.   horizontal price fixing.
d.   vertical price fixing.

8.   Refer to questions 6 and 7. The Department of Justice
brings the case to court, charging a violation of the
antitrust laws. The court will determine if a violation
occurred according to the:

a.   per se rule.
b.   rule of reason.
c.   nolo contendere.
d.   none of the above.

9.   A price fixing agreement may constitute which of the following?

I.   setting a specific price on an item sold by competitors

II.   setting a lower price on an item sold by competitors

III.   stabilizing the price on an item sold by competitors

a.   I only
b.   I and II
c.   II and III
d.   I, II, and III

10. Safe Foods, Inc. is a large chain of grocery stores
throughout the southwest. Safe Foods competes vigorously
with U.S. Foods, Inc. in California, Arizona, and New
Mexico. Both companies spend millions of dollars on
advertising in the states where they compete. Because of
price undercutting, neither company has been very profitable in California and Arizona.

The presidents of both companies meet and agree to segment the market. Safe Foods will sell in California, and

U.S. Foods will sell in Arizona and New Mexico only. Safe Foods has closed all its stores in Arizona and New Mexico, and U.S. Foods has closed its stores in California. The companies have violated which antitrust provision?

a. Section 1 of the Sherman Act
b. Section 2 of the Sherman Act
c. Section 7 of the Clayton Act
d. no provision has been violated.

11. Refer to question 10. The agreement entered into by Safe Foods and U.S. Foods is called a(n):

a. tying arrangement.
b. exclusive dealing.
c. horizontal market division.
d. vertical price fixing.

12. Refer to question 10. The court will determine if a violation has occurred in this case by using the:

a. rule of reason.
b. per se rule.
c. circumstantial evidence.
d. none of the above.

13. Refer to question 10. The Department of Justice decides to prosecute Safe Foods and U.S. Foods for a criminal violation of the antitrust laws. The president of Safe Foods plea bargains with the government and agrees to pay a fine and not to do the activity again. This is called:

a. nolo contendere.
b. consent decree.
c. dissolution.
d. confiscation.

14. Refer to question 10. The Department of Justice criminally prosecutes U.S. Foods under the antitrust laws. The court holds the defendant in violation of the antitrust law. The court may:

  I.   fine the president up to $350,000.
 II.   fine the corporation up to $10 million.
III.   imprison the president up to 25 years.

a. I only
b. I and II

c. I, II, and III
d. II and III

15. A private party that has been injured by a violation of the Sherman or Clayton Acts may sue for damages. The private party may collect:

a. only actual damages.
b. double damages.
c. punitive damages.
d. three times actual damages.

16. The Clayton Act prohibits a merger if the companies that are merging would cause:

  I. a lessening of competition.
 II. a restraint of trade.
III. a tendency to create a monopoly.

a. I only
b. I and II
c. I and III
d. I, II, and III

17. George Wilson is the chairman of the board of Avco Company. George is also a member of the board of directors of Repco, Inc. Both companies compete with each other. Repco, Inc. has total assets of $10 million. George is in violation of which provision of the antitrust law?

a. Section 1 of the Sherman Act
b. Section 2 of the Sherman Act
c. Section 7 of the Clayton Act
d. Section 8 of the Clayton Act

18. The Clayton Act, Section 3, prohibits which of the following arrangements when competition is substantially lessened?

  I. horizontal market division
 II. exclusive dealing agreement
III. vertical price fixing

a. I only
b. II only
c. I and II
d. I, II, and III

19. Which of the following is not exempt from antitrust laws?

a. baseball associations
b. football associations
c. agricultural organizations
d. insurance business

20. The Federal Trade Commission Act covers most activities
prohibited by the Sherman and Clayton Acts. Section 5 of
the Federal Trade Commission Act declares illegal which
of the following?

a. unfair methods of competition
b. interlocking directorates
c. restraints of trade
d. monopolizing

21. Which of the following has the authority to enforce the
Federal Trade Commission Act?

  I. Federal Trade Commission
 II. Department of Justice
III. a private party

a. I only
b. I and II
c. I and III
d. I, II, and III

22. The Fairfax County Bar Association prescribed a minimum-
fee schedule for its member lawyers. The majority of the
members followed the minimum-fee schedule when billing
clients for services. A member who did not follow the
schedule could be disciplined by the bar association.
The Goldfarbs brought suit against the bar association
for violating the antitrust laws. Which provision of the
antitrust law has been violated?

a. Section 1 of the Sherman Act
b. Section 3 of the Clayton Act
c. Section 7 of the Clayton Act
d. no provision has been violated

23. Refer to question 22. The Goldfarbs win the case against
the bar association in court. The Goldfarbs prove they
were injured to the extent of $450. The court will award
what amount of damages?

a. $450
b. $900
c. $1,350
d. $1,800

24. Refer to question 22. The Federal Trade Commission (FTC) finds the bar association in violation of the FTC Act. The FTC may issue:

    a. an injunction.
    b. a dissolution.
    c. a divestiture.
    d. a cease and desist order.

25. The bar association refuses to comply with the FTC order. The FTC may fine the bar association:

    a. up to $500 per day.
    b. up to $1,000 per day.
    c. up to $10,000 per day.
    d. up to $100,000 per day.

Essay Question

1. American Furniture World sells household appliances and furniture. Betterway Store, Inc. also sells household appliances and furniture. Both companies vigorously compete with each other in the Chicago market. American and Betterway agree that American will sell only furniture and Betterway will sell only household appliances. This agreement proved to be profitable for both companies. Have the companies violated any antitrust laws?

Answers to Study Questions

Fill-in-the-Blank Questions

The service station owners and Amoco have entered into an exclusive dealing contract. (p. 511)

The contract may be in violation of the Clayton Act, Section three. (p. 511)

The Sherman Act, Section 1, prohibits restraints of trade which have an adverse effect on competition. (p. 501)

If Amoco will only sell gasoline to the service station owners if they also purchase motor oil, Amoco may have violated Section three of the Clayton Act. (p. 511)

True-False Questions

1. False. The antitrust laws are primarily federal statutes. (p. 513)

2. False. The U.S. Supreme Court has not read the Sherman Act, Section 1, literally. (p. 501)

3. True (p. 500)

4. False. The per se rule concludes an activity is illegal without considering the particular circumstances of a case. (p. 504)

5. True (p. 500)

6. True (p. 517)

7. False. The Clayton Act has no criminal penalties provision. (p. 518)

8. True (p. 516)

9. True (p. 512)

10. True (p. 513)

Multiple-Choice Questions

1. d (p. 500)	14. b (p. 518)	
2. a (p. 500)	15. d (p. 518)	
3. c (p. 500)	16. c (p. 512)	
4. d (p. 501)	17. d (p. 513)	
5. a (p. 501)	18. b (p. 511)	
6. a (p. 504)	19. b (p. 516)	
7. c (p. 504)	20. a (p. 513)	
8. a (p. 504)	21. a (p. 513)	
9. d (p. 504)	22. a (p. 505)	
10. a (p. 505)	23. c (p. 518)	
11. c (p. 505)	24. d (p. 517)	
12. b (p. 505)	25. c (p. 518)	
13. a (p. 519)		

Essay Question

1. Yes, the companies have violated Section 1 of the Sherman Act. The Sherman Act, Section 1, prohibits contracts, combinations, or conspiracies which restrain trade. The

U.S. Supreme Court has declared only unreasonable restraints of trade as illegal. Under the per se rule,
horizontal market division is a per se violation. A per
se activity is conclusively unreasonable and a violation
of Section 1. The parties have entered an agreement to
divide up the market. A market division may divide up
geographic areas, customers, or products being sold.
(p. 506)

Chapter 21
Legislative Control Over Labor and Labor Relations

Major Concepts

The amount of legislation regulating labor has dramatically increased. Congress has enacted a variety of statutes to protect workers and children in the labor force.

The Fair Labor Standards Act has three major provisions. The Act requires an employer to pay a minimum wage, to pay overtime when the employee works over 40 hours per week, prohibits children under 14 from working, and places restrictions on children in the workforce between the ages of 14 and 17. The Act is enforced by the Department of Labor.

Social security is a federal program which provides employees with retirement, disability, and death benefits. The Act requires both the employee and the employer to fund the program.

The Federal Unemployment Tax Act provides benefits to unemployed workers. The program is funded by employers who pay into a trust fund. An employee may collect benefits, if all the requirements are fulfilled.

Two statutes involving worker safety are: state workers' compensation acts and the Occupational Safety and Health Act (OSHA). State workers' compensation acts allow an injured employee to collect benefits automatically from the employer, if the injury is one which arises out of the employment and is in the course of employment. Workers' compensation acts are strict liability statutes and the exclusive remedy of the employee against the employer.

OSHA requires the employer to provide the employee with a work environment free of recognized hazards which may cause death or serious injury. The Act gives employees the right to file a complaint with the Secretary of Labor without fear of reprisal from the employer and the right to refuse a dangerous job assignment.

Unions and collective bargaining are regulated by federal labor law statutes. The most important labor statute is the National Labor Relations Act, also known as the Wagner Act. The Wagner Act gives the employee the right to form a union and the means for doing so. The federal labor laws prohibit unfair labor practices committed by the employer or the union. The process of electing a union as a collective bargaining agent is closely monitored by the National Labor Relations Board.

Chapter Outline

I. Fair Labor Standards Act (FLSA)--The FLSA was enacted in 1938 to protect children in the workplace and assure all individuals a fair wage for services rendered.

    A. Coverage of the Act--The FLSA was passed by Congress under its authority to regulate commerce (i.e., U.S. Constitution, Article I, Section 8). The FLSA covers employees who are either directly engaged in commerce or who are employed by an enterprise engaged in commerce. The employee may produce goods which are put into commerce and qualify for protection of the FLSA. An employer is covered, if he or she employs an employee covered by the Act. The term employer is defined broadly by the Act, including not only the corporation or business entity but also corporate officers in some cases.

        1. Exempt Employees--Several types of employees are exempt from coverage of the Act. Examples of employees exempt from coverage are: agricultural employees, commercial fishing employees, some retail services employees, administrative and professional employees, and casual babysitters.

    B. Major Provisions of the FLSA--The Act has three major sections dealing with wages, hour requirements, and child labor.

1. <u>Minimum Wage Requirements</u>--The FLSA requires all covered employers to pay employees at least a minimum wage of $4.25 per hour. The minimum wage has risen over the years from $.25 in 1938 to its current rate of $4.25 passed by Congress in 1991. A tipped employee, such as a waiter, may be paid less than the minimum wage, if the employee receives more than $30 a month in tips and the employer's credit for tips does not exceed forty percent of the minimum wage.

2. <u>Hour Requirements</u>--The FLSA requires a covered employer to pay an employee for all the hours worked in a week, including the time not actually performing the job but required to be at the place of employment. The employee must also be paid one and one-half times his or her regular hourly rate for any hours worked in excess of forty hours in one week. A person's regularly hourly rate includes a bonus and commissions. The overtime rate is calculated on the employee's regular hourly rate, not the minimum wage.

    The employer must keep records of the employee's compensation. The employer must have on file personal information of the employee, hours expected to work, total hours actually worked, total daily or weekly earnings, and actual payments made to employee, including deductions or additions.

3. <u>Child Labor</u>--The FLSA attempts to protect children from hazardous working conditions and promote a child's well-being. Under the Act, the following restrictions apply to employers hiring children:

    a. 17 years and older have no restrictions on employment.

    b. 16-17 years old may be employed, but some restrictions, if a dangerous industry.

    c. 14-16 years old may be employed in specially approved jobs such as retail stores, restaurants, and service stations.

    d. under 14 years old may not work, unless agricultural work, actor/actress, or performer.

C. <u>Investigation and Enforcement</u>--The FLSA delegates the authority to administer the Act to the Department of Labor. The Wage and Hour Division of the Department of Labor has the primary obligation of enforcement under the FLSA. The Department of Labor may bring an action to collect unpaid wages and/or seek an injunction to restrain further violations. An employer may be criminally prosecuted for willful violations of the Act. The criminal fine is up to $10,000 for the first offense and up to $10,000 plus imprisonment up to 6 months for subsequent offenses.

A private employee may bring a civil action to recover unpaid wages, overtime, liquidated damages, and attorney's fees.

II. <u>Employee Retirement Statutes</u>

A. <u>The Old Age, Survivors, and Disability Insurance (OASDI)</u>--OASDI is known as Social Security, which requires all employers, with limited exceptions, to pay social security tax on employee wages up to a fixed amount. Wages are generally all compensation received in cash or benefits. The social security program's purpose is to provide retirement, survivor, and disability benefits through the social security tax. Upon retirement at age 62 or 65, an individual is entitled to receive monthly retirement benefits, if a sufficient work record exists. In the event a worker dies, the Act provides certain family members with insurance payments. And if an employee is totally disabled and unable to work, he or she may be entitled to monthly payments under social security.

The employer and the employee are each required to pay an equal amount of tax. The employer is required to deduct the employee's contribution from his or her paycheck and remit the amounts to the government. The money is placed into a trust fund and used to pay benefits to millions of individuals already on social security. Part of the tax goes to support the Medicare program. The employee tax is 7.51 percent of the employee's wages up to a maximum contribution of $6,759 per employee. The employer makes a matching payment on the employee's behalf.

B. <u>The Employee Retirement Income Security Act (ERISA)</u>--ERISA was enacted by Congress to protect employees from unfair retirement programs. ERISA protects employees by regulating the creation of private pension plans and pension plan managers. ERISA imposes fiduciary duties on pension plan managers hired by the employer. A fiduciary has the obligation to administer the pension plan in good faith and equitably. ERISA requires the manager to keep accurate records and reports. But the major protection for employees under ERISA are the vesting requirements.

1. Vesting--Vesting is the ownership interest an employee has in contributions made into the pension fund for his or her benefit. Under ERISA, the employee's contributions into the pension fund are 100 percent vested. The employee has the right to receive back all money he or she has contributed. The employer must vest the employee according to ERISA's schedule of vesting for employer contributions. The employee must be vested 100 percent at the end of seven years of employment, according to ERISA's guidelines.

The employer must meet the requirements of ERISA in order to deduct pension contributions as a tax deductible expense.

III. Worker Protection Statutes--The state and federal governments have enacted laws to protect employees from hazardous working conditions and to require compensation to an employee once an injury has occurred.

A. State Workers' Compensation Acts--The states have enacted statutes to provide an employee with benefits once injured. Employees injured while on the job may collect compensation from the employer. Workers' compensation acts provide the employee with an automatic remedy against the employer, if the injury occurred within the course of employment and arises out of the employment.

The courts have broadly interpreted the terms arising out of and in the course of employment. An injury which arises out of the employment is one which the employee was ordinarily subjected to. Every job has certain inherent risks attached to it. For example, a risk inherent in driving a forklift truck is that the employee may inadvertently drive off the loading dock. A risk not inherent in driving a forklift truck is that the driver may be struck by lightning.

In the course of employment is determined in relation to the activity being performed by the employer at the time of the injury. If the employee was acting on behalf of the employer, on work premises, during regular working time, doing something authorized to do, the injury has occurred within the course of employment. In most work situations, the employee is in the course of employment, unless he or she substantially deviated from the job.

Workers' compensation acts are strict liability laws not dependent on the fault of the employer. Whether or not the employer was negligent, the act makes the employer liable for the employee's injury.

Recovery of compensation under such acts are the exclusive remedy of the employee against the employer. The employee is entitled to an automatic recovery, if the requirements are fulfilled. An employer charged with intentional misconduct may be subject to additional common law liability. The employer will not be held liable for the intentionally inflicted injuries of the employee.

B.   The Occupational Safety and Health Act (OSHA)--OSHA was enacted in 1970 to ensure that employees are provided with a safe place to work. OSHA created the Occupational Safety and Health Administration (OSHA), the Occupational Safety and Health Review Commission (OSHRC), and the National Institute for Occupational Safety and Health (NIOSH).

OSHA has the responsibility to promulgate and enforce workers' safety and health standards and conduct investigations of worker complaints. NIOSH has the responsibility of assisting OSHA by providing research data about particular industries. The research data is utilized by OSHA before promulgating a regulation or safety standard.

1.   General Duty Clause--The Act imposes upon each employer a general duty to provide a work environment "free from recognized hazards that are causing or likely to cause death or serious physical harm to employees." The Act allows OSHA to inspect and issue citations to employers who have breached the general duty clause, breached a specific safety or health standard, or failed to keep proper records of all injuries.

2. Investigation and Enforcement--Once a complaint
    has been reported by an employee, OSHA will in-
    vestigate to determine if a violation has
    occurred. If a violation is discovered, OSHA
    will issue a citation, propose a penalty, and
    specify a date the employer must have the condi-
    tion corrected. A citation may be challenged by
    the employer, at which time a hearing will be
    held by the Occupational Safety and Health Re-
    view Commission. An administrative law judge
    will preside over the hearing and determine if a
    violation has occurred. The employer may appeal
    to the commission for review of the administra-
    tive law judge's decision. The decision of the
    commission may be appealed to the United States
    Circuit Court of Appeals. The employer is pro-
    hibited under the Act from discharging an
    employee for filing a complaint with OSHA. In
    addition, the employee has the right to choose
    not to perform an assigned task because of a
    reasonable apprehension of death or serious
    injury, coupled with a reasonable belief that no
    less drastic alternative is available.

3. Penalties--Penalties for violations are both
    civil and criminal. A civil penalty may be as-
    sessed of up to $1,000 per day, while a criminal
    penalty may be up to $10,000 for a willful vio-
    lation. The Secretary of Labor may seek re-
    straining orders to close down a business
    operation which creates an imminent danger of
    death or serious injury to employees.

C. Unemployment Compensation--Congress in 1954 enacted
    the Federal Unemployment Tax Act (FUTA) which estab-
    lished a system whereby employers would pay a fed-
    eral tax of 6.2 percent on the first $7,000 of an
    employee's annual wages. The tax is paid by the em-
    ployer, not the employee, and is considered an ex-
    pense of doing business. The tax goes to provide
    benefits to an unemployed worker who has previously
    worked for a specified period of time, is available
    to work, and out of work involuntarily. The worker
    will not receive benefits if terminated due to mis-
    conduct. Generally, the worker receives benefits
    for 26 weeks.

    The state may implement a program to collect the tax
    and receive a credit under the federal program. The
    employer may pay 5.4 percent to the state and

0.8 percent to the federal government. A particular
employer may lower his or her tax by having a good
employment record (i.e., very few employees having
to collect under the program).

IV. Labor Law--The industrial revolution brought America
into the manufacturing age. Along with technology came
large factories, machinery, and the need for inexpensive
labor. Before 1930, some employers abused employees
with deplorable and unsafe working conditions. The employer had almost complete control over the individual
employee's job.

A. Federal Labor Law Statutes--Labor law is comprised
of four major statutes.

1. Norris-La Guardia Act--In 1932, Congress passed
the Norris-La Guardia Act which protected peace-
ful strikes, picketing, and boycotts. The Act
withdrew the power of the federal courts to
issue injunctions in nonviolent labor disputes.

Prior to 1932, the employer used legal means as
well as physical means to suppress employee
organizations. The employer, in some cases,
argued that the association of employees violated the Sherman Act, Section 1. The Norris-La
Guardia Act declared it a national policy that
labor was to have full freedom to form labor
unions. Many acts were subsequently passed by
Congress to bolster labor's freedom.

2. National Labor Relations Act (NLRA)--The NLRA,
also known as the Wagner Act, was enacted by
Congress in 1935 and established the right of
employees to unionize and engage in collective
bargaining. The NLRA created a federal administrative agency called the National Labor Relations Board (NLRB) to enforce the Act and
protect employee rights. The NLRA guarantees
employees the right to form, join, or assist
labor organizations, to bargain collectively
with the employer, and to engage in concerted
activity for the purpose of collective bargaining or the mutual aid and protection. The
Act also declared certain activities of the
employer illegal. The Act called these illegal
activities unfair labor practices.

3.   The Labor-Management Relations Act--The Labor-
Management Relations Act is known as the Taft-
Hartley Act and was passed in 1947, amending the
Wagner Act. The Taft-Hartley Act gives government the power to eliminate union unfair labor
practices and intervene in strikes, if the
national welfare is at stake. The Act created
the Federal Mediation and Conciliation Service
to assist in resolving labor disputes. The
Taft-Hartley Act also gave the President the
power to ask a federal district court to issue
an 80-day injunction against a work stoppage or
strike which would injure the national health,
welfare, or security of the nation. The Act
prohibited the closed shop. In a closed shop,
union membership is a condition of employment.

4.   The Labor-Management Reporting and Disclosure
Act--The Labor-Management Reporting and Disclosure Act is known as the Landrum-Griffin Act
and was passed by Congress in 1959. The Act
regulates the internal procedures of unions.
The Act attempts to protect the rights and
interests of the individual workers as well as
the public from overly powerful union leader-
ship. The Act makes certain disclosures by the
union mandatory and requires a union to follow
specific election procedures when electing union
leaders.

B.   The National Labor Relations Board (NLRB)--The two
major functions of the NLRB are: to hold representation elections for employees and to decide whether
a certain activity constitutes an unfair labor
practice. The NLRB is divided into two divisions:
the Board itself comprised of five presidentially
appointed members and the Office of the General
Counsel. The General Counsel is in charge of
31 regional offices across the country. The
regional offices are responsible for conducting
representation elections and investigating unfair
labor complaints. The regional office director may
investigate a charge and file a complaint. Complaints are heard by an administrative law judge
within the NLRB. The administrative law judge will
decide if a violation has occurred.

C.   The Representation Election--The collective bargaining agent must file a petition with the NLRB regional office to have a representation election

held. The petition must show that at least 30% of
the employees are interested in having an election
held. Once the petition is verified and the appropriate bargaining unit is determined, the NLRB will
set a date for the election. A bargaining unit is
comprised of employees with similar interests.

The election will be conducted by the NLRB on company premises. The ballot will give the employees
an opportunity to vote for a particular union or no
union at all. If a union receives a majority of the
vote according to a secret ballot, the NLRB will
certify the election results. The union chosen by
the employees will be certified as the collective
bargaining agent by the NLRB.

Once certified, the union cannot be replaced at
least for one year or the term of the collective
bargaining agreement up to a maximum of 3 years. If
the employees vote down the union, no election can
be held for at least 12 months. A union may be de-
certified by the same process.

D. <u>Closed, Union, and Agency Shops</u>--The closed shop is
    illegal under the Taft-Hartley Act. A closed shop
    refuses employment to anyone not a member of the
    union. The union shop requires that an employee
    become a union member within a certain period of
    time after being on the job. Right-to-work laws
    enacted by some states give the employee the right
    to work without having to ever join a union.
    Right-to-work laws prohibit union shops.

    An agency shop does not require union membership at
    any time but does require an employee to pay initia-
    tion fees and union dues.

E. <u>Duty to Bargain in Good Faith</u>--Once the union has
    been certified by the NLRB, the NLRA requires the
    employer and the union to bargain in good faith over
    mandatory topics. The parties must agree to meet at
    reasonable times and negotiate over wages, hours,
    and other terms and conditions of employment. The
    parties do not have to reach an agreement but must
    be willing to negotiate. The employer need not bar-
    gain with the union over nonmandatory topics, such
    as location of the corporate office, a new product
    line, or marketing strategy. A failure to bargain
    in good faith by the employer or the union is an
    unfair labor practice.

F. <u>Unfair Labor Practices</u>--Either the employer or the
    union may commit unfair labor practices. The NLRA
    has defined several employer unfair labor practices.
    If the employer interferes with the employee's right
    to form a union or attempts to dominate the union or
    discriminates against an employee because of union
    affiliation, the employer has committed an unfair
    labor practice.

    The employer may make speeches or statements to em-
    ployees before a representation election is held.
    The employer has the First Amendment right to
    express his or her opinion. But if the employer
    threatens or attempts to coerce the employees to
    vote against the union, an unfair labor practice has
    been committed. The employer may call a mandatory
    meeting of all employees on company time to express
    his or her opinions. The calling of a mandatory
    meeting 24 hours before the election is an automatic
    unfair labor practice. During the period after the
    petition is filed but before the election, the NLRB
    attempts to maintain "laboratory conditions" at the
    work facility. In other words, the NLRB controls
    the work atmosphere such that employees can make an
    independent decision for or against the union.

    The union may also commit unfair labor practices
    under the Taft-Hartley Act. If the union coerces
    employees, discriminates against employees, or
    strikes without approval of the members, an unfair
    labor practice has been committed.

G. <u>Strikes, Picketing, and Lockouts</u>--Whenever negotia-
    tion reaches a point where the parties refuse to
    compromise (i.e., an impasse), the potential for
    economic pressure exists. The union has the right
    to strike and picket to attempt to force the employ-
    er to agree to employee demands. Strikes must be
    nonviolent and voted on by union members. The
    employers may continue to work even though a strike
    has been called, but the union has the right to fine
    or penalize such members. If the strike is for
    economic reasons, the employer may permanently
    replace the striking workers. At the termination of
    the strike, the employer must give striking workers
    priority to open jobs but need not fire any replace-
    ment.

    If the strike is because the employer committed an
    unfair labor practice, the striking workers must
    receive their jobs back once the strike is over.

The employees may also picket the employer peacefully. The picketers cannot block the entrance to
the work facility or make threats to keep others
out.

The employer may lockout the employees to exert economic pressure on the union members.

H.   <u>Remedies</u>--The NLRB has broad authority to design
remedies to fit the purposes of the NLRA. The Board
may issue a cease and desist order. The NLRB may
also reinstate an employee, order back pay, or order
an employer to bargain with the union. If an unfair
labor practice is committed before a representation
election, the Board may order a new election if necessary.

<u>Study Questions</u>

<u>Fill-in-the-Blank Questions</u>

Harvey is considering opening up a supermarket in his home-
town. Harvey is a recent college graduate and knows government regulation protects employees. Harvey expects to employ
approximately 25 employees.

Harvey hires 5 high school students to help around the store.
Harvey must make sure the provisions of the _____
                                            (Fair Labor
_____ are fulfilled.
    Standards Act/Landrum-Griffin Act)

If some of Harvey's employees work over forty hours in one
week, Harvey must pay each of the employees _____
                                            (two/one
_____ times the _____
and one-half)   (minimum wage/employee's
_____.
   regular rate)

Harvey is required to deduct _____
                             (social security/pension
_____ from each employee's weekly paycheck and match
   payments)
the amount up to a stated maximum.

True-False Questions

1. The Fair Labor Standards Act prohibits most children under 14 years old from being employed. _____

2. The minimum wage enacted by Congress in 1981 was $3.35. _____

3. Old Age, Survivors, and Disability Insurance is known as social security. _____

4. Professional employees are exempt from the provisions of the Fair Labor Standards Act. _____

5. Medicare is administered by the Social Security Administration. _____

6. Private pension plans are governed by the Social Security Act. _____

7. State workers' compensation acts allow a worker to collect for intentionally self-inflicted injuries. _____

8. The general duty clause of OSHA requires the employer make the work environment absolutely safe. _____

9. Employees have always had the right to organize unions. _____

10. The Wagner Act is the primary federal statute regulating the formation of organized labor. _____

Multiple-Choice Questions

1. Which one of the following is not a provision of the Fair Labor Standards Act?

    a. minimum age
    b. overtime pay
    c. child work protections
    d. maximum hours able to work

2. Which of the following employees do not have to be paid the minimum wage by the employer?

    a. a sales clerk
    b. a waiter
    c. a truck driver
    d. a factory worker

3. Which of the following jobs may a 15-year-old be employed at?

      I.   a restaurant
     II.   service station
    III.   factory worker

    a. I only
    b. I and II
    c. II and III
    d. I, II, and III

4. Employers are required to keep a file on each employee containing which of the following?

      I.   occupation and birth date of employee
     II.   total overtime pay for a work week
    III.   date of payment and pay period covered

    a. I only
    b. I and II
    c. II and III
    d. I, II, and III

5. Under social security, an individual can receive which of the following benefits, if qualified?

      I.   pension annuity
     II.   total disability payments
    III.   death benefits to surviving family member

    a. I only
    b. I and II
    c. II and III
    d. I, II, and III

6. The Employee Retirement Income Security Act (ERISA) covers the vesting of pension plans for workers in private businesses. Vesting is defined as:

    a. the total amount contributed into the plan.
    b. the employer's contributions only.
    c. the employee's contribution only.
    d. none of the above.

7. Don has been terminated from his job because of poor performance. Don worked for Acme Builders, Inc. for 10 years before he was let go. Don has been out of work for six weeks and desires to receive unemployment compensation. Will Don be able to collect unemployment compensation?

a. Yes, because he is out of work.
b. Yes, because he worked for 10 years.
c. No, because he was terminated for misconduct.
d. No, because Don has not found another job.

8. Dave is a forklift driver at the Store-It-All Warehouse, Inc. Dave has driven a forklift truck for 7 years and has never been injured. Dave, while loading a semi trailer one day, accidentally backs off the loading dock. Dave is seriously injured as a result. Dave may collect damages from his employer under which of the following?

a. Fair Labor Standards Act
b. Workers' Compensation
c. Employee Income Retirement Security Act
d. Dave cannot collect from the employer

9. Refer to question 8. If Dave is allowed to collect from the employer, which of the following must be proven?

I.   The injury was in the course of employment.
II.   The employer was at fault.
III. The employee was not negligent.

a. I only
b. I and II
c. II and III
d. I and III

10. Refer to question 8. Assume Dave properly applied the brake before driving off the end of the loading dock. An investigation reveals the brake on the forklift truck was defective. Dave may collect from which of the following parties?

I.   Store-It-All Warehouse
II.   the manufacturer of the forklift
III. Dave's boss

a. I only
b. I and II
c. II and III
d. I, II, and III

11. Refer to question 8. Which of the following is a defense Store-It-All Warehouse, Inc. may use to avoid paying for Dave's injury?

a. Dave was negligent.
b. Store-It-All was not negligent.

    c.   Dave intentionally drove off the loading dock.

    d.   All of the above.

12.   The Workers' Compensation Act is considered which of the following?

    a.   an exclusive remedy against the employer

    b.   a fault theory of recovery

    c.   a common law rule

    d.   created in favor of the employer

13.   Under the Occupational Safety and Health Act, the employer is required to do which of the following?

    I.   protect the employee from all unsafe conditions

    II.   provide a safe work environment free from recognized hazards

    III.   keep detailed records of worker injuries and illnesses

    a.   I only

    b.   I and II

    c.   II and III

    d.   I, II, and III

14.   Teresa is employed at the local fast food restaurant. The manager tells Teresa to dump a boiling hot vat of grease in the garbage container around back. The vat contains 20 gallons of the hot mixture, and Teresa can barely move it, even though it's on rollers. Teresa may refuse to do the task if:

    I.   she is in reasonable apprehension of death or serious injury.

    II.   she has a reasonable belief that a less drastic alternative is available.

    III.   another employee was injured while performing the same task.

    a.   I only

    b.   I and II

    c.   II and III

    d.   I, II, and III

15.   Which of the following labor statutes created the National Labor Relations Board?

a.   Norris-La Guardia Act
b.   Wagner Act
c.   Taft-Hartley Act
d.   none of the above

16.   The employees at Worldwide Auto Inc. must join the union
      within 30 days after initial employment. Worldwide manu-
      factures small economy automobiles. The Worldwide em-
      ployees are represented by a union. Which of the follow-
      ing is true about Worldwide Auto Inc.?

        I.   The employer may have voluntarily recognized the
             union.

       II.   An election may have been held to vote on union
             representation.

      III.   The employees must unanimously agree on a union.

      a.   I only
      b.   I and II
      c.   II and III
      d.   I, II, and III

17.   Refer to question 16. The Worldwide Auto plant can be
      characterized as which of the following?

      a.   a closed shop
      b.   an agency shop
      c.   a union shop
      d.   none of the above

18.   Refer to question 16. Which of the following would make
      the labor agreement between Worldwide Auto and the em-
      ployees illegal?

      a.   the Fair Labor Standards Act
      b.   Right-to-Work Laws
      c.   Landrum-Griffin Act
      d.   Taft-Hartley Act

19.   Which of the following is a violation of the Wagner Act
      and considered an unfair labor practice?

        I.   the employee's refusal to bargain in good faith
       II.   the employer's refusal to bargain in good faith
      III.   employer's domination of the union

      a.   I only
      b.   I and II

    c.   II and III
    d.   I, II, and III

20.   The Acme Co. employs 5,000 workers at their Dayton, Ohio plant. The employees voted in favor of a union two years ago. The present collective bargaining agreement is about to expire, and the employees are demanding greater benefits. The president of Acme Co. calls the union representative to the bargaining table. At the meeting, the president states he will raise wages to $12.50 per hour. "Take it or leave it." The president then walks out of the meeting and refuses to further discuss wages. The president has:

    a.   properly negotiated with the union.
    b.   discriminated against the union.
    c.   dominated the union.
    d.   failed to bargain in good faith.

21.   Refer to question 20. The union believes an impasse has been reached with the management of Acme. The union may legally do which of the following upon approval of union members?

      I.   strike
     II.   picket Acme
   III.   lockout

    a.   I only
    b.   I and II
    c.   II and III
    d.   I, II, and III

22.   Refer to question 20. During the negotiations between the union and Acme, which of the following items would not have to be bargained over?

    a.   wages
    b.   working conditions
    c.   location of a new factory
    d.   vacation time

23.   When an election is held to determine if the employees want a union to represent them, which of the following will conduct the election?

    a.   Social Security Administration
    b.   Secretary of Labor
    c.   five commissions on the board
    d.   regional office of the General Counsel

24. The union is required to fulfill which of the following
     requirements under the labor laws?

     a. get the employees the longest vacation time
     b. represent employees fairly
     c. go out on strike
     d. all of the above

25. Before a representation election can be held, the Na-
     tional Labor Relations Board must determine which of the
     following?

       I. the bargaining unit
      II. if any unfair labor practices have been committed
     III. the highest wages for employees

     a. I only
     b. I and II
     c. II and III
     d. I, II, and III

Essay Question

1. Mark is employed by the Kolb Company as an engineer.
    Kolb is a multinational corporation manufacturing medical
    equipment. The company sells in 14 different countries.
    The company believes its employees should be physically
    fit and has built a work-out gym and running track for
    employees to use after work or during lunch hours. Mark,
    one day while running his usual 10 miles during lunch,
    tripped and fell on the track at work. Mark broke his
    ankle and will be laid up for at least eight weeks. Can
    Mark collect from Kolb under the Workers' Compensation
    Act?

Answers to Study Questions

Fill-in-the-Blank Questions

Harvey hires 5 high school students to help around the store.
Harvey must make sure the provisions of the Fair Labor Standards Act are fulfilled. (p. 526)

If some of Harvey's employees work over forty hours in one
week, Harvey must pay each of the employees at one and
one-half times the employee's regular rate. (p. 526)

Harvey is required to deduct <u>social security</u> from each employee's weekly paycheck and match the amount up to a stated maximum. (p. 526)

True-False Questions

1.   True (p. 526)

2.   True (p. 525)

3.   True (p. 526)

4.   True (p. 525)

5.   True (p. 527)

6.   False. Private pension plans are governed by the Employee Retirement Income Security Act, if the employee desires to deduct his or her pension contribution. (p. 527)

7.   False. State workers' compensation acts will not compensate an employee for an intentionally self-inflicted injury. (p. 530)

8.   False. The general duty clause of OSHA does not require the employer to make the work premises absolutely safe but free of recognized hazards. (p. 533)

9.   False. Employees did not gain the right to organize as a union until 1935. (p. 534)

10.   True (p. 534)

Multiple-Choice Questions

1.	d (p. 526)	14.	b (p. 532)
2.	b (p. 525)	15.	b (p. 534)
3.	b (p. 526)	16.	b (p. 534)
4.	d (p. 525)	17.	c (p. 534)
5.	c (p. 527)	18.	b (p. 534)
6.	d (p. 527)	19.	c (p. 534)
7.	c (p. 527)	20.	d (p. 535)
8.	b (p. 530)	21.	b (p. 541)
9.	a (p. 530)	22.	c (p. 535)
10.	b (p. 530)	23.	d (p. 535)
11.	c (p. 530)	24.	b (p. 537)
12.	a (p. 530)	25.	b (p. 535)
13.	c (p. 532)		

Essay Question

1. Yes, the workers' compensation act allows an employee to
    recover, if the injury was accidental, occurred in the
    course of employment, and has arisen out of the employ-
    ment. The accident occurred in the course of employment
    since the employer provided the running track for employ-
    ees to use during lunch or after work.

    The company desired to have employees physically fit.
    The accident arose out of the employment since the risk
    of using a running track is that an ankle injury may
    occur.

    Workers' compensation statutes are strict liability laws.
    Such laws are the employee's exclusive remedy against the
    employer. The employee may recover medical benefits and
    disability benefits. (p. 530)

Chapter 22
Employment Law and Equal Opportunity

Major Concepts

Congress in the last twenty-five years has passed comprehensive legislation to protect employees and prospective employees from discrimination. The Civil Rights Act of 1964 was enacted by Congress to eliminate discrimination in housing, public accommodations, and employment. Title VII of the Civil Rights Act of 1964 prohibits discrimination in employment based on race, color, national origin, religion, or sex. Subsequent statutes have also prohibited discrimination based on age and handicap.

Title VII proscribes two types of discrimination: disparate impact and disparate treatment. The courts have determined the elements a discrimination victim must prove. Title VII is administered by the Equal Employment Opportunity Commission (EEOC), a federal administrative agency. The EEOC has the responsibility of investigating complaints of discrimination and attempting to reconcile the parties. An individual must first file with the EEOC before taking his or her case to court.

An employer may discriminate, if the discrimination is based on a bona fide occupational qualification (BFOQ), a bona fide seniority system, or a validated ability test. The Act covers employers, employment agencies, and labor organizations. An employer must have 15 or more employees to be covered by the Act.

The employer may be ordered to implement an affirmative action program. Affirmative action programs have created much controversy since they may result in reverse discrimination.

The Equal Pay Act requires an employer to pay women the same rate as men if performing substantially the same job. The court will carefully consider the substance of the job when making a comparison.

Chapter Outline

I.   The Civil Rights Act of 1964, Title VII--The Civil Rights Act of 1964 is a comprehensive federal statute prohibiting discrimination in housing, public accommodations, and employment. Title VII of the Civil Rights Act of 1964 prohibits discrimination in employment when employers, employment agencies, and labor organizations are involved. The employer must have fifteen or more employees to be covered by Title VII. The Act is premised on Congress's power to regulate commerce under Article I, Section 8, of the U.S. Constitution. Title VII exempts religious associations and religious educational institutions for discrimination based upon religion. Congress, the District of Columbia, and Indian tribes are exempt from the Act.

   A.   Protected Classes--Under Title VII, a covered employer is prohibited from discriminating on the bases of race, color, national origin, religion, or sex. If a person is a member of one of these five categories, he or she is considered part of a protected class. Title VII only protects individuals from discrimination based on a protected class. An employer may legally discriminate against an individual outside of the protected classes.

   B.   Theories of Discrimination Under Title VII--An employer may discriminate against an individual by various means. The employer may refuse to hire, discharge the employee, fail to promote, fail to provide benefits to the employee, or not allow a transfer to another division as a means of effectuating discrimination. The courts have developed two theories for proving a violation of Title VII: disparate impact and disparate treatment.

      1.   Disparate Impact--Since the passage of the Civil Rights Act of 1964, most employers have not overtly practiced discrimination. An

employer may discriminate against a member of a protected class through what seems to be a neutral criteria. Neutral employment criteria may have an adverse effect on a protected class of employees. Title VII proscribes not only overt discrimination but also practices that are fair in form, but discriminatory in operation. If a neutral criteria has the effect of disproportionately rejecting members of a protected class, Title VII has been violated. The victim need only prove he or she is a member of a protected class which has been adversely affected by the criteria. Some examples of neutral criteria are: height and weight requirements, achieving a certain test score, and requiring a college degree or high school diploma.

Once the employee has established a prima facie case of discrimination, the burden shifts to the employer. The employer must prove a business necessity. Business necessity requires the neutral criteria to be substantially related to job performance (e.g., typing test for a secretarial job). If the employer proves a business necessity, no violation exists.

2. Disparate Treatment--Disparate treatment is either a policy or practice of overtly discriminating against a member of a protected class. The employer does not attempt to hide the discrimination.

Employers who have practiced disparate treatment for years may find it difficult to remedy past inequities. In a hiring disparate treatment case, the victim must prove:

a. the plaintiff belongs to a protected class;

b. that he or she applied and was qualified for the job for which the employer was seeking applicants;

c. he or she was rejected; and

d. after rejection, the position remained open and the employer continued to seek applicants from persons of the plaintiff's qualifications.

The employee must prove all four elements to make a prima facie case of disparate treatment. The employee may make a similar prima facie case if discharged or if refused a benefit.

Once the plaintiff has proven a prima facie case, the burden shifts to the employer to prove a legitimate nondiscriminatory reason for the action. The employer may prove the employee was not qualified for the job or that another applicant had superior credentials. Even if the employer proves a legitimate nondiscriminatory reason, the employee may assert it was merely pretext. The employer may cover up discrimination through pretext.
(e.g., Black policemen were discharged from a city police force. The black employees sued under Title VII. The employer responded to the Title VII action by asserting the officers were discharged because they were caught taking bribes. The discharged officers proved pretext by showing that none of the white officers caught taking bribes were discharged.)

II. Administration and Enforcement of Title VII--The Equal Employment Opportunity Commission (EEOC) is a federal administrative agency created to administer Title VII. The EEOC is comprised of a five-member commission appointed by the President with the consent of the Senate for five-year terms. The EEOC has broad powers to investigate complaints of discrimination. The EEOC may hold hearings and require the production of evidence from an employer.

A. EEOC Procedure--An employee must file first with the EEOC within 180 days after the discriminatory action occurred. The state may concurrently regulate employment discrimination. In such case, the aggrieved party may file a complaint with either the state agency or the EEOC. The EEOC will give the state agency an opportunity to resolve the matter.

Ten days after the EEOC receives the complaint the agency will notify the employer and prohibit the employer from retaliating against the employee. The EEOC will then investigate the charges and attempt to reconcile the parties. If the matter cannot be reconciled, the EEOC will either bring an action or allow the employee to sue. The employee will receive a "right to sue" letter from the EEOC. An employee cannot sue under Title VII until receiving the "right to sue" letter from the EEOC.

III. Specific Application of Title VII--Title VII has been expanded to cover a variety of discriminatory activities.

A. Sex Discrimination--Discrimination against a person because of their sex is prohibited. Title VII protects an individual from gender-based discrimination only. A state statute may be invalidated if it attempts to prevent women from undertaking jobs which are too dangerous or strenuous.

Sex-plus discrimination involves discrimination because of sex plus an additional factor, such as a pre-school child. An employer cannot advertise for a particular sex, unless a bona fide occupational qualification exists.

1. Sexual Harassment--Sexual harassment is a violation of Title VII. Examples of sexual harassment are unwelcome sexual advances, requests for sexual favors, verbal conduct of a sexual nature which conditions employment, pay, or a promotion on performance of sexual conduct. If an intimidating, hostile, or offensive environment is created by such harassment, it is illegal. The employer may be held responsible for the employee's sexual harassment, if the employer knows of the activity and fails to act.

2. Pregnancy Discrimination--The Pregnancy Discrimination Act of 1978 amended Title VII to prohibit any activity which discriminated against an employee because of pregnancy, childbirth, or related medical conditions. Health group plans must cover pregnancy, childbirth, and related medical conditions in the same manner as a temporary disability.

If employees are entitled to leave for temporary disability, then pregnant women must receive the same opportunity. A pregnant woman is entitled to continue to work as long as she can perform her job.

3. Pension and Life Insurance--Employers are required to treat women as individuals and not as

a class. Historically, some employers required women to pay greater amounts into pension plans because women, on the average, would draw out greater benefits. The U.S. Supreme Court has held that requiring women to pay more into a retirement program violated Title VII.

B. <u>Discrimination Based on Religion</u>--Title VII makes it unlawful to discriminate against any individual with respect to compensation, terms, conditions, or privileges of employment because of his or her religion. The term religion includes all aspects of religious observance and practice as well as belief. The employer has the additional duty of reasonably accommodating an employee's or prospective employee's religious observance or practice. The employer need only accommodate the employee to the extent of a "de minimis cost." Any accommodation greater than a de minimis cost is considered undue hardship on the employer and not required.

The employer is not required to incur substantial costs or to make changes that require a replacement to be paid higher wages. Nor is the employer required to discriminate against other employees to make an accommodation or breach a collective bargaining agreement. But if the employer can accommodate the employee's religious needs at minimal cost, he or she is required to do so.

The plaintiff in a reasonable accommodation case must prove:

1. the employee has a bona fide religious belief that conflicts with an employment requirement;

2. he or she informed the employer of this belief; and

3. he or she was disciplined for failure to comply with the conflicting employment requirement.

Once the plaintiff has established a prima facie case, the burden shifts to the employer to prove the company cannot reasonably accommodate the employee without incurring undue hardship.

C. <u>Discrimination Based on National Origin</u>--Title VII
    prohibits discrimination based on an individual's
    national origin. National origin is defined as a
    person's place of birth or where a person's ances-
    tors are from. National origin may be manifested
    in physical, cultural, or linguistic characteris-
    tics.

    Requiring an individual to speak English at all
    times while at work is a violation of Title VII,
    based on national origin. Since language is
    closely related to a person's origin, the total
    prohibition of the speaking of a foreign language
    is discriminatory. The employer may require
    employees to speak English while dealing with
    customers.

D. <u>Discrimination Based on Race</u>--Title VII prohibits
    employment discrimination based on a person's race.
    This protection has always applied to nonwhite
    classes. The courts have construed Title VII as
    also applying to the white class. This is called
    reverse discrimination when a black person is
    favored over a white person. The Civil Rights Act
    of 1964 was primarily enacted to abrogate racial
    discrimination.

IV. <u>Statutory Defenses</u>--An employer may assert one of three
    defenses to a Title VII charge.

A. <u>Bona Fide Occupational Qualifications (BFOQs)</u>--The
    employer may be allowed to discriminate if the pro-
    tected class is considered a BFOQ. The employer
    has a BFOQ, if the qualification is reasonably
    necessary to the normal operation of the employer's
    enterprise. The BFOQ defense is a narrowly con-
    strued exception to Title VII. There must be a
    reasonable factual basis for the class limitation.
    The BFOQ is used only if the essence of the busi-
    ness would be affected without it. (e.g., A
    Chinese restaurant may discriminate on the basis of
    national origin by only hiring Chinese waiters
    and/or waitresses.)

    The BFOQ defense is not available for discrimina-
    tion based on race or color. The courts have held
    that customer preference is not enough to make a
    qualification a BFOQ.

B. Bona Fide Seniority System--An employer may provide
    different benefits to employees based on a bona
    fide seniority system. A seniority system usually
    gives a preference to those employees who have been
    employed the longest. In most instances when a
    union is involved, the collective bargaining agree-
    ment outlines a detailed seniority system. Bona
    fide seniority systems must meet the following
    criteria:

    1. the system must apply equally to all persons;

    2. the seniority units must follow industry prac-
        tices and must constitute separate collective
        bargaining units;

    3. the seniority system must not have its origins
        in racial discrimination; and

    4. the system must be maintained free of any il-
        legal racial purpose.

    An employer may provide larger benefits to employ-
    ees with greater seniority status. In addition,
    the employer may lay off employees according to a
    bona fide seniority system in a slowdown.

C. Professionally Developed Ability Tests--The em-
    ployer may utilize professionally developed ability
    tests as a criteria for employment. The test must
    be validated to not violate Title VII. Validation
    requires the test to be job-related. The EEOC has
    formulated guidelines to assist employers in creat-
    ing and using an ability test.

V. The Equal Pay Act--The Equal Pay Act was enacted in
    1963 as an amendment to the Fair Labor Standards Act
    and prohibits discrimination in wages paid for equal
    work on jobs that require equal skills, effort, and
    responsibility held by men and women. The male and
    female must work at the same place of work for the Act
    to apply. The courts may disregard the person's title
    and look to the substance of the job when making the
    comparison. The Act's primary purpose was to create
    equality in wages between men and women.

A. Enforcement--The government and a private party may
    bring an action for violation of the Act. The em-
    ployee may recover back pay for up to two years and
    up to three years if the violation was willful. A

party must bring the lawsuit within two years,
three years for a willful violation. The court may
award the employee liquidated damages equal to the
amount of back pay as a penalty to the employer.
The employer may not have to pay liquidated damages
if he or she can prove reasonable grounds to form a
good faith belief that the act was lawful.

B.   Exceptions--The employer may pay men and women differently, if such differences are based on a
seniority system, merit system, piecework, production bonus systems, or on factors other than sex.
The employer may also pay a premium to those
employees who work certain shifts.

VI.   The Immigration Reform and Control Act of 1986--The Act
prohibits employers from hiring unauthorized aliens.
Employers must verify employees as citizens or authorized aliens. The employer can give a preference to
U.S. citizens over equally qualified authorized aliens,
although a company policy which mandates U.S. citizens
always be given a preference violates antidiscrimina-
tion laws.

VII.   Americans with Disabilities Act of 1990 (ADA)--The ADA
protects persons with disabilities from employment discrimination. In addition, the ADA requires the employer to make reasonable accommodations for persons
with disabilities in the workplace.

The ADA initially applies to employers with 25 or more
employees. In 1994, the employer with 15 or more employees will come under the Act.

VIII.   Affirmative Action--Affirmative action is a program to
eliminate discrimination in employment against women
and minorities. An affirmative action program can be
implemented either voluntarily by the employer, ordered
by the court to correct past incidences of discrimination, or required, if a company sells goods or services
to the government under a contract for $50,000 or more
and the employer has 50 or more employees. An affirmative action program may include quotas and timetables
for increasing the percentages of minorities or women
in an organization's workforce, although strict adherence to a quota violates Title VII.

The employer must communicate the existence of an
affirmative action program to management, employees,
and recruitment sources.

Affirmative action programs, whether voluntary or involuntary, grant racial preferences in hiring and
promotion. Nonminority individuals may be excluded as
a result of the implementation of affirmative action.
The U.S. Supreme Court has held that whites are
entitled to the protections of Title VII. The result
of affirmative action may be "reverse discrimination"
against white male employees and white male applicants.
Affirmative action programs have been upheld despite
potential and actual reverse discrimination.

In a reverse discrimination case, the plaintiff must
prove a prima facie case which will shift the burden to
the employer to articulate nondiscriminatory rationale
for the decision. The employer will then assert the
existence of an affirmative action plan. The burden
then shifts back to the employee to prove the employer's justification was pretext or the plan is invalid.

IX. <u>Privacy Rights of Employees</u>--The U.S. Supreme Court has
interpreted the U.S. Constitution as providing individuals with the right of privacy. The court derived this
concept from the Fourth Amendment's prohibition on
unreasonable search and seizures. The actual term
"privacy" is not found in the Fourth Amendment. The
U.S. Supreme Court has expansively interpreted the
Fourth Amendment to apply not only to criminal cases
but also to the employment area.

A. <u>Drug Testing</u>--Testing employees for drug usage has
created great controversy. Employees argue their
right to privacy is being violated. Employers
argue they have a right to a drug-free workforce.
A private employer has the right to test an employee as a condition of the job or if the employer
believes the employee is under the influence of
alcohol or drugs. The courts have been hesitant to
allow public employers to force an employee to
submit to random drug tests.

B. <u>AIDS Testing</u>--The same concerns are raised in relation to testing employees for the AIDS virus.
Although Title VII does not specifically cover AIDS
victims, some argue that an AIDS victim is considered handicapped and should receive protection
as a protected class. Opponents of classifying
AIDS victims as handicapped argue that the medical
community knows very little about the disease and
its transmission and that in the interests of
safety and health an employer should not be required to employ an AIDS victim.

C.   Employee Records--The employer may not communicate harmful information about a current or prior employee to others, unless the employer is granted a privilege to do so. The employer may be sued by the employee for damage to his or her reputation under the tort of defamation. The employee may collect damages in the amount of the injury to his or her reputation.

The employer may communicate with a prospective new employer about the employee under a limited privilege. The employer should restrict the communication to job title, dates of employment, and ending salary.

Study Questions

Fill-in-the-Blank Questions

The Civil Rights movement began in the early 1940s. The movement culminated in the passage of the Civil Rights Act of 1964. The Act primarily sought to eradicate racial discrimination.

The Civil Rights Act of 1964 prohibits discrimination in housing, public accommodations, and _____.
                                         (sales/employment)

The Act prohibits discrimination in employment under Title

_____.
  (VII/VIII)

An employer is covered under the Act, if he or she employs _____ employees.
        (20 or more/15 or more)

The Act prohibits discrimination based on race, color, national origin, religion, and _____.
                                         (alienage/sex)

True-False Questions

1.   The Civil Rights Act of 1964 prohibits all forms of discrimination in the workplace. _____

2.   A Title VII case of employment discrimination may be proven under the theory of disparate impact. _____

3. Title VII prohibits only overt forms of discrimination in the workplace. _____

4. An employer may violate Title VII by discriminating against pregnant women. _____

5. The employer must reasonably accommodate an employee's religious practices under Title VII. _____

6. The Equal Employment Opportunity Commission has the responsibility of administering Title VII. _____

7. A bona fide occupational qualification is reasonably necessary to the normal operation of a particular business. _____

8. The Equal Pay Act was enacted in 1963 as an amendment to the Civil Rights Act. _____

9. The concept of quotas is mandated by Title VII. _____

10. Reverse discrimination may be the result of an affirmative action program. _____

Multiple-Choice Questions

1. Which of the following situations is not covered by Title VII?

    I.   religious organization hiring an employee on the basis of religion

    II. a Congresswoman hiring only women

    III. an employer with 10 employees hiring two more employees

    a. I only
    b. I and II
    c. II and III
    d. I, II, and III

2. Which of the following practices may appear neutral on the surface but still violate Title VII?

    I.   physical requirements
    II. testing requirements
    III. education requirements

a.   II only
b.   I and II
c.   II and III
d.   I, II, and III

3. The objective of Congress in the enactment of Title VII was to:

   I.   achieve equality of employment opportunities.
  II.   create new jobs for minorities.
 III.   remove barriers which favored white employees.

a.   I only
b.   II only
c.   II and III
d.   I and III

4. Discrimination which involves the treatment of a member of one class differently from the treatment of other employees or applicants is called:

a.   disparate treatment.
b.   disparate impact.
c.   affirmative action.
d.   none of the above.

5. Which of the following is <u>not</u> an element of a prima facie case of discrimination based on religion?

a.   the employee had a bona fide religious belief
b.   the plaintiff had superior qualifications
c.   the plaintiff informed the employer of the belief
d.   validation of tests

6. Once the employee has proven a prima facie case of disparate treatment, the burden shifts to the employer to prove:

a.   pretext.
b.   lack of an injury.
c.   a legitimate nondiscriminatory reason.
d.   all of the above.

7. Shirley, an employee of American International, Inc. (AI) applies for a lower management position within the corporation. The company sells pharmaceutical products worldwide. The company does not have any women in management. Managers are required to deal with foreign nationals who sometimes do not like to deal with women. Shirley applies for the position and is rejected. The position

is filled by Ted, another employee in the company. Shirley argues the company has discriminated against her through:

a.   disparate impact.
b.   disparate treatment.
c.   disproportionate impact.
d.   all of the above.

8.   Refer to question 7. Shirley must prove a prima facie case against AI for what type of discrimination?

a.   national origin
b.   race
c.   sex
d.   color

9.   Refer to question 7. Shirley must file her complaint with the _____ before she can proceed to the federal court.

a.   Department of Labor
b.   Secretary of Labor
c.   Equal Employment Opportunity Commission
d.   Federal Trade Commission

10. Refer to questions 7 and 9. Shirley properly files her complaint and subsequently is given the right to sue in federal court. Shirley proves a prima facie case in federal court. The employer's best defense(s) to the charges would be:

  I.   foreign nationals prefer to deal with men.
 II.   Ted has superior qualification for the position.
III.   Shirley did not meet the qualifications of the job.

a.   I only
b.   I and II
c.   II and III
d.   I and III

11. Refer to questions 7 and 10. American International presents evidence which justifies their actions. Shirley must prove which of the following to refute the defendant's defenses?

a.   pretext
b.   standing
c.   reasonable accommodation
d.   all of the above

12. Which of the following actions by the employer constitutes sexual harassment?

   a. unwelcome sexual advances
   b. verbal conduct of a sexual nature
   c. an intimidating and offensive environment for employees
   d. all of the above

13. Discrimination based on sex includes which of the following?

   I.   pregnancy discrimination
   II. childbirth discrimination
   III. language discrimination

   a. I only
   b. I and II
   c. II and III
   d. I, II, and III

14. The City of Los Angeles employed thousands of employees. The city provided a retirement program for the employees. The program required women to contribute more into the retirement fund than men. The city required women to make greater contributions, because women, on the average, live longer than men and would draw benefits for a longer period of time. The EEOC brings a cause of action against the city of Los Angeles for a violation of Title VII. The city will:

   a. win, because no discrimination occurred.
   b. win, because women live longer.
   c. lose, under Title VII.
   d. lose, because the city has violated the Equal Pay Act.

15. Charlie is employed at a local grocery store as a stocker and maintenance person. The store manager requires Charlie to work all day Sunday from 8 a.m. to 8 p.m. Charlie belongs to the church across the street from the store. The tenets of Charlie's religion requires church attendance on Sunday. Charlie asks his boss for Sunday mornings off so he may attend church. The store must do which of the following?

   a. meet Charlie's needs at all costs
   b. reasonably accommodate Charlie up to a de minimis cost
   c. the store has no obligation at all
   d. none of the above

16. Refer to question 15. Charlie's boss refuses to allow Charlie to take off Sunday mornings. Charlie refuses to work Sunday mornings and is discharged as a result. Charlie desires to file a Title VII claim against the store. Charlie will have to prove which of the following?

   I. He had a bona fide religious belief that conflicts with an employment requirement.

  II. He informed the employer of the conflict.

 III. He obeyed the employment requirement.

  a. I only
  b. I and II
  c. II and III
  d. I, II, and III

17. Refer to questions 15 and 16. Assume Charlie has proven a prima facie case of religious discrimination. The employer may refute the discrimination charge by proving which of the following?

  a. The employee could not be reasonably accommodated without undue hardship.
  b. Other substitutes were available.
  c. Business was poor on Sunday mornings.
  d. All of the above.

18. Refer to questions 15, 16, and 17. Charlie may overcome the employer's defenses by proving which of the following facts?

  I. Substitutes are available at no additional cost.
  II. A collective bargaining agreement exists.
 III. Allowing Charlie off Sunday morning is unreasonable.

  a. I only
  b. I and II
  c. II and III
  d. II only

19. The court may order an employer to follow an affirmative action program. The implementation of an affirmative action program may cause:

  a. reverse discrimination.
  b. minorities to lose out.

c. a preference to white employees.
d. none of the above.

20. Which of the following cannot be a bona fide occupational qualification?

a. sex
b. national origin
c. race
d. religion

21. The First National Bank employs over 25 tellers. The bank has commercial and consumer tellers. The commercial tellers deal only with business accounts. The commercial tellers do basically the same job as a consumer teller but are paid higher wages. The commercial tellers are all men, and most of the consumer tellers are women. Which of the following has probably been violated?

a. affirmative action
b. employee's right of privacy
c. Fair Labor Standards Act of minimum wage
d. Equal Pay Act

22. The employee's right to privacy is derived from:

a. the Fourth Amendment.
b. the Fifth Amendment.
c. the Declaration of Independence.
d. all of the above.

23. An employer may be sued by the employee for communicating harmful information to a third party. The employee will bring the suit under:

a. Equal Pay Act.
b. defamation.
c. affirmative action.
d. all of the above.

24. Which of the following are exempt from Title VII's provision?

a. Congress
b. an employment agency
c. labor union with 15 or more members
d. all of the above

25. Which of the following forms of discrimination involves national origin?

    I.   a prohibition on the speaking of a foreign language while on the job

    II.   a medical condition related to pregnancy which the employer refuses to cover under the health benefit program

    III.   a physical requirement that all employees be six feet tall and 180 pounds or more

    a.   I only
    b.   I and II
    c.   II and III
    d.   I and III

Essay Question

1. Duke Power Company hires individuals to work at one of five divisions within the company. In the construction division, most employees are black. The other four divisions in the company require the employee to have a high school diploma or pass a standardized test. The test has the effect of eliminating 8 of 10 black applicants, whereas only 2 of 10 white applicants are rejected. The black employees in the construction division bring charges for a violation of Title VII. What result?

Answers to Study Questions

Fill-in-the-Blank Questions

The Civil Rights Act of 1964 prohibits discrimination in housing, public accommodations, and <u>employment</u>. (p. 546)

The Act prohibits discrimination in employment under Title <u>VII</u>. (p. 546)

An employer is covered under the Act, if he or she employs <u>15 or more</u> employees. (p. 546)

The Act prohibits discrimination based on race, color, national origin, religion, and <u>sex</u>. (p. 546)

True-False Questions

1. False. The Civil Rights Act of 1964 only prohibits dis-
    crimination where a protected class is involved.
    (p. 546)

2. True (p. 546)

3. False. Title VII prohibits overt and covert forms of
    discrimination. (p. 547)

4. True (p. 549)

5. True (p. 551)

6. True (p. 548)

7. True (p. 554)

8. False. The Equal Pay Act amends the Fair Labor Standards
    Act. (p. 555)

9. False. Employers are only required to attempt to meet
    the goals of affirmative action. (p. 558)

10. True (p. 559)

Multiple-Choice Questions

1.	d (p. 546)	14.	c (p. 551)
2.	d (pp. 546, 547)	15.	b (p. 552)
3.	d (p. 547)	16.	b (p. 553)
4.	a (p. 548)	17.	a (p. 553)
5.	b (p. 553)	18.	a (p. 552)
6.	c (p. 548)	19.	a (p. 559)
7.	b (p. 548)	20.	c (p. 554)
8.	c (p. 548)	21.	d (p. 555)
9.	c (p. 554)	22.	a (p. 561)
10.	c (p. 554)	23.	b (p. 562)
11.	a (p. 548)	24.	a (p. 546)
12.	d (p. 551)	25.	d (p. 553)
13.	b (p. 548)		

Essay Question

1. Duke Power Company has violated Title VII. The company
    has used a neutral criteria to discriminate against black
    employees. This type of discrimination is called dispar-

ate impact.   The employee must prove the policy or
practice of the employer had a disproportionately adverse
effect on members of a protected class, and the plaintiff
is a member of the protected class.   The employer may
attempt to refute the plaintiff's case by proving a business necessity.   (pp. 546, 547)

Chapter 23
Environmental Law

Major Concepts

Environmental law stems primarily from three sources: the
common law, state legislatures, and the federal government.
In the last fifty years, a multitude of federal statutes have
been enacted to protect the environment from pollution and
encourage efficiency in the disposal of waste.

The common law theories deal primarily with the aspects of
property ownership and the protection of the property owner's
right to quiet enjoyment. The theories of nuisance, trespass,
negligence, and strict liability seek to protect the property
owner from interference with his or her property. The common
law rules fail to protect society from the erosion of natural
resources, the pollution of the air and water, and the improper use of toxic substances.

The Environmental Protection Agency (EPA) was created in 1970
to have primary responsibility for environmental concerns.
The EPA enforces and administers a wide variety of federal
statutes aimed at protecting the air and water. The air is
protected by the Clean Air Act and the Noise Control Act.
Water is protected by the Clean Water Act, the Marine Protection, Research, and Sanctuaries Act, and the Drinking Water
Act. Waste disposal is controlled by the Solid Waste Disposal
Act and the Resource Conservation and Recovery Act.

The EPA and state agencies work together to eliminate pollution and enforce specific federal statutes. In some cases, a
violation is determined according to a strict liability stan-

dard.   Most violations carry large penalties and possible
imprisonment.

Chapter Outline

I.   Common Law Regulation--The courts have sought to protect
     the environment from individuals and businesses who pol-
     lute and destroy our natural resources. The common law
     theories were founded primarily on the principle of
     property ownership. The major common law theories are
     nuisance, trespass, negligence, and strict liability.

     A.   Nuisance--A nuisance may be classified as either
          private or public. A private nuisance is when a
          property owner uses his or her property in such a
          way as to inflict harm on others or the property of
          others. The individual's right to quiet and peace-
          ful enjoyment of his or her property is disturbed by
          another's unreasonable and unwarranted use of his or
          her property. A private individual may bring a
          cause of action under the tort theory of nuisance,
          asking the court for an injunction or damages. An
          equity court will only issue an injunction if dam-
          ages are inadequate. (e.g., A neighbor burning
          plastic containers in his backyard which caused
          smoke, soot, and a foul smell to settle in a per-
          son's backyard may be liable under private nui-
          sance.)

          A public nuisance is similar to a private nuisance
          in that the defendant's activity disturbs the prop-
          erty owner, but a public nuisance involves wide-
          spread harm to a substantial segment of the commu-
          nity. (e.g., A corporation is dumping waste mate-
          rials in a river which flows into a lake. The lake
          is being used by the community for recreation and
          drinking water.)

          The court will balance the interests of the plain-
          tiff and the defendant before issuing an injunction.
          The injunction will order the individual or business
          to cease the nuisance. In some cases, a company may
          be shut down altogether as a result of the injunc-
          tion.

     B.   Trespass--Trespass is the intentional invasion of
          another's property, whether or not the interference
          causes damage. The defendant need not physically
          walk/pass over the property as long as the defendant

is responsible for putting in motion an object which passes over another's land. The invasion of land by visible or invisible objects may cause a trespass. Where a company is causing toxic fumes to pass over a person's land, a trespass has occurred. The plaintiff may recover damages or seek an injunction.

C. Negligence--Negligence is an unintentional tort. The plaintiff need not prove the defendant acted with the intent to cause injury. Negligence is defined as the failure to use reasonable care toward an individual which causes a foreseeable injury. A company may have a duty of care under state or federal statute or the common law. If the defendant could reasonably foresee that their action would cause injury, a duty of care then exists. If a company contaminates the water supply of a community by discharging waste, the company may be liable for damages under the theory of negligence.

D. Strict Liability--Strict liability is a no fault theory. The plaintiff need not prove that the defendant did anything wrong. The defendant is automatically liable for the injury of the plaintiff. The most common area the courts apply strict liability is for ultrahazardous activities. Examples of ultrahazardous activities are blasting operations and transporting radioactive materials. The defendant is held responsible for injury resulting from the activity without regard to the amount of care exerted.

II. State Statutory Regulation--A state may impose restrictions on business for the protection of the environment. Many states are attempting to curb air and water pollution through legislative means. Since each state's environmental problems are unique, a wide variety of statutes have been enacted. Some states monitor motor vehicle emissions, transportation of toxic materials, and disposal of waste materials.

Many states have attempted to alleviate solid waste disposal by outlawing certain types of disposable containers. It has been predicted that the majority of landfills across the United States will reach their capacity in about twenty-five years. Companies producing containers which have been prohibited by state statute have challenged the constitutionality of such laws. The courts have upheld environmental statutes, ruling that the problems of litter in public places and solid waste

disposal outweigh the economic benefit to the industry
producing the item. The state's police power in most
cases has been sustained as constitutional.

III. Regulation by the Federal Government--A number of fed-
      eral statutes have been enacted by Congress to protect
      the environment. These statutes place the burden on
      business to act responsibly in relation to the environ-
      ment.

      A. The National Environmental Policy Act (NEPA)--NEPA
          was passed by Congress in 1969 as an attempt to
          unify environmental policy. Congress in 1970
          created the Environmental Protection Agency (EPA) to
          centralize in one agency the enforcement and admin-
          istration of most environmental legislation. The
          EPA may conduct research on pollution and provide
          assistance to state agencies in combatting pollu-
          tion. NEPA requires the federal government to
          prepare an Environmental Impact Statement (EIS) for
          significant actions which affect the quality of the
          environment.

          1. Environmental Impact Statement (EIS)--The EPA
              has been delegated the authority to ensure that
              any proposed federal action which significantly
              affects the quality of the environment is exam-
              ined in an EIS. The EIS must provide detailed
              information describing the environmental impact
              of the proposed action. In addition, the EIS
              must list unavoidable adverse effects, irrevers-
              ible commitments of resources involved, and
              acceptable alternatives to the proposed project.
              The preparation of the EIS can be extremely
              costly, complex, and time-consuming. In some
              cases, the federal agency may have to hire
              experts to assist in completing the EIS. The
              EIS is filed with the EPA.

              The EIS has been utilized by consumer groups,
              businesses, and federal agencies to provide in-
              put for future regulation. A private business
              may be required to prepare and file an EIS, if
              federal funds are involved in the project.
              (e.g., The deployment of the Strategic Defense
              Initiative by the U.S. government might require
              the preparation of an EIS, since the activation
              of the system may have a significant effect on
              the environment.)

B.   The Clean Air Act--The Clean Air Act was initially
     enacted by Congress in 1963 and subsequently amended
     in 1965 and 1967. The Clean Air Act is the primary
     federal statute to combat air pollution. The latter
     amendments to the Act required the establishment of
     ambient (surrounding) air quality standards for dis-
     tinct control regions within state borders. States
     were required to propose State Implementation Plans
     (SIP) to achieve set standards. The Act failed to
     provide specific guidelines to the states.

     In 1970, the Act was amended again, and the EPA was
     given the authority to establish uniform primary
     (health) standards and secondary (welfare) stan-
     dards. The states maintain the responsibility of
     these standards; the EPA makes sure the standards
     are complied with as soon as possible.

     1.   Air Quality Standards--The EPA has the main
          responsibility of establishing standards for
          seven air pollutants: sulfur dioxide, carbon
          monoxide, ozone, hydrocarbons, nitrogen dioxide,
          particulates, and lead. The administrator of
          the EPA established primary standards to protect
          public health. The standards are uniform
          throughout the United States. The states are
          responsible for implementation of a plan which
          would decrease the level of pollutants below the
          national standards. State plans cover only
          stationary sources of pollution and not motor
          vehicles or aircraft. Examples of stationary
          sources of pollution are factories, utilities,
          and mills.

          The EPA has direct responsibility for the reduc-
          tion of air pollutants from aircraft and auto-
          mobiles. The Clean Air Act of 1970 mandated a
          90 percent reduction in the amount of carbon
          monoxide and hydrocarbons emitted from auto-
          mobiles by 1975. The FAA administers similar
          regulations for aircraft. The Act also sets
          standards for automobile manufacturers to reduce
          carbon monoxide emissions.

     2.   Civil and Criminal Penalties--The EPA may insti-
          tute a civil action against a firm that is fail-
          ing to comply with a state implementation plan
          and has been in violation for 30 days. The EPA
          may seek an injunction or a civil penalty up to
          $25,000 per day, or both. A person who know-

ingly and intentionally violates a state plan, an EPA order, or the Clean Air Act may be imprisoned up to 1 year.

C. The Clean Water Act--Congress enacted the Clean Water Act in 1972 as the primary legislation to eliminate water pollution. The Act had three major objectives: (1) to make waters safe for swimming, (2) to protect fish and wildlife, and (3) to eliminate the discharge of pollutants into the water.

   1. Water Quality Standards--Under the Act, municipal and industrial polluters are treated differently. The EPA requires industrial polluters to meet stricter standards. A municipal or industrial polluter is required to apply for a permit before discharging wastes into navigable waters. Specific schedules of compliance were set and extended. The Act requires a firm to use the best conventional treatment control technology.

   2. Civil and Criminal Penalties--The Act allows a private party, the EPA, or state authority to bring a civil suit. The EPA may bring criminal charges, if the firm is in violation for 30 days. In a civil suit, the plaintiff may seek an injunction or damages. Penalties for violations are from $2,500 to $25,000 per day and up to 1 year in prison, or both. The violator may be required to clean up the pollution.

   3. Other Regulations

      a. Marine Protection, Research, and Sanctuaries Act--The Act regulates the discharge of wastes into coastal waters and marine areas by a system of permits.

      b. The Safe Drinking Water Act--In 1974, Congress established regulations which require the states to comply with national standards. Penalties may be imposed on parties who pollute the water.

D. The Noise Control Act--The Noise Control Act was enacted by Congress in 1972 to create an environment free from noise that is injurious to the health and welfare of the public. The Act represents the first major legislation to control excessive noise from

sources the public is continuously exposed to. The
EPA, with the cooperation of the Federal Aviation
Administration and the Department of Transportation,
are to establish noise emission standards for various products. The EPA establishes standards for
equipment, motors, and engines. The Act subjects
federal facilities to state and local standards.

The main emphasis of the Noise Control Act is to
reduce environmental noise in an effort to prevent
long range effects on public health and welfare.

Violations of the Act are punishable by a fine of up
to $25,000 per day and up to 1 year in prison, or
both.

E.   The Toxic Substances Control Act--Congress passed
     the Toxic Substances Control Act in 1976. The Act
     requires the EPA to develop an inventory of existing
     chemicals by requiring manufacturers to report the
     amounts of chemicals they produce. The major thrust
     of the Act is to prohibit the introduction of sub-
     stances that would present an uncontrollable risk.
     Manufacturers must test chemicals and notify the EPA
     when a new substance is being produced. The Act
     provides for testing, warnings, and instructions
     leading to the proper use of toxic substances.

     The EPA may prohibit the production of a new high
     risk substance and may enforce the order through a
     court injunction.

F.   The Federal Environmental Pesticide Act--The Federal
     Environmental Pesticide Act was enacted by Congress
     in 1972 to bolster the Federal Insecticide, Fungi-
     cide, and Rodenticide Act of 1947. A pesticide is
     defined as any substance which is intended for pre-
     venting, destroying, repelling, or mitigating any
     pest. The EPA has the responsibility to control
     pesticides in the environment.

     The Act requires pesticides:

     1.   to be registered before sold,

     2.   be certified and used only for approved applica-
          tions, and

     3.   to only be used in proscribed amounts when ap-
          plied to crops that provide food for people or
          animals.

The EPA is authorized to inspect manufacturing facilities and suspend the use of harmful substances.
The EPA classifies pesticides as either for general
or restricted use. Pesticides classified as restricted can only be applied by a certified applica-
tor. Violations of the Act may subject the violator
to penalties.

G. The Solid Wastes Disposal Act--The Solid Wastes Disposal Act was passed by Congress in 1965 with the
purpose of reducing solid waste disposal by encour-
aging recycling and reuse of materials. The Act was
amended in 1976 as under the Resource Conservation
and Recovery Act. The primary goal of the Act is
more efficient management of waste and its disposal
through financial and technical assistance to state
and local agencies in the production and implementation of new methods of waste disposal. The Office
of Solid Waste is a branch of the EPA and directs
resources to the management and disposal of hazardous waste.

The EPA, under the Resource Conservation and Recovery Act, oversees the issuing of permits for federal
facilities and reviews state permits for use of some
equipment. The EPA may conduct on-site inspections
of hazardous waste generators.

H. The Comprehensive Environmental Response, Compensation, and Liability Act--The Comprehensive Environmental Response, Compensation, and Liability Act is
known as Superfund and was enacted by Congress in
1980. Superfund authorizes the EPA to clean up a
hazardous waste site and recover the costs from the
person who generated the waste disposed at the site,
the person who transported the waste to the site,
the person who owned or operated the waste site at
the time, or the current owner and operator of the
site. Superfund imposes a strict liability standard
and makes the defendants jointly and severally
liable.

IV. Judicial Limits--The courts have given the EPA and other
environmental agencies broad discretion to achieve their
purpose. Some more recent decisions have cut back on
agency authority. A few courts have imposed a cost-
benefit standard on the decisions of the agencies. The
court will weigh the interests of the government to protect the environment against the interests of industry
to operate economically. A firm may argue that the

abatement of all air pollution at their factory is un-
economical. The courts have rejected the cost defense
when it is the sole defense of the firm.

The firm may also argue the statute is unconstitutional
or that the regulation promulgated by the agency is not
supported by substantial evidence in the record.

Study Questions

Fill-in-the-Blank Questions

Universal Manufacturing Inc. produces interior and exterior
paints. The company employs over 500 employees and is located
in a major metropolitan area. The company discharges waste
into a nearby channel which flows into a large lake. The company also emits smoke particles from several smokestacks on
the roof of the factory.

Neighbors complain about the smoke passing over their property. Neighbors may sue Universal under the theory of
_____ for damages to
        (private nuisance/strict liability)
their property.

The state attorney general objects to Universal's disposal of
waste into the lake. The attorney general may sue under the
theory of _____.
            (strict liability/public nuisance)

The _____ may investigate Universal for potential
      (FTC/EPA)
violations of the Clean Air Act.

True-False Questions

1. The common law provides some protection to landowners
    from pollution. _____

2. The tort of trespass may be used by a landowner to re-
    cover damages for a harmful invasion of property. _____

3. A nuisance occurs when a person uses his or her property
    in such a manner as to affect adversely a neighbor's
    property. _____

4. Strict liability is a theory used by plaintiffs injured
    from the defendant's ultrahazardous operation. _____

5. A state may not restrict the amount of emissions from motor vehicles. _____

6. The EPA regulates the preparation of Environmental Impact Statements. _____

7. All private companies are required to file Environmental Impact Statements for actions which affect the environment. _____

8. The EPA has the authority to issue administrative citations. _____

9. The EPA sets the national air quality standards for major pollutants throughout the United States. _____

10. The Clean Water Act attempts to, among other objectives, protect fish and wildlife. _____

Multiple-Choice Questions

1. Which of the following common law theories hold the defendant responsible without proof of fault?

    a. private nuisance
    b. public nuisance
    c. trespass
    d. strict liability

2. Which of the following common law theories requires the plaintiff to prove the defendant acted intentionally?

    a. negligence
    b. trespass
    c. strict liability
    d. all of the above

3. The state of Oregon adopted a law prohibiting the use of nonreturnable containers for soft drinks. The manufacturers of aluminum cans object to the statute and sue the government for a violation of the U.S. Constitution. The can manufacturers claimed which of the following?

      I. a violation of Equal Protection
     II. a violation of Due Process
    III. a violation of the Commerce Clause

    a. I only
    b. I and II

c. II and III
d. I, II, and III

4. Refer to question 3. The state of Oregon will assert
    which of the following arguments to preserve the validity
    of the statute?

    I.   The statute is an attempt to alleviate litter in
         public places.

    II. The statute is an attempt to alleviate solid waste
         disposal problems.

    III. The statute is an attempt to keep out-of-state com-
         panies from selling in the state.

    a. I only
    b. I and II
    c. II and III
    d. I, II, and III

5. Refer to questions 3 and 4. The Oregon court of appeals
    held the statute did not violate the U.S. Constitution.
    The reason for the court's decision was:

    a. the Due Process Clause does not apply to state stat-
        utes.
    b. the companies manufactured aluminum cans and return-
        able bottles.
    c. aluminum cans are ultrahazardous.
    d. none of the above.

6. A property owner may recover from a defendant adjacent
    property owner for damage done to his or her real prop-
    erty under which of the following?

    a. nuisance
    b. strict liability
    c. negligence
    d. all of the above

7. The Amax Company is using dynamite to loosen large
    amounts of bedrock at the site of a new office building.
    Tim Karl owns a home adjacent to the construction site.
    Tim discovers his foundation is beginning to crack and
    crumble in places. Tim should sue Amax under which of
    the following theories?

    a. trespass
    b. negligence

    c.   nuisance
    d.   strict liability

8. Which of the following statements is/are true?

    I.   Negligence is a fault theory of recovery.

    II. Strict liability may allow a plaintiff a recovery for ultrahazardous activity of the defendant.

    III. A landowner has the absolute right to use his or her property.

    a.   I only
    b.   I and II
    c.   II and III
    d.   I, II, and III

9. An Environmental Impact Statement must contain which of the following?

    I.   irreversible effects of the action taken
    II. alternative actions that might be taken
    III. the total cost of preparing the statement

    a.   I only
    b.   I and II
    c.   II and III
    d.   I, II, and III

10. Which of the following parties may be required to file an environmental impact statement with the EPA?

    a.   Department of Defense
    b.   Acme Company, producer of sailboats
    c.   Fairview Company, a retirement village
    d.   none of the above

11. Under the 1970 Clean Air Act, the EPA set primary national ambient air quality standards. The states were required to design a state implementation plan to achieve the standards set by the EPA. If a state failed to implement a plan, the EPA would:

    a.   promulgate one for it.
    b.   sue in court for an injunction.
    c.   sue in court to impose a fine.
    d.   all of the above.

12. Most states have implemented plans to achieve EPA stan-
    dards. The plans are widely different in approach and
    requirements. Ohio promulgated a plan which required
    utility companies in the state to use fuels locally
    available. A Kentucky producer of low-sulfur coal brings
    suit, challenging the Ohio regulation. The Kentucky
    plaintiff is most likely to allege:

    a. a First Amendment violation.
    b. a Fourth Amendment violation.
    c. a violation of the Commerce Clause.
    d. none of the above.

13. Refer to question 12. The court should hold the regula-
    tion:

    a. did not violate the Constitution.
    b. in violation of the Commerce Clause.
    c. in violation of the Due Process Clause.
    d. in violation of the Equal Protection Clause.

14. The Clean Air Act of 1970 required the amount of carbon
    monoxide and hydrocarbons emitted from automobiles be
    reduced. The single largest source of ozone and carbon
    monoxide pollution is:

    a. boats.
    b. motor vehicles.
    c. aircraft.
    d. volcanos.

15. The Clean Air Act of 1970, as amended in 1990, is:

      I. enforced and administered by the EPA.
     II. the only Act dealing with air pollution.
    III. a state statute.

    a. I only
    b. I and II
    c. II and III
    d. I, II, and III

16. Which of the following statutes is/are not an example of
    a federal environmental law administered by the EPA?

    a. Clean Air Act
    b. Clean Water Act
    c. strict liability
    d. Resource Conservation and Recovery Act

17. The Noise Control Act of 1972 established the goal of creating an environment free from noise that is injurious to the health and welfare of the public. The Act is administered by which of the following agencies?

      I.   Federal Aviation Administration
     II.   Department of Transportation
    III.   Environmental Protection Agency

    a.   I only
    b.   I and II
    c.   II and III
    d.   I, II, and III

18. The Federal Environmental Pesticide Control Act of 1972 regulates the production and use of pesticides. Under the Act, pesticides must be:

      I.   sold at a reasonable price.
     II.   registered before sold.
    III.   certified and used only as approved application.

    a.   I only
    b.   I and II
    c.   II and III
    d.   I, II, and III

19. Which of the following federal statutes regulate waste disposal?

      I.   Resource Conservation and Recovery Act
     II.   Superfund
    III.   The Cost-Benefit Standard

    a.   I only
    b.   I and II
    c.   II and III
    d.   I and III

20. The Comprehensive Environmental Response, Compensation, and Liability Act holds which of the following parties responsible for the cleanup of a toxic dump site?

    a.   adjacent landowners to the site
    b.   the person who transported the wastes to the site
    c.   the current owner and operator of the site
    d.   two of the above

21. The National Environmental Policy Act (NEPA) requires which of the following?

a. the preparation of an Environmental Impact Statement
b. the government to eliminate all pollution
c. the states to eliminate all landfills
d. the states to control aircraft pollution

22. The EPA, under the Noise Control Act, has the responsibility of establishing noise emission levels for:

a. aircraft.
b. sports events.
c. equipment.
d. none of the above.

23. A court may impose a cost-benefit analysis to an administrative decision to protect the environment. The court
will:

a. consider the cost of action and compare it to the
benefit of the result.
b. consider only the cost above a certain level.
c. allow all actions where the costs exceed the benefit.
d. none of the above.

24. Which of the following is considered an endangered species under the Endangered Species Act of 1973?

a. Alaskan crab
b. tuna fish
c. sunfish
d. snail darter

25. When a court interprets the meaning of an environmental
law, the court will:

a. hold in favor of Congress.
b. not ignore the ordinary meaning of plain language.
c. consider how the statute should have been written.
d. rule outside of the plain meaning of the statute.

Essay Question

1. The federal government has decided to fund the construction of the largest Atomic Accelerator in the state of
Texas. The accelerator covers a ten-mile radius and is
to be built underground. The project will cost billions
of dollars and employ over 5,000 scientists to study the
effect of atom dissection. What federal requirements
must be met before the project is completed?

Answers to Study Questions

Fill-in-the-Blank Questions

Neighbors complain about the smoke passing over their property. Neighbors may sue Universal under the theory of <u>private nuisance</u> for damages. (p. 570)

The state attorney general objects to Universal's disposal of waste into the lake. The attorney general may sue under the theory of <u>public nuisance</u>. (p. 570)

The <u>EPA</u> may investigate Universal for potential violations of the Clean Air Act. (p. 573)

True-False Questions

1. True (p. 570)

2. True (p. 570)

3. True (p. 570)

4. True (p. 570)

5. False. Some states have legally restricted the amount of emissions from motor vehicles. (p. 571)

6. True (p. 573)

7. False. Private companies need not file an EIS. (p. 573)

8. True (p. 575)

9. True (p. 573)

10. True (p. 576)

Multiple-Choice Questions

1.	d (p. 570)	8.	b (p. 570)
2.	b (p. 570)	9.	b (p. 573)
3.	d (p. 571)	10.	a (p. 573)
4.	b (pp. 571, 572)	11.	a (p. 573)
5.	d (p. 572)	12.	c (p. 571)
6.	d (p. 570)	13.	a (p. 572)
7.	d (p. 570)	14.	b (p. 574)

15. a (p. 573)
16. c (p. 570)
17. d (p. 579)
18. c (p. 579)
19. b (p. 580)
20. d (p. 580)

21. a (p. 573)
22. c (p. 579)
23. a (p. 582)
24. d (p. 583)
25. b (p. 583)

Essay Question

1. Under the National Environmental Policy Act, the project must file an Environmental Impact Statement (EIS) with the EPA. The EIS must contain the environmental impact of the proposed action, any adverse effects to the environment, alternative actions, and what irreversible effects the action might create. The preparation of the EIS is time-consuming and costly. NEPA requires an EIS to be prepared for every major federal action which significantly affects the quality of the environment. (p. 573)

Chapter 24
International Business Law

Major Concepts

This chapter discusses international law as it relates to business transactions. The law of international transactions has many complex aspects due to the difficulty of enforcing a breached contract. The courts of the United States do not have jurisdiction over foreign corporations or governments located outside the United States.

Foreign governments are immune from the jurisdiction of U.S. courts, according to the concept of sovereign immunity. In certain instances, a foreign nation may be subject to the jurisdiction of the United States. If the foreign nation is involved in a commercial activity within the U.S., the court may assert jurisdiction over the foreign nation.

The corporation transacting business internationally must consider the export/import laws and the drafting of the contract. Congress has enacted several acts to promote the exportation of products to foreign nations. Most countries have placed some restrictions on the importation of goods. The General Agreement on Tariffs and Trade (GATT) has attempted to regulate trade between member nations and relax restrictions on imports. A nation may impose a quota or tariff to slow down the importation of foreign goods.

The corporation transacting business with a foreign corporation should carefully draft the contract. International contracts should include Choice of Law, Official Language, and Risk-of-Loss Clauses to protect the parties in the event litigation develops.

Chapter Outline

I.   <u>Sources of International Law</u>--International law is the
     body of law which guides and directs independent
     nations when dealing with each other. A sovereign
     nation cannot be required to obey an international law
     but may voluntarily submit to it. There are three
     primary sources of international law: international
     customs, treaties, and international organizations and
     conferences.

   A.   <u>International Customs</u>--International customs are
        social conventions or traditions carried on by na-
        tions trading with each other. A particular
        behavior or conduct must be generally practiced in
        a nation before it evolves into a custom. The
        United Nations International Court of Justice
        defines international custom as "evidence of a
        general practice accepted as law." If a court
        accepts a practice as custom, it will serve as a
        law.

   B.   <u>Treaties</u>--A treaty is a compact between two or more
        independent nations with a view to the public wel-
        fare. A compact is an agreement reached voluntar-
        ily by the heads of the nations involved. Under
        the U.S. Constitution, Article II, Section 2, the
        President has the authority to negotiate treaties
        with the advice and consent of two-thirds of the
        Senate. Treaties are voluntarily complied with by
        the nations involved.

   C.   <u>International Organizations and Conferences</u>--Hun-
        dreds of international organizations exist and
        attempt to promote international relations. These
        organizations are composed of several member
        nations who agree to follow certain rules and stan-
        dards. These organizations hold conferences to
        adopt resolutions and make declarations. One
        example of an international organization is the
        General Assembly of the United Nations located in
        New York. The United Nations International Court
        of Justice will attempt to resolve disputes which
        involve resolutions passed by the General Assembly.
        Examples of other international organizations are:
        Customs Cooperation Council, Hague Conference on
        Private International Law, International Coffee
        Organization, and the International Bureau of the
        Permanent Court of Arbitration.

II.   Conflicts Between International and National Law--A
      business selling goods or commodities to a foreign
      buyer must consider the conflicts between the laws of
      the two countries involved. Most nations have export
      laws, quotas, customs requirements, and tax laws which
      may affect the international transaction. A nation may
      enact protectionist legislation to shield domestic
      industries from foreign competition.

      The laws of a nation are affected by the culture, his-
      tory, economic well-being, and the political environ-
      ment of the country. Legal systems around the world
      widely differ, causing conflict when international
      disputes arise. The notions of fairness embodied in
      the U.S. Constitution are not universally accepted by
      the nations of the world. If a company does business
      with a foreign buyer, the company's property may not be
      protected from governmental intervention.

III. United States Law Affecting International Business--
      U.S. administrative agencies have the authority to
      regulate international trade. Article I, Section 8 of
      the U.S. Constitution gives Congress the power "to
      regulate Commerce with foreign nations, and among the
      several states." Congress has delegated some of its
      authority to federal agencies. The President has the
      Constitutional authority to negotiate treaties. The
      Senate must ratify any treaty by a two-thirds vote.

      A.   Office of the United States Trade Representative--
           The U.S. trade representative is an ambassador and
           a member of the President's cabinet. The U.S.
           trade representative is the chief representative
           for the United States in international transactions
           concerning the General Assembly on Tariffs and
           Trade.

      B.   United States Customs Service--The customs office
           assesses and collects custom duties, excise taxes,
           fees, and penalties on imported goods. The custom
           service enforces copyright, patent, trademark, and
           maskwork law; quotas and marking requirements for
           imported merchandise.

      C.   International Trade Administration (ITA)--The
           International Trade Commission is a federal agency
           which deals with tariffs and quotas. The Commis-
           sion has broad powers to regulate imported goods as
           they affect U.S. industries.

D. United States Court of International Trade (CIT)--
    The court has similar powers to that of a federal
    district court. Any cause of action against the
    United States involving import transactions are
    held by the Court of International Trade.

IV. Sovereign Immunity--The concept of sovereign immunity
    is described by the phrase, "the sovereign can do no
    wrong." Sovereign immunity exempts a foreign nation
    from the jurisdiction of the United States.

A. Foreign Sovereign Immunities Act (FSIA)--The FSIA
    was enacted by Congress in 1976 to clarify the law
    of sovereign immunity when foreign nations are in-
    volved and expand the rights of creditors seeking
    redress from foreign nations.

    The FSIA gives the federal courts the authority to
    determine claims of foreign sovereign immunity.
    The Act specifies when an action can be brought
    against a foreign nation and if the foreign na-
    tion's property can be attached by creditors. The
    FSIA is the exclusive source of jurisdiction over
    foreign sovereigns. A foreign state is subject to
    the jurisdiction of a U.S. court, if an FSIA excep-
    tion empowers the court to hear the case. A
    plaintiff may sue a foreign sovereign in the U.S.
    for the commission of a tort which caused damage or
    a loss of property to occur in the United States.

    1. Section 1605--Section 1605 of the FSIA outlines
        the major types of claims which may be brought
        against a foreign country in the United States.
        These areas are considered exceptions to the
        foreign nation's sovereign immunity. The Act
        codifies the rule of restrictive sovereign
        immunity.

        The primary exceptions are:

        a. commercial activity of a foreign sovereign
            in the United States;

        b. activities carried on in the United States
            related to the sovereign's commercial busi-
            ness outside the U.S.; and

        c. commercial activities by the foreign sover-
            eign outside the United States which have a
            direct effect within the United States.

V.   <u>Transacting Business Internationally</u>--Companies dealing
     with foreign buyers or sellers must consider the
     import/export laws carefully. A company may sell goods
     or commodities to foreign buyers (i.e., exporting). Or
     a company may buy goods or commodities from foreign
     sellers for use in its manufacturing process
     (i.e., importing).

     A.   <u>Exporting</u>--Several federal statutes govern the ex-
          portation of goods out of the United States.

          1.   <u>The Revenue Act</u>--The Revenue Act was enacted in
               1971 by Congress to provide tax benefits to a
               firm who markets its products overseas through
               a foreign sales corporation. The Act provides
               an incentive for a domestic concern to ship its
               products to a foreign sales corporation owned
               by the company. The income generated by the
               foreign sales corporation is tax exempt.

          2.   <u>Export Trading Company Act</u>--The Export Trading
               Company Act was enacted in 1982 to promote ex-
               ports by small- and medium-sized firms. Under
               the Act, a person, partnership, corporation, or
               any association may file an application for a
               certificate of antitrust immunity. The Secre-
               tary of Commerce is empowered to issue a pro-
               tective certificate, if the applicant can show
               their business activities will not substan-
               tially lessen competition or restrain trade
               within the U.S. nor impact export trade of any
               competitor. Once the certificate is issued and
               as long as the applicant follows its business
               plan, the applicant is immune from antitrust
               prosecution by the Department of Justice.

               The Export Trading Company Act permits banks to
               invest in export trading companies up to 5 per-
               cent of their consolidated capital and surplus
               or to own such companies. This provision
               attempts to promote international trade.

          3.   <u>The Export-Import Bank (Eximbank)</u>--The Eximbank
               assists exporting and importing firms with
               needed funds. The Eximbank makes credit guar-
               antees to commercial banks in the U.S. which,
               in turn, make direct loans to exporting com-
               panies.

4. The Export Administration Act--The Export
    Administration Act was enacted by Congress in
    1979 to regulate exports from the United
    States. The Act provides three types of
    required export licenses:

    a. General License authorizes exports without
        formal application by the exporter.

    b. Qualified General License authorizes mul-
        tiple exports to certain countries.

    c. Validated License authorizes the exporter
        to export a specific item.

    The Export Administration promulgates regula-
    tions which define and implement the Act. The
    regulations specify under what circumstances a
    general license or validated license must be
    obtained. In most cases, the type of commodity
    and the importing country determines which type
    of license is needed. Some countries, such as
    North Korea, Cuba, or Vietnam are closed to
    U.S. exports. The Act controls the exportation
    of technical data and items that would contrib-
    ute to the military of another country.

B. Importing--Several statutes control the importation
    of goods and commodities into the United States.
    Most importing nations restrict the type or number
    of items imported. A nation may restrict the im-
    portation of goods through the following mecha-
    nisms.

    1. Prohibited Items--All countries prohibit cer-
        tain items from entering the country because of
        potential harmful effects. Examples of harmful
        items are cocaine, some drugs, and some agri-
        cultural products. The Trading with the Enemy
        Act was enacted by Congress in 1917 to restrict
        imports from nations considered enemies of the
        United States.

    2. Quotas--Most countries impose quotas on certain
        types of goods being imported. A quota limits
        the number of a particular item that can be
        imported.

    3. Tariffs--A tariff may be imposed on imported
        items. A tariff is a tax which raises the

price of an imported good. The tax may be ad
valorem, which is a percentage of the value of
the imported good or a flat-rate per item.

4. Licensing--A nation may grant a license to a
firm allowing business to be conducted in that
nation. Examples of licenses granted in the
U.S. are patents, copyrights, and trademarks.

C. General Agreement on Tariffs and Trade (GATT)--GATT
attempts to liberalize international trade by providing guidance regarding import restrictions.
GATT was formulated by two dozen countries in 1947.
GATT requires each signatory country to extend
"most favored nation" tariff rates to goods from
other signatory nations and further requires participating nations to provide "national treatment"
to imported goods from other signatory countries.

GATT prohibits discrimination by member nations
through quantitative trade restrictions. Participating nations must equally apply quotas to all
other participating nations. GATT attempts to reduce trade tariff barriers and to increase international trade.

D. The International Monetary Fund (IMF)--The IMF
evolved out of Bretton Woods economic conference
just after the Second World War. The IMF was
created to speed international financial and
economic reconstruction by providing intergovern-
mental loans to stabilize currency exchange rates
and to enable member countries to borrow from the
fund.

VI. International Business Contracts--Companies involved in
international trade must be aware of the different
types of legal systems around the world. Whether the
company is importing, exporting, licensing franchisees,
or involved in a joint venture with another party, a
contract will be created to provide parameters for the
implementation of the transaction. Different legal
systems deal with international contracts in a wide
variety of ways. The three major types of legal systems are: the common law system, the civil law system,
and the socialistic system.

A. Types of Legal Systems

    1. Common Law System--The common law system developed from English law and involves judge-made law and legislative enactments as the primary sources of law. Most English-speaking countries have adopted a common law system, including the United States, Canada, Australia, and New Zealand. The common law system provides great freedom to make contracts and do business.

    2. Civil Law System--A civil law system is composed primarily of codes passed by legislatures. The courts play a minor role in creating the law.

    3. The Socialistic System--The socialistic system controls business activity and the ownership of property. The judiciary is subservient to the government. The freedom to contract is severely limited.

B. Contract Law--Drafting a contract for an international business transaction must be done carefully. The following aspects of contract law should be considered before entering an international contract.

    1. Choice of Law--The parties may agree to use a certain nation's law to settle disputes. The contract will specify which substantive law will be applied and may designate where the dispute is to be litigated.

    The parties may also agree to avoid a court of law by agreeing to an arbitration clause in the contract. In the event of a dispute, the dispute will be submitted to an arbitrator for resolution.

    2. Official Language Clause--A contract may also specify the language to be used in interpreting the terms and conditions of the contract. International contracts may be translated into several languages. If the language of interpretation is not designated, a court may have a difficult time attempting to define terms uniformly among several languages.

The parties should attempt to close all potential gaps by defining all the terms of the
contract, price and manner of payment, and the
acceptable currency for payment.

3. Risk-of-Loss Clause--Risk of loss is a term
used to describe which party will incur a loss
for the value of the goods when the goods are
destroyed or lost. If the goods are destroyed
while being shipped and the risk of loss is on
the buyer, the buyer is still required to pay
the seller for the goods according to the contract. The parties may designate who will have
risk of loss during shipment of the goods.

4. Letter of Credit--A letter of credit is an
instrument used by foreign contracting parties
to facilitate a sale. A letter of credit
assures the seller will be paid, if the seller
performs according to the letter of credit
conditions. Without a letter of credit, a
seller may have the goods delivered to a foreign nation, and the buyer could refuse to pay
for them.

A letter of credit is issued by a bank at the
request of the buyer. The bank (issuer) will
issue the letter of credit, guaranteeing payment if the terms of the contract are complied
with. The letter of credit is sent to the
seller. The seller will then ship the goods to
the buyer. If the goods are delivered to the
buyer and in accordance with the letter of
credit, the seller will be paid by a correspondent bank in his or her own country. The
correspondent bank will then seek payment from
the issuer. If all the documents are in proper
order, the issuer will pay the correspondent
bank. The letter of credit arrangement is independent of the underlying contract between
the buyer and seller.

The terms of the letter of credit are similar
to the terms of the contract but independent of
the contract. The terms of the letter of credit must be reasonably complied with, in order
for the seller to be entitled to payment.

VII. Antitrust Laws in a Transnational Setting--Any restraint of trade which has a substantial effect on U.S.
commerce may violate the Sherman Act, Section 1.

Foreign corporations may violate the antitrust laws, even if the act is committed outside the United States.

A.   <u>Substantial Effect on U.S. Commerce</u>--The federal courts will exert jurisdiction in an antitrust case against a foreign corporation, if a per se violation has occurred or the alleged violation has a substantial effect on U.S. commerce. American firms entering agreements with foreign firms to restrict competition may violate the antitrust laws. Both the American and the foreign firm may be sued for a violation of the Sherman Act and the Federal Trade Commission Act.

VIII.   <u>The European Economic Community (EEC)</u>--The European Economic Community created the European Common Market (ECM). The ECM is composed of twelve Western European nations which have eliminated private and public tariffs and the restrictions on trade among themselves. The ECM attempts to protect itself from outside competition. The member countries of the EEC are Belgium, France, West Germany, Greece, Denmark, Ireland, Italy, United Kingdom, Luxembourg, Netherlands, Spain, and Portugal.

The treaty allows the free movement of workers, goods, and capital between the member nations. Many other economic cooperatives similar to the ECM have been created to promote trade.

Study Questions

Fill-in-the-Blank Questions

The Holmon Company is a publisher of nonfiction books. Holmon desires to market their books in Western Europe. Holmon has the books translated into several different languages for distribution in the appropriate nations.

The president of Holmon negotiates a contract to work with a Western European company called BMX, Co. in marketing and distributing the books. Holmon is involved in _____ (exporting/ _____ goods. importing)

Holmon and BMX agree the contract should be interpreted in English in the event of litigation. This type of contract

provision is called a(n) _____
                                    (choice of law clause/
_____.
    official language clause)

A _____ may restrict the number of books that
    (tariff/quota)
Holmon exports into European nations.

A _____ is a tax which may be placed on books
    (tariff/quota)
imported into European countries by BMX, Co.

True-False Questions

1. International customs are a source of international law
    recognized by the International Court of Justice. _____

2. An example of an international organization is the Gen-
    eral Assembly of the United Nations. _____

3. A convention is a code adopted by an international orga-
    nization. _____

4. An executive agreement is a type of international agree-
    ment. _____

5. The U.S. Trade Representative is responsible for all
    multilateral trade negotiations of the United States.
    _____

6. The International Trade Commission imposes import quotas
    for some industries. _____

7. Licensing gives a business the right to use, lease, sell,
    or distribute goods or services in a foreign market.
    _____

8. The President is not allowed to fast-track a trade agree-
    ment into law. _____

9. The Constitution divides the responsibility for interna-
    tional relations between the President and Congress.
    _____

10. The Omnibus Trade and Competitiveness Act was enacted to
    promote and enhance competitiveness of American industry.
    _____

Multiple-Choice Questions

1. Which of the following is <u>not</u> considered a source of
    international law?

    a. treaties
    b. customs
    c. international organizations
    d. Uniform Commercial Code

2. The International Court of Justice is part of which of
    the following organizations?

    a. International Monetary Fund
    b. General Assembly of the United States
    c. International Jute Organization
    d. Customs Cooperation Council

3. Ireland belongs to the _____ international orga-
    nization.

    a. Association of Southeast Asian nations
    b. Gulf Cooperation Council
    c. Andean Common market
    d. European Community

4. The American Bottlers Company (ABC) has entered into an
    agreement with a German firm to jointly build and operate
    a soft drink factory in Munich, West Germany. ABC has
    invested large sums of money in the construction of the
    facility of which the German firm will operate and assist
    in marketing the product. Which of the following should
    be included in the agreement?

    a. Choice of Laws provision
    b. Risk-of-Loss clause
    c. Official Language clause
    d. all of the above

5. Refer to question 4. The German government decides to
    nationalize all soft drink companies. ABC is required to
    surrender all their interest in the soft drink facility
    and leave the country. The German government can be held
    liable for violating the:

    a. Fourth Amendment.
    b. Fifth Amendment.
    c. Fourteenth Amendment.
    d. none of the above.

6. When a nation treats foreign goods just as it treats
    domestic goods, it is called:

    a. national treatment.
    b. Act of State Doctrine.
    c. expropriation.
    d. none of the above.

7. The Central Company of Costa Rica is selling garments to
    buyers in the U.S. below the price charged in Costa Rica.
    This is called:

    a. infringement.
    b. dumping.
    c. subsidies.
    d. none of the above.

8. Which of the following statement(s) is (are) true con-
    cerning unfair practices?

    I.   Dumping is an attempt to drive out competition.

    II.   Copying of copyrighted works is not illegal or
          unfair.

    III. The International Trade Administration protects
          domestic industries against unfair practices.

    a. I only
    b. I and III
    c. II and III
    d. II only

9. Which of the following is an economic international orga-
    nization?

    I.   World Bank
    II.   International Monetary Fund
    III. Protocol

    a. I only
    b. I and II
    c. II and III
    d. I, II, and III

10. The Amcor Company desires to sell their products in for-
    eign markets. They sell through a company in Austria.
    Amcor is probably entitled to tax benefits under:

    a. the Revenue Act of 1971.
    b. Eximbank regulation.

c.   Fast Track.
d.   Trade Act.

11.   A company may file for a certificate of antitrust immunity under the authority of which act?

a.   Eximbank
b.   The Export Administration Act
c.   International Monetary Fund
d.   The Export Trading Company Act

12.   Which of the following nations have agreed to the North
American Free Trade Agreement?

a.   Canada
b.   United States
c.   Mexico
d.   all of the above

13.   Which of the following terms should be included in an
international sales contract?

  I.   Choice of Law Clause
 II.   Risk-of-Loss Clause
III.   Official Language Clause

a.   I only
b.   I and II
c.   II and III
d.   I, II, and III

14.   A letter of credit may be defined as:

a.   a guarantee by a bank of the buyer that funds for
goods are available to the seller upon meeting the
conditions of the letter.
b.   a contract for the sale of goods.
c.   a contract sent from the bank to the buyer for goods.
d.   none of the above.

15.   The General Agreement on Tariffs and Trade requires which
of the following by member nations?

  I.   an anti-dumping duty on dumped goods
 II.   published tariff schedules
III.   free trade with all member and nonmember nations

a.   I only
b.   I and II
c.   II and III
d.   I, II, and III

16. Which of the following organizations is intended to coor-
    dinate the activities of governments regarding inter-
    national trade and provide institutional structure within
    intergovernmental loans to stabilize currency exchange
    rates?

    a.   International Monetary Fund
    b.   Export Trading Company Act
    c.   General Agreement on Tariffs and Trade
    d.   none of the above

17. Which of the following relationships is based on a letter
    of credit?

    a.   seller and buyer of goods
    b.   buyer and issuing bank
    c.   company president and employee
    d.   all of the above

18. The Acme Corporation desires to sell its products over-
    seas. Acme can avoid paying income tax by selling prod-
    ucts through a foreign sales corporation under the
    authority of which of the following acts?

    a.   The Revenue Act of 1971
    b.   General Agreement on Tariffs and Trade
    c.   The Export Trading Company Act
    d.   none of the above

19. U.S. businessmen may not trade with countries that are
    hostile towards the U.S. Which of the following acts
    prohibits such trade with specified countries?

    a.   General Agreement on Tariffs and Trade
    b.   a quota
    c.   a tariff
    d.   Trading with the Enemy Act

20. A company located in Japan manufactures personal com-
    puters. The company decides to export computers into the
    U.S. The U.S. government assesses a tariff on each com-
    puter as a percentage of the value. Their type of tariff
    is known as:

    a.   ad valorem.
    b.   flat-rate.
    c.   graduated.
    d.   quota.

21. A U.S. manufacturer of weapons in Southern California
    sells its products to a buyer in Kenya. The buyer sells

the same items to a buyer in the Middle East, an embargoed area. The actions of the U.S. manufacturer may violate:

    a.   a tariff.
    b.   GATT.
    c.   the Export Administration Act.
    d.   the Revenue Act.

22. Refer to question 21. If the manufacturer is in violation of federal law, what is the extent of a possible fine?

    a. $1 million
    b. $2 million
    c. $3 million
    d. $4 million

23. Which of the following nations is <u>not</u> a member of the European Community?

    a.   Belgium
    b.   Italy
    c.   Spain
    d.   Liechtenstein

24. The Korean government gives interest-free loans to all manufacturers of sportswear who export their products. In addition, the Korean government guarantees the goods will be sold at a specific price. Which of the following is (are) true?

    I.   The Korean government has committed an unfair practice.

    II.   Interest-free loans are considered a subsidy.

    III. A subsidy distorts the movement of trade in the international community.

    a.   I only
    b.   I and II
    c.   II and III
    d.   I, II, and III

25. The Amersan Company of India copies music of a well-known U.S. country music performer. Amersan does not obtain the permission of the performer and sells the tapes to music distributors. Amersan has done which of the following?

a.   infringed on a copyright
b.   dumped goods on the market
c.   received a subsidy
d.   none of the above

Essay Question

1.   The Automet Company manufactures electronic equipment for
     automobiles and aircraft. The president of Automet, John
     West, desires to ship his company's product overseas.
     John negotiates a $100,000 contract with a Japanese
     buyer. John wants to ship the goods but is hesitant be-
     cause he has no guarantees he will be paid by the buyer.
     What should John do?

Answers to Study Questions

Fill-in-the-Blank Questions

The president of Holmon negotiates a contract to work with a
Western European company called BMX, Co. in marketing and distributing the books. Holmon is involved in <u>exporting</u> goods.
(p. 592)

Holmon and BMX agree the contract should be interpreted in
English in the event of litigation. This type of contract
provision is called an <u>official</u> <u>language clause</u>. (p. 605)

A <u>quota</u> may restrict the number of books that Holmon exports
into European nations. (p. 593)

A <u>tariff</u> is a tax which may be placed on books imported into
European countries by BMX, Co. (p. 593)

True-False Questions

1.   True (p. 592)

2.   True (p. 593)

3.   True (p. 592)

4.   True (p. 592)

5.   True (p. 594)

6.   True (p. 594)

7.   True (p. 595)

8.   False. The President by law may fast-track a trade
     agreement. (p. 600)

9.   True (p. 594)

10. True (p. 599)

Multiple-Choice Questions

1.	d (p. 592)	14.	a (p. 605)
2.	b (p. 592)	15.	b (p. 593)
3.	d (p. 593)	16.	a (p. 593)
4.	d (p. 605)	17.	b (p. 605)
5.	d (p. 592)	18.	a (p. 600)
6.	a (p. 594)	19.	d (p. 600)
7.	b (p. 601)	20.	a (p. 593)
8.	b (p. 601)	21.	c (p. 597)
9.	b (p. 592)	22.	a (p. 597)
10.	a (p. 600)	23.	d (p. 593)
11.	d (p. 600)	24.	d (p. 601)
12.	d (p. 600)	25.	a (p. 601)
13.	d (p. 605)		

Essay Question

1.   John should request the buyer to have a letter of credit
     issued by a Japanese bank and sent to an American bank
     located near Automet. The letter of credit assures John
     will be paid, if the conditions of the letter are ful-
     filled. The letter of credit is a separate contract be-
     tween the issuing bank and the buyer. (p. 605)